THE SUBSTANCE OF SOCIAL DEVIANCE

The Substance of Social Deviance

EDITED BY:
Victoria Lynn Swigert
College of the Holy Cross

Ronald A. Farrell
State University of New York at Albany

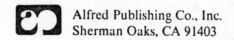
Alfred Publishing Co., Inc.
Sherman Oaks, CA 91403

Alfred Publishing Co., Inc.
15335 Morrison Street
Sherman Oaks, California 91403

Printed in the United States of America

Library of Congress Cataloging in Publication Data
Main entry under title:
The substance of social deviance.

1. Deviant behavior—Addresses, essays, lectures.
2. Deviant behavior—Labeling theory—Addresses,
essays, lectures. I. Swigert, Victoria Lynn.
II. Farrell, Ronald A.

HM291.S857   301.6'2   78-23970
ISBN 0-88284-059-2

Contents

Part Three: Interaction Processes in Labeling Deviance   117

Part Four: Anomie and Adaptation to Strain   211

Part Five: Social and Cultural Support in Learning Deviant Behavior   251

Part Six: Group/Culture Conflict and Deviant Behavior 333

Preface

The study of social deviance is characterized by a proliferation of competing theoretical perspectives. Causal explanations of the origins and maintenance of nonconformity have emerged only to be replaced by alternative paradigms. The product has been the fragmentation of the field into antagonistic orientations. Reflective of this antagonism is the continuous debate and critique regarding the achievements and failures of opposing theoretical schemes. The extent to which this has contributed to the study of human behavior is questionable. A more fruitful direction, we have argued, may lie in a selective application of the several theories to various stages in the deviance process. Such an approach comprised the organizational basis of our earlier work, *Social Deviance* (J. B. Lippincott, 1978). Here, nonconformity is viewed as a sequence of events that shape behavior patterns, personal indentifications, and societal reactions. Within this framework, each major theoretical perspective constitutes an explanation of a particular phase of an overall process.

The Substance of Social Deviance is similarly organized. Guided by the model developed in the earlier volume, substantive articles related to the several theories explore the validity of the processual scheme. The articles presented exemplify descriptive and analytical contributions to functionalism, definitional theory, the interactionist perspective, anomie theory, social and cultural support theory, and theories of group and culture conflict. The attempt is to build toward a general theory of behavior by linking orientations. An overview of this approach is presented in the Introduction. By bringing together basic assumptions of the different theories, this preliminary statement provides a conceptual framework for the text and readings that follow. Each section is also preceded by a discussion of the theoretical foundations of the specific approach and a summary of the selections included. Particular attention is given to the contribution of the perspective to a general understanding of deviance causation. This integrative and comprehensive coverage is intended to provide for a holistic appreciation of deviance as a multi-faceted phenomenon.

We gratefully acknowledge the assistance of Allen Horwitz of Rutgers University for the many helpful comments and suggestions he provided throughout the development of the work. We are also indebted to Kay Flanagan for typing the several drafts of the manuscript. Finally, our thanks to sociology editor Steven Manus of Alfred for the thoughtful attention he has given to the creation and production of *The Substance of Social Deviance*.

Victoria L. Swigert
Worcester, Massachusetts

Ronald A. Farrell
Albany, New York
January, 1979

Introduction

The field of deviance has witnessed the emergence of several distinct theoretical traditions. Yet, no one of these possesses the explanatory power necessary to account for the many social structural and interpersonal aspects of behavior. While most typically viewed as competing and contradictory perspectives, a more fruitful approach may lie in their integration (Farrell and Swigert, 1978). This might be accomplished through a careful consideration of the various conceptual frameworks and those aspects or specific phases of deviance causation treated by each. To the extent that existing theories focus on different stages of the overall process, their integration allows for a more complete understanding of nonconformity as a multifaceted phenomenon. Synthesis, then, rather than comparison, critique, or promotion of particular schemes, becomes the strategy for the creation of a general theory of deviance causation.

The sociological emphasis on collective behavior demands that such an approach most appropriately begin at the macro-level of analysis. Of particular concern is the nature of deviance within the context of social organization and the meaning that it has for systems maintenance. Addressing this issue is the *functionalist approach* to nonconformity. According to this perspective, society is comprised of a number of interrelated parts. Similar to the cells and organs of biological entities, each of society's components works together to maintain the system as a whole (Durkheim, 1893; Parsons, 1951).

A critical aspect of social organization concerns the integration of the membership into a common value system. This occurs, in part, through the mutually reinforcing effects of society's major institutions. The family, religion, education, law, and economy impart shared values by regulating the behavior of group members in the various arenas of social life. As with institutional control, deviance is likewise instrumental in confirming the value system of the collectivity. The designation of certain behaviors as falling outside the limits that will be tolerated by the group calls attention to the standards upon which the system is based (Durkheim, 1904). Thus, property is valued not only because of the respect engendered for it by institutional efforts at socialization, but because the propertyless are shamed and the thief imprisoned (Mead, 1918). In much the same way as the moral leader is exemplary of the cultural ideal, therefore, the deviant exemplifies that to which the culture stands opposed. It is in the repulsion, indignation, and official reaction to his conduct that the group derives its vitality. That is, by calling attention to the sins, pathologies, and crimes of the outcast, the cohesiveness of the group is reinforced and its norms reaffirmed. Since social systems depend upon this process for their very existence, functionalists have argued that they become organized in such a way as to produce required levels of nonconformity (Erikson, 1966).

The means ·by which behavioral boundaries are established are the focus of *definitional theory.* As such, this perspective provides further insight into the relationship between social control and deviance causation. Behavior and events are attributed meaning through the social definition of the situation. It is in this manner that norms and values are communicated to group members. Once these definitions have been internalized, persons are able to interpret their environment. These interpretations, in their turn, become the basis of social action (Thomas, 1923; Merton, 1957).

The definition of the situation, therefore, insofar as it includes expectations for behavior, is self-fulfilling. The assignment of meaning, by precluding alternative definitions and lines of action, serves to produce behavior consistent with original ascriptions (Thomas, 1923; Merton, 1957).

The implications of the definitional process in the case of deviance are clear. Whether through the official activities of agencies of social control, or the informal responses of community relationships, persons are defined as deviant and treated accordingly. Such attribution and reaction set into motion a socially structured process that amplifies the very traits complained of (Tannenbaum, 1938). For, having been assigned to the deviant status, the individual is subject to the normative expectations, sanctions, and anticipated responses that pertain to these positions.

The self-fulfilling nature of deviant definitions, and their social psychological impact on those defined, is further elaborated by the *interactionist perspective,* or *labeling theory.* Developing out of symbolic interactionism, this approach posits that behavioral roles, and the identities upon which they are based, are the product of sustained interaction (Cooley, 1902; Mead, 1934). If imputations of deviance are introduced into this communication, the effect will be for the individual to organize life and identity around the social definition.

While rule violation is virtually universal, the crystallization of this behavior into deviant careers is a product of societal reaction to initial transgressions. These original, or primary deviations would remain transient and often subside without the reinforcing effects of the social response. Progression to the level of secondary, or career deviation is the result of the application of deviance labels (Lemert, 1951; 1967; Becker, 1963).

Society attaches far greater meaning to the deviant status than to other positions individuals normally occupy. Once assigned to this highly salient, master status, the nonconformer is identified and identifies himself as deviant to the exclusion of alternative, more legitimate bases of identification. Age, sex, occupational achievement, and the like become irrelevant to the interaction, and the deviation assumes precedence (Becker, 1963). Given the saliency of the position, individuals become increasingly sensitive to their deviation. In this context of heightened awareness, they react intensely to the most subtle responses of others. Since social relationships are continuously problematic, the deviant identity is further reinforced (Scott and Lyman, 1968).

Also central to labeling and nonconformity is the stereotype that accompanies the deviant status. These popular definitions constitute guiding imageries for action. In much the same manner that roles associated with more traditional statuses dictate socially prescribed behavior, the stereotype provides the normative expectations that attend the deviant status. Such stereotypes are widely diffused and are communicated through mass media depictions and routine interaction (Goffman, 1963; Scheff, 1966).

Individuals defined as deviant are also subject to a redefinition of other aspects of their lives in terms of the deviation. By reinterpreting past and present events to fit the immediate circumstances, biographical consistency is introduced and negative societal response becomes justified (Garfinkel, 1956; Schur, 1971). While such retrospective retelling reduces cognitive conflict among those who would penalize the deviant, it simultaneously obviates the individual's claim to legitimacy in other areas of life.

The net effect of the designation of deviance as a master status, application of a negative stereotype, and retrospective and concurrent reinterpretation, is for the individual to become engulfed in the deviant role, to organize life and identity around the facts of the deviation (Schur, 1971).

We have seen that the stigma that accompanies deviance has important consequences for the self-concepts of persons so labeled. Such stigma also produces stress and a tendency toward adaptation. Exclusion from legitimate roles and relegation to positions on the margins of society implies the loss of social support necessary for positive self-evaluation. Thus, in addition to the behavioral expectations associated with the deviant label, status deprivation is also a motivating factor in deviance causation.

The development of stress and its resolution is the subject of *anomie theory*. Central to the perspective is the concept of referent identifications. Reference groups are those after whom we model our behavior and to whom we look for reward (Merton, 1938). Relationships with such persons are equilibriated when participants are able to comply with the normative expectations that regulate interaction. Since the norms of referent others are internalized to become part of one's own needs, conformity to such expectations is highly motivated. If persons are unable to meet up to these standards, they will experience stress as well as ambivalence regarding the sources of the discomfort (Parsons, 1951). A likely adaptation is to shift referent identifications to those groups wherein one is capable of conformity (Cohen, 1955; 1959). Having been stigmatized as deviant, legitimate referent associations may be precluded. The alternative, therefore, is to seek collective support from those who have been similarly labeled. To the extent that these groups espouse deviant norms, increased commitment to nonconformity will be the outcome.

The learning processes involved in deviant associations are addressed by *social and cultural support theory.* According to this approach, nonconformity is acquired in the same general manner as socially acceptable behavior (Sutherland, 1947). The only distinction concerns the legitimacy or illegitimacy of group norms as defined by the larger society.

Through interaction in groups characterized by a preponderance of normative definitions that encourage and reward nonconformity, persons acquire the motivations, drives, rationalizations, and techniques of deviant behavior (Sutherland, 1947). Central to this learning process is the importance that the individual attaches to these referent associations (Glaser, 1956). We have seen in our discussion of anomie theory that, because of the inability to meet up to the expectations of legitimate groups, the deviant's attachments, commitments, and involvements within the larger society (Hirschi, 1969) became attenuated. The need for acceptance will lead to the development of strong ties with those who share in the experience of stigma. These associations, therefore, are likely to become the circle of significant others. As the only source of social support, conformity to deviant group norms will be of paramount importance. As interaction proceeds, the individual internalizes these norms to become part of his own definition of the situation. Excluded from the opportunities for the enactment of conforming roles and having been socialized to and provided with the means for deviant performance (Cloward and Ohlin, 1960), nonconformity is ensured.

Because they oppose dominant values, deviant subcultures may be viewed as the cumulative result of individual rejection of an unaccepting society. Faced with the inability to conform to dominant expectations, persons engage in defensive reactions involving a redefinition of society's norms as personally unacceptable. This condemnation of condemners functions to protect the self from unattainable demands for conformity. These individual responses then become the basis for subcultural norms and are reinforced for individuals as their interaction within the group continues (Cohen, 1955).

It must also be recalled, however, that those who comprise deviant sub-cultures are individuals to whom the deviant label has been successfully applied. They are persons who have internalized the societal definition of deviance and have come to organize their behavior and identity around the stereotype. It is these popular definitions, as represented in individual self concepts and roles, then, that may underlie the development of the subculture of the deviant group. Through interaction among deviants, individual conceptions feed into the normative structure of the group and become the basis of collective role requirements. We see here, in its classic form, the self-fulfilling nature of deviance definitions. Those whose behavior or attributes are designated as deviant are subject to the interactive and adaptive processes that result in identities and behaviors consistent with original ascriptions.

Behavior, whether conforming or deviant, is group oriented. The myriad of human needs that can be satisfied only through interaction with others implies that commitment to the standards of one's referent associations will be a powerful motivation for conduct (Miller, 1958; Vold, 1958). Individual behavior, therefore, is reflective of the requirements of group cultures.

Modern society is comprised of a proliferation of groups, each with its own distinct culture and needs for survival. In their attempts to satisfy group needs and promote their standards of value, conflict becomes inevitable. The political structure plays an important role in determining competitive outcomes. By gaining access to the institutions of social control, the victors are able to establish their norms and interests as the dominant ones and derogate those that would challenge their position of superiority. Established definitions of deviance and conformity, therefore, are the end result of the dynamic processes involved in group and culture conflict.

Building upon this basic assumption, *conflict theory* proposes that deviance is intimately related to the sociopolitical organization of society. Whether it be the cultural differences found among groups (Wirth, 1931; Sellin, 1938), or the privileges and obligations that accompany the various levels of class, status, and power (Chambliss and Seidman, 1971; Spitzer, 1975), minority populations are subject to deviance defining processes that render their situation and behavior morally reprehensible. These decisions are predicated on efforts by some collectivities to preserve power and maintain the ways of life to which they stand committed.

Conflict theory may be profitably utilized to expand a general approach to deviant behavior. As with minority populations, the culture of deviant groups is in continuous conflict with that of the larger society. Since non-conformity is, by definition, in opposition to existing behavioral codes, contact between enculturated deviants and representatives of legitimate society will be problematic. The consequences of the reactions that ensue from these confrontations are twofold. On the one hand, the need to defend one's self and the position of one's group, reaffirms the deviant's commitment to subcultural associations, associations which ensure the persistence of the original misbehavior. At the same time, conflict legitimates dominant group definitions of deviance. Such encounters and their sanction are visible reminders of the threat of nonconformity to the established order. Similar to the functionalist approach then, it may be argued that deviance, which is itself a product of conflict-derived definitions, contributes to the persistence of social and cultural values over time. It is reasonable to suggest, therefore, that society organizes in such a way as to produce and maintain those very behaviors it seeks to control. Here, we see a sacrificial process involving the relegation of expendable segments of the population to positions of deviance in order that dominant interests may be secured.

REFERENCES

Becker, Howard. *Outsiders.* New York: Free Press, 1963.

Chambliss, William J., and Seidman, Robert B. *Law, Order, and Power.* Reading, Massachusetts: Addison-Wesley, 1971.

Cloward, Richard A., and Ohlin, Lloyd E. *Delinquency and Opportunity: A Theory of Delinquent Gangs.* New York: Free Press, 1960.

Cohen, Albert K. *Delinquent Boys.* New York: Free Press, 1955.

_____. "The Study of Social Disorganization and Deviant Behavior." In *Sociology Today: Problems and Prospects,* edited by Robert K. Merton, Leonard Broom, and Leonard S. Cottrell. New York: Basic Books, 1959.

Cooley, Charles Horton. *Human Nature and the Social Order.* New York: Charles Scribner's Sons, 1902.

Durkheim, Emile. *The Division of Labor in Society.* 1893. Translated by George Simpson. New York: Macmillan, 1933.

_____. *The Rules of Sociological Method.* 1904. Translated by Sarah A. Solovay and John H. Mueller; edited by George E. G. Catlin. New York: Macmillan, 1938.

Erikson, Kai T. *Wayward Puritans: A Study in the Sociology of Deviance.* New York: John Wiley and Sons, 1966.

Farrell, Ronald A., and Swigert, Victoria Lynn. *Social Deviance.* Philadelphia: J. B. Lippincott, 1978.

Garfinkel, Harold. "Conditions of Successful Degradation Ceremonies." *American Journal of Sociology* 61 (1956): 420–24.

Glaser, Daniel. "Criminality Theories and Behavioral Images." *American Journal of Sociology* 61 (1956): 433–44.

Goffman, Erving. *Stigma: Notes on the Management of Spoiled Identity.* Englewood Cliffs, New Jersey: Prentice-Hall, 1963.

Hirschi, Travis. *Causes of Delinquency.* Los Angeles: University of California Press, 1969.

Lemert, Edwin M. *Social Pathology: A Systematic Approach to the Theory of Sociopathic Behavior.* New York: McGraw-Hill, 1951.

_____. *Human Deviance, Social Problems, and Social Control.* Englewood Cliffs, New Jersey: Prentice-Hall, 1967.

Mead, George Herbert. "The Psychology of Punitive Justice." *American Journal of Sociology* 23 (1918): 577–602.

_____. *Mind, Self, and Society.* Chicago: University of Chicago Press, 1934.

Merton, Robert K. "Social Structure and Anomie." *American Sociological Review* 3 (1938): 672–82.

——. *Social Theory and Social Structure.* New York: Free Press, 1957.

Miller, Walter B. "Lower Class Culture as a Generating Milieu for Gang Delinquency." *Journal of Social Issues* 14 (1958): 5–19.

Parsons, Talcott. *The Social System.* New York: Macmillan, 1951.

Scott, Marvin B., and Lyman, Stanford M. "Paranoia, Homosexuality, and Game Theory." *Journal of Health and Social Behavior* 9 (1968): 179–87.

Scheff, Thomas J. *Being Mentally Ill.* Chicago: Aldine, 1966.

Schur, Edwin M. *Labeling Deviant Behavior: Its Sociological Implications.* New York: Harper and Row, 1971.

Sellin, Thorsten. *Culture Conflict and Crime.* Bulletin 41. New York: Social Science Research Council, 1938.

Spitzer, Steven. "Toward a Marxian Theory of Deviance." *Social Problems* 22 (1975): 641–51.

Sutherland, Edwin H. *Principles of Criminology.* Philadelphia: J. B. Lippincott, 1947.

Tannenbaum, Frank. *Crime and the Community.* New York: Columbia University Press, 1938.

Thomas, William I. *The Unadjusted Girl.* Boston: Little, Brown and Co., 1923.

Vold, George B. *Theoretical Criminology.* New York: Oxford University Press, 1958.

Wirth, Louis. "Culture Conflict and Misconduct." *Social Forces* 9 (1931): 484–92.

PART ONE
The Social Functions of Deviance

The functionalist approach to deviant behavior includes as its primary assumption the notion that crime and deviance are fundamental aspects of social systems. Beginning with Emile Durkheim's (1902) observation that nonconformity is and always has been present in all societies, functionalists have sought to specify the origins of deviance in terms of its contributions to social organization. In this regard, it has been argued that nonconformity serves to demarcate the limits of acceptable behavior for all persons sharing membership in a particular group. Since the total range of possible human behavior is virtually limitless, groups must establish such boundaries in order to secure an identity apart from all other systems (Erikson, 1966). These limits are communicated to the membership, not through direct instruction, but through the example set by boundary transgressors. As long as the thief is punished and the sinner excommunicated, acceptable standards of behavior remain visible and a common morality confirmed. Thus, the nonconformer serves as a boundary maintainer for all other members of the collectivity.

The deviant also acts to increase internal solidarity. By uniting against the enemy, individuals assert their own moral superiority, their sense of being citizens and, therefore, their difference from those who have been excluded from the group (Mead, 1918). The rewards of that citizenship become meaningful in light of the negative sanctions applied to those who transgress collective limits (Dentler and Erikson, 1959). In this manner, the inhibitions necessary for continued conformity are ensured.

Similarly, the value of social relationships is a product of the threat posed by the nonconformer. Possessions are dear because there exist those

9

who would take them from us. Chastity is virtuous insofar as promiscuity threatens it. All things valuable, then, become so because we are willing to fight and even die for them (Mead, 1918). Their value has little to do with any inherent worth. Rather, they are prized insofar as they must be protected.

In light of the centrality of deviance to these several aspects of social organization, functionalist theorists have argued that groups may in fact induce, sustain, and permit controlled levels of nonconformity. This is accomplished through both formal and informal mechanisms of social control. Socialization processes, gossip, ostracism, ridicule, as well as the application of official sanctions have the effect of fixing individuals in deviant roles. From this perspective, such reactions are viewed as contributing to the creation of deviants within certain segments of the population in order that nonconformity may be controlled more generally. This sacrificial process allows for a reaffirmation of the normative order of a society by providing clear definitions of acceptable behavior. Without the deviant to mark societal boundaries, the very existence of society would be rendered problematic.

Robert Levy's "The Community Function of Tahitian Male Transvestism" underscores the importance of nonconformity in maintaining organizational boundaries. Within Tahitian villages, the *mahu* is a male who from a very early age is assigned the role of a woman. Throughout his mahu life he wears woman's clothing, cares for the children, learns cooking and weaving skills, and interacts primarily with females. While the mahu is also said to engage in homosexual relations, he is most generally described as one "who does woman's work."

The mahu performs a most important "message function" for the community. Sex role differentiations are minimal in Tahitian culture, although child rearing is the exclusive responsibility of women. In the absence of male role models, the mahu acts to define for Tahitian males the range of their expected performance.

> " ... there clearly, out in the open, is the Mahu, the one man who has taken the female role. I am a non-mahu. Whatever feelings I have about men are no threat to me and to my eventual role as family head. I can see exactly what *he* is, and I am clear about myself in that I am not he."

In "The Group Function of Schizophrenia in the Military," the role of the deviant in sustaining group solidarity is illustrated by Kai T. Erikson's account of the preinstitutionalized psychotic among army trainees. In spite of the deviant's inability to perform his share of the squad's assigned duties, the group acts to protect him from elimination by higher authorities. Through their efforts to cover for the low producer, squad members develop a sense of common concern and shared purpose. The deviant becomes an object about whom "something should be done."

The relationship between nonconformity, boundary maintenance, and cohesion is further specified in Pat Lauderdale's "Deviance and Moral Boundaries," an investigation of group adjustment to external threat. Faced with possible extinction, groups were found to experience an initial crisis of solidarity. In order to reestablish cohesiveness, and to protect themselves from the threat posed to their corporate identity, members became increasingly intolerant of any deviation from the collective norm.

Lauderdale argues that the behavioral boundaries of social systems are flexible and responsive to changing needs. Unthreatened, groups are content to keep their deviants on the fringe. As the objects of controlled hostility, such boundary maintainers provide the means for reaffirming the self-righteousness of conformists. When the continued existence of the collectivity becomes problematic, however, persons become unwilling to tolerate the internal disruptions of its transgressors, expelling them from the group.

The selections by Levy, Erikson, and Lauderdale have focused on the role of nonconformity in small groups. The premodern Tahitian village, the army trainee squad, and the laboratory work group are characterized by limited size and clearly defined goals. Under such conditions, there would likely develop a single set of norms around which behavioral boundaries are established and maintained. The larger society, however, is characterized by social and cultural diversity. Sex, race, age, ethnicity, social class, and the like differentiate the larger collectivity into a heterogeneous assembly of subpopulations. Corresponding differences emerge in the standards and values limiting behavior within these various groups. The concept of boundary maintenance through nonconformity takes on a different meaning in this situation. Given limitations in normative consensus, behavioral boundaries come to represent the successful efforts of some groups to impose their particular values.

Addressing the issue of social pluralism and boundary maintenance, James Inverarity's "Populism and Lynching in Louisiana: Boundary Crises and Repressive Justice" underscores the importance of intergroup conflict in a functionalist approach to deviance. The Populist revolt of the late nineteenth century was indicative of a crisis of solidarity that disrupted traditional boundaries. The South had emerged from the post-Civil War Reconstruction united in its animosity toward northerners and blacks as symbolized by the Republican Party. The consensus of ill will that cut across class lines was threatened by Populist attempts to organize the poor of both races against the wealthy and powerful. The increase of lynchings that occurred during this period was reflective of efforts on the part of southern whites to reassert original boundaries.

From a functionalist perspective, then, deviance is an essential part of social organization. It is boundary maintaining in that it serves to establish and legitimate the behaviors, attitudes, and values upon which organization depends. In small groups, as well as in societies characterized by minimum levels of stratification and complexity, behavioral boundaries approximate a consensually derived ideal. Within modern industrial society, on the other hand, is found a plurality of social and cultural systems, each imposing its expectations for conformity on its membership. Through the competition among groups for access to the institutions of social control, the victors acquire the right to designate their standards and values as the official morality. In this instance, behavioral boundaries represent politically established limits. Such standards are communicated through the boundary maintenance function of deviance and societal reaction to it.

REFERENCES

Dentler, Robert A., and Erikson, Kai T. "The Functions of Deviance in Groups." *Social Problems* 7 (1959): 98–107.

Durkheim, Emile. *The Rules of Sociological Method.* 1904. Translated by Sarah A. Solovay and John H. Mueller; edited by George E. G. Catlin. New York: Macmillan, 1938.

Erikson, Kai T. *Wayward Puritans: A Study in the Sociology of Deviance.* New York: John Wiley and Sons, 1966.

Mead, George Herbert. "The Psychology of Punitive Justice." *American Journal of Sociology* 23 (1918): 577–602.

ROBERT I. LEVY

The Community Function of Tahitian Male Transvestism

At the time of discovery by the West in 1767, Tahiti, like many other non-Western cultures, had an institutionalized form of male homosexuality. As James Morrison, left ashore in 1789 on Tahiti after the mutiny on the Bounty, noted,

> they have a set of men called mahu. These men are in some respects like the Eunuchs in India but are not castrated. They never cohabit with women, but live as they do. They pick their beards out and dress as women, dance and sing with them and are as effeminate in their voice. They are generally excellent hands at making and painting of cloth, making mats, and every other woman's employment. They are esteemed valuable friends in that way and it is said, though I never saw an instance of it, that they converse with men as familiar as women do. This, however, I do not aver as a fact as I never found any who did not detest the thought (Morrison, 1935: 238).

That the mahu did "converse with men as familiar as women do," was attested to by other observers. William Bligh, Morrison's captain, after noting in his journal that the mahus were "particularly selected when boys and kept with the women solely for the caresses of the men," goes on to note that

Source: Levy, Robert I. "The Community Function of Tahitian Male Transvestism: A Hypothesis." *Anthropological Quarterly* 44 (January 1971): 12–21. Permission granted by The Catholic University of America Press.

"those connected with him have their beastly pleasures gratified between his thighs, but are no farther sodomites as they all positively deny the crime" (Bligh, n.d.: 16).

Other early reports from explorers and missionaries added fellatio to the coital forms, the literature giving the impression that it was generally the mahu who performed fellatio on the partner (although there is at least one early report of the reverse).[1]

I spent twenty-six months (during 1961–1964) doing studies of various psychological and anthropological patterns in two Tahitian speaking communities in French Polynesia.[2] The mahu, as a social *type,* still exists. There was one in each of the two communities that I studied. In this paper I will briefly describe the mahu and his relation to others, and propose one of the dynamic factors in the maintenance of the role.

I will base this discussion mostly on the more rural and traditional of the two communities, Piri, a village of about 300 people, with a mixed subsistence (horticulture and fishing) and market (vanilla and copra) economy, on the island of Huahine about 100 miles northwest of Tahiti.

In 1961 there was a sixteen-year-old boy in Piri, who was referred to sometimes by his personal name, sometimes as "the mahu." Although there were photographs of him proudly displayed in his foster mother's house showing him in girls' dancing costume, complete with brassiere, he wore male clothes ordinarily, favoring however the neutral sarong-like *pareu,* worn by both sexes, rather than the Western style trousers now worn frequently by men in the village. His speech and manner were somewhat feminine—resembling feminine style without exaggerating or mocking it. His feminine role-taking was made apparent to the villagers primarily because he performed women's household activities, and because his associations were of feminine type. He cleaned the house, took care of babies, plaited coconut palm leaves into thatching sections, and made decorative patchwork quilts. He associated with the adolescent girls in the village as a peer, walking arm-in-arm with them, gossiping and visiting with them.[3]

There were two other men in Piri who had feminine mannerisms. It was sometimes said about them that they were mahu-like, but they were not said to be mahus. They had wives and children, and performed men's tasks in the

1. There is a note from one of the early (1804) visitors to Tahiti, John Turnbull (quoted by M. Bouge in Journal de la Société des Océanistes, 1955 volume 11 page 147) that the mahu "eagerly swallows [the semen] down as if it were the vigor and force of the other; thinking no doubt thus to restore to himself greater strength." Contemporary Tahitians, describing similar acts, exactly echo Turnbull's incorporation-of-strength thesis to explain why some mahus are so "healthy looking."

2. Some other reports on this work are noted in the references section.

3. The mahu in the other community that I studied, an urban enclave, in the major administrative center, Papeete, was in his fifties. He worked as a maid for a Chinese family. He was accepted as a semi-peer of a group of middle aged Tahitian women.

village. There was also a man in his twenties who had been a mahu in Piri, when the present one was a child. According to the village reports he had given up being a mahu, had gone to Papeete to work, and was now living as an "ordinary man." Mahus were not defined by effeminate behavior alone; they also had to fulfill some aspects of a woman's village role, a role they could give up to become ex-mahus.

It also appeared that many people assumed that Tahitian villages usually had a mahu. Someone would say, "I don't know who the mahu is in X village." When asked, "Then how do you know there is one?" the answer would be something like, "There always is one," or "That's the way things are." When asked if there were ever two mahus in a village, the common answer was, "No, only one." One informant pressed on this said, "When one dies, another replaces him. God arranges it like that. It isn't the nature of things, two mahus in one place. Only one . . . and when that one dies, he is replaced." From what inquiries I was able to make about other villages, although there were periods without a mahu, as there had been in Piri itself, and occasionally two for brief periods, the supposition of "at least one, and no more than one to a community," seemed to stand for an actual tendency. All but one of the villages on Huahine reportedly had one mahu at the time of my study.

Overt homosexual behavior was distinctly not an essential shared part of the community's idea of the mahu's role. The description on which everyone agreed was someone "who did woman's work."

All informants in Piri expressed generally positive feelings about the mahu in this aspect. First, they said he was "natural"; God (Tahitians have been Christian since the early nineteenth century) created him as a mahu—although this does not rule out a later, equally natural relinquishing of the role. Secondly, he was interesting. It was "wonderful" to see a man who had the skills to do women's things. Both men and women spoke with some pride of Piri's mahu's skill. Some men, however, expressed some discomfort about them—in spite of their adherence to a doctrine of approval.

As to his *overt* homosexual behavior, there was a variety of suppositions and of evaluations. Some informants in the village said that most mahus did not engage in sexual activities. Others, mostly the younger men in Piri, stated that all mahus engaged in sexual activity with other males, although they tended to be discreet and secret about it. This latter was the opinion of the mahu in Papeete.[4]

For those who said the mahu did engage in sexual activities, there were differences in opinions as to how many of the village young men were involved with him at one time or another. From the most reliable reports, it

4. The mahu in Piri for various reasons, probably relating to village ambivalences about his sexual life and, thus, to the importance of discreetness, was one of the only two people approached in the village who refused request for life histories.

appears that only a small percentage were involved.[5] The type of sexual activity seems to be limited now (both in Piri and elsewhere) to fellatio, with the mahu being the active partner. Intercourse between the mahu's thighs, with its more clearly feminine sexual role-playing was not reported, and denied when asked about. Anal sodomy was known, but considered to be an unclean perversion introduced by the Europeans, and limited to Papeete.

Those men in Piri who had had contacts with a mahu (either in the village or on visits to Papeete) spoke about it quite openly in interviews. They portrayed the mahu as simply a substitute woman, and described the acts with much the same affect and evaluations that they used for describing casual heterosexual acts. Thus (from a tape recorded interview) an eighteen-year-old man, asked if he felt any shame or embarrassment over it, said, "No, one isn't ashamed. You don't put any particular importance on it. It is like feeding the mahu with your penis. You get more pleasure out of it than they do. . . . For you it is just the same as if you were having intercourse with a woman. You don't take it seriously."

Evaluations by those villagers who denied sexual contact with mahus as to the mahu's sexual behavior and evaluations of the mahu's partner were more complex than the acceptance of nonsexual parts of his behavior. While some villagers were tolerant, repeating that it was just like other kinds of sexual acts, some of the villagers, both men and women, thought that the acts were "disgusting," and that both the mahu and his partner should be ashamed—reflecting Morrison's pre-Christian "I never found any who did not detest the thought." No one, however, ever labeled the partner as a mahu, nor indicated that they thought he was any less manful for his "indecent" behavior.

It is evident that the existence of the mahu role serves various psychological functions. For the mahu himself, it provides a legitimate identity congruent with some of his needs. (The one mahu whom I studied at any length had reported having a feminine self-image from his earliest remembered childhood.) And similarly for the Tahitian men who had occasional physical relations with mahus, a variety of motives, some quite culturally specific, were served.[6]

If we accept the proposition that mahu behavior represents a social role in Tahitian villages, one may ask about its functions, about the social or community purposes that it serves.

5. There were no reports of homosexual relationships between men if neither one was a mahu. Informants said that this "never" happened. In Papeete on the other hand these relationships did exist, and a new term *raerae* had been recently introduced to describe people who engage in preferential homosexual activities, but who are not necessarily mahus.

6. I did not find any examples of exclusive or most-frequent contact of a male with a mahu rather than with women, although semi-legendary stories of men occasionally living with a mahu as a spouse were sometimes told.

The ideal of one and only one mahu to a village would imply not only that somebody was recruited for the role (recall Bligh's remark that mahus were "particularly selected when boys") but that other possible candidates were somehow kept out of the role. This limits the possible function of the role as an acceptable escape from the male role by men whose temperament of aberrant socialization ill-fit them for it. Not only are some candidates kept out, but I have seen in other Tahitian communities very young boys apparently being coaxed into the role where I had the impression that the clues, if any, to which the coaxers were responding were at most related to the possibility of the child playing a transvestite role and not to any strong inclination, and it is possible that the coaxers were acting with no clues at all.

A larger part of the population participated as partners, and this was also part of the use of the role. But for most people the essence of the mahu was his highly visable "doing woman's work" in its public aspects; the private and generally secret sexual acts were considered by some as a perverse aspect of this otherwise acceptable behavior.

I would suggest that the presence and the maintenance of the mahu role have as major aspects a cognitive and message function to the community as audience, particularly to the male members.

Sexual role differentiation has special features and problems for individuals in the communities which I studied. At the cultural level there is relatively little differentiation when compared to Western expectations. The Tahitian language has no grammatical index of gender, the majority of Tahitian first names are not differentiated sexually, there is a relative equality and similarity of much male and female role behavior. To the degree that they are differentiated there is a frequent crossing over in a number of the work roles when necessary, for example, because of the illness of one of the adults in a small household. There is an emphasis in doctrine on playing down sex differences, and this is striking in men's playing down of any special difficulties in women's experience (such as childbirth), or in giving women either any special distinctions or disabilities. The emphasis is on equality, and minimizing of differences.[7]

On a more covert level, identity formation of children growing up in Tahitian households tends to be diffused. Generally the powerful caretakers include a network of older siblings and cousins in a system which is guided in a relatively exterior fashion by the mother, and to which the father is very peripheral except in unusual circumstances. The caretakers are mostly girls and young women, and this, and the fact that her eventual adult roles are those which she witnesses closely every day in the household, seem to make it considerably easier for a girl to establish a sexual identity by modeling and

7. There are clear anxieties underlying this equalizing, but they are not immediately relevant here.

role learning than for a boy.[8] Some indication of the limited differentiation is given by a remark of Gauguin's that Tahitian men seemed to him "androgynous," and that, "there is something virile in the women and something feminine in the men" (Gauguin, 1957:47). Similarly, Henry Adams remarked in a letter from Tahiti in the 1890s that, "the Polynesian woman seems to me too much like the Polynesian man; the difference is not great enough to admit of sentiment, only of physical divergence" (Adams, 1930:484).

There is much homo-erotic play among boys, particularly related to the adolescent boys' life stage in which membership in the village peer group is of central importance. There is much body contact, occasional dancing together, occasional group masturbation, much darting out timidly into heterosexual forays and then a return for bragging and discussion to the peer group.

I propose that in the absence of strong internal shaping toward the self-definition of manhood in its sense of contrast and complementarity to womanhood that there have been developed various external marks or signs which function to clarify that definition.

One is the supercision of the penis which all boys undergo in early puberty. An analysis of the symbolic aspects of this indicates that it marks (as has been often suggested for such rites) both separation from household-parent-child binding and special male status.

I believe that the mahu role, with its clear cut rules, its high visibility, its strictly limited incumbency, and its preempting of homosexual behavior, also has a message function. It says "there, clearly, out in the open, is the mahu, the one man who has taken a female role. I am a non-mahu. Whatever feelings I have about men are no threat to me and to my eventual role as family head. I can see exactly what *he* is, and I am clear about myself in that I am not he."[9]

I suggest that the mahu is a carefully maintained role, building on pre-existing possibilities for a supply of candidates, which carefully presents a behavior complex that serves the important function, among other subsidiary ones, of defining and stabilizing a precarious aspect of identity by a clear negative image—that which I am not, and cannot be . . . .

8. There is no *institutionalized* female homosexuality. There are some male role playing women in Papeete, but this is considered bizarre by the people in Piri.

9. George Devereux (1937) in an article on institutionalized homosexuality of the Mohave Indians suggested that one of the functions of the practice was to create "an 'abscess of fixation' and [to localize] the disorder in a small area of the body social." This seems to be related to the thesis presented here.

REFERENCES

Adams, H. *Letters of Henry Adams*. Boston and New York: Houghton Mifflin Co., 1930.

Bligh, W. *The log of the Bounty*. London: Golden Cockerel Press, n.d.

Devereux, G. "Institutionalized homosexuality of the Mohave Indians." *Human Biology* 9 (1937): 498-527.

Gauguin, Paul. *Noa noa*. New York: Noonday Press, 1957.

Levy, R. "Ma'ohi drinking patterns in the Society Islands." *The Journal of the Polynesian Society* 75 (1966): 304-320.

_____. "Tahitian folk psychotherapy." *International Mental Health Research Newsletter* 9 (1967).

_____. "Child management structure and its implications in a Tahitain family." In *A modern introduction to the family*, edited by E. Vogel and N. Bell. New York: Free Press, 1968a.

_____. "Tahiti observed: early European impressions of Tahitian personal style." *The Journal of the Polynesian Society* 77 (1968b):1: 33-42.

_____. "On getting angry in the Society Islands." In *Mental health research in Asia and the Pacific*, edited by W. Caudill and T. Lin. Honolulu: East West Center Press, 1969a.

_____. "Tahitian adoption as a psychological message." In *Adoption in Eastern Oceania*, edited by V. Carroll. Honolulu: University of Hawaii Press, 1969b.

_____. "Personal forms and meanings in Tahitian Protestantism." *Journal de la Société des Océanistes* 25 (1969c): 125-136.

_____. "Personality studies in Polynesia and Micronesia, stability and change." *Working papers 8, Social Science Research Institute*. Honolulu: University of Hawaii, 1969d.

Morrison, J. *The journal of James Morrison*. London: Golden Cockerel Press, 1935.

ROBERT A. DENTLER AND KAI T. ERIKSON

The Group Function of
Schizophrenia in the Military

[This is a] study of schizophrenia among basic trainees in the U.S. Army . . . .
Through various interview and questionnaire techniques, a large body of data
was collected which enabled the investigators to reconstruct short histories
of the group life shared by the future schizophrenic and his squad prior to the
former's hospitalization. There were eleven subjects in the data under consideration. The bulk of the evidence used for this short report comes from
loosely structured interviews which were conducted with the entire squad in
attendance, shortly after it had lost one of its members to the psychiatric
hospital.

The eleven young men whose breakdown was the subject of the interviews
all came from the northeastern corner of the United States, most of them
from rural or small-town communities. Typically, these men had accumulated
long records of deviation in civilian life: while few of them had attracted
psychiatric attention, they had left behind them fairly consistent records of
job failure, school truancy, and other minor difficulties in the community.
Persons in the community took notice of this behavior, of course, but they
tended to be gently puzzled by it rather than attributing distinct deviant
motives to it.

When such a person enters the service, vaguely aware that his past performance did not entirely live up to expectations current in his community,

Source: Dentler, Robert A., and Erikson, Kai T. "The Functions of Deviance in Groups."
Social Problems 7 (Fall 1959): 104-106. Permission granted by The Society for the
Study of Social Problems and the authors.

he is likely to start negotiating with his squad mates about the conditions of his membership in the group. He sees himself as warranting special group consideration, as a consequence of a deviant style which he himself is unable to define; yet the group has clear-cut obligations which require a high degree of responsibility and coordination from everyone. The negotiation seems to go through several successive stages, during which a reversal of original positions takes place and the individual is fitted for a role which is clearly deviant.

The first stage is characteristic of the recruit's first days in camp. His initial reaction is likely to be an abrupt attempt to discard his entire "civilian" repertoire to free himself for adoption of new styles and new ways. His new uniform for daily wear seems to become for him a symbolic uniform for his sense of identity: he is, in short, overconforming. He is likely to interpret any gesture of command as a literal moral mandate, sometimes suffering injury when told to scrub the floor until his fingers bleed, or trying to consciously repress thoughts of home when told to get everything out of his head but the military exercise of the moment.

The second stage begins shortly thereafter as he fails to recognize that "regulation" reality is different from the reality of group life, and that the circuits which carry useful information are contained within the more informal source. The prepsychotic is, to begin with, a person for whom contacts with peers are not easy to establish, and as he tries to find his way into these circuits, looking for cues to the rhythm of group life, he sees that a fairly standard set of interaction techniques is in use. There are ways to initiate conversation, ways to impose demands, and so on. Out of this cultural lore, then, he chooses different gambits to test. He may learn to ask for matches to start discussion, be ready with a supply of cigarettes for others to "bum," or he may pick up a local joke or expression and repeat it continually. Too often, however, he misses the context in which these interaction cues are appropriate, so that his behavior, in its overliteral simplicity, becomes almost a caricature of the sociability rule he is trying to follow. We may cite the "specialist" in giving away cigarettes:

> I was out of cigarettes and he had a whole pack. I said, "Joe, you got a smoke?" He says "yes," and Jesus, he gave me about twelve of them. At other times he used to offer me two or three packs of cigarettes at a time when I was out.

Or the "specialist" in greetings:

> He'd go by you in the barracks and say, "What do you say, Jake?" I'd say, "Hi, George, how are you?" and he'd walk into the latrine. And he'd come by not a minute later, and it's the same thing all over again, "What do you say, Jake?" It seemed to me he was always saying "hi" to someone. You could be sitting right beside him for ten minutes and he would keep on saying it.

These clumsy overtures lead the individual and the group into the third stage. Here the recruit, almost hidden from group view in his earlier over-conformity, has become a highly visible group object: his behavior is clearly "off beat," anomalous; he has made a presentation of himself to the squad, and the squad has had either to make provisions for him in the group structure or begin the process of eliminating him. The prepsychotic is clearly a low producer, and in this sense he is potentially a handicap. Yet the group neither exerts strong pressures on him to conform nor attempts to expel him from the squad. Instead, he is typically given a wide license to deviate from both the performance and behavior norms of the group, and the group in turn forms a hard protective shell around him which hides him from exposure to outside authorities.

His duties are performed by others, and in response the squad only seems to ask of him that he be at least consistent in his deviation—that he be consistently helpless and consistently anomalous. In a sense, he becomes the ward of the group, hidden from outside view but the object of friendly ridicule within. He is referred to as "our teddy bear," "our pet," "mascot," "little brother," "toy," and so on. In a setting where having buddies is highly valued, he is unlikely to receive any sociometric choices at all. But it would be quite unfortunate to assume that he is therefore isolated from the group or repudiated by it: an accurate sociogram would have the deviant individual encircled by the interlocking sociometric preferences, sheltered by the group structure, and an important point of reference for it.

The examples just presented are weak in that they include only failures of the process described. The shell which protected the deviant from visibility leaked, outside medical authorities were notified, and he was eventually hospitalized. But as a final note it is interesting to observe that the shell remained even after the person for whom it was erected had withdrawn. Large portions of every squad interview were devoted to arguments, directed at a psychiatrist, that the departed member was not ill and should never have been hospitalized.

DISCUSSION

... One aim of this paper is to encourage a functional approach to deviance, to consider the contributions deviant behavior may make toward the development of organizational structures, rather than focusing on the implicit assumption that structures must be somehow in a state of disrepair if they produce deviant behavior.

Any group attempts to locate its position in social space by defining its symbolic boundaries, and this process of self-location takes place not only in reference to the central norms which the group develops but in reference to the *range* of possibilities which the culture makes available. Specialized statuses which are located on the margins of the group, chiefly high-rank leaders and low-rank deviants, become critical referents for establishing the end points of this range, the group boundaries.

As [the] . . . Army illustrations suggest, deviant members are important targets toward which group concerns become focused. Not only do they symbolize the group's activities, but they help give other members a sense of group size, its range and extent, by marking where the group begins and ends in space. In general, the deviant seems to help give the group structure a visible "shape." The deviant is someone about whom something should be done, and the group, in expressing this concern, is able to reaffirm its essential cohesion and indicate what the group is and what it can do.

PAT LAUDERDALE

Deviance and Moral Boundaries

The functional theory of social control conceptualizes social systems as having a social space in which action is defined and evaluated. Within this space there are moral boundaries that give the social system a sense of its identity—that is, identity in terms of what types of entities inhabit it, what types of actions those entities engage in and what types of actions are permissible or moral. To maintain this boundary (and solidarity), the system or parts of the system negatively sanction those entities (e.g., actors or actions) that appear to threaten the boundary. . . .

From a functional perspective, [then,] deviance can be viewed as a regular, integrative and "normal" aspect of any social system, rather than as an irregular, disintegrative and abnormal problem (cf. Durkheim, 1964). Furthermore, it is possible to interpret the "elimination" of deviance not as elimination but, instead, as an attempt to redefine or maintain the moral boundaries that have been symbolically transgressed. Deviance can be thought of as a product of the movement of moral boundaries rather than as a product of the movement of actors across those boundaries. . . .

THEORETICAL ARGUMENT

Our argument is that in order to maintain its moral boundary, its corporate

Source: Lauderdale, Pat. "Deviance and Moral Boundaries." *American Sociological Review* 41, 4 (1976): 661–76. Permission granted by the American Sociological Association and the author.

structure and its solidarity, the social system becomes less tolerant of the internal deviant(s), thereby increasing the level of rejection of the deviants. The redefinition of the deviants as "more deviant," and, therefore, the redefinition of the moral boundaries, creates greater solidarity among the nondeviants of that social system by reaffirming the common corporate membership. That is (1) an external threat to a corporate social system produces an initial, momentary loss of solidarity since the constituents become unsure of the continued existence of the system; (2) in order to ensure its existence as a corporate structure and reestablish its solidarity, the system increases its rejection of the deviants, thereby shifting the moral boundary; (3) the rejection of the deviant and movement of the moral boundary reduce the extent of the internal threat (the deviants) by placing the deviants further from the moral boundary; (4) the rejection of the deviants and movement of the boundary also prepare the system for repulsion of the external threat by bringing divergent (but not deviant and nondeviant) parts into a unified whole, thereby reestablishing solidarity and reaffirming the purity of the nondeviants and the moral boundary of the social system, as well as ensuring the corporate existence of the system. Essentially, we conceive of the external threat as serving as a magnifier of the internal threat—the deviants. That is, the external threat points to the potential dangers of the internal deviants that were not apparent prior to the threat. . . .

The essential hypotheses from our theoretical argument are:

(1) If a threat from the outside challenges the corporateness of a social system, then there will be an increase in the level of rejection of the deviant(s) within that social system.

(2) If a threat from the outside challenges the corporateness of a social system, then the definition of the deviant(s) within that system will become more negative.

(3) If a threat from the outside challenges the corporateness of a social system, then there will be a shift in the moral boundaries of that system.

(4) If there is an increase in the rejection of the deviant(s) within a corporate social system, then there will be an increase in the solidarity of that system. . . .

RESEARCH DESIGN AND PROCEDURES

The Experimental Test

Subjects were solicited to join a social-work group whose ostensible purpose was to review the case histories of juvenile delinquents and to recommend correctional treatment to various authorities.

We chose social-work groups because they can fulfill the requirement of an ongoing, corporate social system. Also, subjects were assigned to groups on the basis of their preliminary interest ratings to ensure that the system will have a minimal level of solidarity.

A brief case history of a juvenile delinquent, distributed at the initial meeting, provided the basis for group discussion. The members were to recommend the best treatment for the delinquent, believing that their recommendations would go to various criminal authorities. An observer, nominally acting as a criminal justice authority and as an expert on the manner in which these groups perform, was present at the meetings to take notes on how the group was progressing. In a typical meeting, after preliminary introductions, each group member read a revised version (i.e., Johnny Martin) of the "Johnny Rocco" case (Evans, 1948), the life history of a juvenile delinquent, which ends as Johnny is waiting sentence for a minor crime. The case was presented as that of a real person. The experimenter (leader) asked the members to discuss and decide on recommendations for the delinquent. A scaled list of alternative recommendations was provided, ranging from extreme love and affection . . . to extreme punishment. . . . Between these two extremes were graded variations of the two points of view. This scale, used to point to the differences of opinion within the group, was introduced to the group members as a convenient device for realizing everyone's position and providing a focal point for the initial part of the discussion.

After reading the case history, each member announced the position on the scale that he had chosen. One confederate, the deviant, chose an extreme position and maintained it throughout the discussion. . . .

The discussion was limited to 55 minutes and was largely concerned with thrashing out differences of opinion among members. After the first 25 minutes, the experimenter took a census to make sure that each member was fully aware of everyone else's position. The last 30 minutes involved further discussion of the problem and, of course, the introduction of our experimental manipulations.

There were 40 groups with a total N of 160. Each group had five members, and in each condition one of these members was the paid confederate (the deviant). The minimal test of our ideas required two conditions: condition 1 consisted of an outside threat and a deviant; condition 2 consisted of no outside threat but a deviant.

In the threat condition, an outside threat was introduced to the group after the first 30 minutes of interaction. The criminal justice authority (observer), who was not involved in the interaction of the group, made a statement to the experimenter (leader) to the effect that "this group should probably not continue." Although this comment was directed to the experimenter, it was made quite audible for the "benefit" of the group members. The observer then, as before, isolated himself from the group's interaction (in fact, at this point he left the meeting). The threat was left ambiguous and the group was allowed to continue. . . .

In the second condition, the criminal justice authority . . . introduced a nonthreatening message to the group after the first 30 minutes to ensure that it was the *threat* that was producing the predicted changes. That is, we wanted to be certain that it was the content of the message that was producing the predicted changes, and that not just any message was sufficient to do so.

In order to assess the change in the boundaries relative to the two conditions, . . . [a scale] was administered. We asked the subjects to select a latitude of acceptance (that segment including the person's own position on the issue, plus the other positions which he would tolerate around that position), a latitude of rejection (that segment including the position on the issue most objectionable to the person, plus other positions also objectionable to the person), and a latitude of noncommitment (that range in which the individual expressed neither acceptance nor rejection). The instrument was administered after the first 20 minutes and again at the conclusion of the group meeting.

In order to assess the change in the internal volume of deviance relative to the two conditions, it was explained to the group members at the conclusion of the meeting that it might be necessary to reduce the number of group members or to break up the group and apportion its members to one of the other groups: therefore, it would be helpful to know which people would like to remain together. They were asked to rank everyone present in order of preference and intensity of that preference for remaining in the same group with them. The specific question was: "To what extent do *you* prefer each other member of your discussion group today to be a member of another similar committee? (Please circle the number that most clearly reflects your preference.)"

In order to assess the level of solidarity, we asked the members at the beginning of the group (i.e., after the initial solidarity manipulation and some five minutes into the meeting) to what extent they were interested in participating in the present judicial study. Also, since we were interested in a measure of solidarity immediately following the threatening or nonthreatening message, we recorded the group interaction on tape and coded that interaction in terms of a solidarity measure. At the conclusion of the meeting, we asked the group members to indicate to what extent they wished to remain in their group and how often they thought the group should meet. At this point, we asked the individual members to stay for a few extra minutes, noting that we were interested in receiving feedback on what type of individual is "best" for this kind of social-work group. This comment was made to each individual privately. We asked each member to indicate on an adjective list (cf. Alexander and Knight, 1971) his impression of that individual to whom he gave the highest preference rating and his impression of that individual to whom he gave the highest preference rating and his impression of that individual to whom he gave the lowest preference rating. The latter impression gave us a measure of the level of negative definition attached to the deviant. As the other measure of the level of stigma attached to the deviant, we asked each member privately, at the conclusion of the post-experimental interview, if there were any people in the group with whom he did not want to work. . . .

Subjects and Facilities

Subjects in the experiment were all males, aged 17 to 25, recruited from various colleges and universities in the Bay Area of Northern California. Each subject was paid for his participation, but not all subjects were aware in advance that they were going to be paid.

RESULTS

The first data are concerned with initial solidarity. After introductions and allowance for "small talk," the group members were asked: "How interested are you in participating in the present judicial study?" The alternatives ranged from "not interested at all" (scored 1) to "extremely interested" (scored 4). The results . . . [indicated that] the levels of group interest for conditions of threat and nonthreat are not significantly different.

Table 1 presents the mean desirability scores for the deviant and other group members. At the end of each meeting the question posed to the group members was: "To what extent do you prefer each other member of your discussion group today to be a member of a similar committee?" The scale ranged from "not at all" (position 1) to "very much" (position 7). The data in Table 1 show that the mean ratings of Others are not significantly different . . . $(Z = 0.001)$ in either threat or nonthreat conditions. The data also show that mean ratings of Deviant are considerably lower . . . than Others in both threat and nonthreat conditions, and that Deviant in the threat condition is much more strongly rejected . . . than Deviant in the nonthreat condition. Therefore, Table 1 supports the first hypothesis: if a threat from the outside challenges the corporateness of a social system, then there will be an increase in the level of rejection of the deviant(s) within that social system.

At the end of the interview, group members were also asked if there were any people in their group with whom they did not want to work. This separate measure of the rejection of the deviant also supported the hypothesis, since three times (30 percent in the threat condition versus 10 percent in the

Table 1: Mean Sociometric Scores for the Deviant and Other Group Members by Condition

CONDITION	N	DEVIANT	OTHERS
THREAT	80	2.800	7.088
NONTHREAT	80	5.275	7.162

Sum of ranks of deviant and others in THREAT condition (Z = –12.337) are significantly different (p < .01) by Mann-Whitney U-Test. Sum of ranks of deviants and others in NONTHREAT condition (Z = –7.503) are significantly different (p < .01) by Mann-Whitney U-Test. Sum of ranks of deviant in THREAT and NONTHREAT conditions (Z = –8.268) are significantly different (p < .01) by Mann-Whitney U-Test. Sum of ranks of others in THREAT and NONTHREAT conditions (Z = 0.0001) are not significantly different by Mann-Whitney U-Test.

nonthreat condition) as many people mentioned the deviant in the threat condition as did those in the nonthreat.

Table 2 supports the second hypothesis: the definition of Deviant becoming more negative when the system is threatened. After the sociometric choices were made, subjects were informed that, in order to be able to organize the advisory groups more efficiently, we were interested in the impressions they had formed of the individuals they preferred the most and the least in their group. The subjects were presented the series of adjective-pairs and asked to: "Please rate this person as best you can in terms of the overall impression you had of him." They were then asked to select the "most relevant" adjectives for describing the person. There were separate forms for most- and least-preferred individuals, and the seven adjective-pairs in Table 2 particularly dominated the relevance selections for the least-preferred individual (in Table 2 the least-preferred individual is synonymous with the deviant). The adjectives were on a scale of 1 to 9, with 1 being the most positive dimension and 9 the most negative. From Table 2, it is evident that the deviant in the threat condition was seen as significantly more Irrational, Rigid, Cold, Insensitive, and somewhat less Honest than the deviant in the nonthreat condition. The deviant was also characterized as slightly Unfriendly and Antisocial in both conditions, but those dimensions were not significantly different between conditions.

It is interesting to note that the most-preferred individual in the threat condition systematically received more positive definitions than the most-preferred individual in the nonthreat. Additionally, the data in Table 2 show that four of the seven dimensions were significantly different: the most-preferred individual in the threat condition was seen as clearly more Friendly, Flexible, Sensitive and Social than the most-preferred individual in the

Table 2:   Mean Scores of the Most Relevant Adjectives that Characterize the Deviant
and the Most Preferred Group Member by Condition[a]

	DEVIANT[b]		MOST-PREFERRED	
ADJECTIVE	THREAT	NONTHREAT	THREAT	NONTHREAT
Rational (1)–	7.649	5.925*	2.267	2.267
Irrational (9)	(N = 37)	(N = 40)	(N = 45)	(N = 45)
Friendly (1)–	6.656	6.415	1.969	2.465*
Unfriendly (9)	(N = 32)	(N = 41)	(N = 32)	(N = 43)
Flexible (1)–	8.250	7.594*	1.771	4.083*
Rigid (9)	(N = 44)	(N = 32)	(N = 35)	(N = 24)
Warm (1)–	7.867	7.242*	2.909	3.421
Cold (9)	(N = 30)	(N = 33)	(N = 11)	(N = 19)
Sensitive (1)–	7.686	4.640*	2.643	4.391*
Insensitive (9)	(N = 35)	(N = 25)	(N = 28)	(N = 23)
Social (1)–	7.469	7.219	2.000	3.429*
Antisocial (9)	(N = 32)	(N = 32)	(N = 11)	(N = 14)
Honest (1)–	4.576	3.069*	2.429	2.581
Dishonest (9)	(N = 33)	(N = 29)	(N = 35)	(N = 43)

[a]The mean scores range from 1 as the most positive characterization to 9 as the most
negative.
[b]In every case, the group member least preferred by the other group members was the
deviant; therefore, in this table, deviant is synonymous with least-preferred.
*T-test yields a significant difference (p < .01) between conditions.

nonthreat condition. A comparison of the data in Table 2 points to the
idea of an evaluative continuum between the threat-nonthreat conditions
and the deviant-most-preferred individual. In the following section, we will
elaborate on possible substantive reasons for this systematic relationship.

The first series of data related to the boundary hypothesis showed the
similarity of the most acceptable and most objectionable positions in the
initial and final measurements of the recommendations concerning the
disposition of "Johnny Martin." For the most acceptable and most objectionable positions, there is little difference from the initial to the final phase
and no significant difference in the boundaries for conditions of threat
and nonthreat.

The next data relevant to the boundary hypothesis concerns the *latitudes*
of acceptance, rejection and noncommitment. These latitudes were computed
by counting the number of *other* positions accepted (excluding the most
acceptable), *others* rejected (excluding the most objectionable) or those not
evaluated by each subject, and by computing means for the three categories
for phases and conditions (cf. Sherif and Sherif, 1965). The latitudes of

Table 3:   Mean Sizes of Latitudes of Rejection*

	Phase	
Condition	Initial	Final
THREAT	1.650	2.125
NONTHREAT	1.712	1.562

*A two-way analysis of variance of . . . the effects of phases and conditions on latitudes of rejection yields nonsignificant F-ratios for main effects and a significant F-ratio for interaction effect (df = 1,316, p < .01).

Table 4:   Mean Sizes of Latitudes of Noncommitment*

	Phase	
Condition	Initial	Final
THREAT	1.988	1.325
NONTHREAT	2.040	2.025

*A two-way analysis of variance of the . . . effects of phases and conditions on latitudes of noncommitment yields nonsignificant F-ratios for main effects and a significant F-ratio for interaction effect (df = 1,316, p < .01).

acceptance data indicated that there is little difference from the initial to the final phase and that there is not a significant difference in the boundaries for conditions of threat and nonthreat. However, a comparison of the latitudes of rejection in Table 3 notes the strong increase in the size of the latitude of rejection for the threat condition versus the nonthreat. That is, the groups in the threat condition rejected significantly more positions in the final phase than did those in the nonthreat. The latitudes of noncommitment presented in Table 4 follow the pattern established by the latitudes of rejection, but inversely. The groups in the threat condition are impressively less noncommittal than those in the nonthreat. The data from Table 4 indicate that groups in the nonthreat condition frequently are more noncommital, thereby having larger latitudes of noncommitment than those groups in the threat condition.

In summary, the average number of *other* acceptable positions does not differ significantly. The systematic variation to be found in the patterns lies in the latitudes of rejection and noncommitment. The latitude of rejection for the threat condition is larger than that for the nonthreat, and the latitude of noncommitment is smaller for the threat condition than that for the nonthreat. We interpret the shift in these latitudes as a constriction of the

Figure 1: Distribution of the Mean Number of Group Solidarity Communications by Conditions of Threat and Nonthreat

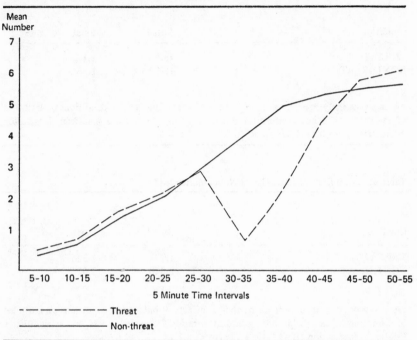

boundary around the position of the deviant ... in the threat condition. Therefore, the data in Tables 3 and 4 lend support to the third hypothesis: if a threat from the outside challenges the corporateness of a social system, then there will be a shift in the moral boundaries of that system. . . .

The first series of data concerning the solidarity hypothesis showed that there is a slightly larger mean interest in remaining in the group in the threat condition; however, that difference is not significant. The question asked of the members to obtain these means was: "To what extent do you wish to remain in the group?" The scale ranged from "not at all interested" (scored 1) to "extremely interested" (scored 4).

The data concerning the solidarity hypothesis were obtained by dividing the meeting into ten-minute intervals and measuring group solidarity communications (as indicated by Bales' [1950] social-emotional interaction process categories) for each interval. . . .

Figure 1 shows the movement of solidarity communications throughout the group meetings in both threat and nonthreat conditions by presenting the distribution of the mean number of group solidarity communications in five-minute intervals. The distribution of the communications in the threat

Table 5:   Solidarity as Indicated by Interest in Future Group Meetings*

		Frequency of Meetings		
Condition	(N)	Twice a Week or More	Once a week	Once Every 2, 3, or 4 Weeks
THREAT	80	25%	49%	26%
NONTHREAT	80	14%	42%	44%

*Chi-square = 16.485, df = 2, p < .01.

condition not only points to the severe loss of solidarity following the threat, but also to the remarkable recovery of solidarity starting with the 35–40 minute interval. This series of solidarity data coupled with the data regarding the rejection of the deviant lends support to the last hypothesis which states that if there is an increase in the rejection of the deviant(s) within a corporate social system, then there will be an increase in the solidarity of that system.

Table 5 also supports the solidarity hypothesis. In this table, the indicator of solidarity is the amount of interest in future group meetings. Subjects were asked to answer: "How often do you think this group should meet?" . . . The threat condition produced significantly . . . more interest in future group meetings than did the nonthreat. The results shown in Table 5 are striking considering that there was such a large loss of solidarity (as indicated by the interaction process categories) in the threat condition some 30 minutes prior to asking this frequency-of-meeting question.

DISCUSSION

. . . Let us turn to the specific relationships between the support of the hypotheses and our theoretical argument. Our first statement was: (1) an external threat to a corporate social system produces an initial, momentary loss of solidarity since the constituents become unsure of the continued existence of the system. The data (especially the distribution of the mean number of group solidarity communications) indicated that the external threat did produce an initial, momentary loss of solidarity, and we *assume* that the loss was due to the constituents' uncertainty concerning the continued existence of the system. It is important to mention that "group solidarity communications" may not be the best indicator of solidarity immediately following the threat, and it would be preferable to have other indicators. However, our pretests showed that the reactivity of other measurements precluded their inclusion.

The next statement was: (2) in order to ensure its existence as a corporate structure and reestablish its solidarity, the system increases its rejection of the deviant(s), thereby shifting the moral boundary. . . . Three times as many people stated that they did not want to work with the deviant in the threat condition versus the nonthreat. This strong rejection of the deviant in the threat condition appears to be directly related to the reestablishment of solidarity following the threat.

We also maintain that the strong rejection of the deviant following the threat is related to the shift in the moral boundaries evident in the threat condition. The groups in the threat condition rejected significantly more positions than did those in the nonthreat. Also, groups in the threat condition were more certain of those positions to which they were committed. We suggest that, since these positions were related to the disposition of a supposedly real juvenile delinquent, they are reasonable indicators of the moral boundary of the group.

We then stated: (3) the rejection of the deviant and movement of the moral boundary reduce the extent of the internal threat (the deviant[s]) by placing the deviant(s) further from [the] moral boundary. The groups in the threat condition did reject more positions around the deviant's position than did those in the nonthreat. That is, in the threat condition the moral boundary was "tightened." The groups in the threat condition were less tolerant of the deviant's moral position; and we suggest that, as a function of this increased intolerance of the deviant's position, they pushed the deviant farther from their moral boundary. We also suggest that this tightening of the boundary and placement of the deviant farther from the boundary was a process that developed throughout the last phase of the threat group.

The next statement in the theoretical argument was: (4) the rejection of the deviants and the movement of the boundary also prepare the system for repulsion of the external threat bringing divergent (but not deviant and nondeviant) parts into a unified whole, thereby reestablishing solidarity and reaffirming the purity of the nondeviants and the moral boundary of the social system, as well as ensuring the corporate existence of the system. All the indicators of solidarity confirm that solidarity was reestablished in the threat groups. In fact, all of the indicators support the notion that solidarity was increasing at a faster rate in the threat condition. We have only indirect indications that the nondeviants in the threat condition were reaffirming their "purity." That is, the groups that followed the threat defined their most preferred member as more Friendly, Flexible, Sensitive, and Social than did those in the nonthreat condition. Another type of response that points to this reaffirmation of purity is the amount and type of interaction produced in the threat group following the threat. . . . Much of the content of that . . . interaction . . . confirmed the righteous nature of the group's existence. . . . The selection of the latitudes of rejection and noncommitment by the groups in the threat condition point to the reaffirmation of the moral boundary. We maintain that the reestablishment of solidarity, the reaffirmation of the purity of the nondeviants and the reaffirmation of the moral boundary by the nondeviants help ensure the corporate existence of the system. . . .

CONCLUSION

. . . We have presented a system of theoretical relationships and corresponding empirical support to explain how the definition and volume of deviance can change in a particular social system independent of the actions of the deviants associated with that system. The evidence from our study supports the contention that deviants, independent of their actions, will be more severely rejected and stigmatized following an external threat to their corporate social system; that rejection and stigmatization has been related to the loss-then-reestablishment of solidarity of that system and the constriction of the moral boundary and, therefore, the further movement of the boundary away from the deviants. . . .

REFERENCES

Alexander, C. Norman, Jr., and Knight, Gordon W. "Situated identities and social psychological experimentation." *Sociometry* 34 (1971): 65–82.

Bales, Robert F. *Interaction Process Analysis.* Cambridge: Addison-Wesley, 1950.

Durkheim, Emile. *The Division of Labor in Society.* New York: Free Press, 1964.

Evans, J. "Johnny Rocco." *Journal of Abnormal and Social Psychology* 43 (1948): 357–83.

Sherif, Muzafer, and Sherif, Carolyn W. *Attitude and Attitude Change.* Philadelphia: Saunders, 1965.

JAMES INVERARITY

Populism and Lynching in Louisiana: Boundary Crises and Repressive Justice

This study seeks to [analyze] . . . lynching in Louisiana during the Populist revolt. This historical phenomenon provides an ideal test case for the [boundary maintenance] argument in three ways. First, lynchings during this period clearly epitomize Durkheim's concept of repressive justice in being ritual punishments "in which the whole society participates in rather large measure" (Durkheim, 1893:76).

> A lynching may be defined as an illegal and summary execution at the hands of a mob, or a number of persons, who have in some degree the public opinion of the community behind them. (Cutler, 1905:276)

. . . Typically, lynchings involved large segments of the community partici-pants in an open, public reaction against an accused criminal. Seldom were any attempts made to disguise the identity of the participants; indeed, in many cases photographs of the participants subsequently appeared in news-papers. Lynchings were carried out with the acquiescence, if not approval, of law enforcement agents; and, in fact, between 1890 and 1900, lynchings out-numbered legal executions by a ratio of 2 to 1 (Bye, 1919:57-8, 64-5). Many prominent white Southerners—publicists, newspaper editors, politicians—

Source: Inverarity, James. "Populism and Lynchings in Louisiana, 1889–1896: A Test of Erikson's Theory of the Relationship between Boundary Crises and Repressive Justice." *American Sociological Review* 41, 2 (April 1976): 263-71, 273-76, 278-80. Permission granted by The American Sociological Association and the author.

viewed lynching as a necessary and legitimate adjunct of the legal system, to maintain law and order, to protect white women and to "keep the niggers in their place" (cf. Collins, 1918). How diffuse these sentiments were in the general white population is difficult to gauge precisely, although as late as the 1930s some 64 percent of the survey respondents in a small Mississippi town agreed that lynching was justified in rape cases (Powdermaker, 1939: 389). . . . [L]ynchings in Louisiana unequivocally involved popular participation and legitimation.

Second, the Populist revolt is a particularly revealing instance of a boundary crisis. The revolt, as will be shown below, was the major breakdown in Southern white solidarity after Reconstruction. Even more significant for our purposes are the ways in which white solidarity was politically institutionalized. In addition to . . . impressionistic assessments of disruption, . . . election statistics provide an explicit, albeit crude, index of the extent of and variation in the boundary crisis.[1] Moreover, the political institutions of this society create a periodicity in the boundary crisis, since conflicts were intensified every two years during election campaigns. This study will capitalize on both these aspects of political institutionalization in arriving at indicators of the magnitude of the boundary crisis that are logically independent of the incidence of repressive justice.

Third, lynchings varied in frequency among a wide range of communities. This opens up the possibility of comparing the reactions of a number of communities differing in their levels of solidarity to a single boundary crisis. . . . Louisiana in the 1890s conveniently provides 59 parishes for comparison.[2]

1. Erikson (1966:89) utilizes data from the gubernatorial election of 1637 to determine the strength of the Antinomian faction.

2. The county in the South was the major political and social unit. As Johnson (1941:3) notes:

> Although every county may have some variation within its borders, the type of underlying economy that dominates tends to enforce itself throughout the country and to be reflected in the characteristic social organization. In many cases . . . the county appears to be a community in itself and to reflect a natural history of development. The open county farming of the section makes it easier for one to say that he is from Jackson County, Georgia, or Green County, Alabama, than from a particular township.

Not only was the county the major social and economic unit, but crime produced the most intense passion among the residents of the county in which it was committed. For example, a lynching failed to occur in the sensational Scottsboro rape case:

> . . . in part, because of the fact that neither of the girls was from Jackson County, Alabama. As Birmingham *News* reporter melodramatically put it: "The homes of Jackson County people were not desecrated. There were no relatives of the girls to feel surging within them the demand for blood vengeance." The question was one of race unheated by personal relationships. (Carter, 1969:10)

The burden of this paper is to show how . . . [the functionalist approach] . . . can be used to generate hypotheses about the relationships between a parish's incidence of lynching and its social and political characteristics. Before considering the systematic empirical analysis, however, it is essential to have some understanding of the sense in which the Populist movement constituted a disruption of solidarity among Southern whites. The following section briefly outlines the basic contours of this history.[3]

The Boundary Crisis in Southern White Solidarity

The familiar idea of the Solid South may be viewed as an instance of mechanical solidarity among Southern whites. As Williams (1961:47) notes:

> In the monolithic Democratic party the whites could thresh out their differences; but these differences would never become troublesome because no issue must be permitted to divide white solidarity. It was an admirable arrangement to head off any economic stirrings on the part of the masses. Indeed, it was understood that there was supposed to be no relationship between politics and economics.

This consensus on values, harmony of interests, and unity of purpose among Southern whites was generated and sustained by two major external threats, the North and the Negro, both of which in the 1890s were politically institutionalized in the Republican party. The sectional conflict and racial issue were of long standing, but the Reconstruction period (c. 1867-1876) provided the real basis for the Solid South. After the Civil War, Congress, dominated by Radical Republicans, reconstituted the state governments of the former Confederacy. Through Constitutional amendment and national legislation, the Negro became not only a citizen but an officeholder as well. The sudden elevation of the Negro, the incursion of Northern adventurers and the occupation of Federal troops (in Louisiana until 1876) galvanized Southern whites around the Democratic party (cf. Turner, 1967).

> The upshot [of Reconstruction] was a suppression of class feeling . . . the like of which has probably not been seen in any other developed society of modern times. (Cash 1941:112)

From the end of Reconstruction to the last decade of the century, the Solid South remained intact. During the Populist revolt of the 1890s, how-

3. Space limitations necessitate sketching the broad contours of this history sufficient for an understanding of the subsequent analysis. Fuller treatment may be found in the references. See especially Lewinson, 1932; Woodward, 1951; Hair, 1969; Cunningham, 1964; Dethloff and Jones, 1968; Howard, 1957; Johnson, 1949.

ever, Southern white solidarity briefly collapsed. In Louisiana "the agrarian revolt was no less than a political and social earthquake" (Degler, 1974:320). The cause of this convulsion lay in the social structure of Southern society. The Solid South was a social myth; the underlying social reality was basically a dichotomous class structure typical of commercial plantation systems (cf. Stinchcombe, 1961). Large planters, merchants, and industrial entrepreneurs constituted a relatively homogeneous class ("the Bourbons"),[4] while most whites were either small farmers or laborers.[5]

The dormant class conflict was increasingly exacerbated by the Bourbon's policy of laissez faire capitalism, which curtailed public education and other social services instituted by the Reconstruction governments and encouraged Northern and British capital to expand the railroad system and exploit the natural resources. Central to this program of economic development was a supply of cheap, docile labor. Although progress was, in the long run, to be beneficial to the whole population, the short run profits were to be used to motivate entrepreneurs while the short run costs were to be borne by the poor whites and the blacks.

The interests of the latter in railroad rate regulation, cheaper credit and higher wages diametrically opposed Bourbon ambitions for a New South. In the 1870s and 1880s, as agricultural prices declined and credit became tighter, lower-class Southern whites began to join farmers throughout the country in a series of national agrarian social and political movements: The Grange, the Farmer's Alliance, The People's (Populist) Party. While most of these organizations sought to work within the framework of existing political parties, the Populists organized as a distinct political entity, which in Louisiana directly confronted the mythology of the Solid South.

The conflict between the two classes of whites was complicated by the racial factor in Southern politics. In Louisiana the blacks were enfranchised in 1868 and overwhelmingly supported the Republican Party. After Reconstruction the Bourbons continued to support franchisement for the blacks. Since black males of voting age outnumbered their white counterparts in many areas, the Bourbons perceived a manipulated black electorate as essential in guaranteeing their position vis-à-vis the poor whites. Moreover, the ability of the Bourbons through economic and physical coercion to deliver

4. The major cleavage in Louisiana's Bourbon class was the split between cotton planters and sugar planters in seven southern parishes who supported the Republican party because its tariff policy promoted their economic interests.

5. In the antebellum South only about 30 percent of the white farmers owned slaves and of these 50 percent owned fewer than five slaves (Woofter, 1936). Except for the threat of black labor competition, most whites, therefore, had little vested interest in the institution of slavery. During the Civil War lower-class whites throughout the South were enraged by Confederate conscription laws (which exempted owners of large plantations) and by war profiteering of their wealthier brethern. Lower-class whites openly rebelled against the Confederacy in several areas (Shugg, 1939; Degler, 1974).

black votes in their districts gave them power in the national Democratic party. Lower-class whites, on the other hand, opposed the black franchise both for the threat it posed to their status and, increasingly, for the power it gave to the Bourbons.

The Populist leaders sought to overcome the racism of the lower-class whites and pragmatically sought to attract the black vote, arguing that " 'the accident of color can make no possible difference in the interest of farmers, croppers, and laborers' " (Woodward, 1951:402). The Populists viewed the ideal of the Solid South as a form of false consciousness and the true interest of the lower-class whites as being not in racial status but in economic position. As the Democratic *Tensas Gazette* editorialized, "We can no longer depend upon the solidarity of the white race" (Hair, 1969:238).

Louisiana's Populists waged strong campaigns in the state and national elections of 1892, the Congressional election of 1894 and the gubernatorial election of 1896. Not only did the Louisiana Populists seek support of the blacks, but they formed coalitions ("fusions") with the Republican Party. The peak of the insurgency was reached in 1896 when the Populists and other anti-Democratic factions won control of 40 percent of the seats in the state General Assembly. Although the Populists carried several parishes, they were unable to win gubernatorial and Congressional contests, for the Democrats controlled both the black votes and the election machinery in too many areas. Frustrated by legitimate means of political opposition many Populists discussed the possibility of open, armed rebellion.

The agrarian revolt, however, died quietly. Many of the supporters of Populism simply withdrew from politics altogether while others returned to the Democratic Party. The latter restored white solidarity in two ways. First, it adopted a major Populist demand, in inflationary monetary policy. (In the Presidential election of 1896 the Populist Party formed a coalition with the Democrats behind free silver advocate William Jennings Bryan.) Second, the Democrats adopted the policy of disenfranchising the blacks.[6] In effect, this policy shifted emphasis from economic interests back to racial status as the basis of political organization.

> Hopes for reform and the political means employed in defiance of tradition and at great cost to emotional attachments . . . met with cruel disappointments and frustration. There had to be a scapegoat. And all along the line signals were going up to indicate that the Negro was an approved object of aggression. (Woodward, 1957:64)

While de facto discrimination and disenfranchisement had been widespread

6. The number of black registered voters was cut from 130,334 in 1896 to 1,342 by 1904. While in 1896 black registered voters outnumbered the whites in 26 parishes, by 1900 whites were the majority in all parishes (Woodward, 1957:68).

Figure 1. Frequency of Lynching in Louisiana, 1889–1900

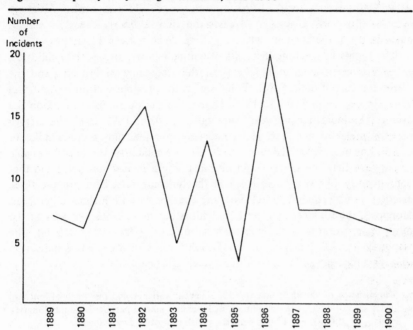

previously, the systematic exclusion of the Negro from social, political, and economic life dates from the collapse of Populism in the latter part of the 1890s (Woodward, 1957; 1971). As a result of this reaffirmation of white supremacy, the boundary crisis precipitated by the Populist movement was resolved and the Solid South restored.

This brief sketch of the historical context suggests that Southern whites in the 1890s experienced a boundary crisis. . . . Reconstruction consolidated the two classes of Southern whites into a one party system, but this unity was broken by a wave of agrarian radicalism. The political failures of Populism resulted in a restoration of the Solid South on a renewed basis of extremist white supremacy. . . .

VARIABLES AND INDICATORS

Lynchings and Repressive Justice

Lynchings will be used in this analysis as the indicator of repressive justice. The data on lynchings were tabulated from a compilation from newspapers made by the N.A.A.C.P. (1919) of victims, date, and location of incident and the alleged offense. Between 1889 and 1896, there were 83 lynchings for which parishes can be identified, an average of 1.41 per parish.[7] Although most victims were black, in 14 cases the victims were white. The unit of analysis here is the incident, which may include as many as 11 victims.

The trends in lynching incidents over time (shown in Figure 1) indicate a fairly systematic relationship between the frequency of lynching and the disruption of the Solid South. Populism, as the previous section showed, was at its apogee from 1892 to 1896. During this period Louisiana had, on the average, 13 incidents per year. Subsequently, from 1897–1918 the average was five incidents per year. This comparison provides only a crude indicator of how lynching responded to the crisis of white solidarity. It seems reasonable to suppose that the crisis would be most severe in election years and that consequently this will be revealed in the lynching rate. Thus, in the three election years (1892, 1894, 1896), the average was 17 incidents per year. Moreover, the sharpest increase in lynchings occurs in 1896, the year of the most bitter contest in the gubernatorial election (Hair, 1969:259 ff). The responsiveness of lynching to the Populist crisis provides some indication that lynching is a valid indicator of repressive justice.[8]

7. The variance of the incidents is 2.52. Since the variance and the mean of lynching incidents are not equal, the distribution of lynchings among parishes is nonrandom (see Spilerman, 1970:632). For 12 incidents the parish cannot be determined.

8. In terms of Erikson's theory, since the strain on white solidarity increased during the elections, the symbolic threat of the criminal correspondingly increased. Groundless accusations became more accepted; when accusations were made, there was much less willingness to allow the law to take its course and a greater need to immediately and ritualistically punish the alleged offender.

Lynching and political conflict, however, might be related more directly, simply as a consequence of the attempts by whites to coerce black voters. Although political violence was widespread during the elections, lynchings do not seem to be simply one manifestation of political violence. If lynchings were used as a form of direct political intimidation, there should be some increase in the victims charged with noncriminal offenses during election years. In the election years (1892, 1894, 1896), only 4 of the 43 victims of lynch mobs were not charged with criminal offenses. Furthermore, 79 percent of the victims were charged with the most serious crimes, murder and rape, during the election years, while only 46 percent of the victims were charged with these offenses in nonelection years. This increase in the proportion of serious offenses during elections is more consistent with Erikson's theory than it is with the interpretation of the increase in lynchings as a direct outgrowth of political violence.

A plausible alternative interpretation is that lynchings were basically a mode of political violence and that the accusations of rape or murder were simply cover-ups designed to conceal the real motive. This is a difficult argument to address with the kinds of evidence available. There are, however, two reasons for rejecting this interpretation. First, political murders were so common that it is difficult to see why indirect methods of political coercion would have been employed. Second, the available descriptive accounts yield no evidence that politically active blacks were accused of crimes and then lynched. In general, it appears victims were possibly not only innocent of the alleged crimes, but innocent of any other offense against the white community. During the 1892 election, white Democrats attempted to lynch a prominent black Populist (Woodward, 1938:240), but this incident seems, on the basis of available evidence, to be isolated.

A further, qualitative indication of the validity of lynching as an index of repressive justice is Woodward's observation that a wave of virulent racism swept the South around the turn of the century, during and after the passage of Jim Crow and disenfranchisement legislation; further, the decline in the rate of lynching was "happily not in conformity with [this] deterioration in race relations" (1951:351). The weight of the evidence, then, suggests that the rate of lynching varies systematically with the disruption of white solidarity and is unaffected by fluctuations in the degree of racist hostility toward blacks.

Solidarity and Parish Characteristics

Published census and electoral data (U. S. Census 1916; 1920; Burnham, 1955; Daniel, 1943) provide a fairly wide range of information about the characteristics of the parishes.[9] The problem for this analysis is to select indicators that can be linked conceptually to the level of solidarity among Southern whites in the parishes.

The discussion of the historical context pointed out that the Solid South arose from the Reconstruction experience of Yankee occupation and "Negro rule." While the actual degree of black participation in Reconstruction governments was minimal, the perceived threat of black domination loomed as a powerful impetus to white solidarity. Moreover, as long as blacks could vote, any split between the whites would hand over the balance of power to the black electorate. It seems reasonable, therefore, to take percent black in the parish as one determinant of the degree of white solidarity; the greater the percent black, the greater the degree of white solidarity.[10]

9. The data on racial composition and urbanization are from the 1900 enumeration (U.S. Bureau of the Census, 1920), those on religious affiliation from the 1916 report. Taking observations from various dates seems justified, given the apparent stabilities in these variables over time. Thus, the average intercensus correlation for percent black from 1890–1920 is $\bar{r} = .947$; for percent urban from 1900 to 1920, $\bar{r} = .899$. It seems unlikely that there were any differential changes in parish characteristics during this period that would materially affect the parameter estimates.

10. Two major caveats must be considered in interpreting percent black as a determinant of white solidarity. First, percent black is in general a powerful explanatory variable statistically (see e.g., Spilerman, 1970; Matthews and Prothro, 1963). Like many variables that provide good statistical explanations, however, percent black is most accurately regarded as a proxy variable for several conceptually distinct processes. Blalock (1967a) suggests some strategies for disentangling threat and competition processes. Reed (1972) reports that the relationship between lynching and percent black is congruent with Blalock's threat hypothesis. In the absence of a more direct index of white fear of black domination, percent black is employed here although it may well represent other aspects of the social organization of the parish.

Second, the effects of percent black are empirically indistinguishable from the

In addition to the racial composition of the parish, two additional determinants of the level of solidarity have been selected. First, urbanization is taken as an index of the extent to which the parish is differentiated, hence organically rather than mechanically solidary. Urban areas are more likely to be ethnically heterogeneous and occupationally diverse (the correlation between percent urban and number of persons engaged in manufacturing is $r = .83$). Since the degree of mechanical solidarity is less in urban areas we should find fewer lynchings in urban than in rural parishes.[11] As Cash (1941: 314) observes:

> It is a part of the general law of the town everywhere that its inhabitants rarely lynch; that the tradition of direct action by mobs natural to the frontier and the open, little policed countryside tends more and more to die out . . . it was largely in the new and growing towns and in the areas in which they stand that lynchings tended to fall off most rapidly.

The third independent variable is an index of religious homogeneity. Louisiana is divided between a French-speaking Catholic white population in the South and an Anglo-Saxon Protestant white population in the North. In any given parish, the degree of solidarity among whites will be contingent on the degree of homogeneity on this characteristic. As Hair (1969:186) points out:

> . . . the commingling of English-speaking and Creole-Cajun cultures had resulted in a milieu of political instability and unusual insensitivity to human rights.

The index of religious homogeneity is calculated by the following formula: $I = 1 - p(1 - p)$, where p denotes the percent Catholic population of the parish. Predominately Catholic or predominately Protestant parishes will have a greater homogeneity since $p(1-p)$ reaches a maximum at .5.

A direct index of the parish's commitment to the Solid South is its level of Democratic vote. Percent Democratic vote in two elections, the 1892

effects of the absolute size of the black and white populations since the percentage variable is an exact linear function of these two variables (cf. Blalock, 1967b). This especially becomes a problem when substantive significance can be attached to effects of both the percentage variable and its components. (In this case, the greater the white population the more potential lynchers; the greater the black population, the greater the potential number of victims.)

11. The distribution of urbanization is markedly skewed among Louisiana's parishes. Only 14 parishes (24 percent) have any urban population. At the other extreme, Orleans parish, containing New Orleans, is 100 percent urban. Consequently, urbanization is a dummy variable that takes on the value 1 if the parish has any urban population and 0 otherwise.

Table 1. Correlation Coefficients for 59 Louisiana Parishes

	1	2	3	4	5	6	7
1. Percent Black	1.0						
2. Urbanization	-.110	1.0					
3. Religious Homogeneity	.231	-.435	1.0				
4. Percent Democratic Vote, 1892 Presidential Election	.324	.098	.246	1.0			
5. Percent Democratic Vote, 1896 Gubernatorial Election	.649	-.058	.178	.496	1.0		
6. Lynchings, 1889–1896	.295	.170	-.014	.253	.213	1.0	
7. Black Population Size	.229	.401	-.224	.111	.230	.418	1.0
Mean	.508	.254	.902	.766	.589	1.41	11,031
Standard Deviation	.213	.439	.082	.210	.229	1.59	11,028

Presidential and the 1896 gubernatorial, will be taken as reflectors of the degree of solidarity.

Table 1 provides the intercorrelations among the variables along with their means and standard deviations.

INCORPORATING THE VARIABLES INTO A CAUSAL MODEL

... The model in Figure 2 states that the level of mechanical solidarity in a given parish is affected by three structural properties of the parish: its percent black; its degree of urbanization; and the extent of its religious homogeneity. Mechanical solidarity should be greater the greater the percent black and the greater the extent of Catholic/Protestant religious homogeneity. On the other hand, urbanization should have a negative impact on the level of mechanical solidarity in the parish. The degree of the parish's mechanical solidarity is reflected by its Democratic vote in two elections.[12] The central thesis of this paper is that mechanical solidarity has a positive impact on repressive justice, which is equated in this model with the incidence of lynching.

12. Note that this does not mean popular support of Southern whites for the Democratic party. First, voting statistics at this time reflect black as well as white votes. Second, voting statistics reflect the capacity of the parties to carry out election fraud. The extent of fraud varies among parishes and among elections. Systematic parish by parish evidence on fraud is not available; but one rough indicator is the magnitude of the correlation between Democratic vote and percent black, since blacks, when given the opportunity, supported the Republican party. In the Presidential election of 1892, this correlation is .324; but in the gubernatorial election of 1896, it nearly doubles (r = .674). In contrast, the Presidential election of 1896, in which the Populists form a coalition with the Democrats and which by contemporary accounts was a fair election, the correlation between Democratic vote and percent black drops to r = -.104.

Figure 2. MIMIC Representation of Durkheim's Thesis Applied to Lynching in Louisiana

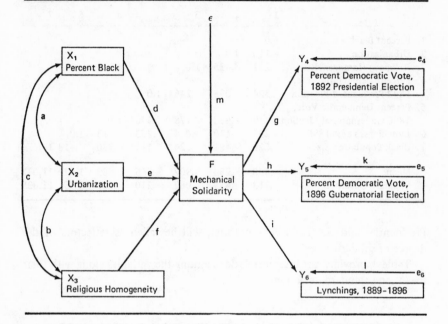

Figure 3. Maximum Likelihood Estimates for Causal Model with Unmeasured Variables

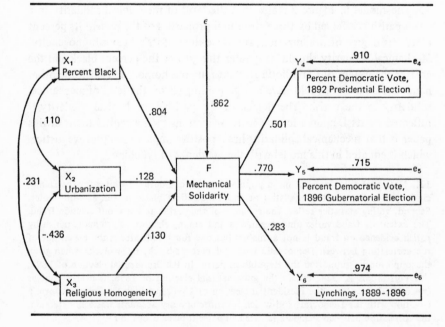

Estimates of the model's parameters are presented in Figure 3.[13] The overwhelming determinant of the level of solidarity is the percent black; the greater the percent black, the greater the level of solidarity. This is congruent with the argument that the threat of black domination was a catalyst for the formation of the Solid South. Urbanization has a small positive impact on solidarity. This is contrary to its anticipated effect since it means that strictly rural parishes have less solidarity than urban areas. This finding may, however, reflect a measurement error arising from using the simple rural/urban dichotomy, which compares primarily rural parishes with parishes that have small towns. Unfortunately, the small number of urban parishes makes it impossible to assess the impact of the *degree* of urbanization on mechanical solidarity, which would capture more realistically the theoretic distinction between mechanical and organic solidarity. Religious homogeneity, on the other hand, does have an anticipated positive impact on solidarity; the greater the homogeneity, the greater the solidarity. But, like urbanization, the magnitude of its impact is not breathtaking, being overshadowed by the impact of percent black.

Turning to the estimated consequences of solidarity, Democratic vote is a strong reflector of the level of solidarity, as would be expected from the substantive significance attached to Democratic voting. Solidarity has a moderate impact on the incidence of lynchings for the period in which the boundary crisis occurred. This is the part of the model that is of greatest theoretic import. It confirms the proposition that the greater the level of solidarity, the greater the incidence of repressive justice. . . .

Given the indicators used and the assumptions built into the model, this test permits us to conclude that the incidence of lynching as a form of repressive justice varied among Louisiana parishes directly with their level of [mechanical] solidarity. . . .

13. Fifteen correlations among the six observed variables may be computed. With nine parameters to be estimated, the model contains six overidentifying restrictions.

Conventional ordinary least squares (OLS) could be used to estimate the parameters of the model. However, OLS will yield alternative estimates for the overidentified parameters and thus, is not efficient (i.e., the variance of OLS estimates fail to converge to zero). Costner (1969) and others advocate a simple averaging of these conflicting estimates. Some estimates, however, will generally be more efficient than others. Where discrepancies among estimates are slight, simple averaging may be the most cost-effective procedure. For cases in which the estimates vary, however, methods for efficiently estimating overidentified models have recently evolved in the literature. These procedures take weighted averages of alternative estimators; the smaller the variance of the estimator, the greater its weight. While this may be done by several techniques, the best developed is the maximum likelihood estimation (MLE) procedure conceived by Jöreskog et al. (1970) and others (Werts et al., 1973; Hauser and Goldberger, 1971; Burt, 1973).

CONCLUSION

... After showing that lynching was a form of repressive justice and that the Populist disruption of the Solid South constituted a major boundary crisis, the study developed a causal model utilizing the configuration of observed relationships among various social and electoral variables to infer the relationship between the degree of mechanical solidarity and the extent of lynching ...

The paper has demonstrated that ... boundary crises ... [and their relationship to] repressive justice can be utilized to account for several peculiarities of lynching during this period (e.g., its tendency to increase during election years, but the failure of the offenses for which the victims were lynched to reflect political conflict directly; and the failure of lynching to increase with racist hostility toward the turn of the century). The study also suggests ... [that] the extent to which a given community responds to a boundary crisis with the exercise of repressive justice depends directly on the magnitude of mechanical solidarity in that community.

REFERENCES

Blalock, Hubert M., Jr. *Toward a Theory of Minority-Group Relations.* New York: John Wiley & Sons, 1967a.

———. "Status inconsistency, social mobility, status integration, and structural effects." *American Sociological Review* 32 (1967b): 790-801.

Burnham, Dean W. *Presidential Ballots, 1836-1892.* Baltimore: Johns Hopkins, 1955.

Burt, Ronald S. "Confirmatory factor-analytic structures and the theory construction process." *Sociological Methods and Research* 2 (1973): 131-90.

Bye, Raymond T. *Capitol Punishment in the United States.* Kenosha, Wi.: Collegiate Press, 1919.

Carter, Dan T. *Scottsboro: A Tragedy of the American South.* Baton Rouge: Louisiana State University Press, 1969.

Cash, Wylbur J. *The Mind of the South.* New York: Knopf, 1941.

Collins, Winfred H. *The Truth about Lynching and the Negro in the South.* New York: Neale, 1918.

Costner, Herbert L. "Theory, deduction, and rules of correspondence." *American Journal of Sociology* 75 (1969): 245-63.

Cutler, James E. *Lynch Law: An Investigation into the History of Lynching in the United States.* New York: Longmans, Greene, 1905.

Cunningham, George E. "The Italian, a hindrance to white solidarity in Louisiana, 1890-1898." *Journal of Negro History,* 1964: 22-36.

Daniel, Lucia E. "The Louisiana People's Party." *Louisiana Historical Quarterly* 26 (1943): 1055-149.

Degler, Carl N. *The Other South: Southern Dissenters in the Nineteenth Century.* New York: Harper & Row, 1974.

Dethloff, Hency R. and Jones, Robert R. "Race relations in Louisiana, 1877-1898." *Louisiana History* 9 (1968): 301-23.

Durkheim, Emile. *The Division of Labor in Society.* (1893) New York: Free Press, 1964.

Erikson, Kai T. *Wayward Puritans: A Study in the Sociology of Deviance.* New York: John Wiley & Sons, 1966.

Hair, William T. *Bourbonism and Agrarian Protest: Louisiana Politics, 1877-1900.* Baton Rouge: Louisiana University Press, 1969.

Hauser, Robert M., and Goldberger, Arthur S. "The Treatment of unobserable variables in path analysis." In *Sociological Methodology,* edited by Herbert L. Costner, pp. 81-117. San Francisco: Jossey-Bass, 1971.

Howard, Perry H. *Political Tendencies in Louisiana, 1812-1952.* Baton Rouge: Louisiana State University Press, 1957.

Johnson, Charles S. *Statistical Atlas of Southern Counties.* Chapel Hill: University of North Carolina Press, 1941.

Johnson, Guion G. "The ideology of white supremacy, 1876-1910." In *Essays in Southern Social History,* edited by Fletcher Green, pp. 124-56. Chapel Hill: University of North Carolina Press, 1949.

Jöreskog, Karl G.; Gruvaneus, Gunner T.; and van Thillo, Marielle. *ACOVS: A General Computer Program for Analysis of Convariance Structures.* Princeton: Educational Testing Service Research Bulletin 70-15, 1970.

Lewinson, Paul. *Race, Class and Party: A History of Negro Suffrage and White Politics in the South.* New York: Oxford University Press, 1932.

Matthews, Donald R., and Prothro, James W. "Political factors and Negro voter registration in the South." *American Political Science Review* 57 (1963): 355-67.

National Association for the Advancement of Colored People (N.A.A.C.P.). *Thirty Years of Lynching in the United States, 1889-1918.* (1919) New York: Arno, 1969.

Powdermaker, Hortense. *After Freedom: A Cultural Study in the Deep South.* New York: Viking, 1939.

Reed, John S. "Percent black: a test of Blalock's theory." *Social Forces* 50 (1972): 356-60.

Shugg, Roger W. *Origins of the Class Struggle in Louisiana: A Social History of White Farmers and Laborers during Slavery and After, 1840-1875.* Baton Rouge: Louisiana State University Press, 1939.

Spilerman, Seymour. "The causes of racial disturbance: a comparison of alternative explanations." *American Sociological Review* 35 (1970): 627-49.

Stinchcombe, Arthur. "Agricultural enterprise and rural class relations." *American Journal of Sociology* 67 (1961): 165-76.

Turner, Ralph H. "Types of solidarity in the reconstituting of groups." *The Pacific Sociological Review* 10 (1967): 60-8.

U.S. Bureau of the Census. *Religious Bodies.* Washington, D.C.: U.S. Government Printing Office, 1916.

———. *Fourteenth Census.* Vols. 1-3, 6. Washington, D.C.: U.S. Government Printing Office, 1920.

Werts, Charles E.; Jöreskog, Karl G.; and Linn, Robert L. "Identification and estimation in path analysis with unmeasured variables." *American Journal of Sociology* 78 (1973): 1469-84.

Williams, T. Harry. *Romance and Realism in Southern Politics.* Athens: University of Georgia Press, 1961.

Woodward, C. Vann. *Tom Watson: Agrarian Rebel.* New York: Rinehart, 1938.

———. *Origins of the New South.* Baton Rouge: Louisiana State University Press, 1951.

_____. *The Strange Career of Jim Crow.* New York: Oxford University Press, 1957.
_____. "The strange career of a historical controversy." In *American Counter-Point: Slavery and Racism in the North-South Dialogue,* edited by C. Vann Woodward, pp. 234-60. Boston: Little, Brown and Co., 1971.
Woofter, Thomas J. *Landlord and Tenant on the Cotton Plantation.* Washington, D.C.: Works Progress Administration, 1936.

PART TWO
Societal Definitions as Self-fulfilling Prophecies

As we have seen, the functionalist approach to deviant behavior suggests that nonconformity is an essential part of social organization. In an attempt to assert unique identities, groups establish moral and behavioral boundaries to demarcate the limits beyond which continued membership may be jeopardized. Boundaries function, that is, to indicate the range of activities that will be tolerated by the group. They become meaningful, however, only insofar as they are repeatedly tested. Through the transgressions of the nonconformer, the criteria of citizenship are made visible. Furthermore, the penalization of the deviant serves to validate the rewards of conformity and to reinforce the internal solidarity of group members. In this manner, the standards and values of social relationships are perpetuated.

The process by which behavioral boundaries are communicated is the focus of definitional theory. The assignment of meaning to particular actions or attributes occurs through collective definitions of the situation (Thomas, 1923). In this manner, group members acquire an understanding and appreciation of society's standards of acceptable behavior. Once these definitions have been internalized, they have a self-fulfilling effect (Merton, 1957). That is, subsequent behavior toward that which has been defined becomes structured in such a way as to produce the very outcome predicted. It is in this sense that William I. Thomas has proposed that "if men define situations as real, they are real in their consequences."

Of particular concern is that institutions designated officially responsible for the control of nonconformity—the police, the courts, and the various treatment and correctional agencies—may actually facilitate the creation of deviance. Such is the theme of Elliott Currie's "Witchcraft and Its Control in Renaissance Europe." Variations in social control measures implemented in England and Continental Europe had important implications for the rates of witchcraft and the kinds of people designated as deviant.

On the Continent, official reaction to witchcraft relied heavily on Inquisitional procedures. Suspension of the legal safeguards of the accused, the use of torture to obtain confessions, and reliance upon impossible dilemmas as proof of guilt produced large numbers of convicted witches. These conviction rates, in their turn, acted to underscore the gravity of the problem and thus led to further relaxation of procedural rules. Added to the unlimited authority of the state was a powerful motive for persecution. Upon conviction, the state had the right to confiscate the property of the witch. Since the use of confessions provided ever-expanding lists of potential accomplices, witchcraft in Continental Europe became a profitable industry, one that depended upon high rates of apprehension and recruitment of offenders from the highest social classes.

The control of witchcraft in England, on the other hand, involved a continued commitment to common law judicial procedures. In addition, while private entrepreneurs may have benefited personally from presumed expertise in the detection of witches, the absence of a state-wide profit motive from property confiscations left little incentive for vigorous pursuit of an offender population. As a result of this more restrained approach, there were not only fewer witches in England and fewer executions but those who were convicted of witchcraft were predominantly females from the lowest social classes.

On the basis of this comparative evidence, Currie has argued that deviance is the self-fulfilled product of institutionalized definitions of the situation. The nature of witchcraft, its extent, and the kinds of people designated as witches were reflective of the social control systems developed to deal with the problem.

A more contemporary illustration of the impact of institutionalized prophecies on behavioral outcomes concerns the role of the criminal record in legal processing. In a selection from our own research, "Prior Offense Record as a Self-Fulfilling Prophecy," we have argued that the accumulation of criminal histories among members of the lower classes is a product, in part, of discriminatory law enforcement and adjudication practices. The use of prior record in subsequent adjudications, then, serves to amplify discretionary decisions made earlier. The presumption of guilt implied by the criminal history leads to a denial of resources necessary for successful defense. Without bail and private counsel, persons frequently receive the more serious dispositions, dispositions which then become part of the official record.

It appears, therefore, that the use of prior record in legal processing constitutes an institutionalization of a self-fulfilling prophecy. Tne lower classes, by virtue of their disadvantaged status, more often accumulate criminal histories. These histories serve ultimately to justify differential treatment in any succeeding adjudications. The cycle is continuous and serves to fulfill the original prediction that the lower classes are prone to crime.

Official policies may also be responsible for creating the very conditions that perpetuate deviant behavior. According to James Spradley's, "Urban Nomads: A World of Strangers Who Are Friends," those qualities associated with urban vagrancy, mobility, alienation, poverty, and survival strategies, are the product of punitive reactions to homeless men.

Repeated arrests and lengthier sentences can be avoided only through continual flight. Similarly, the experience of arrest and incarceration acts to remove the urban nomad from participation in the larger society. Cut off from friends, family, and employers, the vagrant becomes increasingly alienated from the world around him.

Mobility and isolation have consequences for the poverty of the urban nomad. Transient employment and relief constitute the primary income sources of those whose life-styles have been formally designated as deviant. In addition, this poverty not only becomes exacerbated through the payment of bail or fines but becomes the major reason for incarceration. Repeated arrests result in increasing conviction fees. The inability to finance release leads ultimately to extended confinement.

Survival as an urban vagrant depends upon the acquisition of skills and supportive values and attitudes. The jail becomes an ideal locus for the transmission of those techniques, identities, and motives that ensure continued commitment to the nomadic life. The cumulative effect of the criminalization of homelessness, then, is a prophecy fulfilled.

Stereotypes of deviants are especially powerful definitions of the situation. Popularly diffused through mass media depictions and routine interaction, such conceptions serve to shape both informal and formal reactions to nonconformity. The consistency of responses to those who have been defined in terms of the stereotype may ultimately produce behavior that concurs with the original imagery.

Jock Young points out in "Drugs and the Role of the Police as Amplifiers of Deviancy," that the reality of marihuana smoking differs considerably from stereotypic beliefs regarding the drug. Law enforcement policies, however, insofar as they are motivated by popular concern, may act to transform the fantasy into reality. The threat of official reaction tends to isolate those who are defined as deviant. Through a process of association and communication, such persons come to develop norms and values that further accentuate their deviation. The amplification of deviance continues in a cyclical manner as negative reaction ensures increased nonconformity and, therefore, more stringent law enforcement measures.

Experimental evidence of the impact of self-fulfilling prophecies is provided by Robert Rosenthal and Lenore Jacobson's analysis of teacher expectations and student performance, "Pygmalian in the Classroom." Substandard academic achievement by lower-class and minority children has traditionally been attributed to the disadvantaged cultural milieu that precedes their entry into the school system. It is conceivable, however, that it is the expectation of poor performance, rather than the sociocultural conditions of poverty, that lies at the basis of this failure.

In order to assess the effects of achievement expectations on behavior, Rosenthal and Jacobson randomly selected a group of elementary students whom they designated to be "spurters." While such a selection was alleged to be the result of intellectual testing, in fact, the only difference between these children and all others was in the definition that they would show marked acceleration. Periodic retests of both experimental and control groups revealed that the "special" children gained in overall I.Q., performed better on standardized achievement tests, and were rated as better and more adjusted students than the undesignated pupils. Based on the prediction of improved performance, teachers somehow communicated to their "gifted" students the anticipation of intellectual growth. Whether through subtle cues, greater individual attention, or revised instructional techniques, the prophecy became the reality.

Behavioral expectations are communicated to group members through the definition of the situation. The selection of characteristics and activities for informal censure or formal processing serves to identify the range of behavior that will be tolerated by the collectivity. At the same time, once the definition has been assigned, events become structured in such a way as to produce the outcome predicted. Witchcraft and career criminality, urban nomadism, the development of drug subcultures, and academic failure, then, may be less a problem of the tendency toward nonconformity residing within individuals, and more the inevitable result of institutionalized policies and procedures.

REFERENCES

Merton, Robert K. *Social Theory and Social Structure.* New York: Free Press, 1957.
Thomas, William I. *The Unadjusted Girl.* Boston: Little, Brown and Co., 1923.

ELLIOT P. CURRIE

Witchcraft and Its Control
in Renaissance Europe

The sociological study of deviant behavior has begun to focus less on the deviant and more on society's response to him (Becker, 1963; Erikson, 1966; Kitsuse, 1962; Goffman, 1962, 1963; Lemert, 1951; Tannenbaum, 1951). One of several implications of this perspective is that a major concern of the sociology of deviance should be the identification and analysis of different kinds of systems of social control. Particularly important is the analysis of the impact of different kinds of control systems on the way deviant behavior is perceived and expressed in societies.

By playing down the importance of intrinsic differences between deviants and conventional people, and between the social situation of deviants and that of nondeviants, the focus on social response implies much more than the commonplace idea that society defines the kinds of behavior that will be considered odd, disgusting, or criminal. It implies that many elements of the behavior system of a given kind of deviance, including such things as the rate of deviance and the kinds of people who are identified as a deviant, will be significantly affected by the kind of control system through which the behavior is defined and managed.

In this paper, I attempt to add to the rather small body of research on kinds of social control systems and their impact (Schur, 1962). The subject is witchcraft in Renaissance Europe, and in particular, the way in which

Source: Currie, Elliot P. "Crimes Without Criminals: Witchcraft and Its Control in Renaissance Europe." *Law and Society Review* 3 (October 1968): 7–28. Permission granted by The Law and Society Association.

the phenomenon of witchcraft differed in England and in continental Europe,[1] as a result of differences in their legal systems. I will show that the English and the continental legal systems during this period represented the two ends of a continuum along which different social control systems may be placed, and I will suggest some general ways in which each kind of control system affects the deviant behavior systems in which it is involved. Along the way, however, I will also suggest that the *degree* to which a social control system can influence the character of a deviant behavior system is variable and depends in part on the *kind* of behavior involved and the particular way it is socially defined.

WITCHCRAFT AS DEVIANCE

Something labeled witchcraft can be found in many societies, but the particular definition of the crime of witchcraft which emerged in Renaissance Europe was unique. It consisted of the individual's making, for whatever reason and to whatever end, a pact or covenant with the Devil, thereby gaining the power to manipulate supernatural forces for antisocial and un-Christian ends. What was critical was the pact itself; not the assumption or use of the powers which it supposedly conferred, but the willful renunciation of the Faith implied by the act of Covenant with the Devil. Thus, on the Continent, witchcraft was usually prosecuted as a form of heresy, and in England as a felony whose essence was primarily mental.[2] Witchcraft, then, came to be defined as a sort of thought-crime. It was not necessarily related to the practice of magic, which was widespread and had many legitimate forms. There were statutes forbidding witchcraft before the Renaissance, but the new conception of witchcraft involved important changes in both the nature and the seriousness of the crime. Early legislation, throughout Europe, had tended to lump witchcraft and magic in the same category, and to deal with them as minor offenses. In ninth-century England, the Law of the Northumbrian Priests held that if anyone "... in any way love witchcraft, or worship idols, if he be a king's thane, let him pay X half-marks; half to Christ, half to the king. We are all to love and worship one god, and strictly hold one Christianity, and renounce all heathenship." (Murray, 1962:22; Ewen, 1929:1-5.)

1. Erikson, 1966, discusses some aspects of witchcraft in America, which unfortunately cannot be discussed here without unduly lengthening the paper. For the curious, though, it should be noted that the American experience was in general much closer to the English than to the continental experience, particularly in terms of the small number of witches executed. For anyone interested in American witchcraft, Erikson's discussion and bibliography is a good place to start.

2. Elizabeth's statute of 1563 made witchcraft punishable by death only if it resulted in the death of the bewitched; witchcraft unconnected with death was a lesser offense. However, in 1604 James I revised the statute to invoke the death penalty for witchcraft regardless of result. On this point see Davies, 1947:15, 41-42.

Similar mildness is characteristic of other early English legislation, while the Catholic Church itself, in the thirteenth century, explicitly took the position that the belief in witchcraft was an illusion.[3] In no sense were witches considered by ecclesiastical or secular authorities to be a serious problem, until the fifteenth century.

I cannot speculate here on the process through which the early conception of witchcraft as, essentially, the witch's delusion evolved to the point where the witch was believed to have actual powers. Suffice it to say that such a shift in definition did take place;[4] that during the fifteenth and sixteenth centuries a new theological and legal conception of witchcraft emerged, which amounted to an official recognition of a hitherto unknown form of deviance. In 1484, Pope Innocent IV issued a Bull recognizing the seriousness of the crime of witchcraft, affirming its reality, and authorizing the use of the Holy Inquisition to prosecute it with full force. As an indication of the state of thinking on witchcraft at this time, this document serves admirably.

It has recently come to our attention, not without bitter sorrow, that ... many persons of both sexes, unmindful of their own salvation and straying from the Catholic Faith, have abandoned themselves to devils ... and by their ... accursed charms and crafts, enormities and horrid offenses, have slain unborn infants and the offspring of cattle, have blasted the produce of the earth ... these wretches furthermore afflict and torment men and women ... with terrible and piteous pains.... Over and above this they blasphemously renounce the Faith which is theirs by the Sacrament of Baptism, and do not shrink from committing and perpetrating the foulest abominations and filthiest excesses ... (Davies, 1947:4.)

A few years later, the new conception of witchcraft was given practical impetus with the publication of a manual known as the *Malleus Maleficarum,* or Witch-Hammer, written by two German Inquistors under Papal authorization, which set forth in systematic form the heretofore diffuse beliefs on

3. This position was formulated in a document known as the CAPITULUM EPISCOPI, apparently written in 1215, which molded Church policy for over 200 years. It reads in part as follows:

Some wicked women ... seduced by the illusions and phantasms of demons, believe and profess that they ride at night with Diana on certain beasts with an innumerable company of women, passing over immense distances ... priests everywhere should preach that they know this to be false, and that such phantasms are sent by the Evil Spirit, who deludes them in dreams ... (Lea, 1888:Vol 3, 493;Murray, 1962:22.)

4. The shift, however, did not take place all at once, nor did it take place without important ideological struggles both within and beyond the Church; a number of important figures remained skeptical throughout. Interesting materials on this process can be found in Lea, 1939:Vol. 1.

the nature and habits of witches, means for their discovery, and guidelines for their trial and execution (Sprenger and Kramer, 1948). At this point, the witch persecutions in continental Europe entered a peak phase which lasted into the eighteenth century. Estimates of the number of witches executed in Western Europe vary, but half a million is an average count (Kittredge, 1907:59). Although there were consistently dissident voices both within and outside of the Church, the prevalence of witches was a fact widely accepted by the majority, including a number of the most powerful intellects of the time. Luther and Calvin were believers, as was Jean Bodin, who wrote an extremely influential book on witches in which he argued, among other things, that those who scoffed at the reality of witches were usually witches themselves (Davies, 1947:25, 5-9). Witchcraft was used as an explanation for virtually everything drastic or unpleasant that occurred; leading one Jesuit critic of the persecutions, Father Friedrich Spee, to declare: "God and Nature no longer do anything; witches, everything." (Kittredge, 1907:47.) In the fifteenth century, a delayed winter in the province of Treves brought over a hundred people to the stake as witches (Lea, 1888:Vol. 3, 549).

Once officially recognized, the crime of witchcraft presented serious problems for those systems of control through which it was to be hunted down and suppressed. The fact that no one had ever been seen making a pact with the Devil made ordinary sources of evidence rather worthless. Ordinary people, indeed, were in theory unable to see the Devil at all; as an eminent jurist, Sinistrari, phrased the problem, "There can be no witness of that crime, since the Devil, visible to the witch, escapes the sight of all beside." (Parrinder, 1958:76.) The attendant acts—flying by night, attending witches' Sabbaths, and so on—were of such nature that little reliable evidence of their occurrence could be gathered through normal procedures. The difficulty of proving that the crime had ever taken place severely taxed the competence of European legal institutions, and two different responses emerged. In England, the response to witchcraft took place within a framework of effective limitations on the suppressive power of the legal order and a relatively advanced conception of due process of law; on the Continent, the response took place within a framework of minimal limitations on the activity of the legal system, in which due process and legal restraint tended to go by the board.

CONTINENTAL EUROPE: REPRESSIVE CONTROL

In continental Europe, people accused of witchcraft were brought before the elaborate machinery of a specialized bureaucratic agency with unusual powers and what amounted to a nearly complete absence of institutional restraints on its activity. Originally, the control of witchcraft was the responsibility of the Inquisition. After the disappearance, for practical purposes, of the Inquisition in most of Western Europe in the sixteenth century, witches were tried before secular courts which retained for the most part the methods which the Inquisition had pioneered (Lea, 1939:Vol. 1, 244). This was as true of the Protestant sectors of Europe—England excepted—as it was of those which remained Catholic (Burr, 1891:11). The methods were effective and extreme.

Ordinary continental criminal procedure approximated the "inquisitorial" process, in which accusation, detection, prosecution, and judgment are all in the hands of the official control system, rather than in those of private persons; and all of these functions reside basically in one individual (Esmein, 1913:8 passim). The trial was not, as it was in the "accusatorial" procedure of English law, a confrontative combat between the accuser and the accused, but an attack by the judge and his staff upon the suspect, who carried with him a heavy presumption of guilt. Litigation was played down or rejected (Esmein, 1913:9).

> The system of procedure called inquisitorial is more scientific and more complex than the accusatory system. It is better adapted to the needs of social repression. Its two predominant features are the secret inquiry to discover the culprit, and the employment of torture to obtain his confession. (Esmein, 1913:8.)

Above and beyond the tendencies to repressive control visible in the inquisitorial process generally, the establishment of the Holy Inquisition in the thirteenth century as a weapon against heresy ushered in a broadening of the powers of the control system vis-à-vis the accused. Ecclesiastical criminal procedure had always been willing to invoke extraordinary methods in particularly heinous crimes, especially those committed in secret (Esmein, 1913:128). With the coming of the Inquisition a good many procedural safeguards were systematically cast aside, on the ground that the Inquisition was to be seen as "an impartial spiritual father, whose functions in the salvation of souls should be fettered by no rules." (Lea, 1958:Vol. 1, 405.) Thus, in the interest of maintaining the ideological purity of Christendom, the legal process became conceived as a tool of the moral order, whose use and limits were almost entirely contingent on the needs of that order.

Nevertheless, certain powerful safeguards existed, in theory, for the accused. Chief among these was a rigorous conception of proof, especially in the case of capital crimes. In general, continental criminal procedure, at least from the fifteenth century onward, demanded a "complete proof" as warrant for capital punishment. "Complete proof" generally implied evidence on the order of testimony of two eyewitnesses to the criminal act or, in the case of certain crimes which otherwise would be difficult to establish, like heresy or conspiracy against the Prince, written proofs bound by rigorous standards of authenticity (Esmein, 1913:622-23). In most cases of heresy and of witchcraft generally, proof of this order was hard, if not impossible, to come by, for obvious reasons. As a result, it was necessary to form a complete proof through combining confession, which was strong but not complete evidence, with another indication, such as testimony by one witness (Esmein, 1913:625).[5] The result was tremendous pressure for confession at all costs, as well as a pressure for the relaxation of standards for witnesses and other sources of lesser evidence. The pressure for confession put a premium on the regular and systematic use of torture. In this manner, the procedural safeguard of rigorous proof broke down in practice through the allowance of extraordinary procedures which became necessary to circumvent it (Esmein, 1913:625).[6]

In theory, there were some restraints on the use of torture, but not many. One sixteenth-century German jurist argued that it could not be used without sufficient indication of guilt, that it could not be used "immoderately," and that it should be tempered according to the strength, age, sex, and condition of the offender. German officials, when approving the use of torture, usually added the phrase *Doch Mensch-oder-Christlicher Weise,*—roughly, "In humane or Christian fashion." (Lea, 1939:Vol. 2, 854-55.) In theory, confessions under torture had to be reaffirmed afterward by the accused; but torture, though it could not lawfully be repeated, could be "continued" indefinitely after interruption, and few accused witches could maintain a denial of their confession after several sessions (Lea, 1939:Vol. 2, 427-28; Esmein, 1913: 113-14).

Besides being virtually required for the death penalty, confession was useful in two other important ways, which consequently increased the usefulness of torture. First, confession involved the denunciation of accomplices, which assured a steady flow of accused witches into the courts (Lea, 1939: Vol. 2, 885). Secondly, confessions were publicly read at executions, and distributed to the populace at large, which reinforced the legitimacy of the trials themselves and re-created in the public mind the reality of witchcraft

5. It would still, of course, have been difficult to get even one reliable witness to an act of witchcraft; in practice, the testimony of one accused, under torture, was used for this purpose.

6. In a study of the criminal process in China, Cohen relates, in a similar vein, that the requirement of confession for conviction in Manchu China reinforced the temptation to use torture on the accused (Cohen, 1966:473). It should be noted that the employment of torture by the Inquisition was a retrograde step in continental criminal procedure. The Church explicitly condemned torture; after it had been used by the Romans, torture was not again a standard procedure in Western Europe until it was reactivated in the 1200s in the offensive against heresy (Esmein, 1913:9). It was early laid down as an accepted rule of Canon Law that no confession should be extracted by torment; but the elimination of trials by ordeal in the thirteenth century, coupled with the rise of powerful heretical movements, put strong pressure on the Church to modify its approach. Originally, torture was left to the secular authorities to carry out, but a Bull of Pope Alexander IV in 1256 authorized Inquisitors to absolve each other for using it directly, and to grant each other dispensation for irregularities in its use (Lea, 1888:421).

itself. If people *said* they flew by night to dance with the Devil, then surely there was evil in the land, and the authorities were more than justified in their zeal to root it out. In extorting confessions from accused witches, the court also made use of means other than torture. Confession was usually required if the accused were to receive the last sacraments and avoid damnation (Lea, 1888:Vol. 3, 506), and the accused, further, were frequently promised pardon if they confessed, a promise which was rarely kept (Lea, 1888:Vol. 3, 514; 1939:Vol. 2, 895).[7]

In line with the tendency to realx other standards of evidence, there was a considerable weakening of safeguards regarding testimony of witnesses. Heretics could testify, which went against established ecclesiastical policy; so could excommunicates, perjurors, harlots, children and others who ordinarily were not allowed to bear witness. Witnesses themselves were liable to torture if they equivocated or appeared unwilling to testify; and, contrary to established procedure in ordinary continental courts, names of witnesses were withheld from the accused (Esmein, 1913:91-94; Lea, 1958:Vol. 1, 434-37).

In general, prisoners were not provided with information on their case (Esmein, 1913:129). Most of the proceedings were held in secret (Lea, 1958: Vol. 1, 406). The stubborn prisoner who managed to hold to a denial of guilt was almost never released from custody (Lea, 1958:Vol. 1, 419) and frequently spent years in prison (Lea, 1958:Vol. 1, 419). Acquittal, in witchcraft and heresy cases, was virtually impossible. Lacking enough evidence for conviction, the court could hold an accused in prison indefinitely at its discretion. In general, innocence was virtually never the verdict in such cases; the best one could hope for was "not proven." (Lea, 1958:Vol. 1, 453.)[8]

Legal counsel for the accused under the Inquisition was often prohibited, again contrary to ordinary continental procedure (Esmein, 1913:91-94).[9]

7. Deception by the court in witchcraft cases was widely approved. Bodin argued that the court should use lying and deception of the accused whenever possible; the authors of the MALLEUS MALEFICARUM felt that it was a good idea for the courts to promise life to the accused, since the fear of execution often prevented confession.

8. The following quote from the period shows one important motive behind the absence of outright release:

> If by torture he will say nothing nor confess, and is not convicted by witnesses ... he should be released at the discretion of the judge on pain of being attainted and convicted of the matters with which he is charged and of which he is presumed guilty ... for if he be freed absolutely, *it would seem that he had been held prisoner without charge.*

Quoted in Esmein, 1913:130 (emphasis added).

9. This was particularly critical in continental procedure, where presumption of guilt made the defense difficult in any case; it was less critical in England, where the burden of proof was on the court. The Church well knew the vital importance of counsel in criminal trials; *free* counsel was provided, in many kinds of ordinary cases, to those unable to afford it. *See* Lea, 1958:Vol. 1, 444-45.

Where counsel was allowed, it was with the disturbing understanding that successful or overly eager defense laid the counsel himself open to charges of heresy or of conspiracy to aid heretics (Sprenger and Kramer, 1948:218; Lea, 1958:Vol. 1, 444-45). Moreover, counsel was appointed by the court, was warned not to assume a defense he "knew to be unjust," and could be summoned by the court as a witness and made to turn over all his information to the court (Lea, 1958:Vol. 2, 517-18).

Lesser indications of guilt were supplied through the court's use of impossible dilemmas. If the accused was found to be in good repute among the populace, he or she was clearly a witch, since witches invariably sought to be highly thought of; if in bad repute, then he or she was also clearly a witch, since no one approves of witches. If the accused was especially regular in worship or morals, it was argued that the worst witches made the greatest show of piety (Lea, 1939:Vol. 2, 858). Stubbornness in refusing to confess was considered a sure sign of alliance with the Devil, who was known to be taciturn (Lea, 1888:Vol. 3, 509). Virtually the only defense available to accused witches was in disabling hostile witnesses on the grounds of violent enmity; this provision was rendered almost useless through the assumption that witches were naturally odious to everyone, so that an exceptionally great degree of enmity was required (Lea, 1888:Vol. 3, 517).

A final and highly significant characteristic of the continental witch trial was the power of the court to confiscate the property of the accused, whether or not he was led to confess (Lea, 1939:Vol. 2, 808-11; 1958:Vol. 1, 529). The chief consequence of this practice was to join to a system of virtually unlimited power a powerful motive for persecution. This coincidence of power and vested interest put an indelible stamp on every aspect of witchcraft in continental Europe.

All things considered, the continental procedure in the witch trials was an enormously effective machine for the systematic and massive production of confessed deviants. As such, it approximates a type of deviance-management which may be called repressive control. Three main characteristics of such a system may be noted, all of which were present in the continental legal order's handling of the witch trials:

1. Invulnerability to restraint from other institutions;
2. Systematic establishment of extraordinary powers for suppressing deviance, with a concomitant lack of internal restraints;
3. A high degree of structured interest in the apprehension and processing of deviants.

The question at hand is what the effects of this type of control structure are on the rate of deviance, the kinds of people who become defined as deviant, and other aspects of the system of behavior that it is designed to control. This will be considered after a description of the English approach to the control of witchcraft, which, having a very different character, led to very different results.

ENGLAND: RESTRAINED CONTROL

There was no Inquisition in Renaissance England, and the common law tradition provided a variety of institutional restraints on the conduct of the witch trials. As a consequence, there were fewer witches in England, vastly fewer executions, and the rise of a fundamentally different set of activities around the control of witchcraft.

Witchcraft was apparently never prosecuted as a heresy in England, but after a statute of Elizabeth in 1563 it was prosecuted as a felony in secular courts.[10] The relatively monolithic ecclesiastical apparatus, so crucial in the determination of the shape of witch trials on the Continent, did not exist in England; the new definition of witchcraft came to England late and under rather different circumstances.[11] English laws making witchcraft a capital crime, however, were on the books until 1736 although executions for witchcraft ceased around the end of the seventeenth century (Ewen, 1929: 43; Stephen, 1883:436). Nevertheless, the English laws were enforced in a relatively restrained fashion through a system of primarily local courts of limited power, accountable to higher courts and characterized by a high degree of internal restraint.

---

10. The statute is 5 Eliz., c. 16 (1563); see Davies, 1947:15, for a partial quote of this statute; and p. 42, for a quote from James I's 1604 statute making witchcraft per se, without involving the death of another person, a capital offense.

    An earlier statute (33 Hen. 8, c. 8 [1541]) made witchcraft a felony, but was repealed in 1547 and probably used only sporadically and for largely political purposes. Before that, too, there were occasional trials for witchcraft or sorcery, and witchcraft of a sort, as I have shown, appears in the earliest English law. But this was the older conception of witchcraft, blurring into that of magic; and it was not until Elizabeth's statute that witch trials began in earnest. See Notestein, 1911:Chap. 1.

11. Two of these circumstances may be mentioned. One was the general atmosphere of social and political turmoil surrounding the accession of Elizabeth to the throne; another was the return to England, with Elizabeth's crowning, of a number of exiled Protestant leaders who had been exposed to the witch trials in Geneva and elsewhere and had absorbed the continental attitudes toward witchcraft. One of these, Bishop John Jewel of Salisbury, argued before the Queen that

> This kind of people (I mean witches and sorcerers) within the last few years are marvelously increased within your Grace's realm. These eyes have seen the most evident and manifest marks of their wickedness. Your Grace's subjects pine away even unto death, their color fadeth, their speech is benumbed, their senses are berefit. Wherefore your poor subject's most humble petition to your Highness is, that the laws touching such malefactors may be put in due execution." Davies, 1947:17; cf. Notestein, 1911.

With a few exceptions, notably the Star Chamber, English courts operated primarily on the accusatory principle, stressing above all the separation of the functions of prosecution and judgment, trial by jury, and the presumption of the innocence of the accused.[12] Accuser and accused assumed the role of equal combatants before the judge and jury; prosecution of offenses generally required a private accuser (Esmein, 1913:107, 336). The English trial was confrontative and public, and the English judge did not take the initiative in investigation or prosecution of the case (Esmein, 1913:3, 6). Again unlike the situation on the Continent, the accused witch could appeal to higher authority from a lower court, and could sue an accuser for defamation; such actions frequently took place in the Star Chamber (cf. Ewen, 1938). Reprieves were often granted (Ewen, 1929:32). From the middle of the seventeenth century, the accused in capital cases could call witnesses in their defense (Esmein, 1913:342). In general, the English courts managed to remain relatively autonomous and to avoid degeneration into a tool of ideological or moral interests: Voltaire was to remark, in the eighteenth century, that "In France the Criminal Code seems framed purposely for the destruction of the people; in England it is their safeguard." (Esmein, 1913:361.)

There were, nevertheless, important limitations to this picture of the English courts as defenders of the accused. Accusatory ideals were not always met in practice, and many elements of a developed adversary system were only latent. Defendants were not allowed counsel until 1836 (Esmein, 1913: 342). In general, since the defendant entered court with a presumption of innocence, the English courts did not demand such rigorous proofs for conviction as did the continental courts. Testimony of one witness was usually sufficient for conviction in felony cases; children were frequently allowed to testify (Ewen, 1929:58). In practice, however, this worked out differently than might be expected. The lack of complex, rigid standards of proof in English courts meant that there was little pressure to subvert the series of safeguards surrounding the accused through granting the court extraordinary powers of interrogation, and it went hand-in-hand with a certain care on the part of the courts for the rights of the defendent. Torture, except in highly limited circumstances as an act of Royal prerogative, was illegal in England, and was never lawfully or systematically used on accused witches in the lower courts.[13]

12. Esmein (1913:Introduction) notes the similarity between the politically-oriented Star Chamber and the typical continental court. A few cases of witchcraft, notably those with political overtones, were processed there; *see* Ewen, 1938:11.

13. Torture may have been used on some witches in the Star Chamber. Notestein, 1911:167, 204 suggests that it may have been used illegally in a number of cases; nevertheless, torture was not an established part of English criminal procedure, except in the limited sense noted above (Stephen, 1883:434; Ewen, 1929:65). It was allowed in Scotland, where, predictably, there were more executions; several thousand witches were burned there during this period (Black, 1938:13-8; Notestein, 1911:95-96).

Given the nature of the crime of witchcraft, witnesses were not always easily found; given the illegality of torture, confessions were also relatively rare. In this difficult situation, alternative methods of obtaining evidence were required. As a consequence, a variety of external evidence emerged.

Three sources of external evidence became especially significant in English witch trials. These are pricking, swimming, and watching (Ewen, 1929:60-71; Notestein, 1911). Pricking was based on the theory that witches invariably possessed a "Devil's Mark," which was insensitive to pain. Hence, the discovery of witches involved searching the accused for unusual marks on the skin and pricking such marks with an instrument designed for that purpose. If the accused did not feel pain, guilt was indicated. Often, pricking alone was considered sufficient evidence for conviction.

Swimming was based on the notion that the Devil's agents could not sink in water, and was related to the "ordeal by water" common in early European law (Hopkins, 1928:38).

The victim was stripped naked and bound with her right thumb to her right toe, and her left thumb to her right toe, and was then cast into the pond or river. If she sank, she was frequently drowned; if she swam she was declared guilty without any further evidence being required.[14]

The third source of evidence, watching, reflected the theory that the Devil provided witches with imps or familiars which performed useful services, and which the witch was charged with suckling. The familiars could therefore be expected to appear at some point during the detention of the suspected witch, who was therefore placed in a cell, usually on a stool, and watched for a number of hours or days, until the appointed watchers' observed familiars in the room.

A number of other kinds of evidence were accepted in the English trials. Besides the testimony of witnesses, especially those who claimed to have been bewitched, these included the discovery of familiars, waxen or clay images, or other implements in the suspect's home, and of extra teats on the body, presumably used for suckling familiars (Ewen, 1929:68).

These methods were called for by the lack of more coercive techniques of obtaining evidence within the ambit of English law. In general, the discovery and trial of English witches was an unsystematic and inefficient process, resembling the well-oiled machinery of the continental trial only remotely. The English trial tended to have an ad hoc aspect in which new practices, techniques, and theories were continually being evolved or sought out.

Finally, the confiscation of the property of suspected witches did not occur in England, although forfeiture for felony was part of English law

14. Ewen (1929:68) argues, though, that swimming alone was probably not usually sufficient evidence for the death penalty.

until 1870.[15] As a consequence, unlike the continental authorities, the English officials had no continuous vested interest in the discovery and conviction of witches. Thus, they had neither the power nor the motive for large-scale persecution. The English control system, then, was of a "restrained" type, involving the following main characteristics:

1. Accountability to, and restraint by, other social institutions;
2. A high degree of internal restraint, precluding the assumption of extraordinary powers;
3. A low degree of structured interest in the apprehension and processing of deviants.

The English and continental systems, then, were located at nearly opposite ends of a continuum from restrained to repressive control of deviance. We may now look at the effects of these differing control systems on the character of witchcraft in the two regions.

WITCHCRAFT CONTROL AS INDUSTRY: THE CONTINENT

On the Continent, the convergence of a repressive control system with a powerful economic motive created something very much like a large-scale industry based on the mass stigmatization of witches and the confiscation of their property. This gave distinct character to the *rate* of witchcraft in Europe, the kinds of people who were convicted as witches, and the entire complex of activities which grew up around witchcraft.

The Inquisition, as well as the secular courts, were largely self-sustaining; each convicted witch, therefore, was a source of financial benefit through confiscation.[16] "Persecution," writes a historian of the Inquisition, "as a steady and continuous policy, rested, after all, upon confiscation. It was this which supplied the fuel to keep up the fires of zeal, and when it was lacking the business of defending the faith languished lamentably." (Lea, 1958: Vol. 1, 529.)

The witchcraft industry in continental Europe was a large and complex business which created and sustained the livelihoods of a sizable number of people. As such, it required a substantial income to keep it going at all.

15. Forfeiture grew out of the feudal relation between tenant and lord. A felon's lands escheated to the lord, and his property also was forfeited to the lord. A later development made the King the recipient of forfeited goods in the special case of treason; this was struck down in the Forfeiture Act of 1870 (Pollack and Maitland, 1895:332). This is, of course, a very different matter from the direct confiscation of property for the court treasury which was characteristic of the Continent.

16. Self-sustaining control systems often view presumptive deviants as a source of profit. On a smaller scale, it has been noted that some jurisdictions in the American south have been known to make a practice of arresting Negroes en masse in order to collect fees (Johnson, 1962).

As a rule, prisoners were required to pay for trial expenses and even for the use of instruments of torture (Lea, 1888:Vol. 3, 524; 1939:Vol. 3, 1080). Watchmen, executioners, torturers and others, as well as priests and judges, were paid high wages and generally lived well (Lea, 1939:Vol. 3, 1080). A witch-judge in seventeenth-century Germany boasted of having caused 700 executions in three years, and earning over 5,000 gulden on a per-capita basis (Lea, 1939:Vol. 3, 1975). A partial account of costs for a single trial in Germany reads as follows (Lea, 1939:Vol. 3, 1162):

	Florins	Batzen	Pfennige
For the Executioner.	14	7	10
For the Entertainment and Banquet of the Judges, Priests and Advocate	32	6	3
For Maintenance of the Convicts and Watchmen.	33	6	6

A total of 720,000 florins were taken from accused witches in Bamberg, Germany, in a single year (Lea, 1939:Vol. 3, 1177-78). Usually, the goods of suspected witches were sold after confiscation to secular and ecclesiastical officials at low prices (Lea, 1939:Vol. 3, 1080). Of the prosecutions at Trier, a witness wrote that: "Notaries, copyists, and innkeepers grew rich. The executioner rode on a blooded horse, like a courtier, clad in gold and silver; his wife vied with noble dames in the richness of her array . . . not till suddenly, as in war, the money gave out, did the zeal of the Inquisitors flag." (Burr, 1891:55.) During a period of intense witch-hunting activity at Trier, secular officials were forced to issue an edict to prevent impoverishment of local subjects through the activities of the Inquisitors (Burr, 1891:55 fn).

Like any large enterprise, the witchcraft industry was subject to the need for continual expansion in order to maintain its level of gain. A mechanism for increasing profit was built into the structure of the trials, whereby, through the use of torture to extract names of accomplices from the accused, legitimate new suspects became available.

The creation of a new kind of deviant behavior was the basis for the emergence of a profit-making industry run on bureaucratic lines, which combined nearly unlimited power with pecuniary motive and which gave distinct form to the deviant behavior system in which it was involved.

Its effect on the scope or rate of the deviance is the most striking at first glance. Several hundred thousand witches were burned in continental Europe during the main period of activity, creating a picture of the tremendous extent of witchcraft in Europe. The large number of witches frightened the population and legitimized ever more stringent suppression. Thus, a cycle developed in which rigorous control brought about the appearance of high rates of deviance, which were the basis for more extreme control, which in turn sent the rates even higher, and so on.

A second major effect was the selection of particular categories of people for accusation and conviction. A significant proportion of continental witches were men, and an even more significant proportion of men and women were people of wealth and/or property. This is not surprising, given the material advantages to the official control apparatus of attributing the crime to heads of prosperous households.

In trials of Offenburg, Germany, in 1628, witnesses noted that care was taken to select for accusation "women of property." (Lea, 1939:Vol. 3, 1163.) A document from Bamberg at about the same time lists the names and estimated wealth of twenty-two prisoners, nearly all of whom are propertied, most male, and one a burgher worth 100,000 florins (Lea, 1939:Vol. 3, 1177-78). In early French trials, a pattern developed which began with the conviction of a group of ordinary people, and then moved into a second stage in which the wealthy were especially singled out for prosecution (Lea, 1958: Vol. 1, 523-27). In German trials, the search for accomplices was directed against the wealthy, with names of wealthy individuals often supplied to the accused under torture (Lea, 1939:Vol. 1, 235). At Trier, a number of burgomasters, officials, and managers of large farms were executed as witches (Burr, 1891:29, 34). An eyewitness to the trials there in the late sixteenth century was moved to lament the fact that "[b]oth rich and poor, of every rank, age and sex, sought a share in the accursed crime." (Burr, 1891:19.) Apparently, resistance or dissent, or even insufficient zeal, could open powerful officials to accusation and almost certain conviction.[17]

Thus, though it was not the case that all continental witches were well-to-do or male, a substantial number were. The witch population in England, to be considered shortly, was strikingly different.

The mass nature of the witchcraft industry, the high number of witches in Europe, and the upper-income character of a sufficient proportion of them,[18] were all due to the lack of restraints on court procedure—especially, of the systematic use of torture—coupled with the legal authority to confiscate property, which added material interest to unrestrained control. That the prevalence of witches in continental Europe was a reflection of the peculiar structure of legal control is further implied by the fact that when torture and/or confiscation became from time to time unlawful, the number of witches decreased drastically or disappeared altogether. In Hesse, Phillip the Magnificent forbade torture in 1526 and, according to one witness, "nothing more was heard of witchcraft till the half-century was passed." (Lea, 1939:Vol. 3, 1081.) In Bamberg, pressure from the Holy Roman

17. This fact is graphically presented in Burr's Chronicle of Dietrich Flade, a powerful court official at Trier whose ultimate execution for witchcraft was apparently in part the result of his failure to zealously prosecute witches in his district.

18. That a greater percentage of wealthy witches did not appear is due in part to the fact that wealthy families often paid a kind of "protection" to local officials to ensure that they would not be arrested (Lea, 1939:Vol. 3, 1080).

Emperor to abandon confiscation resulted in the disappearance of witchcraft arrests in 1630 (Lea, 1939:Vol. 3, 1173-79).[19] The Spanish Inquisitor Salazar Frias issued instructions in 1614 requiring external evidence and forbidding confiscation; this move marked the virtual end of witchcraft in Spain (Parrinder, 1958:79). It was not until criminal law reform began in earnest in the eighteenth century that witches disappeared, for official purposes, from continental Europe.

A form of deviance had been created and sustained largely through the efforts of a self-sustaining bureaucratic organization dedicated to its discovery and punishment, and granted unusual powers which, when removed, dealt a final blow to that entire conception of deviant behavior. In England too, witches existed through the efforts of interested parties,[20] but the parties were of a different sort.

WITCHCRAFT CONTROL AS RACKET: ENGLAND

The restrained nature of the English legal system precluded the rise of the kind of mass witchcraft industry which grew up on the Continent. What the structure of that system did provide was a context in which individual entrepreneurs, acting from below, were able to profit through the discovery of witches. Hence, in England, there developed a series of rackets through which individuals manipulated the general climate of distrust, within the framework of a control structure which was frequently reluctant to approve of their activities. Because of its accusatorial character, the English court could not systematically initiate the prosecution of witches; because of its limited character generally, it could not have processed masses of presumed witches even had it had the power to initiate such prosecutions; and because of the absence of authority to confiscate witches' property, it had no interest in doing so even had it been able to. Witch prosecutions in England were

19. In part, also, the decrease in arrests was due to the occupation of the area by an invasion of the somewhat less zealous Swedes.

20. It should be stressed that quite probably, a number of people, both in England and on the Continent, did in fact believe themselves to be witches, capable of doing all the things witches were supposed to be able to do. Some of them, probably, had the intent to inflict injury or unpleasantness on their fellows, and probably some of these were included in the executions. This does not alter the fact that the designation of witches proceeded independently of such beliefs, according to the interests of the control systems. Some students of witchcraft have suggested that the promotion of witch beliefs by the official control systems provided a kind of readymade identity, or role, into which some already disturbed people could fit themselves. This is a more subtle aspect of the creation of deviance by control structures, and has, I think, applicability to certain contemporary phenomena. The images of deviance provided by newspapers and police may provide a structured pattern of behavior and an organized system of deviant attitudes which can serve as an orienting principle for the otherwise diffusely dissatisfied.

initiated by private persons who stood to make a small profit in a rather precarious enterprise. As a result, there were fewer witches in England than on the Continent, and their sex and status tended to be different as well.

Given the lack of torture and the consequent need to circumvent the difficulty of obtaining confessions, a number of kinds of external evidence, some of which were noted above, became recognized. Around these sources of evidence there grew up a number of trades, in which men who claimed to be expert in the various arts of witchfinding—pricking, watching, and so on—found a ready field of profit. They were paid by a credulous populace, and often credulous officials, for their expertise in ferreting out witches. In the seventeenth century, the best-known of the witchfinders was one Matthew Hopkins, who became so successful that he was able to hire several assistants (Hopkins, 1928:57). Hopkins, and many others, were generalists at the witchfinding art; others were specialists in one or another technique. Professional prickers flourished. A Scottish expert who regularly advertised his skill was called to Newcastle-upon-Tyne in 1649 to deal with the local witch problem, with payment guaranteed at twenty shillings per convicted witch. His technique of selecting potential witches was ingenious and rather efficient, and indicates how the general climate of fear and mistrust could be manipulated for profit. He sent bell-ringers through the streets of Newcastle to inquire if anyone had a complaint to enter against someone they suspected of witchcraft. This provided a legitimate outlet for grievances, both public and private, against the socially marginal, disapproved, or simply disliked, and was predictably successful; thirty witches were discovered, most of whom were convicted (Ewen, 1929:62). Several devices were used by prickers to increase the probability of discovery and conviction. One was the use of pricking knives with retractable blades and hollow handles, which could be counted on to produce no pain while appearing to be embodied in the flesh—thus demonstrating the presence of an insensible "Devil's Mark." (Ewen, 1929:62.)

Professional "watchers," too, thrived in this climate. A voucher from a Scottish trial in 1649 is indicative (Black, 1938:59):[21]

	Pounds	Shillings
Item: In the first, to Wm. Currie and Andrew Gray; for the watching of her the space of 30 days, each day 30 shillings—	45	0
Item: More to John Kincaid for brodding (pricking) of her—	6	0
More for meat and drink and wine for him and his men—	4	0

21. This is apparently unusual for a Scottish trial, since these methods of evidence were less crucial, given the frequent use of torture.

An essential characteristic of all these rackets was their precariousness. To profess special knowledge of the demonic and its agents opened the entrepreneur to charges of fraud or witchcraft; money could be made, but one could also be hanged, depending on the prevailing climate of opinion. The Scottish pricker of Newcastle was hanged, and many other prickers were imprisoned (Ewen, 1929:63); the witchfinder Hopkins continually had to defend himself against charges of wizardry and/or fraud, and may have been drowned while undergoing the "swimming" test.[22] People who professed to be able to practice magic—often known as "cunning folk"—frequently doubled as witchfinders, and were especially open to the charge of witchcraft (Notestein, 1911:chap. 1).

The peculiar and restrained character of the English control of witches led to characteristic features of the behavior system of English witchcraft. The lack of vested interest from above, coupled with the absence of torture and other extraordinary procedures, was largely responsible for the small number of witches executed in England from 1563 to 1736 (cf. Ewen, 1929: 112; Kittredge, 1907:59). Of those indicted for witchcraft, a relatively small percentage was actually executed—again in contrast to the inexorable machinery of prosecution in continental Europe. In the courts of the Home Circuit, from 1558 to 1736, only 513 indictments were brought for witchcraft; of these, only 112, or about 22 per cent, resulted in execution (Ewen, 1929:100).

Further, English witches were usually women and usually lower class. Again, this was a consequence of the nature of the control structure. English courts did not have the power or the motive to systematically stigmatize the wealthy and propertied; the accusations came from below, specifically from the lower and more credulous strata or those who manipulated them, and were directed against socially marginal and undersirable individuals who were powerless to defend themselves. The process through which the witch was brought to justice involved the often reluctant capitulation of the courts to popular sentiment fueled by the activities of the witchfinders; the witches were usually borderline deviants already in disfavor with their neighbors. Household servants, poor tenants, and others of lower status predominated. Women who worked as midwives were especially singled out, particularly when it became necessary to explain stillbirths. Women who lived by the practice of magic—cunning women—were extremely susceptible to accusation. Not infrequently, the accused witch was a "cunning woman" whose accusation

22. Hopkins, 1928:45. Summers, the editor of Hopkins' work, denies that Hopkins was drowned in this fashion. Hopkins' pamphlet includes a lengthy question-and-answer defense of his trade, part of which (p. 49) reads as follows: "Certaine queries answered, which have been and are likely to be objected against Matthew Hopkins, in his way of finding out Witches. Querie 1. That hee must needs be the greatest Witch, Sorcerer, and Wizzard himselfe, else hee could not doe it. Answer: If Satan's Kingdome be divided against itselfe, how shall it stand?"

was the combined work of a witchfinder and a rival "cunning woman." In the prevailing atmosphere, there was little defense against such internecine combat, and the "cunning" trade developed a heavy turnover (Notestein, 1911:82). In general, of convicted witches in the Home Circuit from 1564-1663, only 16 of a total of 204 were men (Ewen, 1929:102-108; Murray, 1962:255-70), and there is no indication that any of these were wealthy or solid citizens.

The decline of witchcraft in England, too, was the result of a different process from that on the Continent, where the decline of witchcraft was closely related to the imposition of restraints on court procedure. In England, the decline was related to a general shift of opinion, in which the belief in witchcraft itself waned, particularly in the upper strata, as a result of which the courts began to treat witchcraft as illusory or at best unprovable. English judges began refusing to execute witches well before the witch laws were repealed in 1736; and although there were occasional popular lynchings of witches into the eighteenth century, the legal system had effectively relinquished the attempt to control witchcraft (Davies, 1947:182-203). With this shift of opinion, the entire structure of witchcraft collapsed, for all practical purposes, at the end of the seventeenth century.[23]

CONCLUSION

If one broad conclusion emerges from this discussion, it is that the phenomenon of witchcraft in Renaissance Europe strongly reinforces on one level the argument that deviance is what officials say it is, and deviants are those so designated by officials. Where the deviant act is nonexistent, it is necessarily true that the criteria for designating people as deviant do not lie in the deviant act itself, but in the interests, needs, and capacities of the relevant official and unofficial agencies of control, and their relation to extraneous characteristics of the presumptive deviant. Witchcraft was invented in continental Europe, and it was sustained there through the vigorous efforts of a system of repressive control; in England it was sustained, far less effectively, through the semi-official efforts of relatively small-time entrepreneurs. In both cases, witchcraft as a deviant behavior system took its character directly from the nature of the respective systems of legal control. On the Continent, the system found itself both capable of and interested in defining large numbers of people, many of whom were well-to-do, as

23. An incident supposedly involving the anatomist, William Harvey, is indicative of this change of opinion. Harvey, on hearing that a local woman was reputed to be a witch, took it upon himself to dissect one of her familiars, which took the shape of a toad; he found it to be exactly like any other toad, and a minor blow was struck for the Enlightenment (Notestein, 1911:111).

witches; therefore, there *were* many witches on the Continent and many of these were wealthy and/or powerful. In England, the control system had little interest in defining anyone as a witch, and consequently the English witches were those few individuals who were powerless to fend off the definition supplied by witchfinders on a base of popular credulity. Witches were, then, what the control system defined them to be, and variation in the behavior system of witchcraft in the two regions may be traced directly to the different legal systems through which that definition was implemented . . . .

REFERENCES

Becker, H. S. *Outsiders.* New York: Free Press, 1963.

Black, G. F. *A Calendar of Cases of Witchcraft in Scotland, 1510-1727.* New York: The New York Public Library, 1938.

Burr, G. L. "The Fate of Dietrich Flade." *Papers of the American Historical Association* 3 (July 1891).

Cohen, J. A. "The Criminal Process in the People's Republic of China: an Introduction." *Harvard Law Review* 79 (1966).

Davies, R. T. *Four Centuries of Witch Beliefs.* New York: Arno Publishers, 1947.

Erikson, K. T. *Wayward Puritans.* New York: John Wiley & Sons, 1966.

Esmein, A. *A History of Continental Criminal Procedure.* Translated by John Simpson. New York: Kelley, 1913.

Ewen, C. L'Estrange. *Witch Hunting and Witch Trials.* London: K. Paul, Trench, Trubner and Co., Ltd., 1929.

——. *Witchcraft in the Star Chamber.* London: Ewen, 1938.

Goffman, E. *Asylums.* Chicago: Aldine, 1962.

——. *Stigma.* Englewood Cliffs, New Jersey: Prentice-Hall, 1963.

Hopkins, M. *The Discovery of Witches.* London: The Cayne Press, 1928.

Johnson, G. B. "The Negro and Crime." In *The Sociology of Crime and Delinquency,* edited by M. Wolfgang, L. Savitz and N. Johnson. New York: John Wiley & Sons, 1962.

Kitsuse, J. I. "Societal Response to Deviance: Some Problems of Theory and Method." *Social Problems* 9 (Winter 1962).

Kittredge, G. L. *Notes on Witchcraft.* Worchester, Mass.: Davis Press, 1907.

Lea, H. C. *A History of the Inquisition in the Middle Ages.* New York: Russell and Russell, 1888.

——. *Materials Toward a History of Witchcraft.* Arranged and edited by Arthur C. Howland. Philadelphia: University of Pennsylvania Press, 1939.

——. *A History of the Inquisition in the Middle Ages.* New York: Russell and Russell, 1958.

Lemert, E. M. *Social Pathology.* New York: McGraw-Hill, 1951.

Murray, M. *The Witch-Cult in Western Europe.* Magnolia, Mass.: Peter Smith, 1962.

Notestein, W. *A History of Witchcraft in England.* New York: Apollo, 1911.

Parrinder, G. *Witchcraft: European and African.* New York: Barnes & Noble, 1958.

Pollack, I. F., and Maitland, W. A. *A History of English Law Before the Time of Edward I.* London: Cambridge University Press, 1895.

Schur, E. M. *Narcotic Addiction in Britain and America; The Impact of Public Policy.*
    Bloomington, Indiana: Indiana University Press, 1962.
Sprenger, J., and Institoris, H. *Malleus Maleficarum.* Translated by M. Summers. London:
    Anglo Books, 1948.
Stephen, Sir J. F. *History of the Criminal Law in England.* New York: B. Franklin, 1883.
Tannenbaum, F. *Crime and the Community.* New York: Columbia University Press,
    1951.

RONALD A. FARRELL AND VICTORIA LYNN SWIGERT
Prior Offense Record
as a Self-Fulfilling Prophecy

The use of official records of arrest and conviction as indices of criminality
has long been a controversial issue in sociology. Many studies utilizing such
documents have shown that lower-class persons are overrepresented in criminal populations (Shaw, 1929; Shaw and McKay, 1931; Caldwell, 1931;
Glueck and Glueck, 1934). Based on these findings a theoretical tradition has
developed that explains crime and delinquency in terms of the characteristics
of lower-class life (Merton, 1938; Shaw and McKay, 1942; Kobrin, 1951;
Cohen, 1955; Miller, 1958; Cloward and Ohlin, 1960). Differentials in legitimate and illegitimate opportunities, institutional disorganization, the conflict
of cultural values, and the predominance of norms conducive to criminal
behavior have all been offered as explanations of official rates of criminality
among the poor.

At the same time, however, it has been argued that law enforcement
agencies exercise selective bias against lower-class and minority populations
(Robison, 1936; Warner and Lunt, 1941; Useem et al., 1942; Sutherland,
1949; Stinchcombe, 1963; Goldman, 1963; Cameron, 1964; Chambliss and
Liell, 1966; UCLA Law Review, 1966:686; Skolnick, 1966; Chevigny, 1969;
Black, 1970). Saturated patrol of slums and lower-class neighborhoods,
detention of suspicious persons, and harassment of deviant and delinquent
groups are illustrative. The self-fulfilling effects of these practices appear in

Source: Farrell, Ronald A. and Swigert, Victoria Lynn. "Prior Offense Record as a
Self-Fulfilling Prophecy." *Law and Society Review* 12 (1978):3. Permission granted by
The Law and Society Association.

the form of inflated arrest rates and criminal records among the black and the poor (Robison, 1936:228; Swett, 1969:93). In this view, official statistics become indicators of official processing decisions rather than of actual criminality.

Evidence generated by self-report and victimization surveys lends support to this argument (Nye, *et al.*, 1958; Akers, 1964; Empey and Erickson, 1966; Gold, 1966; Ennis, 1967; Blankenburg, 1976). These studies suggest that crime levels are several times greater than the officially recorded rates, and that there may in fact be no significant relationship between criminal behavior and socioeconomic status. Statistical differences in criminal involvement, therefore, may only reflect variations in the reporting of offenses and differential law enforcement practices.

In spite of the questionable validity of official data, explorations of differential justice continue to treat arrest and conviction records as indicators of prior criminality. Such studies conclude that apparent relationships between class, race, and legal treatment are explained by the more extensive criminal histories accumulated by lower-class and minority groups, and not by overt discrimination (Green, 1961; 1964; D'Esposito, 1969; Willick *et al.*, 1975; Burke and Turk, 1975).

Such a conclusion overlooks the fact that the explanatory variable— criminal history—may itself be a product of differential justice. For "although a disproportionately large number of...lower [status] offenders have a prior...record, there is at least the possibility that the legal treatment initially given these offenders was influenced by their social status." (Farrell, 1971:57).

An understanding of prior record and its role in the legal process requires an exploration of the factors that lead to a determination of guilt. Unfortunately, research on differential legal treatment has focused almost exclusively on sentencing (for a review and discussion of the literature, see Swigert and Farrell, 1976:15–17; Greenberg, 1977). An exception, however, is the work of Chiricos, Jackson, and Waldo (1972), who have studied adjudication itself, thereby making the construction of what will become a "prior record" a dependent variable. Their analysis indicates that where judges have the option of not entering a felony conviction on a defendant's record, persons who have a prior record, as well as those who are older, black, poorly educated, and defended by appointed counsel, are more likely to be denied this privilege. Thus, in addition to the social characteristics of defendants, prior contact with the law itself affected subsequent elaboration of a criminal record.

These findings have important implications. Since present adjudications influenced by status criteria, become part of criminal histories, it may be inferred that prior record is itself a product of the differential dispensation of justice. It would appear, furthermore, that the official designation of individuals as career offenders may influence subsequent decisions of law enforcement agents. Once criminality becomes the dominant prophecy, a sequence of events may be set into motion that serves to preclude outcomes inconsistent with the original presumption of guilt. Guided by the theoretical tradition of W. I. Thomas (1923) and Robert K. Merton (1957:421-36), we would suggest that prior offense records, as public definitions (prophecies or predictions), become an integral part of the situation and affect subsequent developments, regardless of the factual basis upon which these definitions are built.

The focus of the present work is an examination of the antecedents of criminal adjudication. Using the convictions of defendants as the dependent variable, an effort will be made to specify the process by which prior records are constructed.

THE SAMPLE

The data utilized for this research were part of a larger study of the differential legal treatment of homicide defendants. Cases were drawn from the files of a diagnostic and evaluation clinic attached to the court, and from the indictment records maintained by the Office of the Clerk of Courts in a large urban jurisdiction in the northeastern United States. Four hundred and forty-four defendants were selected for analysis, a 50 percent random sample of all persons arrested on general charges of murder from 1955 through 1973.

As an offense type, criminal homicide provides a valuable opportunity for the study of legal treatment. Homicide defendants are more representative of persons who commit homicide than are defendants accused of any other crime [representative] of persons who commit that crime. The visibility of the offense and the high clearance rate of deaths due to homicide suggest that individuals charged with murder exemplify persons who actually commit murder; other offenses display a much greater disparity between crimes known to the police and arrests recorded.[1]

The seriousness of the offense is also controlled by the use of a single offense type. This is particularly true in the jurisdiction in which this study was conducted, where defendants are arrested on general charges of murder and indicted for both murder and voluntary manslaughter. The degree of the offense, along with guilt or innocence, is determined at the trial.

The court clinic from which the records were obtained is charged with the evaluation of all persons arrested for homicide. Within 72 hours of the alleged offense, extensive psychiatric and social histories are compiled for each defendant. If the accused is subsequently adjudged insane, proceedings

---

1. Of all homicides known to the police, 82 percent are eventually cleared by arrest. Clearance rates for other crimes are much lower: forcible rapes—57 percent, aggravated assaults—66 percent, robbery—30 percent, burglary—19 percent, larceny—20 percent, auto theft—17 percent (see Quinney, 1975:19).

are initiated for his commitment to a mental hospital. Otherwise, the clinic report is summarized and forwarded to the presiding judge for use in pre-sentence investigation. If the defendant is found not guilty, or if the case is dismissed, the sealed evaluation is returned to the clinic unopened.

The clinic files included information from a number of diverse sources. FBI and police reports; military, occupational, and educational records; medical histories; social service investigations; and psychiatric evaluations were available for all defendants.

Information regarding the legal aspects of the case was obtained from the Office of the Clerk of Courts, and included the type of legal representation, results of bail hearings, plea, and conviction.[2]

METHODS

Previous research concerning the effects of prior record on legal treatment has traditionally noted the presence or absence of a criminal record (Farrell, 1971; Burke and Turk, 1975) or the number of crimes of which the defendant was found guilty (Bullock, 1961; Green, 1964; Chiricos *et al.,* 1972). Given the reported significance of the variable, a more sensitive index seemed desirable. In the present study it has been operationalized as the sum of the maximum penalties prescribed for each prior conviction. The selection of this measure was guided by a number of considerations. The legislatively determined maximum sentence constitutes the most objective determination of the severity of an offense. Robbery is more serious than bookmaking because the State authorizes a maximum penalty of 20 years for the former and 5 years for the latter. Records of previous arrests or time actually served introduce subjective considerations. Arrest records are affected by adminis-trative practices such as stacking (the filing of multiple charges in preparation for bargained settlements). Sentence actually served, on the other hand, is a product of the bargaining skills of defense, the capacity of the system to absorb new prisoners, and the presentence evaluation of the defendant's characteristics and circumstances. To be sure, conviction is also a product of the nature of the original arrest and agreements between prosecution and defense. Yet in all succeeding adjudications, the official determination of guilt of a particular offense stands as a decontextualized indicator of prior criminality. The seriousness of a record measured in this fashion describes the crime itself, as legislatively quantified, and not the special circumstances affecting time served. The second degree murderer who serves 5 years and the one who serves 10 years are equally guilty of an offense carrying the maxi-

2. The characteristics of the sample and the circumstances of the offense did not differ significantly from those reported by earlier studies, cf. Wolfgang (1958); Bensing and Schroeder (1960); Porkorny (1965); Voss and Hepburn (1968).

mum penalty of 20 years. We maintain that the records of both are equally serious from the point of view of legal officials.[3]

The severity of a prior record was measured by summing the maximum penalties for each conviction. A defendant with an earlier conviction for robbery (maximum penalty 20 years) and one for bookmaking (maximum penalty 5 years) would receive a score of 25. Penalties ranged from 0 to 20 years; no defendant had a prior conviction for first degree murder. Sentences of less than a year were given fractional scores.[4]

In the first stage of the analysis we assessed the impact of the prior offense record and social characteristics of defendants, including age, sex, race, and occupational prestige,[5] upon conviction severity. Since defendants were sometimes found guilty of charges other than the two degrees of murder and two degrees of manslaughter, the disposition was scaled as first degree murder, first degree felony (including second degree murder), second degree felony (including voluntary manslaughter), first degree misdemeanor (including involuntary manslaughter), acquittal, and dismissal (including *nolle*

---

3. Evidence that this is actually the court's logic can be found in the fact that the record of relevant *convictions* is utilized by this jurisdiction during bail hearings to determine eligibility and amount.

4. Defendant scores ranged from 0 to 219.25, with a mean of 17.12 and a standard deviation of 31.675.

5. The distribution of the social characteristics of defendants is presented below. Occupational prestige was measured in terms of Treiman's (1977) classification system.

Race and Sex of Defendants

	Male		Female		Total	
Race	n	%	n	%	n	%
White	134	30.5	26	5.9	160	36.4
Black	215	49.0	64	14.6	279	63.6
Total	349	79.5	90	20.5	439	100.0

Age and Occupational Prestige of Defendants

	Range	Mean	Standard Deviation
Age	13-81	35.73	14.796
Occupational Prestige	5-71	25.34	11.606

prosequi and demurrer sustained.[6]

The second stage of the analysis sought to specify the influence of criminal record within the legal process. Here, we tried to determine the role of private attorney, bail, and trial by jury in mediating the effects of prior convictions upon disposition.

The highly structured nature of the judicial system lends itself to a systematic analysis of legal processing. The discrete ordering of events—the social characteristics of the defendants prior to their entry into the system, their accumulated criminal histories, the type of legal representation, pretrial release, the mode of adjudication, and final disposition—constitutes a series of stages that allows the researcher to assert the causal sequence of relationships. The path analytic technique is particularly suited to such an exploration. Having established causal priority among a system of variables, paths of direct as well as indirect influence may be assessed. Based on multiple regression techniques, path coefficients represent the relative contributions of the several independent variables to predicting the dependent variable (Lin, 1976:315). Where a coefficient failed to reach 0.100 the variable was dropped from the equation and all coefficients were recalculated.

In addition to standardized path coefficients, the multiple correlation coefficient (R^2) is also presented. This statistic indicates the total portion of the dependent variable explained by the combined effects of all independent variables.

FINDINGS

The path model presented in Figure 1 depicts the relationships among the social characteristics of defendants, the severity of their prior convictions, and the final dispositions.

6. Although disposition is ordinally scaled, multiple regression techniques appear to be robust enough to handle the violation of the method's interval assumption, *see* Bohrnstedt and Carter (1971). The distribution of cases across the dependent variable is depicted below:

	Disposition	
	n	%
Dismissed	38	8.96
Acquitted	67	15.80
First degree misdemeanor	40	9.44
Second degree felony	126	29.72
First degree felony	110	25.94
First degree murder	43	10.14
Total	424	100

Table 1: Correlation Coefficients Among All Variables Included in the Analysis

Variables	2	3	4	5	6	7	8	9	10	11
1. Age (L-H)*	-.056	.006	.077	.221	-.050	-.064	-.046	.209	-.057	-.052
2. Sex (F-M)*	—	.080	.057	.151	.034	-.065	.093	.155	.024	.167
3. Race (B-W)*		—	.352	-.081	.057	.042	.034	.160	-.063	-.032
4. Occupational Prestige (L-H)			—	-.131	.316	.153	.104	-.302	.306	-.237
5. Prior Conviction Severity (L-H)				—	-.162	-.161	-.010	.738	-.155	.215
6. Private Attorney (No-Yes)					—	.230	.016	-.199	.607	-.165
7. Bail (No-Yes)						—	.108	-.212	.681	-.293
8. Jury Trial (No-Yes)							—	-.030	.549	-.171
9. Occupational Prestige and Prior Conviction Severity (P-N)*								—	-.201	.267
10. Legal Resources (L-H)									—	-.306
11. Final Disposition (L-H)										—

*(L-H) = low to high   (B-W) = black-white
 (F-M) = female-male   (P-N) = positive to negative

Figure 1. Final Disposition By Defendant Characteristics and Prior Conviction Severity

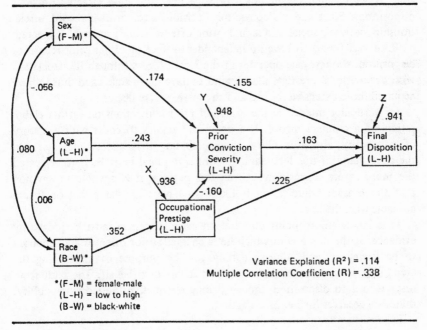

Variance Explained (R²) = .114
Multiple Correlation Coefficient (R) = .338

*(F-M) = female-male
(L-H) = low to high
(B-W) = black-white

Age and sex are antecedents of a defendant's prior record. Males and older defendants are more likely to have severe conviction histories. These relationships are presumably the result of the greater opportunity that older persons have had to accumulate conviction histories and of the more frequent application of criminal labels to men. Whether the latter reflects criminal activity (cf. Adler, 1975) or the unwillingness of legal authorities to recognize female criminality (cf. Harris, 1977) requires further investigation. We have argued elsewhere (Swigert and Farrell, 1977) that the overrepresentation of males in offender populations may be a function of the applicability of a criminal imagery to this group (*see also* Harris, 1977). The relationship between sex and disposition lends support to this argument: even when males and females are charged with the same offense, males are more likely to be convicted of more serious charges. In this way the imagery of the violent male is reinforced by statistics concerning violent criminality, statistics which themselves reflect the failure of officials to perceive and label females involved in violent crimes.

Occupational prestige also influences the development of a prior offense record. There are two competing explanations of this relationship: lower-status persons may actually have committed more crime, or their more extensive records may indicate differential treatment in the past. In order to choose between these explanations, it is sufficient to observe that, in the present adjudication, defendants of lower status still receive more severe sanctions when we control for prior record. Given this finding, it is reasonable to assume that occupational prestige may also have affected previous dispositions. Since today's conviction decision is tomorrow's record, a relationship between social status and prior offense record must be expected.

Race was found to have no independent effect on either prior record or disposition. Rather, race operates in the legal process through its association with occupational prestige. Blacks tend to have lower status and thus to have acquired more extensive records and to receive severe dispositions.

Of particular interest is the effect of prior convictions on further elaboration of a criminal record. If a defendant comes to court with a history of criminality, the probability of exacerbating that history increases. On the other hand, if the defendant's record is minimal he is likely to be spared the more severe dispositions. Given this pattern, it is possible to envision that the present adjudication is likely to have a similar effect on future contacts with the law.

It is important to point out that an accused person must be judged by evidence of the crime with which he is charged; prior offenses are supposed to be irrelevant, and admissible only for the purpose of impeaching the credibility of a defendant who testifies in his own behalf. The path from prior record to disposition, though it may reflect that limited admissibility, therefore deserves further investigation.

In order to specify the effects of criminal record on disposition, it was necessary to examine several intervening events: the type of counsel retained, whether the defendant was released on bail, and the mode of adjudication.[7] The influence of each of these variables on disposition has received abundant empirical support. The differential resources available to private and public attorneys for investigation of the case have been shown to affect the outcome of legal proceedings (Ehrmann, 1962; Chiricos et al., 1972). Similarly, studies have shown that, among defendants charged with similar offenses, those jailed before trial are more often convicted than those released on bail or on their own recognizance (Foote, 1959:47; Louisiana Law Review, 1961; Ares et al., 1963:83; cf. Clarke and Koch, 1976:83). Finally, the defendant has a right to trial by jury, but may also choose to be tried by a judge or to plead guilty. In fact, more than 90 percent of all convictions involve the negotiation of a guilty plea between defense and prosecution (Newman, 1956; Blumberg, 1967; Alschuler, 1968). This may defeat the ends of justice, for not only are the guilty neither prosecuted nor sanctioned for the offense originally charged, but the innocent are often encouraged to enter a plea of guilt and accept a certain but slight penalty rather than run the risk of a more serious conviction (Rosett, 1967).

In an effort to determine the interrelationships among prior record, the several legal variables, and disposition, a second path model was generated. As shown in Figure 2, prior record is an important determinant of the ability to retain private counsel and to secure pretrial release, but not of the mode of adjudication.

7. Type of attorney is a two-catagory variable: privately retained and state subsidized. The latter category includes court appointed private attorneys who are compensated by the state at a fixed rate per case, and salaried public defenders.

Persons without pretrial release may remain incarcerated either because bail was denied or because it was set at a prohibitive level.

Mode of adjudication was dichotomized into jury trial and no jury trial. In most cases, the absence of a jury trial was the product of the defendant's plea to the original or reduced charges. In a few, it represented a decision to be tried by a judge. The distribution of cases across each of these variables is as follows:

	Intervening Events					
	Private Attorney		Bail		Trial by Jury	
	n	%	n	%	n	%
Yes	192	48.7	125	33.0	147	39.8
No	202	51.3	254	67.0	222	60.2
Total	394	100	379	100	369	100

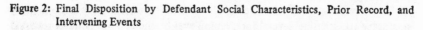

Figure 2: Final Disposition by Defendant Social Characteristics, Prior Record, and Intervening Events

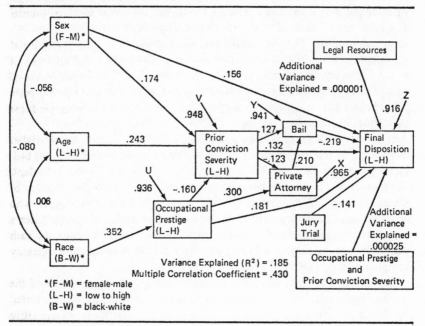

The influence of prior record on access to a private attorney is independent of the defendant's occupational status and may be a product of the presumption of guilt implied by a criminal history. Private attorneys, sensitive to the importance of prior record in arriving at negotiated settlements and fearful of loss of payment when incarceration appears to be the inevitable outcome, may refuse to accept defendants whose earlier experiences with the law are seen as predictive of career criminality. But occupational prestige also exerts a strong independent influence on access to private counsel. It becomes apparent, then, that the failure of lower-class persons to retain private counsel is a product of their financial inability to purchase such services as well as of the more extensive criminal histories found in this group.

A defendant with a record of serious convictions is also more likely to be detained before trial. Such a pattern may likewise be a consequence of the presumption of guilt created by a criminal record. The belief that individuals previously convicted of violating the law are more likely to be guilty of the present offense is institutionalized in the standards recommended for granting bail.[8] Access to bail is also influenced by the type of legal representation: private attorneys are more successful in securing pretrial release.

An assessment of the effects of bail on disposition reveals that pretrial release directly results in greater leniency. The effects of type of attorney on disposition, on the other hand, are not direct but mediated by the ability of private counsel to secure pretrial release for their clients. Persons with private attorneys are more often awarded bail, a resource which in turn produces the more favorable dispositions.

There are no significant relationships between the social characteristics of defendants, prior conviction severity, access to a private attorney, and bail, on the one hand, and the mode of adjudication selected by the defendant, on the other.[9] Persons who waive their right to a jury *are* found guilty of more serious charges. But it must be remembered that most defendants who waive a jury trial plead guilty to the original or a reduced charge. Since a plea of guilty is virtually synonymous with an adjudication of guilt, the path coefficient between this variable and conviction severity would necessarily link more serious convictions to nonjury trials.[10]

On the basis of these findings, it is possible to assert the nature of the relationships that exist among prior offense record, intervening legal variables, and adjudication severity. Defendants with histories of repeated criminality have less access to a private attorney and bail. This latter relationship is not only a product of the immediate influence of criminal record, but is also an

---

8. In the jurisdiction studied, because the degree of the offense is determined at the time of the trial, homocide defendants are eligible for pretrial release. The purpose of bail is to insure the presence of the defendant at subsequent proceedings. The official standards include:

    i.   the nature of the offense charged and any mitigating or aggravating factor that may bear upon the likelihood of conviction and possible penalty;

    ii.   the defendant's employment status and history and his financial condition;

    iii.   the nature of his family relationships;

    iv.   his age, character, reputation, mental condition, *record of relevant convictions*, and whether addicted to alcohol or drugs; and

    v.   any other facts relevant to whether the defendant has strong ties with the community or is likely to flee the jurisdiction.

[Criminal Code Manual issued by the state in which this study was conducted; italics added]

9. Elsewhere we have shown that the extent to which the defendant resembles criminal stereotypes affects the availability of a jury trial (Swigert and Farrell, 1976, 1977).

10. An analysis of the effects of mode of adjudication on sentence severity, not reported here, shows that persons who are found guilty following a jury trial are penalized more severely. This supports the contention that defendants who make greater demands on the scarce resources of the legal system are treated more harshly (Tiffany *et al.*, 1975).

indirect result of the inability of defendants represented by publicly paid counsel to obtain pretrial release. Finally, persons who are incarcerated pending adjudication are convicted of more serious charges.

It should be emphasized that though part of the impact of criminal history on disposition is mediated, a significant direct effect remains evident. Explanations of this relationship must remain speculative, given the limitations of the data. It may be suggested, however, that though the law requires a determination of guilt without reference to a defendant's background, such information actually influences the legal process at a number of stages. Prosecutors, defense attorneys, and judges do have access to the prior record. The vehemence with which defense counsel will press for acquittal and the prosecutor for conviction, or the weight a judge accords to evidence in a bench trial, may in fact be influenced by their familiarity with the defendant's criminal history. It is an issue certainly deserving of empirical attention.

The remainder of the analysis involves an assessment of the interactive effects of several variables on disposition. A significant interaction was anticipated between occupational prestige and prior record—that dispositions for persons from the lowest occupational levels would be most affected by extensive criminal histories. For while the imagery of guilt created by prior criminal involvement might lead to a less favorable disposition, both directly and through the mediating variables, persons of higher status might be able to compensate for these disadvantages. Likewise, we thought that the combined influence of private attorney, bail, and jury trial upon disposition might exceed the sum of the effects of each. In both cases, however, the additional variance explained is insignificant. This would suggest that the effects of each variable are additive, which supports our original interpretation.

CONCLUSION

In their study of the application of the felony label, Chiricos *et al.* (1972: 569-70) have noted:

> the privileged status of first offenders before the law is neither surprising nor uncommon. In fact, many statutes explicitly provide harsher penalties for repeat offenders. A reasonable—though not necessarily correct— interpretation of these findings would be that judges recognize the self- fulfilling character of the formal convict label and purposely withhold it from first offenders in the interests of possible "rehabilitation."

But the pattern observed in this research has even more important implications. The use of a prior record as meaningful information in the disposition of a criminal case compounds the discretion of prior adjudications.

We have seen that lower-status offenders are more likely to have accumulated long histories of criminal conviction. Similar observations have led researchers to conclude that the relationship of class to differential criminal justice is explained by the greater involvement of lower-status persons in lives of crime. Thus it is argued that if blacks and members of the lower classes are more severely sanctioned for their offenses, it is because of the judicial decision to penalize the repeat offender.

We have also seen, however, that each criminal conviction is itself influenced by class. Lower-status defendants, independent of their prior criminal involvement, receive more severe dispositions. The relationship between social status and prior record is therefore not simply the result of a tendency toward criminality on the part of the lower classes, but is also a reflection of the influence of class on those previous convictions. Furthermore, prior record, both independently and through the three mediating legal variables, was found to be associated with the severity of disposition. Since occupational prestige affects severity of disposition both directly and indirectly through its historical influence on prior record, the introduction of that record into the criminal process may amplify its class bias.

The influence of prior record within the legal system produces a cyclic reconfirmation of criminality. Prior record, itself partly a product of discretionary treatment, becomes a salient factor in the accumulation of additional convictions. This occurs not only through its direct effect on disposition but also through its influence on access to private counsel and bail, themselves important determinants of outcome.

Such findings are obviously significant for the criminal justice system. Prior record is presently an important source of information at a number of stages in the legal process. The use of previous convictions in habitual offender laws, in eligibility for suspension of sentence and probation, in the standards for granting of bail, and as evidence of a defendant's credibility are an official sanction of discretionary treatment. More important, such practices constitute an institutionalization of prior record as a self-fulfilling prophecy. The lower classes, by virtue of social and economic disadvantages, more often accumulate more serious convictions. These convictions, in their turn, serve to justify differential treatment in any succeeding adjudication. The process is continuous and serves to fulfill the original prediction that the lower classes are dangerous classes, prone to lives of criminality.

REFERENCES

Adler, Freda. *Sisters in Crime: The Rise of the New Female Criminal.* New York: Mc-Graw-Hill, 1975.

Akers, Ronald L. "Socioeconomic Status and Delinquent Behavior: A Retest." *Journal of Research in Crime and Delinquency* 1 (1964): 38-46.

Alschuler, Albert W. "The Prosecutor's Role in Plea Bargaining." *University of Chicago Law Review* 36 (1968): 50-112.

Ares, Charles E.; Rankin, Anne; and Sturz, Herbert. "The Manhattan Bail Project: An Interim Report on the Use of Pre-Trial Parole." *New York University Law Review* 38 (1963): 67-95.

Bensing, Robert C., and Schroeder, Jr., Oliver. *Homicide in an Urban Community.* Springfield, Ill.: Thomas, 1960.

Black, Donald J. "Production of Crime Rates." *American Sociological Review* 35 (1970): 733-48.

Blankenburg, Erhard. "The Selectivity of Legal Sanctions: An Empirical Investigation of Shoplifting." *Law & Society Review* 11 (1976): 109-30.

Blumberg, Abraham S. "The Practice of Law as a Confidence Game: Organizational Cooptation of a Profession." *Law & Society Review* 1 (1967): 15-39.

Bohrnstedt, George W., and Carter, T. Michael. "Robustness in Regression Analysis." In *Sociological Methodology,* edited by Herbert L. Costner, pp. 118-46. San Francisco: Jossey-Bass, 1971.

Bullock, Henry Allen. "Significance of the Racial Factor in the Length of Prison Sentences." *Journal of Criminal Law, Criminology and Police Science* 52 (1961): 411-17.

Burke, Peter J., and Turk, Austin T. "Factors Affecting Post-Arrest Dispositions: A Model for Analysis." *Social Problems* 22 (1975): 313-32.

Caldwell, Morris G. "The Economic Status of the Families of Delinquent Boys in Wisconsin." *American Journal of Sociology* 37 (1931): 231-39.

Cameron, Mary Owen. *The Booster and the Snitch: Department Store Shoplifting.* New York: Free Press of Glencoe, 1964.

Chambliss, William J., and Liell, John T. "The Legal Process in the Community Setting: A Study of Law Enforcement." *Crime and Delinquency* 12 (1966): 310-17.

Chevigny, Paul. *Police Power: Police Abuses in New York City.* New York: Vintage Books, 1969.

Chiricos, Theodore G.; Jackson, Phillip D.; and Waldo, Gordon P. "Inequality in the Imposition of a Criminal Label." *Social Problems* 19 (1972): 553-72.

Clarke, Stevens H., and Koch, Gary G. "The Influence of Income and Other Factors on Whether Criminal Defendants Go to Prison." *Law & Society Review* 11 (1976): 57-92.

Cloward, Richard A., and Ohlin, Lloyd E. *Delinquency and Opportunity: A Theory of Delinquent Gangs.* Glencoe, Ill.: Free Press, 1960.

Cohen, Albert K. *Delinquent Boys: The Culture of the Gang.* Glencoe, Ill.: Free Press, 1955.

D'Esposito, Julian C., Jr. "Sentencing Disparity: Causes and Cures." *Journal of Criminal Law, Criminology and Police Science* 60 (1969): 182-95.

Ehrmann, Sara B. "For Whom the Chair Waits." *Federal Probation* 26 (1962): 14-25.

Empey, Lamar T., and Erickson, Maynard. "Hidden Delinquency and Social Status." *Social Forces* 44 (1966): 546-54.

Ennis, Phillip H. "Crime, Victims, and the Police." *Trans-Action* 4 (1967): 36-44.

Farrell, Ronald A. "Class Linkages of Legal Treatment of Homosexuals." *Criminology* 9 (1971): 49–68.

Foote, Caleb. "The Bail System and Equal Justice." *Federal Probation* 23 (1959): 43–48.

Glueck, Sheldon, and Glueck, Elanor T. *One Thousand Juvenile Delinquents: Their Treatment by Court and Clinic.* Cambridge, Mass.: Harvard University Press, 1934.

Gold, Martin. "Undetected Delinquent Behavior." *Journal of Research in Crime and Delinquency* 3 (1966): 27–46.

Goldman, Nathan. *The Differential Selection of Juvenile Offenders for Court Appearance.* New York: National Research and Information Center, National Council on Crime and Delinquency, 1963.

Green, Edward. *Judicial Attitudes in Sentencing.* New York: St. Martin's Press, 1961.

———. "Inter- and Intra-Racial Crime Relative to Sentencing." *Journal of Criminal Law, Criminology and Police Science* 55 (1964): 348–58.

Greenberg, David F. "Socioeconomic Status and Criminal Sentences: Is There an Association?" *American Sociological Review* 42 (1977): 174–76.

Harris, Anthony R. "Sex and Theories of Deviance: Toward a Functional Theory of Deviant Type-Scripts." *American Sociological Review* 42 (1977): 3–16.

Kobrin, Solomon. "The Conflict of Values in Delinquency Areas." *American Sociological Review* 16 (1951): 653–61.

Lin, Nan. *Foundations of Social Research.* New York: McGraw-Hill, 1976.

Louisiana Law Review. "The Institution of Bail as Related to Indigent Defendants." *Louisiana Law Review* 21 (1961): 627.

Merton, Robert K. "Social Structure and Anomie." *American Sociological Review* 3 (1938): 672–82.

———. *Social Theory and Social Structure.* Glencoe, Ill.: Free Press, 1957.

Miller, Walter B. "Lower Class Culture as a generating Milieu of Gang Delinquency." *The Journal of Social Issues* 14 (1958): 5–19.

Newman, Donald J. "Pleading Guilty for Considerations: A Study of Bargain Justice." *Journal of Criminal Law, Criminology and Police Science* 46 (1956): 780–90.

Nye, F. Ivan; Short, James F., Jr.; and Olson, Virgil J. "Socioeconomic Status and Delinquent Behavior." *American Journal of Sociology* 63 (1958): 381–89.

Porkorny, Alex D. "A Comparison of Homicides in Two Cities." *Journal of Criminal Law, Criminology and Police Science* 56 (1965): 479.

Quinney, Richard. *Criminology: Analysis and Critique of Crime in America.* Boston: Little, Brown & Co., 1975.

Robison, Sophia. *Can Delinquency be Measured?* New York: Columbia University Press, 1936.

Rosett, Arthur. "The Negotiated Guilty Plea: An Evaluation." *Annals of the American Academy of Political and Social Science* 374 (1967): 70–81.

Shaw, Clifford R. *Delinquency Areas.* Chicago: University of Chicago Press, 1929.

Shaw, Clifford R., and McKay, Henry D. "Social Factors in Juvenile Delinquency." In *Report on the Causes of Crime. Washington, D. C.: National Commission on Law Observance and Enforcement* 13 (1931).

———. *Juvenile Delinquency and Urban Areas.* Chicago: University of Chicago Press, 1942.

Skolnick, Jerome H. *Justice Without Trial: Law Enforcement in Democratic Society.* New York: Wiley, 1966.

Stinchcombe, Arthur L. "Institutions of Privacy in the Determination of Police Administrative Practice." *American Journal of Sociology* 69 (1963): 150–59.

Sutherland, Edwin H. *White Collar Crime.* New York: Dryden Press, 1949.

Swett, Daniel H. "Cultural Bias in the American Legal System." *Law & Society Review* 4 (1969): 79–110.

Swigert, Victoria Lynn, and Farrell, Ronald A. *Murder, Inequality, and the Law.* Lexington, Mass.: Lexington Books, 1976.

――――. "Normal Homicides and the Law." *American Sociological Review* 42 (1977): 16–32.

Thomas, William I. *The Unadjusted Girl.* Boston: Little, Brown & Co., 1923.

Tiffany, Lawrence; Avichai, Yakov; and Peters, Geoffrey. "A Statistical Analysis of Sentencing in Federal Courts." *Journal of Legal Studies* 4 (1975): 369–90.

Treiman, Donald J. (ed.) *Occupational Prestige in Comparative Perspective.* New York: Academic Press, 1977.

UCLA Law Review. "The Consenting Adult Homosexual and the Law: An Empirical Study of Enforcement and Administration in Los Angeles County (part III - Enforcement Techniques)." *UCLA Law Review* 13 (1966): 686–742.

Useem, John; Tangent, Pierre; and Useem, Ruth. "Stratification in a Prairie Town." *American Sociological Review* 7 (1942): 331–42.

Voss, Harwin L., and Hepburn, John R. "Patterns in Criminal Homicide in Chicago." *Journal of Criminal Law, Criminology and Police Science* 59 (1968): 499–508.

Warner, W. Lloyd, and Lunt, Paul S. *The Social Life of a Modern Community.* New Haven: Yale University Press, 1941.

Willick, Daniel H.; Gehlker, Gretchen; and Watts, Anita McFarland. "Social Class as a Factor Affecting Judicial Disposition: Defendants Charged with Criminal Homosexual Acts." *Criminology* 13 (1975): 57–77.

Wolfgang, Marvin E. *Patterns in Criminal Homicide.* Philadelphia: University of Pennsylvania Press, 1958.

JAMES P. SPRADLEY

Urban Nomads: A World
of Strangers Who Are Friends

Each year in the United States more arrests are made for public drunkenness than for any other crime. Although these arrests are made at the discretion of the police, they express and symbolize the way our society evaluates those whose style of life does not conform to the mainstream of American culture. The drunk charge covers a multitude of sins—sleeping in public places, urinating in alleys, drinking on docks, sitting in bars, begging on streets, claiming the public places of our cities as one's home. The drunk charge sweeps many into jail who are quickly released for a few dollars. The urban nomad has little money, cannot beat the drunk charge in court, and so must pay for his style of life by doing time. He is punished for the crime of poverty —he doesn't have a $20 license fee for drinking. And his punishment may reach grotesque proportions as he does a life sentence on the installment plan for living by the tramp culture. . . .

The urban nomad culture is characterized by *mobility, alienation, poverty,* and a unique set of *survival strategies.* Some men enter this way of life by choice, others are pushed toward it by personal problems, and still others are drawn to some scenes in this culture because that is where the action is. Whatever the initial impetus, once a man moves to the edge of this world he will be thrust to its center by repeated incarceration.

Source: Spradley, James P. "A World of Strangers Who Are Friends," in *You Owe Yourself a Drunk: An Ethnography of Urban Nomads.* Boston: Little, Brown & Co., 1970: 252-58. Copyright © 1970 by Little, Brown & Company (Inc.). Reprinted by permission.

Urban nomads have developed a style of life based on *mobility*. They travel from town to town, job to job, and mission to mission. They ride freight trains in circuits which cover the continent. They go from one harvest to another in broken-down automobiles. They walk the streets of the city in search of a spot job or a place to sleep. The fact that they wander continuously from place to place is not nearly so important as the fact that mobility has been internalized as part of their social identity. These men see themselves and others who are like them according to nomadic criteria. The significant features of social identity in this culture involve the extent to which one travels, how he travels, and how he lives when he travels. The tramp is on a perpetual journey and the trip is more important than the destination. The wanderings of any tramp have boundaries: for some it is the world; to others it is the nation; and still others move about within a single city with only occasional forays beyond its streets. Many complex motivations lie behind their mobility, but one is predominant. The structure of our law enforcement institutions makes travel a necessity for these men. Repeated arrests mean a growing criminal record which cuts a man off from jobs and friends. With each succeeding arrest, the length of time he must serve in jail is increased. The only sure way to maintain a good record is to leave town. As the number of days hanging grows over a period of repeated arrests and a man begins to contemplate the imminent necessity of leaving town, he may be apprehended yet another time and receive a long, suspended sentence. That day in court will mark his last in *that* city for at least six months. Even the homeguard tramp who patiently does his time on each sentence will sooner or later become too valuable as a trusty, or become a marked man for some other reason, and so be driven to mobility. Others find themselves loaded on a boxcar and shipped out of town by the police when the harvest is over. Whereas most Americans are *drawn* to a destination when they travel, urban nomads are *pushed from* a destination by these forces. In a multitude of ways, then, the practices of the police and courts, which are intended to control and punish, actually perpetuate the core of this culture — a nomadic style of life.

Although they live in our cities, urban nomads are *alienated* from the rest of society. They are stereotyped by others as bums and common drunkards. Whether looking for a job or a place to sleep, they will move with great care and expect rejection at every turn. Rejection and alienation demand constant vigilance, attempts to become invisible, and carefully constructed definitions of those who will surely interfere with one's life. The tramps' sense of alienation may have begun with friends and kinsmen because of excessive drinking or failure to hold down a steady job, but the gap is widened dramatically when they make the bucket.* They lose self-respect when labeled as "drunken bums" and "Skid Road bastards." Their jail record becomes

* Bucket is a slang term for jail.

known to employers and friends, further separating them from civil society. An identity vacuum is created within as items of personal property, symbols of their identity, disappear. As they are worked over at the call box, on the elevator, or in jail, they find that autonomy and executive command over their lives are slowly dissolving. In the grey confines of the drunk tank their communication with the outside world is cut off. They appear in court after days of waiting, are made to feel like bums, and by their very appearance lose the right to be considered innocent until proven guilty. They may even have the blood drawn from their veins before they are relased from jail. Most important, as they are cut off from former jobs, families, and friends, they lose those roles which gave them respectable identities. With each repeated arrest they may have less to lose, less which binds them to the larger society. For most men the stripping process works more deeply each time until finally the alienation has become permanent and their personal identities are thoroughly spoiled for a meaningful life anywhere except in the tramp world. And thus our institutions perform a rite of passage for these men, moving them out of the larger society and transforming their identities without providing a way for them to move back again or to alleviate the sting of rejection.

But there is another side to the alienated status of urban nomads. The forces which wrench them from one social network thrust them into another. The tramp world is especially suited for those with spoiled identities. Acceptance in that culture is based on rejection from the other and the life-style which was held to be despicable has now become an asset. A nomadic way of life not only hides what others may consider to be personal failures, but it is a world of strangers who are friends. . . . [T] ramps define their strategies for survival in jail by the criteria of reciprocity. There is a "brotherhood of the road" in this culture which is often entered while in jail. Of course liquor, which is defined in American culture as a social lubricant, is widely used by urban nomads. When strangers meet they become friends more quickly when they have had a few drinks. Aside from the physiological effects of alcohol, drinking rituals, bottle gangs, and sharing a drink with another are powerful symbols of acceptance and comradeship among those who have known the opposite from outsiders. Skid Road bars are not simply places to drink, they are institutions where strangers with spoiled identities can meet and find security in their common humanity as tramps. But even as a man finds companionship on Skid Road he is reminded of his vulnerability to the police and so, after a few months, he must move on, knowing, however, that in the next town there will be kindred souls on Skid Road who will share a jug with him, show him some good flops, and warn him of the local police practices. After thirty days in jail a tramp owes himself a drunk, not simply because he desires to gratify those impulses which have been denied while incarcerated, but because drinking and drunkenness are the prime symbols of acceptance for the man who has come through a ritual experience of alienation.

The lives of urban nomads are marked by periodic *poverty*. They work at spot jobs, make the harvest for a few months, or live off meager pension checks. Their poverty is often increased by bailing out of jail or paying off fines. When arrested they are especially vulnerable to being robbed, rolled, or clipped. Because they are bums they do not deserve property receipts. These men not only *lose* their money when they make the bucket, but their poverty becomes the major reason for doing time in jail. With each arrest their sentences are lengthened while those with money pay the same amount. Drunk drivers are often given fines which can be worked off by doing time but tramps are seldom arrested for driving while drunk and they are not fined. When a tramp repeatedly compares $20 bail with the months he does in jail he comes to realize the deep significance of his poverty. As he goes to court and sees others, who are earning money from steady jobs, released because they have steady jobs, he is again reminded that monetary considerations are primary in our system of justice. Whereas poverty may hamper a man who aspires to a middle-class way of life, except for the lack of bail money it poses little difficulty for a tramp. In fact, a nomadic way of life almost requires that one have few material possessions. As one is socialized into this world he learns that the most respected kinds of tramps are those with the fewest possessions, those who can travel "streamline" and yet survive by their wits. The lack of possessions takes on a new meaning for such a man and each time he is released from jail without a penny in his pocket he learns anew the importance of other tramps who share this world where poverty need not deter him from participating in the culture.

In order to be a successful urban nomad it is necessary to learn the *strategies for survival* in this culture. Whether panhandling, junking, boosting, or peddling, each way of making it requires learning certain skills. If a man is to be mobile he cannot depend upon a single vocation but will need a variety of ways to earn a living. If a man is alienated he will have trouble holding down a steady job even if he wants one — sooner or later the stigma of his past will color his relationships with employers and colleagues. But since the skills needed in this culture are based on different values and norms, they require deep changes in personality rather than the simple acquisition of new techniques. The self-reliance which inhibits begging by most Americans must be altered to allow for this way of earning a living; values placed upon honesty, pride of accomplishment, and the virtue of hard work must all be transformed to pave the way for junking, boosting, conning, and peddling. New risks are encountered in all these ways of making it and must be considered by those who use these strategies, but the jail setting provides the ideal situation for learning to survive in the other scenes of this culture. After months of hustling or observing others hustle in the bucket, survival as an urban nomad becomes a viable alternative to other ways of life. A man may lose a great deal when he goes to jail on a drunk charge but if he is being drawn into this culture he has also gained invaluable skills.

As these men repeatedly make the bucket and do their time, *dynamic* processes are at work to change their perception of themselves and teach them styles of living which are alien to most Americans. They acquire new identities, skills, and motivations. These men have been to school where they have been taught *who* they are, *how* they should act, and given the *desire* to do so: Skid Road bums to the outsider, tramps to the insider, and urban nomads to the anthropologist. Making the bucket effects deep and lasting changes in these men. The difference between this experience and identity change rituals in most societies, our own included, is that most schools for changing identities and teaching new roles elevate a person to a higher status—they are graduation ceremonies. The one described [there] ... lowers a man into a world and culture which is held in disrepute. He has not been graduated but demoted. He has not gone through a promotion ceremony but a degradation ritual.

JOCK YOUNG

Drugs and the Role of the Police as Amplifiers of Deviancy

The starting point of this article is W. I. Thomas's famous statement that a situation defined as real in a society will be real in its consequences. In terms, then, of those individuals whom society defines as deviants, one would expect that the stereotypes that society holds of them would have very real consequences on both their future behavior and the way they perceive themselves.

I wish to describe the manner in which society's stereotypes of the drug-taker fundamentally alter and transform the social world of the marihuana smoker. To do this I draw from a participant observation study of drug-taking in Notting Hill which I carried out between 1967 and 1969. I will focus on the effect of the beliefs and stereotypes held by the police about the drug-taker, as important characteristics of our society are that there is an increasing segregation between social groups, and that certain individuals are chosen to mediate between the community and deviant groups. Chief of these individuals are the police, and I want to suggest:

   (i) that the policeman, because of his isolated position in the community, is peculiarly susceptible to the stereotypes, the fantasy notions that the mass media carry about the drug-taker;

Source: Young, Jock. "The Role of the Police as Amplifiers of Deviancy, Negotiators of Reality, and Translators of Fantasy." In *Images of Deviance,* edited by Stanley Cohen. Middlesex, England: Penguin Books, Ltd., 1971: 27–28, 33–37, 39–52, 60. Copyright © 1971 Penguin Books, Ltd. Reprinted by permission of Penguin Books, Ltd.

Figure 1: Feedback Loop of Deviance Amplification

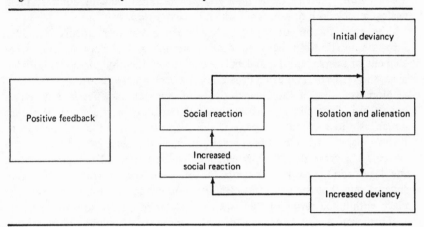

(ii) that in the process of police action—particularly in the arrest situation, but continuing in the courts—the policeman because of his position of power inevitably finds himself negotiating the evidence, the reality of drug-taking, to fit these preconceived stereotypes;

(iii) that in the process of police action against the drug-taker changes occur within drug-taking groups involving an intensification of their deviance and in certain important aspects a self-fulfillment of these stereotypes. That is, there will be an amplification of deviance, and a translation of stereotypes into actuality, of fantasy into reality. . . .

The major exponent of . . . [the] concept [of deviance amplification] is the criminologist Leslie Wilkins, who notes how when society defines a group of people as deviant it tends to react against them so as to isolate and alienate them from the company of 'normal' people. In this situation of isolation and alienation, the group—because of various reasons which I will discuss later—tends to develop its own norms and values, which society perceives as even more deviant than before. As a consequence of this increase in deviancy, social reaction increases even further, the group is even more isolated and alienated, it acts even more deviantly, society acts increasingly strongly against it, and a spiral of deviancy amplification occurs (Wilkins, 1965). Thus diagrammatically see Figure 1:

. . . The determining factor in our treatment of individuals is the type of information we receive about them. In modern urban societies there is extreme social segregation between different groups which leads to information being obtained at second hand through the mass media rather than directly by face-to-face contact. The type of information which the mass media portray is that which is "newsworthy." They select events which are *atypical,* present them in a *stereotypical* fashion and contrast them against a backcloth of normality which is *over-typical.* . . .

The twin factors of social segregation and the mass media introduce into the relationship between deviant groups and society an important element of misperception; and the deviancy amplification process is initiated always in terms of, and often because of, incorrect perceptions.

Moreover, one of the characteristics of complex societies is that certain people are allocated special roles in the process of social control. The roles —such as those of the policeman, the magistrate, and the judge—tend to involve people who themselves exist in specially segregated parts of the system. I suggest that the particular individuals assigned to administrating the legal actions against deviants inhabit their own particular segregated spheres, and that the processes of arrest, sentencing, and imprisonment take place within the terms of their own particular misperceptions of deviancy.

Furthermore, our knowledge of deviants not only is stereotypical because of the distortions of the mass media but is also, unlike in small-scale societies, one-dimensional. For example, we know very little of the methylated-spirits drinker as a person in terms of his attitudes to the world. We know him merely by the label "meths-drinker" and the hazy stereotype of activities which surrounds this phrase. Rarely—or not at all—have we even seen or talked to him in the early hours of the morning. . . .

THE POSITION OF THE POLICEMAN IN A SEGREGATED SOCIETY

Because of . . . [their relative] segregation [from society,] the police are particularly exposed to the stereotypical accounts of deviants prevalent in the mass media. They have, of course, by the very nature of their role, a high degree of face-to-face contact with deviants; but these contacts, as I will argue later, are of a type which, because of the policeman's position of power, make for a reinforcement rather than an elimination of mass-media stereotypes. Indeed a person in a position of power vis-à-vis the deviant tends to negotiate reality so that it fits his preconceptions. As a consequence of the isolation of the police and their awareness of public suspicion and hostility, there is a tendency for the police officer to envisage his role in terms of enacting the will of society, and representing the desires of a hypothesized "normal" decent citizen. In this vein, he is sensitive to the pressures of public opinion as represented in the media, and given that the police are grossly incapable because of their numbers of dealing with all crime, he will focus his attention on those areas where public indignation would seem to be greatest and which at the same time are in accord with his own preconceptions. He is thus a willing instrument—albeit unconsciously—of the type of moral panics about particular types of deviancy which are regularly fanned by the mass media. The real conflict between police and drug-taker in terms of direct interests and moral indignation is thus confirmed, distorted and structured by the specified images presented in the mass media.

THE FANTASY AND REALITY OF DRUG-TAKING

I wish to describe the social world of the marihuana smoker in Notting Hill, as it was in 1967, contrasting it with the fantasy stereotype of the drug-taker available in the mass media.

1. It is a typical bohemian "scene," that is, it is a highly organized community involving tightly interrelated friendship nets and especially intense patterns of visiting.

The stereotype held in the mass media is that of the isolated drug-taker living in a socially disorganized area, or at the best, a drifter existing in a loose conglomeration of misfits.

2. The values of the hippie marihuana smoker are relatively clear-cut and in opposition to the values of the wider society. The focal concerns of the culture are short-term hedonism, spontaneity, expressivity, disdain for work. These are similar to what David Matza [and Gresham Sykes (1961) have] . . . called the subterranean values of society.

The stereotype held is of a group of individuals who are essentially asocial, who *lack* values, rather than propound alternative values. An alternative stereotype is of a small group of ideologically motivated antisocial individuals (the corruptors) who are seducing the innocent mass of young people (the corrupted). I will elaborate this notion of the corruptors and the corrupted later on.

3. Drug-taking is—at least to start with—essentially a peripheral activity of hippie groups. That is, it does not occupy a central place in the culture: the central activities are concerned with the values outlined (for example dancing, clothes, aesthetic expression). Drug-taking is merely a vehicle for the realization of hedonistic, expressive goals.

Drugs hold a great fascination for the non-drug-taker, and in the stereotype drugs are held to be the primary concern of such groups. That is, a peripheral activity is misperceived as a central group activity.

4. The marihuana user and the marihuana seller are not fixed roles in the culture. At one time a person may sell marihuana, at another he may be buying it. This is because at street level supply is irregular, and good "connections" appear and disappear rapidly. The supply of marihuana derives from two major sources: tourists returning from abroad, and "hippie" or immigrant entrepreneurs. The latter are unsystematic, deal in relatively small quantities and make a restricted and irregular profit. The tourist's total contribution to the market is significant. Both tourists and entrepreneurs restrict their criminal activities to marihuana importation. The dealer in the street buys from these sources and sells in order to maintain himself in drugs and sustain subsistence living. He is well thought of by the

group, is part of the "hippie" culture, and is not known as a "pusher." The criminal underworld has little interest in the entrepreneur, the tourist or the dealer in the street.

The stereotype, in contrast, is on the lines of the corruptor and the corrupted, that is the "pusher" and the "buyer." The pusher is perceived as having close contacts with the criminal underworld and being part of a "drug pyramid."

5. The culture consists of largely psychologically stable individuals. The stereotype sees the drug-taker essentially as an immature, psychologically unstable young person corrupted by pushers who are criminals with weak superegos, and a near psychopathic nature.

6. The marihuana user has in fact a large measure of disdain for the heroin addict. There is an interesting parallel between the marihuana user's perception of the businessman and of the heroin addict. Both are considered to be "hung-up," obsessed and dominated by money or heroin respectively. Hedonistic and expressive values are hardly likely to be realized by either, and their way of life has no strong attraction for the marihuana user. Escalation, then, from marihuana to heroin is a rare phenomenon which would involve a radical shift in values and life-style.

In the stereotype the heroin addict and the marihuana user are often indistinguishable, the values of both are similar, and escalation is seen as part of a progressive search for more effective "kicks."

7. The marihuana user is widely prevalent in Notting Hill. A high proportion of young people in the area have smoked pot at some time or another.

The stereotype based on numbers known to the police is small compared to the actual number of smokers, yet is perceived as far too large at that and increasing rapidly.

8. The effects of marihuana are mildly euphoric; psychotic effects are rare and only temporary.

The stereotypical effects of marihuana range from extreme sexuality, through aggressive criminality, to wildly psychotic episodes.

THE POLICEMAN AS A NEGOTIATOR OF REALITY

We live in a world which is as I have suggested segregated in terms not so much of distance but of meaningful contact and empirical knowledge. The stereotype of the drug-taker—drug-seller relationship is available to the public via the mass media. This stereotype is constructed according to a typical explanation of deviancy derived from consensual notions of society: namely, that the vast majority of individuals in society share common values and agree on what is conformist and what is deviant. In these terms the deviant is a fringe phenomenon consisting of psychologically inadequate individuals who live in socially disorganized or anomic areas. The emergence of large numbers of young people indulging in deviant activities such as drug-taking in particular areas such as Notting Hill would seem to clash with this notion, as it is impossible to postulate that all of them are psychologically inadequate and that their communities are completely disorganized socially. To circumvent this, consensual theories of society invoke the notion of the corrupted and the corruptor: healthy youngsters are being corrupted by a few psychologically disturbed and economically motivated individuals. This is a subtype of the type of conspiracy theory that suggests all strikes are caused by a few politically motivated, psychologically disturbed individuals. Thus the legitimacy of alternative norms—in this case drug-taking—arising of their own accord in response to certain material and social pressures is circumvented by the notion of the wicked drug-pusher corrupting innocent youth. This allows conflicts of direct interest and moral indignation to be easily subsumed under the guise of humanitarianism. The policeman—like the rest of the public—shares this stereotype, and his treatment of individuals suspected of drug-taking is couched in terms of this stereotype.

The individual found in possession of marihuana is often—and in Notting Hill frequently—ignored by the police. They are after the real enemy, the drug-pusher. In order to get at him they are willing to negotiate with the individual found in possession. Thus they will say, "We are not interested in you, you have just been stupid, we are interested in the person who sold you this stuff. Tell us about him and we will let you off lightly." Moreover, if the individual found in possession of marihuana actually finds himself in the courts he is in a difficult position: if he tells the truth and says that he smokes marihuana because he likes it and because he believes that it does no harm and that therefore the law is wrong, he will receive a severe sentence. If, on the other hand, he plays the courts' game and conforms to their stereotype—say, he claims that he got into bad company, that somebody (the pusher) offered to sell him the stuff, so he thought he would try it out, that he knows he was foolish and won't do it again—the courts will let him off lightly. He is not then in their eyes the true deviant. He is not the dangerous individual whom the police and the courts are really after. Thus the fantasy stereotypes of drug-taking available to the police and the legal profession are reinforced and reenacted in the courts, in a process of negotiation between the accused and the accusers. T. Scheff (1968) has described this as the process of "negotiating reality." The policeman continues with evangelical zeal to seek the pusher, with the forces of public opinion and the mass media firmly behind him. As a result the sentences for possession and for sale become increasingly disparate. In a recent case that I know of, the buyer of marihuana received a fine of £5 while the seller received a five-year jail sentence. A year previously the individual who in this case was buying was selling marihuana to the person who was sentenced in this case for selling.

The negotiation of reality by the policeman is exhibited in the widespread practice of perjury. This is not due to policemen's Machiavellianism, but rather to their desire, in the name of administrative efficiency, to jump the gap between what I will term theoretical and empirical guilt. For example a West Indian who wears dark glasses, who has no regular employment, and who mixes with beatniks would quite evidently conform to their idea of a typical drug-pusher. If he is arrested, then it is of no consequence that no marihuana is found in his flat, nor is it morally reprehensible to plant marihuana on his person. For all that is being done is to aid the course of justice by providing the empirical evidence to substantiate the obvious theoretical guilt. That the West Indian might really have sold marihuana only a few times in the past, that he mixes with hippies because he likes their company, and that he lives on his national assistance payments, all this is ignored; the stereotype of the pusher is evident, and the reality is unconsciously negotiated to fit its requirements.

THE AMPLIFICATION OF DEVIANCE AND THE TRANSLATION OF FANTASY INTO REALITY

Over time, police action on the marihuana smoker in Notting Hill results in (i) the intensification of the deviancy of the marihuana user, that is the consolidation and accentuation of his deviant values in process of deviancy amplification; and (ii) a change in the life-style and reality of marihuana use, so that certain facets of the stereotype become actuality. That is a translation of fantasy into reality.

I wish to consider the various aspects of the social world of the marihuana user . . . and note the cumulative effects of intensive police action:

1. Intensive police action serves to increase the organization and cohesion of the drug-taking community, uniting its members in a sense of injustice felt at harsh sentences and mass media distortions. The severity of the conflict compels bohemian groups to evolve theories to explain the nature of their position in society, thereby heightening their consciousness of themselves as a group with definite interests over and against those of the wider society. Conflict welds an introspective community into a political faction with a critical ideology, and deviancy amplification results.

2. A rise in police action increases the necessity for the drug-taker to segregate himself from the wider society of non-drug-takers. The greater his isolation the less chance there is that the informal face-to-face forces of social control will come into operation, and the higher his potentiality for further deviant behavior. At the same time the creation by the bohemian of social worlds centering around hedonism, expressivity, and drug-use makes it necessary for the non-drug-taker, the "straight" person, to be excluded not only for reasons of security but also to maintain definitions of reality unchallenged by the outside world. Thus after a point in the process of exclusion of the deviant by society, the deviant himself will cooperate in the policy of separation.

3. The further the drug-taker evolves deviant norms, the less chance there is of his reentering the wider society. Regular drug-use, bizarre dress, long hair, and lack of a workaday sense of time, money, rationality and rewards, all militate against his reentry into regular employment. To do so after a point would demand a complete change of identity; besides modern record systems would make apparent any gaps which have occurred in his employment or scholastic records, and these might be seen to indicate a personality which is essentially shiftless and incorrigible. Once he is out of the system and labeled by the system in this manner, it is very difficult for the penitent deviant to reenter it especially at the level of jobs previously open to him. There is a point therefore beyond which an ossification of deviancy can be said to occur.

4. As police concern with drug-taking increases, drug-taking becomes more and more a secret activity. Because of this, drug-taking in itself becomes of greater value to the group as a symbol of their difference, and of their defiance of perceived social injustices. Simmel (1906), writing on the "Sociology of Secrecy," has outlined the connection between the social valuation of an activity and the degree of secrecy concerned with its prosecution.

This is what Goffman (1968:274) referred to as overdetermination. "Some illicit activities," he notes, "are pursued with a measure of spite, malice, glee, and triumph and at a personal cost that cannot be accounted for by the intrinsic pleasure of consuming the product." That is, marihuana comes to be consumed not only for its euphoric effects but as a symbol of bohemianism and rebellion against an unjust system. In addition to this, given that a desire for excitement is one of the focal concerns of the community, the ensuing game of cops and robbers is positively functional to the group. What the "fuzz" are investigating, who they have "busted" recently, become ubiquitous topics yielding unending interest and excitement.

Drug-taking and trafficking thus move from being peripheral activities of the groups, a mere vehicle for the better realization of hedonistic, expressive goals, to become a central activity of great symbolic importance. The stereotype begins to be realized, and fantasy is translated into reality.

5. The price of marihuana rises, the gains to be made from selling marihuana become larger and the professional pusher begins to emerge as police activity increases. Importation becomes more systematized, long-term and concerned with large regular profits. Because of increased vigilance at the customs, the contribution of returning tourists to the market declines markedly. International connections are forged by importers linking supply countries and profitable markets and involving large sums of capital. Other criminal activities overlap with marihuana importation, especially those dealing in other saleable drugs. On the street level the dealer becomes more of a "pusher," less part of the culture, and motivated more by economic than social and subsistence living considerations. The criminal underworld becomes more interested in the drug market, overtures are made to importers; a few pushers come under pressure to buy from them and to sell a wider

range of drugs, including heroin and methedrine. A drug pyramid, as yet embryonic, begins to emerge. Once again fantasy is being translated into reality.

6. The marihuana user becomes increasingly secretive and suspicious of those around him. How does he know that his activities are not being observed by the police? How does he know that seeming friends are not police informers? Ugly rumours fly around about treatment of suspects by the police, long terms of imprisonment, planting and general social stigmatization. The effects of drugs are undoubtedly related to the cultural milieu in which drugs are taken. A Welsh rugby club drinks to the point of aggression, an all-night party to the point of libidinousness; an academic sherry party unveils the pointed gossip of competitiveness lurking under the mask of a community of scholars. Similarly, the effects of marihuana being smoked in the context of police persecution invite feelings of paranoia and semipsychotic episodes. As Allen Ginsberg (1968) astutely notes:

> It is no wonder ... that most people who have smoked marihuana in America often experience a state of anxiety, of threat, of paranoia in fact, which may lead to trembling or hysteria, at the microscopic awareness that they are breaking a Law, that thousands of Investigators all over the country are trained and paid to smoke them out and jail them, that thousands of their community are in jail, that inevitably a few friends are 'busted' with all the hypocrisy and expense and anxiety of that trial and perhaps punishment—jail and victimage by the bureaucracy that made, propagandized, administers, and profits from such a monstrous law.
>
> From my own experience and the experience of others I have concluded that most of the horrific effects and disorders described as characteristic of marihuana 'intoxication' by the U.S. Federal Treasury Department's Bureau of Narcotics are quite the reverse, precisely traceable back to the effects on consciousness not of the narcotic but of the law and the threatening activities of the U.S. Bureau of Narcotics itself. Thus, as Buddha said to a lady who offered him a curse, the gift is returned to the giver when it is not accepted.

This relates to Tigani el Mahi's (1962) hypothesis that making a drug illegal, and failing to institutionalize its use through controls and sanctions, produce adverse psychic effects and bizarre behavior when the drug is taken. Thus stereotypical effects become in part reality.

7. As police activity increases, the marihuana user and the heroin addict begin to feel some identity as joint victims of police persecution. Interaction between heroin addicts and marihuana users increases. The general social feeling against all drugs creates a stricter control of the supply of heroin to the addict. He is legally bound to obtain his supplies from one of the properly authorized clinics. Lack of personnel who are properly trained, or who even

have an adequate theoretical knowledge of dealing with the withdrawal problems of the heroin addict, results in the alienation of many from the clinics. The addict who does attend either is kept on maintenance doses or else has his supply gradually cut. Either way euphoria becomes more difficult to obtain from the restricted supply, and the "grey market" of surplus National Health heroin, which previously catered for addicts who required extra or illicit supplies, disappears. In its place a sporadic black market springs up, often consisting of Chinese heroin diluted with adulterants. This provides a tentative basis for criminal underworld involvement in drug selling and has the consequence of increasing the risks of overdosage (because the strength is unknown) and infection (because of the adulterants).

But the supply of black-market heroin alone is inadequate. Other drugs are turned to in order to make up the scarcity, the precise drugs varying with their availability, and the ability of legislation to catch up with this phenomenon of drug displacement. Chief of these are methadone, a drug addictive in its own right and which is used to wean addicts off heroin, and freely prescribed barbiturates. As a result of displacement, a body of methadone and barbiturate addicts emerges; the barbiturates are probably more dangerous than heroin and cause even greater withdrawal problems. For a while the over prescription by doctors creates, as once occurred with heroin, an ample grey market of methadone and barbiturates. But pressure on the doctors restricts at least the availability of methadone, and the ranks of saleable black-market drugs are increased in the process. Because many junkies share some common bohemian traditions with hippies (they often live in the same areas, smoke pot, and affect the same style of dress), the black market of heroin, methadone, barbiturates *and* marihuana will overlap. The heroin addict seeking money in order to maintain his habit at a desirable level and the enterprising drug-seller may find it profitable to make these drugs available to marihuana smokers.

Some marihuana users will pass on to these hard drugs, but let me emphasize *some*, as, in general, *heavy* use of such drugs is incompatible with hippie values. For full-blown physical addiction involves being at a certain place at a certain time every day, it involves an obsession with one substance to the exclusion of all other interests, it is anathema to the values of hedonism, expressivity, and autonomy. But the number of known addicts in Britain is comparatively small (just over 2,000 heroin addicts in March 1970), while the estimates of the marihuana smoking population range up to one million and beyond. Thus it would need only a minute proportion of marihuana smokers to escalate for the heroin addiction figures to rise rapidly. Besides, the availability of methadone and barbiturates gives rise to alternative avenues of escalation. Methadone, once a palliative for heroin addicts, becomes a drug of addiction for individuals who have never used heroin. To this extent increased social reaction against the drug-taker would make real the stereotype held by the public about escalation. But the transmission of addiction, unlike the transmission of disease, is not a matter of contact, it is a process that is dictated by the social situation and values of the person who is in contact with the addict. The values of marihuana smokers and the achievement of subterranean goals are not met by intensive heroin use. Escalation to heroin (or methadone and the barbiturates) will occur only in atypical cases where the structural position of the marihuana user changes sufficiently to necessitate the evolution of values compatible with heroin use as solutions to his newly emergent problems. I have discussed this problem elsewhere, suffice it to say here that it is a product of contradictions between the subterranean goals and the limited economic and material base of the bohemian culture, which are considerably aggravated in situations where social reaction is particularly intensive. On the face of things, escalation to other, equally dangerous drugs, especially intravenous amphetamine use, is a more likely occurrence. Amphetamines, particularly methedrine or "speed," are particularly appropriate to hedonistic and expressive cultures. It is to drugs such as these that the deviancy amplification of marihuana users might well result in escalation in the type of drugs taken.

8.   As the mass media fan public indignation over marihuana use, pressure on the police increases: the public demands that they solve the drug problem. As I have mentioned previously, the number of marihuana users known to the police is a mere tip of the iceberg of actual smokers. Given their desire to behave in accordance with public opinion and to legitimize their position, the police will act with greater vigilance and arrest more marihuana offenders. All that happens is that they dig deeper into the undetected part of the iceberg; the statistics for marihuana offenders soar; the public, the press, and the magistrates view the new figures with even greater alarm. Increased pressure is put on the police, the latter dig even deeper into the iceberg, the figures increase once again, and public concern becomes even greater. We have entered what I term a fantasy crime wave, which does not necessarily involve at any time an actual increase in the number of marihuana smokers. Because of the publicity, however, the notion of marihuana smoking occurs for the first time to a larger number of people, and through their desire to experiment there will be some slight real increase. We must not overlook here the fact that moral panic over drug-taking results in the setting-up of drug squads which by their very bureaucratic creation will ensure a regular contribution to the offense figures which had never been evidenced before.

Police action not only has a deviancy amplification effect because of the unforeseen consequences of the exclusion of the marihuana smoker from "normal" society; it has also an effect on the content of the bohemian culture within which marihuana smoking takes place.

I have discussed a process which has been going on over the last three years, to some extent accentuating the contrasts in an ideal typical fashion in order to make more explicit the change. The important feature to note is that there has been change, and that this has been in part the product of

Figure 2: Spiral of Theoretical Misperceptions and Empirical Confirmations

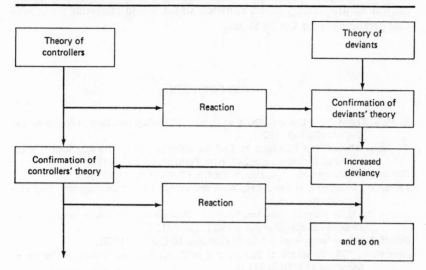

social reaction. For many social commentators and policy makers, however, this change has merely reinforced their initial presumptions about the nature of drug-takers: individuals with near psychopathic personalities, a weak superego, an unrealistic ego, and inadequate masculine identification. Inevitably these people, it is suggested, will pass on to heroin, and the figures show that this has actually occurred. Similarly the police, convinced that drug-use is a function of a few pushers, will view the deviancy amplification of the bohemian and the emergence of a drug pyramid as substantiation of their theory that we have been too permissive all along. False theories are evolved and acted upon in terms of a social reaction, resulting in changes which, although merely a *product* of these theories, are taken by many to be a proof of their initial presumptions. Similarly, the drug-taker, evolving theories as to the repressive nature of the police, finds them progressively proven as the gravity of the situation escalates. As Figure 2 shows, there can occur a spiral of theoretical misperceptions and empirical confirmations very similar to the spiral of interpersonal misperceptions described by Laing, Phillipson and Lee in *Interpersonal Perceptions* (1966).

What must be stressed is that we are dealing with a delicately balanced system of relationships between groups, and between values and social situations, which can be put, so to speak, out of gear by the overreaction of public and police. It is my contention that the tendency to unnecessary over-reaction is part of the nature of modern large-scale urban societies, and that a proper understanding of the nature of deviancy amplification and moral panic is a necessary foundation for the basis of rational social action. We could quite easily launch ourselves, through faulty mismanagement of the control of drug-taking, into a situation which would increasingly resemble that pertaining in the United States.

REFERENCES

El Mahi, Tigani. "The Use and Abuse of Drugs." *WHO Reg. Off. Eastern Mediterranean* EM/RC 12/6XVI (1962).

Ginsberg, Allen. "First Manifesto to End the Bringdown." In *The Marihuana Papers,* edited by D. Soloman, p. 242. New York: Signet Books, 1968.

Goffman, E. *Asylums.* Harmondsworth, England: Penguin Books, 1968.

Laing, R.; Phillipson, H.; and Lee, A. *Interpersonal Perception.* London: Tavistock Publications, 1966.

Matza, David, and Sykes, Gresham. "Juvenile Delinquency and Subterranean Values." *American Sociological Review* 26 (1961): 712 ff.

Scheff, T. "Negotiating Reality." *Social Problems* 16 (Summer 1968).

Simmel, G. "The Sociology of Secrecy and of Secret Societies." *American Journal of Sociology* 11 (1906): 441 ff.

Wilkins, L. "Some Sociological Factors in Drug Addiction Control." In *Narcotics,* edited by D. Wilner and G. Kassebaum. New York: McGraw-Hill, 1965.

Young, L. *The Drugtakers: The Social Meaning of Drug Use.* London: McGibbon & Kee and Paladin, 1971.

ROBERT ROSENTHAL AND LENORE F. JACOBSON

Pygmalion in the Classroom

It is usually in September that school opens, and thousands of near-six-year-olds from every conceivable kind of home start first grade. It is an anxious time for them, a mixture of uncertainty and excitement, confused with anticipatory feelings. "Will the teacher like me? When will I learn to read? Will she like *me*?"

Entering the first-grade classroom is a big step for a child. It can be a glowing or a devastating experience. The teacher smiles at the children, looking at them to see what the year will bring. The well-groomed white boys and girls will probably do well. The black- and brown-skinned ones are lower-class and will have learning problems unless they look exceptionally clean. All the whites who do not look tidy and need handkerchiefs will have trouble. If the teacher sees a preponderance of lower-class children, regardless of color, she knows her work will be difficult and unsatisfying. The teacher wants her children to learn, all of them, but she knows that lower-class children do not do well in school, just as she knows that middle-class children do do well. All this she knows as she smiles at her class for the first time, welcoming them to the adventure of first grade, measuring them for success or failure against the yardstick of middle-classness. The children smile back at her, unaware as yet that the first measurements have been taken. The yardstick will be used again when they speak to her, as she hears words spoken clearly or snuffled or stammered

Source: Rosenthal, Robert, and Jacobson, Lenore F. *Pygmalion in the Classroom: Teacher Expectation and Pupil Intellectual Development.* New York: Holt, Rinehart, and Winston, 1968: 47-48, 174-180. Copyright ©1968 Holt, Rinehart, and Winston. Reprinted by permission of the publisher.

or spoken with an accent. And later they will be measured for readiness for reading or intelligence. Many times that first year the children will be examined for what they are, for what they bring with them when they come to school.

Down the hall, the second-grade teacher knows that most of *her* lower-class students are behind those of the middle class. All through the schools that first day in September the teachers look at their classes and know which children will and will not do well during the year. Sometimes the results of formal and informal measurement modify that first day's perception; a dirty child may be very bright, a brown child may learn rapidly, a black child may read like an angel, and a tidy middle-class child may be hopelessly dull. Sometimes. Usually, the teacher is right when she predicts that middle-class children generally succeed in school and lower-class children generally lag behind and eventually fail....

[It] might also be true that school children believed by their teachers to be brighter would become brighter because of their teachers' beliefs. Oak School became the laboratory in which an experimental test of that proposition was carried out.

Oak School is a public elementary school in a lower-class community of a medium-size city. The school has a minority group of Mexican children who comprise about one-sixth of the school's population. Every year about 200 of its 650 children leave Oak School, and every year about 200 new children are enrolled.

Oak School follows an ability-tracking plan whereby each of the six grades is divided into one fast, one medium, and one slow classroom. Reading ability is the primary basis for assignment to track. The Mexican children are heavily overrepresented in the slow track.

On theoretical grounds it would have been desirable to learn whether teachers' favorable or unfavorable expectations could result in a corresponding increase or decrease in pupils' intellectual competence. On ethical grounds, however, it was decided to test only the proposition that favorable expectations by teachers could lead to an increase in intellectual competence.

All of the children of Oak School were pretested with a standard nonverbal test of intelligence. This test was represented to the teachers as one that would predict intellectual "blooming" or "spurting." The IQ test employed yielded three IQ scores: total IQ, verbal IQ, and reasoning IQ. The "verbal" items required the child to match pictured items with verbal descriptions given by the teacher. The reasoning items required the child to indicate which of five designs differed from the remaining four. Total IQ was based on the sum of verbal and reasoning items.

At the very beginning of the school year following the schoolwide pretesting, each of the eighteen teachers of grades one through six was given the names of those children in her classroom who, in the academic year ahead, would show dramatic intellectual growth. These predictions were allegedly made on the basis of these special children's scores on the test of academic blooming. About 20 percent of Oak School's children were alleged to be potential spurters. For each classroom the names of the special children had actually been chosen by means of a table of random numbers. The difference between the special children and the ordinary children, then, was only in the mind of the teacher.

All the children of Oak School were retested with the same IQ test after one semester, after a full academic year, and after two full academic years. For the first two retests, children were in the classroom of the teacher who had been given favorable expectations for the intellectual growth of some of her pupils. For the final retesting all children had been promoted to the classes of teachers who had not been given any special expectations for the intellectual growth of any of the children. That follow-up testing had been included so that we could learn whether any expectancy advantages that might be found would be dependent on a continuing contact with the teacher who held the especially favorable expectation.

For the children of the experimental group and for the children of the control group, gains in IQ from pretest to retest were computed. Expectancy advantage was defined by the degree to which IQ gains by the "special" children exceeded gains by the control-group children. After the first year of the experiment a significant expectancy advantage was found, and it was especially great among children of the first and second grades. The advantage of having been expected to bloom was evident for these younger children in total IQ, verbal IQ, and reasoning IQ. The control-group children of these grades gained well in IQ, 19 percent of them gaining twenty or more total IQ points. The "special" children, however, showed 47 percent of their number gaining twenty or more total IQ points.

During the subsequent follow-up year the younger children of the first two years lost their expectancy advantage. The children of the upper grades, however, showed an increasing expectancy advantage during the follow-up year. The younger children who seemed easier to influence may have required more continued contact with their influencer in order to maintain their behavior change. The older children, who were harder to influence initially, may have been better able to maintain their behavior change autonomously once it had occurred.

Differences between boys and girls in the extent to which they were helped by favorable expectations were not dramatic when gains in total IQ were considered. After one year, and after two years as well, boys who were expected to bloom intellectually bloomed more in verbal IQ; girls who were expected to bloom intellectually bloomed more in reasoning IQ. Favorable teacher expectations seemed to help each sex more in that sphere of intellectual functioning in which they had excelled on the pretest. At Oak School boys normally show the higher verbal IQ while girls show the higher reasoning IQ.

It will be recalled that Oak School was organized into a fast, a medium, and a slow track system. We had thought that favorable expectations on the part of teachers would be of greatest benefit to the children of the slow track. That was not the case. After one year, it was the children of the medium track who showed the greatest expectancy advantage, though children of the other tracks were close behind. After two years, however, the children of the medium track very clearly showed the greatest benefits from having had favorable expectations held of their intellectual performance. It seems surprising that it should be the more average child of a lower-class school who stands to benefit more from his teacher's improved expectation.

After the first year of the experiment and also after the second year, the Mexican children showed greater expectancy advantages than did the non-Mexican children, though the difference was not significant statistically. One interesting minority-group effect did reach significance, however, even with just a small sample size. For each of the Mexican children, magnitude of expectancy advantage was computed by subtracting from his or her gain in IQ from pretest to retest, the IQ gain made by the children of the control group in his or her classroom. These magnitudes of expectancy advantage were then correlated with the "Mexican-ness" of the children's faces. After one year, and after two years, those boys who looked more Mexican benefited more from their teachers' positive prophecies. Teachers' preexperimental expectancies for these boys' intellectual performance were probably lowest of all. Their turning up on a list of probable bloomers must have surprised their teachers. Interest may have followed surprise and, in some way, increased watching for signs of increased brightness may have led to increased brightness.

In addition to the comparison of the "special" and the ordinary children on their gains in IQ it was possible to compare their gains after the first year of the experiment on school achievement as defined by report-card grades. Only for the school subject of reading was there a significant difference in gains in report-card grades. The children expected to bloom intellectually were judged by their teachers to show greater advances in their reading ability. Just as in the case of IQ gains, it was the younger children who showed the greater expectancy advantage in reading scores. The more a given grade level had benefited in over-all IQ gains, the more that same grade level benefited in reading scores.

It was the children of the medium track who showed the greatest expectancy advantage in terms of reading ability just as they had been the children to benefit most in terms of IQ from their teachers' favorable expectations.

Report-card reading grades were assigned by teachers, and teachers' judgments of reading performance may have been affected by their expectations. It is possible, therefore, that there was no real benefit to the earmarked children of having been expected to bloom. The effect could very well have been in the mind of the teacher rather than in the reading performance of the child. Some evidence was available to suggest that such halo effects did not occur. For a number of grade levels, objective achievement tests had been administered. Greater expectancy advantage were found when the

assessment was by these objective tests than when it was by the more subjective evaluation made by the teacher. If anything, teachers' grading seemed
to show a negative halo effect. It seemed that the special children were
graded more severely by the teachers than were the ordinary children. It is
even possible that it is just this sort of standard-setting behavior that is
responsible in part for the effects of favorable expectations.

The fear has often been expressed that the disadvantaged child is further
disadvantaged by his teacher's setting standards that are inappropriately low
(Hillson and Myers, 1963; Rivlin, n.d.). Wilson (1963) has presented compelling evidence that teachers do, in fact, hold up lower standards of achievement for children of more deprived areas. It is a possibility to be further
investigated that when a teacher's expectation for a pupil's intellectual
performance is raised, she may set higher standards for him to meet (that
is, grade him tougher). There may be here the makings of a benign cycle.
Teachers may not only get more when they expect more; they may also
come to expect more when they get more.

All teachers had been asked to rate each of their pupils on variables
related to intellectual curiosity, personal and social adjustment, and need
for social approval. In general, children who had been expected to bloom
intellectually were rated as more intellectually curious, as happier, and,
especially in the lower grades, as less in need of social approval. Just as had
been the case with IQ and reading ability, it was the younger children who
showed the greater expectancy advantage in terms of their teachers' perceptions of their classroom behavior. Once again, children of the medium
track were most advantaged by having been expected to bloom, this time in
terms of their perceived greater intellectual curiosity and lessened need
for social approval.

When we consider expectancy advantages in terms of perceived intellectual
curiosity, we find that the Mexican children did not share in the advantages
of having been expected to bloom. Teachers did not see the Mexican children
as more intellectually curious when they had been expected to bloom. There
was even a slight tendency, stronger for Mexican boys, to see the special
Mexican children as less curious intellectually. That seems surprising, particularly since the Mexican children showed the greatest expectancy advantages
in IQ, in reading scores, and for Mexican boys, in overall school achievement.
It seemed almost as though, for these minority-group children, intellectual
competence may have been easier for teachers to bring about than to believe.

Children's gains in IQ during the basic year of the experiment were correlated with teachers' perceptions of their classroom behavior. This was done
separately for the upper- and lower-track children of the experimental and
control groups. The more the upper-track children of the experimental
group gained in IQ, the more favorably they were rated by their teachers.
The more the lower-track children of the control group gained in IQ, the
more unfavorably they were viewed by their teachers. No special expectation

had been created about these children, and their slow-track status made it unlikely in their teachers' eyes that they would behave in an intellectually competent manner. The more intellectually competent these children became, the more negatively they were viewed by their teachers. Future research should address itself to the possibility that there may be hazards to "unwarranted," unpredicted intellectual growth. Teachers may require a certain amount of preparation to be able to accept the unexpected classroom behavior of the intellectually upwardly mobile child.

There are a number of alternative "theories" available to account for our general findings. One such class of theories, the "accident" theories, maintain that artifacts are responsible for the results obtained, that there is really nothing to explain. The problems of test unreliability and of pretest IQ differences were discussed and found wanting as explanations of our results. The possibility that teachers treated the special children differently only during the retesting process itself was considered. The patterning of results, the fact that a "blind" examiner obtained even more dramatic expectancy effects than did the teachers, teachers' poor recall of the names of their "special" children, and the fact that the results did not disappear one year after the children left the teachers who had been given the expectations, all weaken the plausibility of that argument. Most important to the tenability of the hypothesis that teachers' expectations can significantly affect their pupils' performance are the preliminary results of three replications all of which show significant effects of teacher expectations. These replications also suggest, however, that the effects of teacher expectations may be quite complicated and affected both as to magnitude and direction by a variety of pupil characteristics and by situational variables in the life of the child.

It might reasonably be thought that the improved intellectual competence of the special children was bought at the expense of the ordinary children. Perhaps teachers gave more time to those who were expected to bloom. But teachers appeared to give slightly less time to their special children. Furthermore, those classrooms in which the special children showed the greatest gains in IQ were also the classrooms in which the ordinary children gained the most IQ. The robbing-Peter theory would predict that ordinary children gain less IQ where special children gain more IQ.

On the basis of other experiments on interpersonal self-fulfilling prophecies, we can only speculate as to how teachers brought about intellectual competence simply by expecting it. Teachers may have treated their children in a more pleasant, friendly, and encouraging fashion when they expected greater intellectual gains of them. Such behavior has been shown to improve intellectual performance, probably by its favorable effect on pupil motivation.

Teachers probably watched their special children more closely, and this greater attentiveness may have led to more rapid reinforcement of correct responses with a consequent increase in pupils' learning. Teachers may also have become more reflective in their evaluation of the special children's intellectual performance. Such an increase in teachers' reflectiveness may have led to an increase in their special pupils' reflectiveness, and such a change in cognitive style would be helpful to the performance of the non-verbal skills required by the IQ test employed.

To summarize our speculations, we may say that by what she said, by how and when she said it, by her facial expressions, postures, and perhaps by her touch, the teacher may have communicated to the children of the experimental group that she expected improved intellectual performance. Such communications together with possible changes in teaching techniques may have helped the child learn by changing his self-concept, his expectations of his own behavior, and his motivation, as well as his cognitive style and skills.

REFERENCES

Hilson, H. T., and Meyers, F. C. *The Demonstration Guidance Project: 1957-1962.* New York: New York City Board of Education, 1963.

Rivlin, H. N. *Teachers for Our Big City Schools. New York Anti-Defamation League of B'Nai B'Rith,* undated.

Wilson, A. B. "Social Stratification and Academic Achievement." In A. H. Passow (Ed.) *Education in Depressed Areas.* New York: Bureau of Publications, Teachers College of Columbia University, pp. 217-35, 1963.

PART THREE
Interaction Processes in Labeling Deviance

The definition of the situation is the medium through which behavioral boundaries are established. These definitions come to have personal meaning for group members given the reliance of individuals on significant others. This dependence includes not only the satisfaction of life-sustaining needs but the development of identities as well. For, the awareness of self is made possible only by the symbolic communication of individuals in sustained interaction with one another. This fundamental assumption underlies the symbolic interactionist approach to behavior (Cooley, 1902; Mead, 1934). Through the perception of the attitudes of others toward them, persons come to identify with the statuses and roles that comprise self-concept and motivate behavior.

Developing out of this general, social psychological approach is the interactionist, or labeling perspective on deviance. Central to the theory is the proposition that persons who are responded to as deviant are likely to define themselves as such. Society's attempts at controlling nonconformity, therefore, may actually ensure its existence. To the extent that negative sanctions preclude legitimate sources of identification, individuals will reorganize their lives and identities around the deviant status.

An important distinction, in this regard, is that between primary and secondary deviations. Primary deviations are the original, specific, and frequently transient instances of rule violation that are found universally. Whether from accident, experimentation, or group pressure, virtually all possess attributes or engage in behaviors that may elicit negative sanction. Deviations remain primary as long as they are viewed as incidental to the individual's more total life situation. They become secondary when, as a result of societal response, persons begin the think of themselves, and behave, in terms of the deviant status. The sequence of events leading to secondary deviation may be visualized as:

" ... (1) primary deviation; (2) social penalties; (3) further primary deviation; (4) stronger penalties and rejections; (5) further deviation, perhaps with hostilities and resentment beginning to focus on those doing the penalizing; (6) crisis reached in the tolerance quotient, expressed in formal action by the community stigmatizing of the deviant; (7) strengthening of the deviant conduct as a reaction to the stigmatizing and penalties; (8) ultimate acceptance of deviant social status and efforts at adjustment on the basis of the associated role." (Lemert, 1951:77).

Given the highly salient nature of the deviant status (Becker, 1963; Scott and Lyman, 1968), the attribution to that status of a distinct role defined in terms of the public stereotype (Goffman, 1963; Scheff, 1966), and the negative redefinition of other statuses and identifications through concurrent and retrospective interpretation (Garfinkel, 1956; Schur, 1971), the deviation comes to take precedence over other aspects of an individual's life and serves to guide subsequent behavior.

Negative societal reaction is contingent upon the nature of the behavior, the characteristics of the nonconformer, and the situation in which the deviation occurs. Ronald Farrell and Thomas Morrione point out in "Social Interaction and Stereotypic Responses to Homosexuals," that homosexuals are more likely to perceive rejection in secondary group settings. That is, the more impersonal contacts that characterize public encounters will tend to rely on the stereotype of the deviation when dealing with the homosexual. Since interaction in this setting is incomplete, the homosexual is effectively prevented from presenting those aspects of himself that would facilitate a more legitimate basis of communication. Among the intimate associations of primary groups, however, interaction is far more complete. Here, reliance on the stereotype can be expected to recede.

Farrell and Morrione also point out that social class is an important determinant of interpersonal responses. Homosexuals from lower-status positions elicit the more negative reactions. It appears that this relationship is a product of the closer approximation of the lower-class individual to the popular imagery of homosexuality. Overt effeminacy in manner and dress among such persons renders their deviation more visible and thus more susceptible to negative sanction.

Once an individual has been identified as deviant, the responses of others may act to exclude him from more meaningful interaction. Such is the focus of Edwin Lemert's "Paranoia and the Dynamics of Exclusion." A reciprocal process, paranoia represents the end product of the failure of communication.

The cycle most typically begins with an experience of sudden status loss or repeated disappointment. As toleration for behavior evaporates, strategies emerge to restrict the individual from full group participation. Efforts at exclusion are conspiratorial in nature and serve to limit the feedback necessary to correct the original misconduct. The paranoid becomes accusatory and aggressive in his attempts to get any reaction from his associates at all. Far from a pseudocommunity, the world of the paranoid is in fact populated by persons who are solidary and deliberate in their exclusionary tactics.

Fred Davis' "Deviance Disavowal: Management of Strained Interaction by the Visibly Handicapped" addresses the problem of exclusion from the perspective of the deviant. In our society, a visible handicap operates as a stigma to discredit the normality of its bearer. Public encounters tend to occur in terms of a fictional, or polite acceptance, that belies a sincere attribution of equality. In such a situation, the deviation becomes a master status in that the disabled is defined solely in its terms. If interaction is to proceed beyond this superficial level, reciprocal role-taking around a normalized projection of self must occur. Referred to by Davis as "breaking through," this process involves overcoming the initial fictional acceptance and, eventually, institutionalization within the relationship of a definition of self that is essentially normal.

If the relationship is not normalized, the deviant may come to occupy a token position in interaction with others. Rosabeth Kanter's "Tokenism as Deviance, " an analysis of women in predominantly male work forces, is illustrative. The visibility of women in such a situation, the resultant exaggeration of sex-based differences, and reliance on stereotypes when dealing with tokens act to shape the behavioral responses of such persons. Visibility, for example, is associated with heightened performance pressures. Attempts to adapt to these expectations may lead to either aggressive overachievement or concerted efforts to limit professional visibility. The polarization of differences between males and females, while providing for the increased solidarity of dominant group members, similarly requires a response from the token. In this case, acceptance of a position of isolation or overt participation in downgrading other members of the deviant's category will be the likely outcomes. Finally, reliance on stereotypes in interaction with the token produces a tendency toward the entrapment of females into caricaturized roles. Whether as "mother," "seductress," "pet," or "iron maiden," such roles become the only basis for sustained interaction with dominant others while resistance may result in only further rejection.

The importance of societal reactions in determining behavioral outcomes is the focus of Anthony Harris' article, "Imprisonment and Criminal Choice," regarding the impact of imprisonment on expectations for future criminality. On the basis of interviews conducted with incarcerated juveniles, Harris found that length of confinement is strongly related to the possibility of deviant careers. While there are rehabilitative effects associated with the initial period of incarceration, these are quickly surpassed by the criminalizing influences of extended sentences. This pattern is particularly evident in the case of white juveniles. Susceptibility to the amplifying effects of deviance designations, therefore, may be differentially distributed on the basis of the social characteristics of nonconformers.

Being designated as deviant is an unpleasant experience. If nonconformity cannot be avoided or concealed, the deviant may attempt to relieve stress by seeking out others who share the stigma. This was the pattern that emerged in Thomas Moriarty's experimental investigation of opinion divergence, "Stigma in the Experience of Deviance." Upon learning that their responses differed from those of most other members of the group, individuals indicated a desire to change their opinions to concur with collective norms. Not being able to do so, these persons not only expressed greater liking for fellow minority members, but demonstrated a willingness to conform to deviant others in succeeding laboratory tasks. It appears, therefore, that nonconformity may be perpetuated by those very efforts designed to censure and control it.

A sequential analysis of homosexual secondary deviation by Ronald Farrell and James Nelson, "A Causual Model of Secondary Deviance," elaborates this process by focusing on the relationship between rejection of deviants and increased nonconformity. The perception of negative responses by homosexuals leads to association with those similarly labeled. These associations may provide the support and acceptance necessary for the maintenance of positive self-concept. The end product of participation in homosexual groups, however, is further commitment to the original behavior. The isolating effects of societal rejection, therefore, may be seen as precluding conformity to conventional norms, on the one hand, while providing the motivation for adherence to deviant standards, on the other.

Once individuals have been designated as deviant, interaction between them and conforming others act to reinforce the original behavior. With claims to legitimacy denied them and the responses of others guided by the stereotype of the deviation, persons may come to identify with the only status and role available, that of the secondary deviant.

REFERENCES

Becker, Howard S. *Outsiders.* New York: Free Press, 1963.

Cooley, Charles Horton. *Human Nature and the Social Order.* New York: Charles Scribner's Sons, 1902.

Garfinkel, Harold. "Conditions of Successful Degradation Ceremonies." *American Journal of Sociology* 61 (1956): 420–24.

Goffman, Erving. *Stigma: Notes on the Management of Spoiled Identity.* Englewood Cliffs, New Jersey: Prentice-Hall, 1963.

Lemert, Edwin M. *Social Pathology: A Systematic Approach to the Theory of Sociopathic Behavior.* New York: McGraw-Hill, 1951.

Mead, George Herbert. *Mind, Self and Society.* Chicago: University of Chicago Press, 1934.

Scheff, Thomas J. *Being Mentally Ill.* Chicago: Aldine, 1966.

Schur, Edwin M. *Labeling Deviant Behavior: Its Sociological Implications.* New York: Harper & Row, 1971.

Scott, Marvin B., and Lyman, Stanford M. "Paranoia, Homosexuality and Game Theory." *The Journal of Health and Social Behavior* 9 (1968): 179–87.

RONALD A. FARRELL AND THOMAS J. MORRIONE

Social Interaction and Stereotypic Responses to Homosexuals

INTRODUCTION

Although societal reaction theorists have emphasized that deviance results from the interaction between the deviant and significant others, most research in this area has paid little direct attention to the nature of this interaction or to the structural elements surrounding and influencing it. Instead, the focus has been on the effects of such interaction on the self-definition and behavior of individuals. Pointing out this general problem in *Homosexuals and the Military,* Williams and Weinberg (1971, pp. 182–183) suggest that it partially results from the lack of adequate research methods to handle the dynamics of social interaction, a problem that besets research based on symbolic interactionism, the body of sociological theory from which this approach to deviance has been drawn. In any event, it is suggested that more attention should be given to the kinds of interaction that occur between the deviant and those around him. Although adequate methods are not presently available to handle the more dynamic aspects of interaction (i.e., the *process* by which symbols are created and communicated and shared meanings developed), this research addresses the problem by dealing with the less dynamic structural elements impinging on this process. In so doing, the analysis focuses on (1) the variations in societal responses perceived by

Source: Farrell, Ronald A. and Morrione, Thomas J. "Social Interaction and Stereotypic Responses to Homosexuals." *Archives of Sexual Behavior* 3, 5 (1974): 425–42. Permission granted by Plenum Publishing Corporation.

deviants in different group settings of interaction and (2) the relationship of these responses to their social status and related behavioral characteristics.

THE LITERATURE

Among those known to have committed deviant acts, only a segment are labeled deviant, and of those labeled there are significant differences with regard to the severity of the negative reactions experienced. Thus the likelihood of a definition of deviance and more severe societal reactions seems to show systematic variation among different groups and depending on different circumstances.

Social Distance

The first question to which we address ourselves is whether ... [negative] responses to deviance are more likely to occur in primary or secondary group settings. This question is not easily answered in the existing literature. Rather, in this area we find a limited and somewhat contradictory body of evidence. On the one hand, studies show that the labeling process is more likely to occur in intimate primary group relations, while on the other, there are those who hold that impersonal secondary group contacts are more subject to such responses.

Data that may be interpreted as support for the first point of view are offered by Mechanic (1962), who found that the definition of mental illness is more likely to be made in primary groups, and by Strerfert (1965), who reports that attitudes toward a deviant group member become more unfavorable as interaction distance decreases. Implicit in these findings is the notion that those in regular and intimate contact with the deviant find it more difficult to accept him than those who are not required to share his stigma or spend a great deal of time exerting tact and care regarding it.

Those who hold that impersonal contacts between strangers are particularly subject to stereotypic responses, on the other hand, view such responses as a form of limited, almost "one-way" symbolic communication, characterized by an absence of reaction on the part of the individual being stereotyped (see especially Goffman, 1963, pp. 51-52). Goffman states that as persons become more familiar with each other this categoric approach recedes and gradually sympathy, understanding, and a realistic assessment of personal qualities take its place. He points out that people with a bodily stigma, for example, report that "normals" with whom they interact gradually come to accept or ignore the disability, so that something like a daily round of normalization may occur. Although there are bound to be instances wherein persons experience more rejection in primary group relations, the notion that . . . [negative] responses are largely a secondary group phenomenon is most consistent with the interactionist perspective and would seem to apply in most instances of social deviance (support for this view is also offered by Rubington and Weinberg, 1968).

Social Class

A point which clearly stands out in the empirical literature is that lower-class persons are more susceptible to the labeling process. Synthesis of the findings and logical implications of this literature suggest that this is a result of a combination of at least three influences: (1) the subcultural groups in which lower-class persons interact reject deviants more than do those of the middle class (e.g., *see* Kitsuse, 1962, p. 101,[1] and Dohrenwend and Chin-Shong, 1967[2]); (2) those responsible for enforcing the norms apply more negative sanctions to lower-class persons (e.g., *see* Gallo *et al.*, 1965-1966, p. 740,[3] and Farrell, 1971[4]); and (3) the personal characteristics of lower-class persons and the circumstances under which they conduct their behavior are more likely to bring their deviations to the attention of others (e.g., *see* Leznoff and Westley, 1955, p. 260, and Myerhoff and Myerhoff, 1964). Also, related to these last findings is evidence which suggests that the likelihood of a definition of deviance and more severe societal reactions is greater when the behavior increases in (1) intensity (Terry, 1967), (2) frequency (Mechanic, 1962; Terry, 1967), (3) visibility (Mechanic, 1962), and (4) unfavorability of the place and situations in which acts occur (Terry, 1967); at least most of these are behavior patterns that seem to be more prevalent among the lower classes.

1. Kitsuse found a relative absence of extreme and overtly expressed negative sanctions against homosexuals among his more educated middle-class subjects.

2. Dohrenwend and Chin-Shong report that when both lower- and high-status groups define a pattern of behavior as seriously deviant, lower-status groups are less tolerant.

3. In a study of the legal treatment of consenting adult homosexuals, Gallo *et al.* found that a disproportionately small number of the defendants were "professional men" and that in one small upper-class community studied there were no arrests for homosexual offenses during a 2-year period.

4. This study of the legal treatment of homosexuals showed that a disproportionately large number of persons who were arrested and held for court were from the lower classes and that they received more severe legal treatment than higher-status persons, even when guilty of roughly similar offenses.

PROPOSITIONS

Based on the existing literature and its theoretical implications, the following propositions were set forth:

1. Because of interactional factors, ... [negative] responses to deviance are more likely to occur in secondary as opposed to primary group settings.

2. Lower-class persons are more susceptible to ... [negative] responses because of (a) their subcultural group associations, (b) discriminatory enforcement patterns by the middle class, and (c) their personal attributes and the circumstances under which they conduct their behavior.

THE SAMPLE

Data Collection

These propositions were tested by using data collected from a sampling of 148 male homosexuals in and around a large midwestern city.[5] The data were obtained as part of a broader social psychological study and by the use of a questionnaire distributed through four homosexual bars and social clubs,[6] two different organizations for homosexuals, and individual contact with persons from various social class backgrounds. By tapping the homosexual community at various organizational and social class levels and taking whatever cases came to hand, it was felt that a sample could be obtained that more nearly resembled the homosexual population. Furthermore, by distributing questionnaires through individual contacts, an attempt was made to reach persons who neither frequented gay bars and clubs nor were involved in the activities of homophile organizations.[7] To complement this method of data collection, a period of roughly one year was also spent conducting field study in the homosexual community. . . .

5. In 1970, this standard metropolitan statistical area had a population in excess of 1 million inhabitants.

6. For a discussion of the precedent for such sampling and its implications, see Weinberg (1970).

7. Altogether 656 questionnaires were distributed, of which the 148 were returned. This gives a response rate of 22 percent. Twenty-two percent of the returned protocols obtained through organizations for homosexuals, 48 percent from social clubs and bars, and 30 percent through individual contacts. Although the return rate is low, it is not at all surprising. In addition to the problems of using a lengthy questionnaire and sampling a

METHODOLOGY

The composite scales to tap the various concepts were first developed from information obtained from the existing literature and field study. The items were then revised after pretesting the questionnaire. Following the return of the 148 questionnaires, each scale's items were tested for their internal consistency and those with low reliability levels were omitted.[8] Scale scores were then computed for each person based on his combined responses to a given scale's items. For each of these scales, the median has been established as the cutting point between the high and low scores. (The rationale for operationalizing each concept and the scale items and their α coefficient are given in the footnotes.)

In dealing with the issue of the use of significance tests with nonprobability samples, we have followed Winch and Campbell's (1969) and Gold's (1969) suggestions that the χ^2 test be reported for the reader's information and then have supplemented this test with a measure of association as suggested by Duggan and Dean (1968, p. 46). Cramér's V has been selected as the measure of association since it can attain unity regardless of the size of the table being tested.[9]

RESULTS

Social Distance

The first proposition holds that because of interactional factors, . . . [negative] responses to deviance are more likely to occur in secondary as opposed to primary group settings.[10] Judging from the findings of this study, this proposition

population whose behavior is subject to strong taboos, in attempting to obtain a more nearly representative sample, methods of distribution were used which lend themselves to low response rates. These include distributing questionnaries under the unfavorable circumstances of the bar situation and the related difficulties in carrying out any kind of systematic followup to encourage persons to return their questionnaires.

8. Coefficient α was used to obtain the exact coefficient of equivalence for each composite scale. This statistical procedure provides a measure of internal consistency, taking into account the number of items, by giving the average split-half correlation for all possible ways of dividing the test into two parts (*see* Cronbach, 1951).

9. Although it is not possible to attach a precise meaning to Cramér's V, since the values for this measure will range from 0 to 1 even in those instances in which the number of rows and columns is not equal, it serves as a very useful measure for comparing the relative strength of the various relationships (*see* Blalock, 1960, p. 230).

10. Perceived societal reactions were considered in terms of the patterned and recurrent experiences of social acceptance or rejection in informal encounters. With this in mind,

appears to be supported in the case of homosexuality. Table 1 shows the relationship between the perceived reactions of others and the group setting of interaction. The figures show that 76 percent of the sample fell into the "acceptance" category in reporting on the reactions from "people who knew them" (i.e., members of their primary groups). Unlike this situation in primary group relations, 50 percent perceived "acceptance" in their more impersonal public encounters. Furthermore, the data show that 21 percent of the sample perceived rejection in secondary group settings, while only 2 percent reported such responses in primary group encounters. Accordingly, stigma, at least in this instance, is something that pertains primarily to public life, to contact between strangers and mere acquaintances—generally to secondary group relations.

These findings may be explained in terms of symbolic interaction theory (*see* especially Blumer, 1966, 1969; Morrione, 1971; Rubington and Weinberg, 1968; Turner, 1962; Wilson, 1970). According to the interactionist perspective, human association is a continual process of interpretation and reinterpretation of indications. On the basis of their interaction, people form meanings on which they act; they define the situation through the interaction process. Impersonal contacts, however, are representative of incomplete interaction. In essence, what is lacking and the factor whose lack facilitates stereotyping is the "feedback process" in the interaction (Buckley, 1967). Stereotypic responses are almost unidirectional, with an absence of opportunity

two scales were developed, one to tap primary group reactions and the other for secondary group reactions. The scale of perceived primary group reactions was based on Cooley's (1909, pp. 23-24) classical description of the primary group, which emphasized the features of intimacy and mutual identification characteristic of the family, play group, neighborhood, and community. Since we were dealing with adults, we substituted the more appropriate *work group* for Cooley's *play group*. The items that comprised this scale were as follows: (1) Please indicate what each of these groups or persons think of you (think very well of me; think well of me; do not accept or reject me; think poorly of me; think very poorly of me): (a) your community acquaintances; (b) your neighbors; (c) people you work/worked with; (d) your relatives. Now indicate how friendly or unfriendly each of these groups or persons is toward you (very friendly; friendly; somewhat friendly; somewhat unfriendly; unfriendly; very unfriendly). (α coefficient = 0.66.) The perceived secondary group reaction scale attempts to deal with informal public encounters. Adjectives used in the literature on symbolic interactionism that are thought to describe responses to deviance in impersonal relations were used in constructing the statements that make up this scale (*see* especially Cooley, 1902, pp. 258-260, and Thomas, 1923, pp. 49-50). Persons were asked to respond to these statements in the following terms: agree strongly; agree moderately; agree slightly; disagree slightly; disagree moderately; disagree strongly. (1) Straight people are cold toward me; (2) I have noticed that they wink, shrug, or nudge at one another about me; (3) They degrade me; (4) They laugh at me; (5) Straight people gossip about me; (6) They refer to me as being odd or strange; (7) They call me names such as fairy and queer; (8) I have noticed that they give me "the once over"; (9) Straight people act as though they are better than me. (α coefficient = 0.91.)

Table 1: Perceived Societal Reaction by Group Setting of Interaction

| | Group setting of interaction | | | |
| | Primary groups | | Secondary groups | |
Perceived societal reaction (with level of scaled score)	n	Percent	n	Percent
Acceptance (first quartile)	(113)	76	(74)	50
Moderate acceptance (second quartile)	(31)	21	(43)	29
Moderate rejection (third quartile)	(3)	2	(19)	13
Rejection (fourth quartile)	(0)	–	(12)	8
Not known	(1)	1	(0)	–
Total	(148)	100	(148)	100

$$x^2 = 33.713 \text{ with 3 df}, p < 0.001$$
$$V = 0.338$$

for reaction by the deviant. When interaction is of this nature, meanings neither are created via the process of definition, evaluation, and reinterpretation nor do they change as the interaction proceeds. The "interactors" interact only on the basis of the meanings which they bring into the situation (the stereotype). Impersonal contacts lack the empathic dimension precipitated by reciprocal role-taking.

In impersonal relations, the situation might often be exemplified by the following hypothetical dialogue: Stereotyper: "I *see* you are a homosexual." Homosexual: "I know you *see* I am a homosexual, but that's only a *part* of my life. Let me interact with you and explain my case." Stereotyper: "What do you mean *explain* your case? You *are* the case!" In actuality, these words may never be spoken due to the physical and social exigencies of the situation. However, the net effect of the attitude they represent results in rejection of the homosexual. Impersonal contacts, by definition, and the stereotypes they perpetuate do not facilitate communication based on shared symbols.

When social conditions facilitate face-to-face interaction of extended duration, however, the probability of the emergence of shared symbols or definitions increases.[11] Concomitantly, the rationale for divergent definitions held by actors becomes evident to those participating in the interaction and a

11. Although this theoretical proposition may be noted in the writings of many social psychological theorists, it is perhaps most cogently stated by George Homans (1950: 133): "the more frequently persons interact with one another, the stronger their sentiments of friendship for one another are apt to be."

Table 2: Perceived Societal Reaction by Social Class

Perceived societal reaction	Social class						Total
	I and II		III		IV and V		
	n	Percent	n	Percent	n	Percent	n
Low acceptance	(12)	26	(30)	54	(32)	70	(74)
High acceptance	(34)	74	(26)	46	(14)	30	(74)
Total	(46)	100	(56)	100	(46)	100	(148)

$x^2 = 17.851$ with 2 df, $p < 0.001$
$V = 0.347$

more "total" perspective of the motives of behavior is obtained. Individuals who can interact on such a non-secondary-group level are thus viewed by others in light of a more inclusive ideological and role-expectational system. In this situation, stereotypic responses and definitions are deemphasized, less frequent, and not required as prerequisites for developing meanings.

Social Status

The second proposition states that lower-class persons are more susceptible to . . . [negative] responses because of (1) their subcultural group associations, (2) discriminatory enforcement patterns by the middle class, and (3) their personal attributes and the circumstances under which they conduct their behavior. Since the preceding findings seem to have shown that stigma in the case of homosexuality pertains primarily to public life, *secondary group responses* were used as the dependent variable in testing this proposition. As a first step in the analysis, Table 2 shows the relationship between the social class of individuals and their perceived reaction of others in secondary group settings.[12] Based on this relationship, the data from this study offer support for the proposition. The table shows a very strong relationship between low social class and low perceived societal acceptance. The figures indicate that while 70 percent of the persons from the two lower classes (IV and V) perceived a low degree of acceptance, only 26 percent from the upper classes (I and II) reported such responses.

Based on the existing literature, the second proposition has suggested that this relationship is a result of a combination of (1) subcultural, (2) discriminatory, and (3) personal and circumstantial influences. Although the data from this study do not lend themselves to systematic analyses of these first two

12. Hollingshead's "Two Factor Index" (combining occupation and education) was used to measure social class (*see* Bonjean *et al.*, 1967, pp. 381–385).

Table 3: Perceived Societal Reaction by Homosexual Image

	Homosexual image				
Perceived societal reaction	High stereotypic		Low stereotypic		Total
	n	Percent	n	Percent	n
Low acceptance	(49)	65	(25)	34	(74)
High acceptance	(26)	35	(48)	66	(74)
Total	(75)	100	(73)	100	(148)

$x^2 = 14.300$ with 1 df, $p < 0.001$
$V = 0.311$

influences in the case of homosexuality, it was possible to identify important factors relating to the third. This was done first by examining the relationship between persons' perceived societal reactions to their deviance and the social image that they presented. This social image was considered in terms of its degree of correspondence with the homosexual stereotype, particularly in regard to overt and effeminate behavior patterns. Thus a scaled set of items was used which dealt with the personal attributes of the individual and the circumstances under which he conducted his behavior.[13] Again, perceived societal reactions were considered in terms of secondary group responses.

Table 3 shows the relationship between the perceived societal reaction and homosexual image of the members of the sample. The data show that those who possessed additional qualities concurring with the stereotypic image of the homosexual were more likely to perceive low acceptance. The figures indicate that 65 percent of the persons who presented a high stereotypic image perceived low acceptance, while 34 percent of those who presented a low stereotypic image reported such responses.

Further analysis also showed that the effects of a homosexual image on societal response are confined largely to these more impersonal public encounters. Very little correspondence was found between the reactions that persons perceived in primary group relations and their image as a homosexual.

13. The homosexual image scale consists of the following items (persons were asked to respond to the first four statements in these terms: very often; often; fairly often; rarely; very rarely; never). Items 1 and 5 are modifications from a scale used by Weinberg (1970). (1) One dances "slow" dances with other males; (2) One speaks in the homosexual slang; (3) One uses feminine nicknames when referring to his friends and acquaintances; (4) One wears facial "makeup;" . . . (5) One dresses in women's clothing (almost daily; one or more times a week; once or twice a month; few times a year; on an isolated occasion or so; not at all). (α coefficient = 0.64.) Although some of the items that make up this scale would seem to apply to behavior that would occur only in homosexual groups, it is our impression that they are part of a more general behavior pattern that does, in fact, carry over into public encounters.

Table 4:   Homosexual Image by Social Class

Homosexual image	Social class						
	I and II		III		IV and V		Total
	n	Percent	n	Percent	n	Percent	n
High stereotypic	(14)	30	(34)	61	(27)	59	(75)
Low stereotypic	(32)	70	(22)	39	(19)	41	(73)
Total	(46)	100	(56)	100	(46)	100	(148)

$x^2 = 10.981$ with 2 df, $p < 0.01$
$V = 0.272$

Therefore, it is suggested that as normals interact with the homosexual over an extended period of time, they not only redefine the meanings that they had originally brought into the relationship but, as Goffman (1963, pp. 51–52) points out, they also come to accept or ignore even his *visible deviation* to the extent that interaction proceeds in a more normal fashion.

Next the analysis addressed itself to the question of whether lower-class homosexuals were more likely to present a more stereotypic image. If the data showed this to be the case, then it could be inferred that lower-class persons are more susceptible to stereotypic responses because of their personal attributes and the circumstances under which they conduct their behavior. Table 4 shows the relationship between the homosexual image and social class of the respondents. The data show that lower-class persons were in fact more likely to present a more stereotypic image. While 59 percent of the persons from the two lower classes possessed such characteristics, 30 percent of those from the two upper classes possessed them.

To determine further if overt and effeminate behavior alone might explain the relationship between lower social class and rejection, the original relationship was reexamined while holding homosexual image constant. The results of this analysis showed that the relationship was retained for both those who were high and those who were low in their level of stereotypic image. Thus it would seem that although the more overt and effeminate behavior of lower-class persons contributes to their rejection, it is probably only one of several class-related factors that influence this response. As the second proposition suggests, other factors that are presumably operating are (1) membership of lower-class persons in groups that are more likely to reject those who are deviant and (2) discriminatory enforcement patterns by the middle class. Unfortunately, the data from this study did not lend themselves to analyses of these proposed influences.

Before accepting even the testable explanation for the second proposition, however, further analysis was done to determine if the relationship between a high stereotypic image and lower social class might be operating through a third important variable. Simon and Gagnon (1969, pp. 19-20) say that effeminate behavior tends to appear after "coming out" and then apparently diminishes with time.[14] They explain that after coming out, "many homosexuals go through a crisis of femininity; that is, they act in relatively public places in a relatively effeminate manner and some, in a transistory fashion, wear female clothing. . . . This crisis is partially structured by the already existing homosexual culture in which persons already in the crisis stage become models for those who are newer to their commitment to homosexuality. . . . The tendency is . . . for this kind of behavior to be a transitional experiment for most homosexuals. . . . " Thus it could be argued that (1) if effeminate behavior is transitional and (2) if the older homosexuals in the sample are from the higher social classes, the relationship between homosexual image and social class may be a spurious one that is in fact operating through age. Given this possibility, it was necessary to explore the joint relationship between these variables. The results of this analysis offer support for Simon and Gagnon's contention. It was found that overt and effeminate behavior (a high stereotypic image) seems to increase at about 21 years of age and then begins to diminish after 30. This is probably because most male homosexuals enter the "gay world" during their early 20s and then decrease their participation in it after 30. As might be expected, the analysis of the relationship between social class and age showed also that older persons in the sample were more likely to be members of the higher classes.

Thus these findings support the notion of the importance of controlling for age in analyzing the relationship between homosexual image and social class. This control was introduced by reexamining the relationship within each of four age groups. Table 5 shows these relationships. Although the data are meager in that there are very few cases in some of the categories, they seem to indicate that a high stereotypic image was more likely to be characteristic of the lower classes for all but those between 26 and 30 years of age. Although the relationship is in the predicted direction for this last age group, persons were or were not overt and effeminate apart from any *significant* influence of social class. However, even after further analysis the question of why this is so remains unanswered.[15] Nevertheless, it appears for

14. Although it has slightly different meanings in the homosexual argot, Simon and Gagnon (1969, p. 19) use the term "coming out" as it refers to "that point in time when there is self-recognition of one's identity as a homosexual and the first major entry into exploration of the homosexual community."

15. In attempting to answer this question, the sample was divided into two groups: those between 26 and 30 and those of all other ages. Other variables were then identified that were thought to be related to the development of overt and effeminate behavior. Those considered (among others) were number of years involved in the "gay world," level of homosexual association, and frequency of attendance at "gay" bars. These variables were "run" in relation to the two age groups in order to determine whether persons

Table 5: Homosexual Image by Social Class Among Different Age Groups

	Social class: 20 years of age and under (n = 30)					
	I and II		III		IV and V	
	n	Percent	n	Percent	n	Percent
High stereotypic image	(0)	0	(4)	44	(7)	44
Low stereotypic image	(5)	100	(5)	56	(9)	56
Total	(5)	100	(9)	100	(16)	100

x^2 = 3.475 with 2 df, $p < 0.20$
V = 0.340

	Social class: 21–25 years of age (n = 57)					
	I and II		III		IV and V	
	n	Percent	n	Percent	n	Percent
High stereotypic image	(1)	10	(21)	72	(12)	67
Low stereotypic image	(9)	90	(8)	28	(6)	33
Total	(10)	100	(29)	100	(18)	100

x^2 = 12.573 with 2 df, $p < 0.01$
V = 0.470

	Social class: 26–30 years of age (n = 33)					
	I and II		III		IV and V	
	n	Percent	n	Percent	n	Percent
High stereotypic image	(8)	53	(8)	67	(4)	67
Low stereotypic image	(7)	47	(4)	33	(2)	33
Total	(15)	100	(12)	100	(6)	100

x^2 = 0.609 with 2 df, $p < 0.50$
V = 0.136

	Social class: 31 years of age and over (n = 28)					
	I and II		III		IV and V	
	n	Percent	n	Percent	n	Percent
High stereotypic image	(5)	31	(1)	17	(4)	67
Low stereotypic image	(11)	69	(5)	83	(2)	33
Total	(16)	100	(6)	100	(6)	100

x^2 = 3.591 with 2 df, $p < 0.20$
V = 0.358

at least 78 percent of the sample that lower-class homosexuals are more likely to perceive a low degree of societal acceptance because they do not exercise as much self-possession and are more effeminate in mannerisms and appearance.

DISCUSSION

Based on the analysis of the data and findings described in the preceding pages, we have concluded that (1) ... [negative] responses to homosexuals are more likely to occur under the interactional prescripts characteristic of secondary as opposed to primary groups and (2) lower-class homosexuals are more likely to perceive ... [negative] responses than are upper-class homosexuals. Although the data did not lend themselves to analyses of all three factors proposed to be responsible for this latter relationship, it was found that one factor did have a significant influence. Thus the data showed that lower-class persons seem to have contributed to their rejection by manifesting behavior which is more characteristic of the homosexual stereotype. Beyond the prima facie conclusion that the lower-class homosexual manifesting a more stereotypic image is the homosexual most likely to perceive rejection in a secondary group setting, what other conclusions are indicated by this study?

First, it would seem that stereotypic responses are more likely to occur in secondary group settings due to the impersonal and almost "one-way" interaction which characterizes them. When two individuals meet, they interact in an attempt to define each other's social positions, roles, and statuses. In primary groups, interaction will most likely continue beyond the level dictated by apriori conceptualizations of these elements of social action. In secondary groups, however, there is a relative absence of reciprocated communication directed toward accurate as well as sensitive mutual definition. Such curtailed interaction does not allow one to test his conception or definition of the other via interactional feedback, thus the process of redefinition or reconceptualization is severely, if not completely, restricted. This situation is similar to what Glaser and Strauss (1964) refer to as a "closed awareness context." In such a context, one interactant does not know the other's whole identity. Thus the stereotyper who rejects the homosexual in a secondary group setting rejects him to the extent that stereotyping presents an interaction barrier to continued communication. Social action of the stereotyper in the post-stereotyping period of interaction, then, is most likely

between 26 and 30 were significantly different in any respect. The results showed that there were virtually no differences. Thus the relationship for this age group may have occurred simply as a result of sampling error. Further explanation at any rate would only be pure conjecture.

to follow a pattern similar to ritualized avoidance. As in any ritualized situation, one then *follows* the rules or normative prescripts governing the behavior in the situation; one does not discuss them with the idea of changing them. As the likelihood of reciprocated interaction in the secondary group setting decreases, so also does the probability that there will be acceptance of the homosexual contingent on the stereotyper's understanding of him.

It might be reasoned further that ritualized avoidance also fosters the development and maintenance of stereotypes. It seems that, subsequent to initial interaction, persistent ritualized avoidance inhibits an actor's ability to use symbols that would enable him to understand and accept the deviant. In this situation, the "symbol pool" necessary for understanding and acceptance, as well as the ability to engage in the process of redefinition of symbols itself, may atrophy to the extent that communication in future interaction is severely restricted. This curtailment of input elements into the interaction system may begin at the individual level and then feed back into the normative system of the group. Thus normative systems taking on these characteristics would be lacking in symbols necessary for more positive interaction with deviants. In this case, individual symbols or the lack of them (as manifested in stereotypic responses and ritualized avoidance) are reinforced and perpetuated by the normative patterns which they foster. This is more likely to occur in secondary group settings due to their greater reliance on existing definitions (i.e., in the case of deviance, stereotypes) for defining situations in interaction.

In addition to the interactional limitations inherently characteristic of secondary groups, attention also was given to another factor which facilitates stereotyping. This factor is *social class*. The findings of this study showed that (1) homosexuals from the lower classes were much less likely to perceive societal acceptance and (2) the difference in perceived acceptance among the classes may be due to the lower-class person's closer approximation to the stereotypic image of the homosexual.... [The] lower-class homosexual is *most visible* due to this closer approximation to the stereotype. Therefore, he is most apt to suffer the consequences of labeling because of the overt manifestation of his homosexuality.

A question which represents an extrapolation of this analysis is, simply put: Why does the behavior of lower-class homosexuals more closely approximate the homosexual stereotype than does the action of upper-class homosexuals? Although this query may most easily be relegated to the position of "suggested for further research," we would like to offer the following speculation. This is an extension of an explanation offered by some to the effect that upper-class homosexuals have "more to lose" and are therefore more covert or careful about manifesting behavior which is liable to reveal their homosexuality (*see* Leznoff and Westley, 1955).[16] Our guess is based on two related propositions: (1) lower-class homosexuals are more prone to identify themselves as members of the "homosexual community" and (2) as members of the lower classes such individuals are subject to social patterns conducive to the adoption of sex role stereotypic expectations. Such identifications, then, may become salient factors in influencing subsequent action.

Exhibiting behavior which closely approximates the stereotype may be a manifestation of the lower-class homosexual's desire to be clearly identified as a member of his group. In such groups, the usual criteria for social differentiation (i.e., occupational and educational levels of achievement) are often deemphasized and new ones which are more readily accessible are established. Therefore, although close approximation to the homosexual stereotype may facilitate societal rejection, it may also serve to more positively define the individual's position relative to other homosexuals of similar social background. This identification, in turn, serves the purpose of "crystallizing" his position vis-a-vis other homosexual groups. Such identification locates him in society and gives his action meaning.

Also, the life experiences of the lower-class homosexual, particularly occupationally and educationally dependent ones, are relatively restricted. As a consequence, he may think of himself as a homosexual *first* and as an assembly line worker, a laborer, or a dishwasher second. Furthermore, the alternatives open to a self-definition other than the one dependent on the homosexual criterion may be more "distasteful" or less rewarding for him to consider. Thus behavior which closely approximates the homosexual stereotype also may provide for a meaningful self-definition unattainable in the larger society. The middle-class person, on the other hand, usually occupies a number of socially rewarding positions, any or several of which he may identify with. As one such individual explained: "I cannot see myself as a homosexual first. True, it is a very important thing in my life, as anyone's sex life is, but I strive to keep it more than that. I am a homosexual, but I am also an urban designer, a pacifist, a conservationist, a socialist, and a unitarian. . . . I have few 'swish' friends and none as partners in sex; I feel I am quite tender and affectionate in a completely masculine way."

Among its other functions, the homosexual community offers the individual social support, the sense of identity, and an opportunity for upward mobility (Hacker, 1971, p. 86). If the above line of reasoning is valid, these

16. It should be noted that there are also higher-status homosexuals who exhibit overt and effeminate behavior. As Humphreys (1970, pp. 120, 131-133) points out, some upper-class men can be more open about their homosexuality because they possess so many resources for self-protection. Although there are these cases and this explanation for their existence is quite plausible, our data would suggest that they represent a substantially small proportion of the persons in these classes (see Table 4).

functions would be of greater importance to lower-class homosexuals. The availability of alternative reference groups in which to anchor one's self-image and to achieve a sense of identity and opportunity for upward mobility is more pronounced in the case of the upper-class homosexual. For the lower-class homosexual, association in the homosexual community and definite unequivocal identification as a member of it (via closely approximating the homosexual stereotype) may become a central concern due to the paucity of opportunity to achieve acceptance and a positive self-image in the larger society.

Furthermore, among the lower classes a great deal of importance is given to sex roles, and these roles are stereotypically and unequivocally defined. A male is required to be masculine and a female to be feminine; there is a relatively low level of tolerance of conduct that deviates from these prescriptions. In this situation, if a male is homosexual and therefore like a female in sexual preference, he is also expected to behave socially as a woman. Lower-class homosexuals who do not conform to these expectations, but instead are marginal in this regard, are likely to experience cognitive dissonance. The dissonance in this case results from the inconsistency between their perceived role and manifest behavior. Since the evaluation of the self is based on the performance of prescribed roles, such inconsistency would also result in low self-esteem. As alternatives to this dilemma, individuals may assume a masculine identity and enact only the dominant role in sex relations (e.g., hustlers, jailhouse wolves, and other "insertors"), or they may adopt a female identity and project that identity through the enactment of overt effeminate behavior. In our sample, the majority of lower-class persons seem to have chosen the latter alternative.[17]

Thus the sex role socialization patterns of the lower classes, coupled with the fact that there are relatively few viable alternative roles for the lower-class homosexual to enact, would appear to necessitate adopting overt and effeminate behavior in order to maintain a positive self-definition. Such behavior may be construed as role-playing directed in part toward the preservation, as well as the achievement, of a self consistent with one's perceived role. There is then the possibility of performing a necessary or accepted role in the eyes of the nonhomosexual members of their same social class, as well

17. We are grateful to Laud Humphreys (personal communication, 1972) for having suggested an interpretation of our findings similar in emphasis to the position we have noted here. According to Humphreys, overt and effeminate behavior on the part of lower-class homosexuals may be due to their having been "socialized into a world in which sex role stereotypical expectations are much more strongly dichotomized than with the upper classes in contemporary America. . . . In the lower strata of society, it is extremely difficult to maintain identity as 'just a little bit gay,' as this results in too much cognitive dissonance from the machismo expectations. If one is to break from his prescribed sex role, he must do so clearly and unmistakably."

as for their homosexual associates. For the upper-class homosexual manifesting stereotypic behavior, the results may be disastrous. For the lower-class homosexual, it is, perhaps, an attractive alternative in view of his position in the larger society.

REFERENCES

Blalock, H. M. *Social Statistics.* New York: McGraw-Hill, 1960.

Blumer, H. "Sociological implications of the thought of George Herbert Mead." *American Journal of Sociology* 71 (1966): 535–544.

––––––. *Symbolic Interactionism: Perspective and Method.* Englewood Cliffs, New Jersey: Prentice-Hall, 1969.

Bonjean, C. M.; Hill, R.; and McLemore, S. *Sociological Measurement.* San Francisco: Chandler, 1967.

Buckley, W. *Sociology and Modern Systems Theory.* Englewood Cliffs, New Jersey: Prentice-Hall, 1967.

Cooley, C. H. *Human Nature and the Social Order.* New York: Charles Scribner's Sons, 1902.

––––––. *Social Organization.* New York: Charles Scribner's Sons, 1909.

Cronbach, L. J. "Coefficient alpha and the internal structure of tests." *Psychometrika* 16 (1951): 297–334.

Dohrenwend, B. P., and Chin-Shong, E. "Social status and attitudes toward psychological disorder: The problem of tolerance of deviance." *American Sociological Review* 32 (1967): 417–433.

Duggan, T., and Dean, C. "Common misinterpretations of significance levels in sociological journals." *American Sociologist* 3 (1968): 45–46.

Farrell, R. A. "Class linkages of legal treatment of homosexuals." *Criminology* 9 (1971): 49–68.

Gallo, J. J., et al. "The consenting adult homosexual and the law." *UCLA Law Review* 13 (1965-66): 686–742.

Glaser, B. G., and Strauss, A. Awareness contexts and social interaction. *American Sociological Review* 29 (1964): 669–679.

Goffman, E. *Stigma: Notes on the Management of Spoiled Identity.* Englewood Cliffs, New Jersey: Prentice-Hall, 1963.

Gold, D. "Statistical tests and substantive significance." *American Sociologist* 4 (1969): 42–46.

Hacker, H. M. Homosexuals: Deviant or minority group? In *The Other Minorities*, edited by E. Sagarin, pp. 65–92. Waltham, Massachusetts: Ginn, 1971.

Homans, G. *The Human Group.* New York: Harcourt Brace, 1950.

Humphreys, L. *Tearoom Trade: Impersonal Sex in Public Places.* Chicago: Aldine, 1970.

Kitsuse, J. "Societal reaction to deviant behavior: Problems of theory and method." *Social Problems* 9 (1962): 247–256.

Leznoff, M., and Westley, W. "The homosexual community." *Social Problems* 3 (1965): 257–263.

Mechanic, D. "Some factors in identifying and defining mental illness." *Mental Hygiene* 46 (1962): 66–74.

Morrione, T. J. "The omission of the "i": A clue to understanding the link between social action theory and symbolic interactionism." Paper presented at the 1971 Annual Meeting of the Pacific Sociological Society.

Myerhoff, H. L., and Myerhoff, B. G. "Field observation of middle class gangs." *Social Forces* 42 (1964): 328-336.

Rubington, E., and Weinberg, M. S. "The social deviant. Part I," in *Deviance: The Interactionist Perspective.* New York: Macmillan, 1968.

Simon, W., and Gagnon, J. Homosexuality: The formulation of a sociological perspective. In *The Same Sex,* edited by R. W. Weltge. Philadelphia: Pilgrim Press. Originally printed in *Journal of Health and Social Behavior* 8(3), 1967.

Strerfert, S. "Communicator importance and interpersonal attitudes toward conforming and deviant group members." *Journal of Personal Social Psychology* 2 (1965): 242-246.

Terry, R. M. "The screening of juvenile offenders." *Journal of Criminal Law, & Criminology, Police Science* 58 (1967): 173-181.

Thomas, W. I. *The Unadjusted Girl.* Boston: Little, Brown and Co., 1923.

Turner, R. Role-taking: Process versus conformity. In *Human Behavior and Social Process: An Interactionist Approach,* edited by A. M. Rose. Boston: Houghton Mifflin, 1962.

Weinberg, M. S. "Homosexual samples: Differences and similarities. *Journal of Sex Research* 6 (1970): 312-325.

Williams, C. J., and Weinberg, M. S. *Homosexuals and the Military.* New York: Harper & Row, 1971.

Wilson, T. P. "Conceptions of interaction and forms of sociological explanation." *American Sociological Review* 35 (1970): 697-710.

Winch, R., and Campbell, D. "Proof? No. Evidence? Yes. The significance of tests of significance." *American Sociologist* 4 (1969): 140-143.

EDWIN M. LEMERT
Paranoia and the
Dynamics of Exclusion

One of the few generalizations about psychotic behavior which sociologists
have been able to make with a modicum of agreement and assurance is that
such behavior is a result or manifestation of a disorder in communication
between the individual and society. The generalization, of course, is a large
one, and, while it can be illustrated easily with case history materials, the
need for its conceptual refinement and detailing of the process by which
disruption of communication occurs in the dynamics of mental disorder has
for some time been apparent. Among the more carefully reasoned attacks
upon this problem is Cameron's formulation of the paranoid pseudocommunity (1943).

In essence, the conception of the paranoid pseudocommunity can be
stated as follows:[1]

Paranoid persons are those whose inadequate social learning leads them
in situations of unusual stress to incompetent social reactions. Out of the
fragments of the social behavior of others the paranoid person symbolically
organizes a pseudocommunity whose functions he perceives as focused on
him. His reactions to this *supposed community* of response which he sees
loaded with threat to himself bring him into open conflict with the actual

---

1. In a subsequent article Cameron (1959) modified his original conception, but not of
the social aspects of paranoia, which mainly concern us.

Source: Lemert, Edwin M. "Paranoia and the Dynamics of Exclusion." *Sociometry*
25, 1 (March 1962): 2-15, 19-20. Permission granted by The American Sociological
Association and the author.

community and lead to his temporary or permanent isolation from its affairs. The "real" community, which is unable to share in his attitudes and reactions, takes action through forcible restraint or retaliation *after* the paranoid person "bursts into defensive or vengeful activity" (Cameron, 1943).

That the community to which the paranoid reacts is "pseudo" or without existential reality is made unequivocal by Cameron when he says:

"As he (the paranoid person) begins attributing to others the attitudes which he has towards himself, he unintentionally organizes these others into a functional community, a group unified in their supposed reactions, attitudes and plans with respect to him. He in this way organizes individuals, some of whom are actual persons and some only inferred or imagined, into a whole which satisfies for the time being his immediate need for explanation but which brings no assurance with it, and usually serves to increase his tensions. The community he forms not only fails to correspond to any organization shared by others but actually contradicts this consensus. More than this, the actions ascribed by him to its personnel are not actually performed or maintained by them; *they are united in no common undertaking against him*" (Cameron, 1943 :Italics ours).

The general insightfulness of Cameron's analysis cannot be gainsaid and the usefulness of some of his concepts is easily granted. Yet a serious question must be raised, based upon empirical inquiry, as to whether in actuality the insidious qualities of the community to which the paranoid reacts are pseudo or a symbolic fabrication. There is an alternative point of view, which is the burden of this paper, namely that, while the paranoid person reacts differentially to his social environment, it is also true that "others" react differentially to him and this reaction commonly if not typically involves covertly organized action and conspiratorial behavior in a very real sense. A further extension of our thesis is that these differential reactions are reciprocals of one another, being interwoven and concatenated at each and all phases of a process of exclusion which arises in a special kind of relationship. Delusions and associated behavior must be understood in a context of exclusion which attenuates this relationship and disrupts communication.

By thus shifting the clinical spotlight away from the individual to a relationship and a process, we make an explicit break with the conception of paranoia as a disease, a state, a condition, or a syndrome of symptoms. Furthermore, we find it unnecessary to postulate trauma of early childhood or arrested psychosexual development to account for the main features of paranoia—although we grant that these and other factors may condition its expression.

This conception of paranoia is neither simple a priori theory nor is it a proprietary product of sociology. There is a substantial body of writings and empirical researches in psychiatry and psychology which question the sufficiency of the individual as primary datum for the study of paranoia. . . . More precisely, a number of studies have ended with the conclusions that external circumstances—changes in norms and values, displacement, strange environments, isolation, and linguistic separation—may create a paranoid disposition in the absence of any special character structure (Pederson, 1946). The recognition of paranoid reactions in elderly persons, alcoholics, and the deaf adds to the data generally consistent with our thesis. The finding that displaced persons who withstood a high degree of stress during war and captivity subsequently developed paranoid reactions when they were isolated in a foreign environment commands special attention among data requiring explanation in other than organic or psychodynamic terms (Kine, 1951; Listivan, 1956). . . .

DATA AND PROCEDURE

The first tentative conclusions which are presented here were drawn from a study of factors influencing decisions to commit mentally disordered persons to hospitals, undertaken with the cooperation of the Los Angeles County Department of Health in 1952. This included interviews by means of schedules with members of 44 families in Los Angeles County who were active petitioners in commitment proceedings and the study of 35 case records of public health officer commitments. In 16 of the former cases and in seven of the latter, paranoid symptoms were conspicuously present. In these cases family members and others had plainly accepted or "normalized" paranoid behavior, in some instances longstanding, until other kinds of behavior or exigencies led to critical judgments that "there was something wrong" with the person in question, and, later, that hospitalization was necessary. Furthermore, these critical judgments seemed to signal changes in the family attitudes and behavior toward the affected persons which could be interpreted as contributing in different ways to the form and intensity of the paranoid symptoms.

In 1958 a more refined and hypothesis-directed study was made of eight cases of persons with prominent paranoid characteristics. Four of these had been admitted to the state hospital at Napa, California, where they were diagnosed as paranoid schizophrenic. Two other cases were located and investigated with the assistance of the district attorney in Martinez, California.

One of the persons had previously been committed to a California state hospital, and the other had been held on an insanity petition but was freed after a jury trial. Added to these was one so-called "White House case," which had involved threats to a President of the United States, resulting in the person's commitment to St. Elizabeth's Hospital in Washington, D. C. A final case was that of a professional person with a history of chronic job difficulties, who was designated and regarded by his associates as "brash," "queer," "irritating," "hypercritical," and "thoroughly unlikeable." . . .

The investigation of the cases were as exhaustive as it was possible to make them, reaching relatives, work associates, employers, attorneys, police, physicans, public officials and any others who played significant roles in the lives of the persons involved. As many as 200 hours each were given to collecting data on some of the cases. Written materials, legal documents, publications and psychiatric histories were studied in addition to the interview data. Our procedure in the large was to adopt an interactional perspective which sensitized us to sociologically relevant behavior underlying or associated with the more apparent and formal contexts of mental disorder. In particular we were concerned to establish the order in which delusions and social exclusion occur and to determine whether exclusion takes conspiratorial form.

THE RELEVANT BEHAVIOR

In another paper (Lemert, 1946) we have shown that psychotic symptoms as described in formal psychiatry are not relevant bases for predictions about changes in social status and social participation of persons in whom they appear. Apathy, hallucinations, hyperactivity, mood swings, tics, tremors, functional paralysis, or tachycardias have no intrinsic social meanings. By the same token, neither do such imputed attributes as "lack of insight," "social incompetence" or "defective role-taking ability" favored by some sociologists as generic starting points for the analysis of mental disorders. Rather, it is behavior which puts strain on social relationships that leads to status changes: informal or formal exclusion from groups, definition as a "crank," or adjudication as insane and commitment to a mental hospital (Lemert, 1946). This is true even where the grandiose and highly bizarre delusions of paranoia are present. Definition of the socially stressful aspects of this disorder is a minimum essential, if we are to account for its frequent occurrence in partially compensated or benign form in society, as well as account for its more familiar presence as an official psychiatric problem in a hospital setting.

It is necessary, however, to go beyond these elementary observations to make it preeminently clear that strain is an emergent product of a relationship in which the behaviors of two or more persons are relevant factors, and in which the strain is felt both by ego and *alter* or *alters*. The paranoid relationship includes reciprocating behaviors with attached emotions and meanings which, to be fully understood, must be described cubistically from at least two of its perspectives. On one hand the behavior of the individual must be seen from the perspective of others or that of a group, and conversely the behavior of others must be seen from the perspective of the involved individual.

From the vantage of others the individual in the paranoid relationship shows:

1.   A disregard for the values and norms of the primary group, revealed by giving priority to verbally definable values over those which are implicit, a lack of loyalty in return for confidences, and victimizing and intimidating persons in positions of weakness.

2.   A disregard for the implicit structure of groups, revealed by presuming to privileges not accorded him, and the threat or actual resort to formal means for achieving his goals.

The second items have a higher degree of relevancy than the first in an analysis of exclusion. Stated more simply, they mean that, to the group, the individual is an ambiguous figure whose behavior is uncertain, whose loyalty can't be counted on. In short, he is a person who can't be trusted because he threatens to expose informal power structures. This, we believe, is the essential reason for the frequently encountered idea that the paranoid person is "dangerous" (Dentler and Erikson, 1959).

If we adopt the perceptual set of ego and see others or groups through his eyes, the following aspects of their behavior become relevant:

1.   the spurious quality of the interaction between others and himself or between others interacting in his presence;
2.   the overt avoidance of himself by others;
3.   the structured exclusion of himself from interaction.

The items we have described thus far—playing fast and loose with the primary group values by the individual, and his exclusion from interaction—do not alone generate and maintain paranoia. It is additionally necessary that they emerge in an interdependent relationship which requires trust for its fulfillment. The relationship is a type in which the goals of the individual can be reached only through cooperation from particular others, and in which the ends held by others are realizable if cooperation is forthcoming from ego. This is deduced from the general proposition that cooperation rests upon perceived trust, which in turn is a function of communication (Loomis, 1959). When communication is disrupted by exclusion, there is a lack of mutually perceived trust and the relationship becomes dilapidated or paranoid. We will now consider the process of exclusion by which this kind of relationship develops.

THE GENERIC PROCESS OF EXCLUSION

The paranoid process begins with persistent interpersonal difficulties between the individual and his family, or his work associates and superiors, or neighbors, or other persons in the community. These frequently or even typically arise out of bona fide or recognizable issues centering upon some actual or threatened loss of status for the individual. This is related to such things as the death of relatives, loss of a position, loss of professional certification, failure to be promoted, age and physiological life cycle changes, mutilations, and changes in family and marital relationships. The status changes are distinguished by the fact that they leave no alternative acceptable to the individual, from whence comes their "intolerable" or "unendurable" quality. For example: the man trained to be a teacher who loses his certificate, which means he can never teach; or the man of 50 years of age who is faced with loss of a promotion which is a regular order of upward mobility in an organization, who knows that he can't "start over"; or the wife undergoing hysterectomy, which mutilates her image as a woman.

In cases where no dramatic status loss can be discovered, a series of failures often is present, failures which may have been accepted or adjusted to, but with progressive tension as each new status situation is entered. The unendurability of the current status loss, which may appear unimportant to others, is a function of an intensified commitment, in some cases born of an awareness that there is a quota placed on failures in our society. Under some such circumstances, failures have followed the person, and his reputation as a "difficult person" has preceded him. This means that he often has the status of a stranger on trial in each new group he enters, and that the groups or organizations willing to take a chance on him are marginal from the standpoint of their probable tolerance for his actions.

The behavior of the individual—arrogance, insults, presumption of privilege, and exploitation of weaknesses in others—initially has a segmental or checkered pattern in that it is confined to status-committing interactions. Outside of these, the person's behavior may be quite acceptable—courteous, considerate, kind, even indulgent. Likewise, other persons and members of groups vary considerably in their tolerance for the relevant behavior, depending on the extent to which it threatens individual and organizational values, impedes functions, or sets in motion embarrassing sequences of social actions. In the early generic period, tolerance by others for the individual's aggressive behavior generally speaking is broad, and it is very likely to be interpreted as a variation of normal behavior, particularly in the absence of biographical knowledge of the person. At most, people observe that "there is something odd about him," or "he must be upset," or "he is just ornery," or "I don't quite understand him" (Cumming and Cumming, 1957).

At some point in the chain of interactions, a new configuration takes place in perceptions others have of the individual, with shifts in figure-ground relations. The individual, as we have already indicated, is an ambiguous figure, comparable to textbook figures of stairs or outlined cubes which reverse themselves when studied intently. From a normal variant the person becomes "unreliable," "untrustworthy," "dangerous," or someone with whom others "do not wish to be involved." An illustration nicely apropos of this came out in the reaction of the head of a music department in a university when he granted an interview to a man who had worked for years on a theory to compose music mathematically:

> When he asked to be placed on the staff so that he could use the electronic computers of the University *I shifted my ground* . . . when I offered an objection to his theory, he became disturbed, so I changed my reaction to "yes and no."

As is clear from this, once the perceptual reorientation takes place, either as the outcome of continuous interaction or through the receipt of biographical information, interaction changes qualitatively. In our words it becomes *spurious,* distinguished by patronizing, evasion, "humoring," guiding conversation onto selected topics, underreaction, and silence, all calculated either to prevent intense interaction or to protect individual and group values by restricting access to them. When the interaction is between two or more persons in the individual's presence it is cued by a whole repertoire of subtle expressive signs which are meaningful only to them.

The net effects of spurious interaction are to:

1. stop the flow of information to ego;
2. create a discrepancy between expressed ideas and affect among those with whom he interacts;
3. make the situation or the group image an ambiguous one for ego, much as he is for others.

Needless to say this kind of spurious interaction is one of the most difficult for an adult in our society to cope with, because it complicates or makes decisions impossible for him and also because it is morally invidious.[2]

The process from inclusion to exclusion is by no means an even one. Both individuals and members of groups change their perceptions and reactions, and vacillation is common, depending upon the interplay of values, anxieties and guilt on both sides. Members of an excluding group may decide they have been unfair and seek to bring the individual back into their confidence. This overture may be rejected or used by ego as a means of further attack. We have also found that ego may capitulate, sometimes abjectly, to others and seek group reentry, only to be rejected. In some cases compromises are struck and a partial reintegration of ego into informal social relations is achieved. The direction which informal exclusion takes depends upon ego's reactions, the degree of communication between his interactors, the

2. The interaction in some ways is similar to that used with children, particularly the *"enfant terrible."* The function of language in such interaction was studied by Sapir (1915) years ago.

composition and structure of the informal groups, and the perceptions of "key others" at points of interaction which directly affect ego's status.

ORGANIZATIONAL CRISIS AND FORMAL EXCLUSION

Thus far we have discussed exclusion as an informal process. Informal exclusion may take place but leave ego's formal status in an organization intact. So long as this status is preserved and rewards are sufficient to validate it on his terms, an uneasy peace between him and others may prevail. Yet ego's social isolation and his strong commitments make him an unpredictable factor; futhermore the rate of change and internal power struggles, especially in large and complex organizations, means that preconditions of stability may be short-lived.

Organizational crises involving a paranoid relationship arise in several ways. The individual may act in ways which arouse intolerable anxieties in others, who demand that "something be done." Again, by going to higher authority or making appeals outside the organization, he may set in motion procedures which leave those in power no other choice than to take action. In some situations ego remains relatively quiescent and does not openly attack the organization. Action against him is set off by growing anxieties or calculated motives of associates—in some cases his immediate superiors. Finally, regular organizational procedures incidental to promotion, retirement or reassignment may precipitate the crisis.

Assuming a critical situation in which the conflict between the individual and members of the organization leads to action to formally exclude him, several possibilities exist. One is the transfer of ego from one department, branch, or division of the organization to another, a device frequently resorted to in the armed services or in large corporations. This requires that the individual be persuaded to make the change and that some department will accept him. While this may be accomplished in different ways, not infrequently artifice, withholding information, bribery, or thinly disguised threats figure conspicuously among the means by which the transfer is brought about. Needless to say, there is a limit to which transfers can be employed as a solution to the problem, contingent upon the size of the organization and the previous diffusion of knowledge about the transferee.

Solution number two we call encapsulation, which, in brief, is a reorganization and redefinition of ego's status. This has the effect of isolating him from the organization and making him directly responsible to one or two superiors who act as his intermediators. The change is often made palatable to ego by enhancing some of the material rewards of his status. He may be nominally promoted or "kicked upstairs," given a larger office, or a separate secretary, or relieved of onerous duties. Sometimes a special status is created for him.

This type of solution often works because it is a kind of formal recognition by the organization of ego's intense commitment to his status and in part a victory for him over his enemies. It bypasses them and puts him into direct communication with higher authority who may communicate with him in a more direct manner. It also relieves his associates of further need to connive against him. This solution is sometimes used to dispose of troublesome corporation executives, high-ranking military officers, and academic personae non gratae in universities.

A third variety of solutions to the problem of paranoia in an organization is outright discharge, forced resignation or nonrenewal of appointment. Finally, there may be an organized move to have the individual in the paranoid relationship placed on sick leave, or to compel him to take psychiatric treatment. The extreme expression of this is pressure (as on the family) or direct action to have the person committed to a mental hospital.

The order of the enumerated solutions to the paranoid problem in a rough way reflects the amount of risk associated with the alternatives, both as to the probabilities of failure and of damaging repercussions to the organization. Generally, organizations seem to show a good deal of resistence to making or carrying out decisions which require expulsion of the individual or forcing hospitalization, regardless of his mental condition. One reason for this is that the person may have power within the organization, based upon his position, or monopolized skills and information,[3] and unless there is a strong coalition against him the general conservatism of administrative judgments will run in his favor. Herman Wouk's novel of *The Caine Mutiny* dramatizes some of the difficulties of cashiering a person from a position of power in an essentially conservative military organization. An extreme of this conservatism is illustrated by one case in which we found a department head retained in his position in an organization even though he was actively hallucinating as well as expressing paranoid delusions.[4] Another factor working on the individual's side is that discharge of a person in a position of power reflects unfavorably upon those who placed him there. Ingroup solidarity of administrators may be involved, and the methods of the opposition may create sympathy for ego at higher levels.

Even when the person is almost totally excluded and informally isolated within an organization, he may have power outside. This weighs heavily when the external power can be invoked in some way, or when it automatically leads to raising questions as to the internal workings of the organization. This touches upon the more salient reason for reluctance to eject an uncooperative and retaliatory person, even when he is relatively unimportant to the organization. We refer to a kind of negative power derived from the vulnerability

3. For a systematic analysis of the organizational difficulties in removing an "unpromotable" person from a position *see* Levenson, 1961.
4. One of the cases in the first study.

of organizations to unfavorable publicity and exposure of their private lives that are likely if the crisis proceeds to formal hearings, case review or litigation. This is an imminent possibility where paranoia exists. If hospital commitment is attempted, there is a possibility that a jury trial will be demanded, which will force leaders of the organization to defend their actions. If the crisis turns into a legal contest of this sort, it is not easy to prove insanity, and there may be damage suits. Even if the facts heavily support the petitioners, such contests can only throw unfavorable light upon the organization.

THE CONSPIRATORIAL NATURE OF EXCLUSION

A conclusion from the foregoing is that organizational vulnerability as well as anticipations of retaliations from the paranoid person lay a functional basis for conspiracy among those seeking to contain or oust him. Probabilities are strong that a coalition will appear within the organization, integrated by a common commitment to oppose the paranoid person. This, the exclusionist group, demands loyalty, solidarity and secrecy from its members; it acts in accord with a common scheme and in varying degrees utilizes techniques of manipulation and misrepresentation.

Conspiracy in rudimentary form can be detected in informal exclusion apart from an organizational crisis. This was illustrated in an office research team in which staff members huddled around a water cooler to discuss the unwanted associate. They also used office telephones to arrange coffee breaks without him and employed symbolic cues in his presence, such as humming the "Dragnet" theme song when he approached the group. An office rule against extraneous conversation was introduced with the collusion of supervisors, ostensibly for everyone, actually to restrict the behavior of the isolated worker. In another case an interview schedule designed by a researcher was changed at a conference arranged without him. When he sought an explanation at a subsequent conference, his associates pretended to have no knowledge of the changes.

Conspiratorial behavior comes into sharpest focus during organizational crises in which the exclusionists who initiate action become an embattled group. There is a concerted effort to gain consensus for this view, to solidify the group and to halt close interaction with those unwilling to completely join the coalition. Efforts are also made to neutralize those who remain uncommitted but who can't be kept ignorant of the plans afoot. Thus an external appearance of unanimity is given even if it doesn't exist.

Much of the behavior of the group at this time is strategic in nature, with determined calculations as to "what we will do if he does this or that." In one of our cases, a member on a board of trustees spoke of the "game being played" with the person in controversy with them. Planned action may be carried to the length of agreeing upon the exact words to be used when confronted or challenged by the paranoid individual. Above all there is continuous, precise communication among exclusionists, exemplified in one case by mutual exchanging of copies of all letters sent and received from ego.

Concern about secrecy in such groups is revealed by such things as carefully closing doors and lowering of voices when ego is brought under discussion. Meeting places and times may be varied from normal procedures; documents may be filed in unusual places and certain telephones may not be used during a paranoid crisis.

The visibility of the individual's behavior is greatly magnified during this period; often he is the main topic of conversation among the exclusionists, while rumors of the difficulties spread to other groups, which in some cases may be drawn into the controversy. At a certain juncture steps are taken to keep the members of the ingroup continually informed of the individual's movements and, if possible, of his plans. In effect, if not in form, this amounts to spying. Members of one embattled group, for example, hired an outside person unknown to their accuser to take notes on a speech he delivered to enlist a community organization on his side. In another case, a person having an office opening onto that of a department head was persuaded to act as an informant for the nucleus of persons working to depose the head from his position of authority. This group also seriously debated placing an all-night watch in front of their perceived malefactor's house.

Concomitant with the magnified visibility of the paranoid individual, come distortions of his image, most pronounced in the inner coterie of exclusionists. His size, physical strength, cunning, and anecdotes of his outrages are exaggerated, with a central thematic emphasis on the fact that he is dangerous. Some individuals give cause for such beliefs in that previously they have engaged in violence or threats, others do not. One encounters characteristic contradictions in interviews on this point, such as: "No, he has never struck anyone around here—just fought with the policemen at the State Capitol," or "No, I am not afraid of him, but one of these days he will explode."

It can be said parenthetically that the alleged dangerousness of paranoid persons storied in fiction and drama has never been systematically demonstrated. As a matter of fact, the only substantial data on this, from a study of delayed admissions, largely paranoid, to a mental hospital in Norway, disclosed that "neither the paranoiacs nor paranoids have been dangerous, and most not particularly troublesome" (Ödegard, 1958). Our interpretation of this, as suggested earlier, is that the imputed dangerousness of the paranoid individual does not come from physical fear but from the organizational threat he presents and the need to justify collective action against him.

However, this is not entirely tactical behavior—as is demonstrated by anxieties and tensions which mount among those in the coalition during the more critical phases of their interaction. Participants may develop fears quite analogous to those of classic conspirators. One leader in such a group spoke of the period of the paranoid crisis as a "week of terror," during which he was wracked with insomnia and "had to take his stomach pills." Projection was revealed by a trustee who, during a school crisis occasioned by discharge of an aggressive teacher, stated that he "watched his shadows," and "wondered if all would be well when he returned home at night." Such tensional states, working along with a kind of closure of communication within the group, are both a cause and an effect of amplified group interaction which distorts or symbolically rearranges the image of the person against whom they act.

Once the battle is won by the exclusionists, their version of the individual as dangerous becomes a crystallized rationale for official action. At this point misrepresentation becomes part of a more deliberate manipulation of ego. Gross misstatements, most frequently called "pretexts," become justifiable ways of getting his cooperation, for example, to get him to submit to psychiatric examination or detention preliminary to hospital commitment. This aspect of the process has been effectively detailed by Goffman, with his concept of a "betrayal funnel" through which a patient enters a hospital (1959). We need not elaborate on this, other than to confirm its occurrence in the exclusion process, complicated in our cases by legal strictures and the ubiquitous risk of litigation.

THE GROWTH OF DELUSION

The general idea that the paranoid person symbolically fabricates the conspiracy against him is in our estimation incorrect or incomplete. Nor can we agree that he lacks insight, as is so frequently claimed. To the contrary, many paranoid persons properly realize that they are being isolated and excluded by concerted interaction, or that they are being manipulated. However, they are at a loss to estimate accurately or realistically the dimensions and form of the coalition arrayed against them.

As channels of communication are closed to the paranoid person, he has no means of getting feedback on consequences of his behavior, which is essential for correcting his interpretations of the social relationships and organization which he must rely on to define his status and give him identity. He can only read overt behavior without the informal context. Although he may properly infer that people are organized against him, he can only use confrontation or formal inquisitorial procedures to try to prove this. The paranoid person must provoke strong feelings in order to receive any kind of meaningful communication from others—hence his accusations, his bluntness, his insults. Ordinarily this is nondeliberate; nevertheless, in one complex case we found the person consciously provoking discussions to get readings from others on his behavior. This man said of himself: "Some people would describe me as very perceptive, others would describe me as very imperceptive."

The need for communication and the identity which goes with it does a good deal to explain the preference of paranoid persons for formal, legalistic, written communications, and the care with which many of them preserve records of their contracts with others. In some ways the resort to litigation is best interpreted as the effort of the individual to compel selected others to interact directly with him as equals, to engineer a situation in which evasion is impossible. The fact that the person is seldom satisfied with the outcome of his letters, his petitions, complaints, and writs testifies to their function as devices for establishing contact and interaction with others, as well as "setting the record straight." The wide professional tolerance of lawyers for aggressive behavior in court and the nature of Anglo-Saxon legal institutions, which grew out of a revolt against conspiratorial or star-chamber justice, mean that the individual will be heard. Furthermore his charges must be answered; otherwise he wins by default. Sometimes he wins small victories, even if he loses the big ones. He may earn grudging respect as an adversary, and sometimes shares a kind of legal camaraderie with others in the courts. He gains an identity through notoriety.

REFERENCES

Cameron, N. "The Paranoid Pseudocommunity." *American Journal of Sociology* 46 (1943): 33–38.

_____. "The Paranoid Pseudocommunity Revisited." *American Journal of Sociology* 65 (1959): 52–58.

Cumming, E., and Cumming, J. *Closed Ranks.* Cambridge, Massachusetts: Harvard Press, 1957, Chap. 6.

Dentler, R. A., and Erikson, K. T. "The Functions of Deviance in Groups." *Social Problems* 7 (1959): 102.

Goffman, E. "The Moral Career of the Mental Patient." *Psychiatry* 22 (1959): 127 ff.

Kine, F. F. "Aliens' Paranoid Reaction." *Journal of Mental Science* 98 (1951): 589–594.

Lemert, E. "Legal Commitment and Social Control." *Sociology and Social Research* 30 (1946): 370–378.

Levenson, G. "Bureaucratic Succession." In *Complex Organization,* edited by A. Etzioni, pp. 362–395. New York: Holt, Rinehart and Winston, 1961.

Listivan, I. "Paranoid States: Social and Cultural Aspects." *Medical Journal of Australia* 1956, 776–778.

Loomis, J. L. "Communications, The Development of Trust, and Cooperative Behavior." *Human Relations* 12 (1959): 305–315.

Ödegard, O. "A Clinical Study of Delayed Admissions to a Mental Hospital." *Mental Hygiene* 42 (1958): 66–77.

Pederson, S. "Psychological Reactions to Extreme Social Displacement (Refugee Neuroses)." *Psychoanalytic Review* 36 (1946): 344–354.

Sapir, E. "Abnormal Types of Speech in Nootka." *Canada Department of Mines, Memoir* 62, 1915, no. 5.

FRED DAVIS

Deviance Disavowal:
Management of Strained Interaction
by the Visibly Handicapped

In interviews I conducted with a small number of very articulate and socially skilled informants who were visibly handicapped[1] I inquired into their handling of the imputation that they were not "normal, like everyone else." This imputation usually expresses itself in a pronounced stickiness of interactional flow and in the embarrassment of the normal by which he conveys the all to obvious message that he is having difficulty in relating to the handicapped person[2] as he would to "just an ordinary man or woman." Frequently he will make *faux pas*, slips of the tongue, revealing gestures and inadvertent remarks which overtly betray this attitude and place the handicapped person in an even more delicate situation (*see* Goffman, 1956; 1957; 1959). The triggering of such a chain of interpersonal incidents is

---

1. Six were orthopedically handicapped, three blind and two facially disfigured. Additional detailed biographical and clinical materials were secured on one blind and four facially disfigured persons, making for a total of sixteen records.

2. Throughout this paper, whether or not the term 'handicap' or 'handicapped' is joined by the qualifier 'visible,' it should be read in this way. Unfortunately, it will not be possible to discuss here that which sociologically distinguishes the situation of the visibly handicapped from that of persons whose physical handicaps are not visible or readily apparent, and how both differ from what is termed the 'sick role.' These are though important distinctions whose analysis might illuminate key questions in the study of deviance.

Source: Davis, Fred. "Deviance Disavowal: The Management of Strained Interaction by the Visibly Handicapped." *Social Problems* 9, 3 (Fall 1961): 121-122, 125-131. Permission granted by The Society for the Study of Social Problems and the author.

more likely with new persons than with those with whom the handicapped have well-established and continuing relations. Hence, the focus here is on more or less sociable occasions, it being these in which interactional discomfort is felt most acutely and coping behavior is brought into relief most sharply. . . .

[T]he analysis will attempt to delineate in transactional terms the stages through which a sociable relationship with a normal typically passes, assuming, of course, that the confrontation takes place and that both parties possess sufficient social skill to sustain a more than momentary engagement.

For present purposes we shall designate these stages as: 1) fictional acceptance, 2) the facilitation of reciprocal role-taking around a normalized projection of self and 3) the institutionalization in the relationship of a definition of self that is normal in its moral dimension, however qualified it may be with respect to its situational contexts. As we shall indicate, the unfolding of these stages comprises what may be thought of as a process of deviance disavowal or normalization,[3] depending on whether one views the process from the vantage point of the "deviant" actor or his alters.[4]

FICTIONAL ACCEPTANCE

In Western society the overture phases of a sociable encounter are to a pronounced degree regulated by highly elastic fictions of equality and normalcy. In meeting those with whom we are neither close nor familiar, manners dictate that we refrain from remarking on or otherwise reacting too obviously to those aspects of their persons which in the privacy of our thoughts betoken important differences between ourselves. In America at least, these fictions tend to encompass sometimes marked divergencies in social status as well as a great variety of expressive styles; and, it is perhaps the extreme flexibility of such fictions in our culture rather than, as is mistakenly assumed by many foreign observers, their absence that accounts for the seeming lack of punctiliousness in American manners. The point is nicely illustrated in the following news item:

3. As used here the term 'normalization' denotes a process whereby alter for whatever reason comes to view as normal and morally acceptable that which initially strikes him as odd, unnatural, "crazy," deviant, etc., irrespective of whether his perception was in the first instance reasonable, accurate or justifiable. Cf. Schwartz, 1957.

4. Because of the paper's focus on the visibly handicapped person, in what follows his interactional work is highlighted to the relative glossing over of that of the normal. Actually, the work of normalization calls for perhaps as much empathic expenditure as that of deviance disavowal and is, obviously, fully as essential for repairing the interactional breach occasioned by the encounter.

NUDE TAKES A STROLL IN MIAMI

MIAMI, Fla., Nov. 13 (UPI)—A shapely brunette slowed traffic to a snail's pace here yesterday with a 20-minute nude stroll through downtown Miami. . . .

"The first thing I knew something was wrong," said Biscayne Bay bridgetender E. E. Currey, who was working at his post about one block away, "was when I saw traffic was going unusually slow."

Currey said he looked out and called police. They told him to stop the woman, he said.

Currey said he walked out of his little bridge house, approached the woman nervously, and asked, "Say, girl, are you lost?"

"Yes," she replied. "I'm looking for my hotel."

Currey offered help and asked, "Say, did you lose your clothes?"

"No," he said the woman replied, "Why?"

Currey said that he had to step away for a moment to raise the bridge for a ship and the woman walked away. . . . (*San Francisco Chronicle,* November 14, 1960)

Unlike earlier societies and some present day ones in which a visible handicap automatically relegates the person to a caste-like, inferior, status like that of mendicant, clown or thief—or more rarely to an elevated one like that of oracle or healer—in our society the visibly handicapped are customarily accorded, save by children,[5] the surface acceptance that democratic manners guarantee to nearly all. But, as regards sociability, this proves a mixed blessing for many. Although the polite fictions do afford certain entrée rights, as fictions they can too easily come to serve as substitutes for "the real thing" in the minds of their perpetrators. The interaction is kept starved at a bare subsistence level of sociability. As with the poor relation at the wedding party, so is the reception given the handicapped person in many social situations: sufficient that he is here, he should not expect to dance with the bride.

At this stage of the encounter, the interactional problem confronting the visibly handicapped person is the delicate one of not permitting his identity to be circumscribed by the fiction while at the same time playing along with it and showing appropriate regard for its social legitimacy. For, as transparent and confining as the fiction is, it frequently is the only basis

---

5. The blunt questions and stares of small children are typically of the 'Emperor's Clothes' variety. "Mister, why is your face like that?" "Lady, what are you riding around in that for? Can't you walk?" Nearly all of my informants spoke of how unnerving such incidents were for them, particularly when other adults were present. Nonetheless, some claimed to value the child's forthrightness a good deal more than they did the genteel hypocrisy of many adults.

upon which the contact can develop into something more genuinely sociable. In those instances in which the normal fails or refuses to render even so small a gesture toward normalizing the situation, there exists almost no basis for the handicapped person to successfully disavow his deviance.[6] The following occurrence related by a young female informant is an apt, if somewhat extreme, illustration:

> I was visiting my girl friend's house and I was sitting in the lobby waiting for her when this woman comes out of her apartment and starts asking me questions. She just walked right up. I didn't know her from Adam, I never saw her before in my life. "Gee, what do you have? How long have you been that way? Oh gee, that's terrible." And so I answered her questions, but I got very annoyed and wanted to say, "Lady, mind your own business."

"BREAKING THROUGH"—FACILITATING NORMALIZED ROLE-TAKING

In moving beyond fictional acceptance what takes place essentially is a redefinitional process in which the handicapped person projects images, attitudes, and concepts of self which encourage the normal to identify with him (i.e., "take his role") in terms other than those associated with imputations of deviance (Mead, 1934; Strauss, 1959:44-88). Coincidentally, in broadening the area of minor verbal involvements, this also functions to drain away some of the stifling burden of unspoken awareness that, as we have seen, so taxes ease of interaction. The normal is cued into a larger repertoire of appropriate responses, and even when making what he, perhaps mistakenly, regards as an inappropriate response (for example, catching himself in the use of such a word as cripple or blind) the handicapped person can by his response relieve him of his embarrassment. One young informant insightfully termed the process "breaking through":

6. On the other side of the coin there are of course some handicapped persons who are equally given to undermining sociable relations by intentionally flaunting the handicap so that the fiction becomes extremely difficult to sustain. An equivalent of the "bad nigger" type described by Strong (1946), such persons were (as in Strong's study) regarded with a mixture of admiration and censure by a number of my informants. Admiration, because the cruel stripping away of pretenses and forcing of issues was thought morally refreshing, especially since, as the informants themselves recognized, many normals refuse to grant anything more than fictional acceptance while at the same time imagining themselves ennobled for having made the small sacrifice. Censure, because of the conviction that such behavior could hardly improve matters in the long run and would make acceptance even more difficult for other handicapped persons who later came into contact with a normal who had received such treatment.

The first reaction a normal individual or good-legger has is, "Oh gee, there's a fellow in a wheelchair," or "there's a fellow with a brace." And they don't say, "Oh gee, there is so-and-so, he's handsome" or "he's intelligent," or "he's a boor," or what have you. And then as the relationship develops they don't see the handicap. It doesn't exist any more. And that's the point that you as a handicapped individual become sensitive to. You know after talking with someone for a while when they don't see the handicap any more. That's when you've broken through.

What this process signifies from a social psychological standpoint is that as the handicapped person expands the interactional nexus he simultaneously disavows the deviancy latent in his status; concurrently, to the degree to which the normal is led to reciprocally assume the redefining (and perhaps unanticipated) self-attitudes proffered by the handicapped person, he comes to normalize (i.e., view as more like himself) those aspects of the other which at first connoted deviance for him. (Sometimes, as we shall see, the normal's normalizing is so complete that it is unwittingly applied to situations in which the handicapped person cannot possibly function "normally" due to sheer physical limitations.) These dynamics might also be termed a process of identification. The term is immaterial, except that in "identifying" or "taking the role of the other" much more is implicated sociologically than a mere subjective congruence of responses. The fashioning of shared perspectives also implies a progressively more binding legitimation of the altered self-representations enacted in the encounter; that is, having once normalized his perception of the handicapped person, it becomes increasingly more compromising—self-discrediting, as it were—for the normal to revert to treating him as a deviant again.

The ways in which the visibly handicapped person can go about disavowing deviance are, as we have stated, many and varied. These range from relatively straightforward conversational offerings in which he alludes in passing to his involvement in a normal round of activities, to such forms of indirection as interjecting taboo or privatized references by way of letting the normal know that he does not take offense at the latter's uneasiness or regard it as a fixed obstacle toward achieving rapport. In the above quote, for example, the informant speaks of "good-leggers," an ingroup term from his rehabilitation hospital days, which along with "dirty normals" he sometimes uses with new acquaintances "because it has a humorous connotation . . . and lots of times it puts people at their ease."[7]

7. Parallel instances can easily be cited from minority group relations as, for example, when a Jew in conversation with a non-Jew might introduce a Yiddish phrase by way of suggesting that the other's covert identification of him as a Jew need not inhibit the interaction unduly. In some situations this serves as a subtle means of declaring, "O.K., I know what's bothering you. Now that I've said it, let's forget about it and move on to something else."

Still other approaches to disavowing deviance and bridging fictional acceptance include: an especially attentive and sympathetic stance with respect to topics introduced by the normal, showing oneself to be a comic, wit, or other kind of gifted participant, and, for some, utilizing the normalization potential inherent in being seen in the company of a highly presentable normal companion (Gowman, 1956). These, and others too numerous to mention, are not of course invariably or equally successful in all cases; neither are such resources equally available to all handicapped persons, nor are the handicapped equally adept at exploiting them. As a class of corrective strategies however, they have the common aim of overcoming the interactional barrier that lies between narrow fictional acceptance and more spontaneous forms of relatedness.

Inextricably tied in with the matter of approach are considerations of setting, activity and social category of participants, certain constellations of which are generally regarded as favorable for successful deviance disavowel and normalization while others are thought unfavorable. Again, the ruling contingencies appear to be the extent to which the situation is seen as containing elements in it which: 1) contextually reduce the threat posed by the visible handicap to the rules and assumptions of the particular sociable occasion, and 2) afford the handicapped person opportunities for "breaking through" beyond fictional acceptance.

The relevance of one or both of these is apparent in the following social situations and settings about which my informants expressed considerable agreement as regards their preferences, aversions and inner reactions. To begin with, mention might again be made of the interactional rule violations frequently experienced at the hands of small children. Many of the informants were quite open in stating that a small child at a social occasion caused them much uneasiness and cramped their style because they were concerned with how, with other adults present, they would handle some bare-faced question from the child. Another category of persons with whom many claimed to have difficulty is the elderly. Here the problem was felt to be the tendency of old people to indulge in patronizing sympathy, an attitude which peculiarly resists redefinition because of the fulsome virtue it attributes to itself. In another context several of the informants laid great stress on the importance of maintaning a calm exterior whenever the physical setting unavoidably exposed them to considerable bodily awkwardness. (At the same time, of course, they spoke of the wisdom of avoiding, whenever possible, such occasions altogether.) Their attitude was that to expressively reflect gracelessness and a loss of control would result in further interactional obstacles toward assimilating the handicapped person to a normal status.

It makes me uncomfortable to watch anyone struggling, so I try to do what I must as inconspicuously as possible. In new situations or in strange places, even though I may be very anxious, I will maintain a deadly calm.

For example, if people have to lift the chair and I'm scared that they are going to do it wrong, I remain perfectly calm and am very direct in the instructions I give.

As a final example, there is the unanimity with which the informants expressed a strong preference for the small, as against the large or semipublic social gathering. Not only do they believe that, as one handicapped person among the nonhandicapped, they stand out more at large social gatherings, but also that in the anonymity which numbers further there resides a heightened structural tendency for normals to practice avoidance relations with them. The easy assumption on such occasions is that "some other good soul" will take responsibility for socializing with the handicapped person. Even in the case of the handicapped person who is forward and quite prepared to take the initiative in talking to others, the organization and ecology of the large social gathering is usually such as to frustrate his attempts to achieve a natural, nondeviant, place for himself in the group. As one young man, a paraplegic, explained:

The large social gathering presents a special problem. It's a matter of repetition. When you're in a very large group of people whom you don't know, you don't have an opportunity of talking to three, four or five at a time. Maybe you'll talk to one or two usually. After you've gone through a whole basic breakdown in making a relationship with one—after all, it's only a cocktail party—to do it again, and again, and again, it's wearing and it's no good. You don't get the opportunity to really develop something.

INSTITUTIONALIZATION OF THE
NORMALIZED RELATIONSHIP

In "breaking through" many of the handicapped are confronted by a delicate paradox, particularly in those of their relationships which continue beyond the immediate occasion. Having disavowed deviance and induced the other to respond to him as he would to a normal, the problem then becomes one of sustaining the normalized definition in the face of the many small amendments and qualifications that must frequently be made to it. The person confined to a wheelchair, for example, must brief a new acquaintance on what to do and how to help when they come to stairs, doorways, vehicle entrances, etc. Further briefings and rehearsals may be required for social obstructions as well: for example, how to act in an encounter with—to cite some typical situations at random—an overly helpful person, a waitress who communicates to the handicapped person only through his companion, a person who stares in morbid fasciination (Gowman, 1956).

Generally, such amendments and special considerations are as much as possible underplayed in the early stages of the relationship because, as in the case of much minority group protest, the fundamental demand of the handicapped is that they first be granted an irreducibly equal and normal status, it being only then regarded as fitting and safe to admit to certain incidental incapacities, limitations and needs. At some point however, the latter must be broached if the relationship to the normal is to endure in viable form. But to integrate effectively a major claim to "normalcy" with numerous minor waivers of the same claim is a tricky feat and one which exposes the relationship to the many situational and psychic hazards of apparent duplicity: the tension of transferring the special arrangements and understandings worked out between the two to situations and settings in which everyone else is "behaving normally"; the sometimes lurking suspicion of the one that it is only guilt or pity that cements the relationship, of the other that the infirmity is being used exploitatively, and of on-lookers that there is something "neurotic" and "unhealthy" about it all.[8]

From my informants' descriptions it appears that this third, "normal, but ... " stage of the relationship, if it endures, is institutionalized mainly in either one of two ways. In the first, the normal normalizes his perceptions to such an extent as to suppress his effective awareness of many of the areas in which the handicapped person's behavior unavoidably deviates from the normal standard. In this connection several of the informants complained that a recurring problem they have with close friends is that the latter frequently overlook the fact of the handicap and the restrictions it imposes on them. The friends thoughtlessly make arrangements and involve them in activities in which they, the handicapped, cannot participate conveniently or comfortably.

The other major direction in which the relationship is sometimes institutionalized is for the normal to surrender some of his normalcy by joining the handicapped person in a marginal, half-alienated, half-tolerant, outsider's orientation to "the Philistine world of normals."[9] Gowman (1956) nicely describes the tenor and style of this relationship and its possibilities for sharply disabusing normals of their stereotyped approaches to the handicapped. *Épater le bourgeois* behavior is often prominently associated with it,

8. The rhetoric of race relations reflects almost identical rationalizations and "insights" which are meant among other things to serve as cautions for would-be transgressors. "Personally I have nothing against Negroes [the handicapped], but it would be bad for my reputation if I were seen socializing with them." "She acts nice now, but with the first argument she'll call you a dirty Jew [good-for-nothing cripple]." "Regardless of how sympathetic you are toward Negroes [the disabled], the way society feels about them you'd have to be a masochist to marry one."

9. Students of race relations will recognize in this a phenomenon closely akin to "inverse passing" as when a white becomes closely identified with Negroes and passes into a Negro subculture.

as is a certain strictly ingroup license to lampoon and mock the handicap in a way which would be regarded as highly offensive were it to come from an uninitiated normal. Thus, a blind girl relates how a sighted friend sometimes chides her by calling her "a silly blink." A paraplegic tells of the old friend who tries to revive his flagging spirits by telling him not to act "like a helpless cripple." Unlike that based on over-normalization, the peculiar strength of this relationship is perhaps its very capacity to give expressive scope to the negative reality of the larger world of which it is inescapably a part while simultaneously removing itself from a primary identification with it.

REFERENCES

Goffman, Erving. "Embarrassment and Social Organization." *American Journal of Sociology* 62 (November 1956): 264-71.
———. "Alienation from Interaction." *Human Relations* 10 (1957): 47-60.
———. *Presentation of Self in Everyday Life.* New York: Doubleday and Co., 1959.
Gowman, Alan G. "Blindness and the Role of the Companion." *Social Problems* 4 (July 1956).
Mead, George H. *Mind, Self and Society.* Chicago: University of Chicago Press, 1934.
Schwartz, Charlotte G. "Perspectives on Deviance—Wives' Definitions of their Husbands' Mental Illness." *Psychiatry* 20 (August 1957): 275-91.
Strauss, Anselm. *Mirrors and Masks.* Glencoe, Illinois: Free Press, 1959.
Strong, Samuel M. "Negro—White Relations as Reflected in Social Types." *American Journal of Sociology* 52 (July 1946): 24.

ROSABETH MOSS KANTER

Tokenism as Deviance

The analysis presented here deals with interaction in face-to-face groups with highly skewed sex ratios. More specifically, the focus is upon what happens to women who occupy token statuses and are alone or nearly alone in a peer group of men. This situation is commonly faced by women in management and the professions, and it is increasingly faced by women entering formerly all-male fields at every level of organizations. But proportional scarcity is not unique to women. Men can also find themselves alone among women, blacks among whites, very old people among the young, straight people among gays, the blind among the sighted. The dynamics of interaction (the process) is likely to be very similar in all such cases, even though the content of interaction may reflect the special culture and traditional roles of both token and members of the numerically dominant category.

Use of the term "token" for the minority member rather than "solo," "solitary," or "lone" highlights some special characteristics associated with that position. Tokens are not merely deviants or people who differ from other group members along any one dimension. They are people identified by ascribed characteristics (master statuses such as sex, race, religion, ethnic group, age, etc.) or other characteristics that carry with them a set of assump-

Source: Kanter, Rosabeth Moss. "Some Effects of Proportions on Group Life: Skewed Sex Ratios and Responses to Token Women." *American Journal of Sociology* 82, 5 (1977): 967–985, 989–990. Copyright © 1977 by The University of Chicago Press. Permission granted. Some of this material appears in R. M. Kanter, *Men and Women of the Corporation*. New York: Basic Books, 1977.

tions about cultures, status, and behavior highly salient for majority category members. They bring these "auxiliary traits," in Hughes's (1944) term, into situations in which they differ from other people not in ability to do a task or in acceptance of work norms but only in terms of these secondary and informal assumptions. The importance of these auxiliary traits is heightened if members of the majority group have a history of interacting with the token's category in ways that are quite different from the demands of task accomplishment in the present situation—as is true of men with women. Furthermore, because tokens are by definition alone or virtually alone, they are in the position of representing their ascribed category to the group, whether they choose to do so or not. They can never be just another member while their category is so rare; they will always be a hyphenated member, as in "woman-engineer" or "male-nurse" or "black-physican."

People can thus be in the token position even if they have not been placed there deliberately for display by officials of an organization. It is sufficient to be in a place where others of that category are not usually found, to be the first of one's kind to enter a new group, or to represent a very different culture and set of interactional capacities to members of the numerically dominant category. The term "token" reflects one's status as a symbol of one's kind. However, lone people of one type among members of another are not necessarily tokens if their presence is taken for granted in the group or organization and incorporated into the dominant culture, so that their loneness is merely the accidental result of random distributions rather than a reflection of the rarity of their type in that system.[1]

While the dynamics of tokenism are likely to operate in some form whenever proportional representation in a collectivity is highly skewed, even if the dominant group does not intend to put the token at a disadvantage, two conditions can heighten and dramatize the effects, making them more visible to the analyst: (1) the token's social category (master status) is physically obvious, as in the case of sex, and (2) the token's social type is not only rare but also new to the setting of the dominants. The latter situation may or may not be conceptually distinct from rarity, although it allows us to see the development of patterns of adjustment as well as the perception of and response to tokens. Subsequent tokens have less surprise value and may be thrust into token roles with less disruption to the system. . . .

---

1. As an anonymous reviewer pointed out, newness is more easily distinguished from rarity conceptually than it may be empirically, and further research should make this distinction. It should also specify the conditions under which "accidental loneness" (or small relative numbers) does not have the extreme effects noted here: when the difference is noted but not considered very important, as in the case of baseball teams that may have only one or two black members but lack token dynamics because of the large number of teams with many black members.

THE FIELD STUDY

The forms of interaction in the presence of token women were identified in a field study of a large industrial corporation, one of the *Fortune 500* firms (see Kanter [in press] for a description of the setting). The sales force of one division was investigated in detail because women were entering it for the first time. The first saleswoman was hired in 1972; by the end of 1974, there had been about 20 in training or on assignment (several had left the company) out of a sales force of over 300 men. The geographically decentralized nature of sales meant, however, that in training programs or in field offices women were likely to be one of 10 or 12 sales workers; in a few cases, two women were together in a group of a dozen sales personnel. Studying women who were selling industrial goods had particular advantages: (1) sales is a field with strong cultural traditions and folklore and one in which interpersonal skills rather than expertise count heavily, thus making informal and cultural aspects of group interaction salient and visible even for members themselves; and (2) sales workers have to manage relations not only with work peers but with customers as well, thus giving the women two sets of majority groups with which to interact. Sixteen women in sales and distribution were interviewed in depth. Over 40 male peers and managers were also interviewed. Sales-training groups were observed both in session and at informal social gatherings for approximately 100 hours. Additional units of the organization were studied for other research purposes.

THEORETICAL FRAMEWORK

The framework set forth here proceeds from the . . . assumption that form determines process, narrowing the universe of interaction possibilities. The form of a group with a skewed distribution of social types generates certain perceptions of the tokens by the dominants. These perceptions determine the interaction dynamics between tokens and dominants and create the pressures dominants impose on tokens. In turn, there are typical token responses to these pressures.

The proportional rarity of tokens is associated with three perceptual phenomena: visibility, polarization, and assimilation. First, tokens, one by one, have higher visibility than dominants looked at alone: they capture a larger awareness share. A group member's awareness share, averaged over shares of other individuals of the same social type, declines as the proportion of total membership occupied by the category increases, because each individual becomes less and less surprising, unique, or noteworthy; in Gestalt terms, they more easily become "ground" rather than "figure." But for tokens there is a "law of increasing returns": as individuals of their type come to represent a *smaller* numerical proportion of the group, they potentially capture a *larger* share of the group members' awareness.

Polarization or exaggeration of differences is the second perceptual tendency. The presence of a person bearing a different set of social characteristics makes members of a numerically dominant group more aware both of their commonalities with and their differences from the token. There is a tendency to exaggerate the extent of the differences, especially because tokens are by definition too few in number to prevent the application of familiar generalizations or stereotypes. It is thus easier for the commonalities of dominants to be defined in contrast to the token than it would be in a more numerically equal situation. One person can also be perceptually isolated and seen as cut off from the group more easily than many, who begin to represent a significant proportion of the group itself.

Assimilation, the third perceptual tendency, involves the use of stereotypes or familiar generalizations about a person's social type. The characteristics of a token tend to be distorted to fit the generalization. If there are enough people of the token's type to let discrepant examples occur, it is possible that the generalization will change to accommodate the accumulated cases. But if individuals of that type are only a small proportion of the group, it is easier to retain the generalization and distort the perception of the token. . . .

Visibility, polarization, and assimilation are each associated with particular interaction dynamics that in turn generate typical token responses. These dynamics are similar regardless of the category from which the token comes, although the token's social type and history of relationships with dominants shape the content of specific interactions. Visibility creates performance pressures on the token. Polarization leads to group boundary heightening and isolation of the token. And assimilation results in the token's role entrapment.

PERFORMANCE PRESSURES

The women in the sales force I studied were highly visible, much more so than their male peers. Managers commonly reported that they were the subject of conversation, questioning, gossip, and careful scrutiny. Their placements were known and observed throughout the sales unit, while those of men typically were not. Such visibility created a set of performance pressures: characteristics and standards true for tokens alone. Tokens typically perform under conditions different from those of dominants.

Public Performance

It was difficult for the women to do anything in training programs or in the field that did not attract public notice. The women found that they did not have to go out of their way to be noticed or to get the attention of management at sales meetings. One woman reported, "I've been at sales meetings where all the trainees were going up to the managers—'Hi, Mr. So-and-So'—

trying to make that impression, wearing a strawberry tie, whatever, something that they could be remembered by. Whereas there were three of us [women] in a group of 50, and all we had to do was walk in, and everyone recognized us."

Automatic notice meant that women could not remain anonymous or hide in the crowd; all their actions were public. Their mistakes and their relationships were known as readily as any other information. It was impossible for them to have any privacy within the company. The women were always viewed by an audience, leading several to complain of "over-observation."

Extension of Consequences

The women were visible as category members, and as such their acts tended to have added symbolic consequences. Some women were told that their performance could affect the prospects for other women in the company. They were thus not acting for themselves alone but carrying the burden of representing their category. In informal conversations, they were often measured by two yardsticks: how *as women* they carried out the sales role and how *as salesworkers* they lived up to images of womanhood. In short, every act tended to be evaluated beyond its meaning for the organization and taken as a sign of "how women do in sales." The women were aware of the extra symbolic consequences attached to their acts.

Attention to a Token's Discrepant Characteristics

A token's visibility stems from characteristics—attributes of a master status—that threaten to blot out other aspects of the token's performance. While the token captures attention, it is often for discrepant characteristics, for the auxiliary traits that provide token status. No token in the study had to work hard to have her presence noticed, but she did have to work hard to have her achievements noticed. In the sales force, the women found that their technical abilities were likely to be eclipsed by their physical appearance, and thus an additional performance pressure was created. The women had to put in extra effort to make their technical skills known, to work twice as hard to prove their competence. Both male peers and customers would tend to forget information women provided about their experiences and credentials, while noticing and remembering such secondary attributes as style of dress.

Fear of Retaliation

The women were also aware of another performance pressure: to avoid making the dominants look bad. Tokenism sets up a dynamic that makes tokens afraid of outstanding performance in group events and tasks. When a token does well enough to show up a dominant, it cannot be kept a secret, because all eyes are on the token. Therefore it is difficult in such a situation to avoid the public humiliation of a dominant. Thus, paradoxically, while the token women felt they had to do better than anyone else in order to be seen as competent and allowed to continue, they also felt in some cases that their successes would not be rewarded and should be kept secret. One woman had trouble understanding this and complained of her treatment by managers. They had fired another woman for not being aggressive enough, she reported; yet she, who succeeded in doing all they asked and had brought in the largest amount of new business during the past year, was criticized for being too aggressive, too much of a hustler.

Responses of Tokens to Performance Pressures

There are two typical ways tokens respond to these performance pressures. The first involves overachievement. Aware of the performance pressures, several of the saleswomen put in extra effort, promoted themselves and their work at every opportunity, and let those around them know how well they were doing. These women evoked threats of retaliation. On the gossip circuit, they were known to be doing well but aspiring too high too fast; a common prediction was that they would be cut down to size soon.

The second response is more common and is typical of findings of other investigators. It involves attempts to limit visibility, to become socially invisible. This strategy characterizes women who try to minimize their sexual attributes so as to blend unnoticeably into the predominant male culture, perhaps by adopting "mannish dress" (Hennig, 1970, chap. 6). Or it can include avoidance of public events and occasions for performance—staying away from meetings, working at home rather than in the office, keeping silent at meetings. Several of the saleswomen deliberately kept such a low profile, unlike male peers who tended to seize every opportunity to make themselves noticed. They avoided conflict, risks, and controversial situations. Those women preferring social invisibility also made little attempt to make their achievements publicly known or to get credit for their own contributions to problem solving or other organizational tasks. They are like other women in the research literature who have let others assume visible leadership (Megaree, 1969) or take credit for their accomplishments (Lynch, 1973; Cussler, 1958). These women did blend into the background, but they also limited recognition of their competence.

This analysis suggests a reexamination of the "fear of success in women" hypothesis. Perhaps what has been called fear of success is really the token woman's fear of visibility. The original research identifying this concept created a hypothetical situation in which a woman was at the top of her class in medical school—a token woman in a male peer group. Such a situation puts pressure on a woman to make herself and her achievements invisible, to deny success. Attempts to replicate the initial findings using settings in which women were not so clearly tokens produced very different results. And in other studies (e.g., Levine and Crumrine, 1975), the hypothesis that fear of success is a female-linked trait has not been confirmed. (*See* Sarason [1973] for a discussion of fear of visibility among minorities.)

BOUNDARY HEIGHTENING

Polarization or exaggeration of the token's attributes in contrast to those of the dominants sets a second set of dynamics in motion. The presence of a token makes dominants more aware of what they have in common at the same time that it threatens that commonality. Indeed it is often at those moments when a collectivity is threatened with change that its culture and bonds become evident to it; only when an obvious outsider appears do group members suddenly realize their common bond as insiders. Dominants thus tend to exaggerate both their commonality and the token's difference, moving to heighten boundaries of which previously they might not even have been aware.[2]

Exaggeration of Dominants' Culture

Majority members assert or reclaim group solidarity and reaffirm shared in-group understandings by emphasizing and exaggerating those cultural

2. This awareness often seemed to be resented by the men interviewed in this study, who expressed a preference for less self-consciousness and less attention to taken-for-granted operating assumptions. They wanted to "get on with business," and questioning definitions of what is "normal" and "appropriate" was seen as a deflection from the task at hand. The culture in the managerial/technical ranks of this large corporation, like that in many others, devalued introspection and emphasized rapid communication and ease of interaction. Thus, although group solidarity is often based on the development of strong in-group boundaries (Kanter, 1972), the stranger or outsider who makes it necessary for the group to pay attention to its boundaries may be resented not only for being different but also for giving the group extra work.

elements which they share in contrast to the token. The token becomes both occasion and audience for the highlighting and dramatization of those themes that differentiate the token as outsider from the insider. Ironically, tokens (unlike people of their type represented in greater proportion) are thus instruments for under*lining* rather than under*mining* majority culture. In the sales-force case, this phenomenon was most clearly in operation in training programs and at dinner and cocktail parties during meetings. Here the camaraderie of men, as in other work and social settings (Tiger, 1969), was based in part on tales of sexual adventures, ability with respect to "hunting" and capturing women, and off-color jokes. Secondary themes involved work prowess and sports. The capacity for and enjoyment of drinking provided the context for displays of these themes. According to male informants' reports, they were dramatized more fervently in the presence of token women than when only men were present. When the men introduced these themes in much milder form and were just as likely to share company gossip or talk of domestic matters (such as a house being built), as to discuss any of the themes mentioned above, this was also in contrast to the situation in more equally mixed male-female groups, in which there were a sufficient number of women to influence and change group culture in such a way that a new hybrid based on shared male-female concerns was introduced. (*See* Aries [1973] for supportive laboratory evidence.)

In the presence of token women, then, men exaggerated displays of aggression and potency: instances of sexual innuendo, aggressive sexual teasing, and prowess-oriented "war stories." When one or two women were present, the men's behavior involved showing off, telling stories in which masculine prowess accounted for personal, sexual, or business success. The men highlighted what they could do, as men, in contrast to women. In a set of training situations, these themes were even acted out overtly in role plays in which participants were asked to prepare and perform demonstrations of sales situations. In every case involving a woman, men played the primary, effective roles, and women were objects of sexual attention. In one, a woman was introduced as president of a company selling robots; she turned out to be one of the female robots, run by the male company sales manager.

The women themselves reported other examples of testing to see how they would respond to the "male" culture. They said that many sexual innuendos or displays of locker-room humor were put on for their benefit, especially by the younger men. (The older men tended to parade their business successes.) One woman was a team leader and the only woman at a workshop when her team, looking at her for a reaction, decided to use as its slogan "The [obscenity] of the week." By raising the issue and forcing the woman to choose not to participate in the workshop, the men in the group created an occasion for uniting against the outsider and asserting dominant-group solidarity.

Interruptions as Reminders of "Difference"

Members of the numerically dominant category underscore and reinforce differences between tokens and themselves, ensuring that the former recognize their outsider status by making the token the occasion for interruptions in the flow of group events. Dominants preface acts with apologies or questions about appropriateness directed at the token; they then invariably go ahead with the act, having placed the token in the position of interrupter or interloper. This happened often in the presence of the saleswomen. Men's questions or apologies were a way of asking whether the old or expected cultural rules were still operative—the words and expressions permitted, the pleasures and forms of release indulged in. (Can we still swear? Toss a football? Use technical jargon? Go drinking? Tell in jokes? *See* Greenbaum [1971, p. 65] for other examples.) By posing these questions overtly, dominants make their culture clear to tokens and state the terms under which tokens interact with the group.

The answers almost invariably affirm the understandings of the dominants, first because of the power of sheer numbers. An individual rarely feels comfortable preventing a larger number of peers from engaging in an activity they consider normal. Second, the tokens have been put on notice that interaction will not be "natural," that dominants will be holding back unless the tokens agree to acknowledge, permit, and even encourage majority cultural expressions in their presence. (It is important that this be stated, of course, for one never knows that another is holding back unless the other lets a piece of the suppressed material slip out.) At the same time, tokens have also been given the implicit message that majority members do *not* expect those forms of expression to be natural to the tokens' home culture; otherwise majority members would not need to raise the question. (This is a function of what Laws [1975] calls the "double deviance" of tokens: deviant first because they are women in a man's world and second because they aspire inappropriately to the privileges of the dominants.) Thus the saleswomen were often in the odd position of reassuring peers and customers that they could go ahead and do something in the women's presence, such as swearing, that they themselves would not be permitted to do. They listened to dirty jokes, for example, but reported that they would not dare tell one themselves. Via difference-reminding interruptions, then, dominants both affirm their own shared understandings and draw the cultural boundary between themselves and tokens. The tokens learned that they caused interruptions in "normal" communication and that their appropriate position was more like that of audience than full participant.

Overt Inhibition: Informal Isolation

In some cases, dominants do not wish to carry out certain activities in the presence of a token; they have secrets to preserve. They thus move the locus of some activities and expressions away from public settings to which tokens have access to more private settings from which they can be excluded. When information potentially embarrassing or damaging to dominants is being exchanged, an outsider audience is not desirable because dominants do not know how far they can trust tokens. As Hughes (1944, 1958) pointed out, colleagues who rely on unspoken understandings may feel uncomfortable in the presence of "odd kinds of fellows" who cannot be trusted to interpret information in just the same way or to engage in the same relationships of trust and reciprocity (*see* also Lorber, 1975). The result is often quarantine —keeping tokens away from some occasions. Thus some topics of discussion were never raised by men in the presence of many of the saleswomen, even though they discussed these topics among themselves: admissions of low commitment to the company or concerns about job performance, ways of getting around formal rules, political plotting for mutual advantage, strategies for impressing certain corporate executives. As researchers have also found in other settings, women did not tend to be included in the networks by which informal socialization occurred and politics behind the formal system were exposed (Wolman and Frank, 1975; O'Farrell, 1973; Hennig, 1970; Epstein, 1970). In a few cases, managers even avoided giving women information about their performance as trainees, so that they did not know they were the subject of criticism in the company until they were told to find jobs outside the sales force; those women were simply not part of the informal occasions on which the men discussed their performances with each other. (Several male managers also reported their "fear" of criticizing a woman because of uncertainty about how she would receive it.)

Loyalty Tests

At the same time that tokens are often kept on the periphery of colleague interaction, they may also be expected to demonstrate loyalty to the dominant group. Failure to do so results in further isolation; signs of loyalty permit the token to come closer and be included in more activities. Through loyalty tests, the group seeks reassurance that tokens will not turn against them or use any of the information gained through their viewing of the dominants' world to do harm to the group. They get this assurance by asking a token to join or identify with the majority against those others who represent competing membership or reference groups; in short, dominants pressure tokens to turn against members of the latter's own category. If tokens collude, they make themselves psychological hostages of the majority group. For token women, the price of being "one of the boys" is a willingness to turn occasionally against "the girls."

There are two ways by which tokens can demonstrate loyalty and qualify for closer relationships with dominants. First, they can let slide or even participate in statements prejudicial to other members of their category. They can allow themselves to be viewed as exceptions to the general rule that others of their category have a variety of undesirable or unsuitable characteristics. Hughes (1944) recognized this as one of the deals token blacks might make for membership in white groups. Saleswomen who did well were told they were exceptions and were not typical women. At meetings and training sessions, women were often the subjects of ridicule or joking remarks about their incompetence. Some women who were insulted by such innuendos found it easier to appear to agree than to start an argument. A few accepted the dominant view fully. One of the first saleswomen denied in interviews having any special problems because she was a woman, calling herself skilled at coping with a man's world, and said the company was right not to hire more women. Women, she said, were unreliable and likely to quit; furthermore, young women might marry men who would not allow them to work. In this case, a token woman was taking over "gate-keeping" functions for dominants (Laws, 1975), letting them preserve their illusion of lack of prejudice while she acted to exclude other women.

Tokens can also demonstrate loyalty by allowing themselves and their category to provide a source of humor for the group. Laughing with others, as Coser (1960) indicated, is a sign of a common definition of the situation; to allow oneself or one's kind to be the object of laughter signals a further willingness to accept others' culture on their terms. Just as Hughes (1946, p. 115) found that the initiation of blacks into white groups might involve accepting the role of comic inferior, the saleswomen faced constant pressures to allow jokes at women's expense, to accept kidding from the men around them. When a woman objected, men denied any hostility or unfriendly intention, instead accusing the woman by inference of lacking a sense of humor. In order to cope, one woman reported, "You learn to laugh when they try to insult you with jokes, to let it roll off your back." Tokens thus find themselves colluding with dominants through shared laughter.

Responses of Tokens to Boundary Heightening

Numerical skewing and polarized perceptions leave tokens with little choice about whether to accept the culture of dominants. There are too few other people of the token's kind to generate a counterculture or to develop a shared intergroup culture. Tokens have two general response possibilities. They can accept isolation, remaining an audience for certain expressive acts of dominants, in which case they risk exclusion from occasions on which informal socialization and political activity take place. Or they can try to become insiders, proving their loyalty by defining themselves as exceptions and turning against their own social category.

The occurrence of the second response on the part of tokens suggests a reexamination of the popularized "women-prejudiced-against-women" hypothesis or the "queen bee syndrome" for possible structural (numerical) rather than sexual origins. Not only has this hypothesis not been confirmed in a variety of settings (e.g., Ferber and Huber, 1975), but the analysis offered here of the social psychological pressures on tokens to side with the majority also provides a compelling explanation for the kinds of situations most likely to produce this effect, when it does occur.

ROLE ENTRAPMENT

The third set of interaction dynamics centering around tokens stems from the perceptual tendency toward assimilation: the distortion of the characteristics of tokens to fit preexisting generalizations about their category. Stereotypical assumptions and mistaken attributions made about tokens tend to force them into playing limited and caricatured roles in the system.

Status Leveling

Tokens are often misperceived initially as a result of their statistical rarity: "statistical discrimination" (U.S. Council of Economic Advisers, 1973, p. 106) as distinguished from prejudice. That is, an unusual woman may be treated as though she resembles women on the average. People make judgments about the role played by others on the basis of probabilistic reasoning about the likelihood of what a particular kind of person does. Thus the saleswomen, like other tokens, encountered many instances of mistaken identity. In the office, they were often taken for secretaries; on the road, especially when they traveled with male colleagues, they were often taken for wives or mistresses; with customers, they were usually assumed to be substituting for men or, when with a male peer, to be assistants; when entertaining customers, they were assumed to be wives or dates.

Such mistaken first impressions can be corrected. They require tokens to spend time untangling awkward exchanges and establishing accurate and appropriate role relations, but they do permit status leveling to occur. Status leveling involves making adjustments in perception of the token's professional role to fit the expected position of the token's category—that is, bringing situational status in line with master status, the token's social type. Even when others knew that the token saleswomen were not secretaries, for example, there was still a tendency to treat them like secretaries or to make demands of them appropriate to secretaries. In the most blatant case, a woman was a sales trainee along with three men; all four were to be given positions as summer replacements. The men were all assigned to replace salesmen; the woman was asked to replace a secretary—and only after a long, heated discussion with the manager was she given a more professional assignment. Similarly, when having professional contacts with customers and managers, the women felt themselves to be treated in more wifelike or datelike ways than a man would be treated by another man, even though the situation was clearly professional. It was easier for others to make their perception of the token women fit their preexisting generalizations about women than to change the category; numerical rarity provided too few examples to contradict the generalization. Instances of status leveling have also been noted with regard to other kinds of tokens such as male nurses (Segal, 1962), in the case of tokens whose master status is higher than their situational status, leveling can work to their advantage, as when male nurses are called "Dr."

Stereotyped Role Induction

The dominant group can incorporate tokens and still preserve their generalizations about the tokens' kind by inducting them into stereotypical roles; these roles preserve the familiar form of interaction between the kinds of people represented by the token and the dominants. In the case of token women in the sales force, four role traps were observed, all of which encapsulated the women in a category the men could respond to and understand. Each centered on one behavioral tendency of the token, building upon this tendency an image of her place in the group and forcing her to continue to live up to the image; each defined for dominants a single response to her sexuality. Two of the roles are classics in Freudian theory: the mother and the seductress. Freud wrote of the need of men to handle women's sexuality by envisioning them as either madonnas or whores—as either asexual mothers or overly sexual, debased seductresses. (This was perhaps a function of Victorian family patterns, which encouraged separation of idealistic adoration of the mother and animalistic eroticism [Rieff, 1963; Strong, 1973].) The other roles, termed the pet and the iron maiden, also have family counterparts in the kid sister and the virgin aunt.

Mother. A token woman sometimes finds that she has become a mother to a group of men. They bring her their troubles, and she comforts them.

The assumption that women are sympathetic, good listeners, and can be talked to about one's problems is common in male-dominated organizations. One saleswoman was constantly approached by her all-male peers to listen to their domestic problems. In a variety of residential-sales-training groups, token women were observed acting out other parts of the traditional nurturant-maternal role: cooking for men, doing their laundry, sewing on buttons.

The mother role is a comparatively safe one. She is not necessarily vulnerable to sexual pursuit (for Freud it was the very idealization of the madonna that was in part responsible for men's ambivalence toward women), nor do men need to compete for her favors, because these are available to everyone. However, the typecasting of women as nurturers has three negative consequences for a woman's task performance: (1) the mother is rewarded by her male colleagues primarily for service to them and not for independent action. (2) The mother is expected to keep her place as a noncritical, accepting, good mother or lose her rewards because the dominant, powerful aspects of the maternal image may be feared by men. Since the ability to differentiate and be critical is often an indicator of competence in work groups, the mother is prohibited from exhibiting this skill. (3) The mother becomes an emotional specialist. This provides her with a place in the life of the group and its members. Yet at the same time, one of the traditionally feminine characteristics men in positions of authority in industry most often criticize in women (*see* Lynch, 1973) is excess emotionality. Although the mother herself might not ever indulge in emotional outbursts in the group, she remains identified with emotional matters. As long as she is in the minority, it is unlikely that nurturance, support, and expressivity will be valued or that a mother can demonstrate and be rewarded for critical, independent, task-oriented behaviors.

Seductress.   The role of seductress or sexual object is fraught with more tension than the maternal role, for it introduces an element of sexual competition and jealousy. The mother can have many sons; it is more difficult for a sex object to have many lovers. Should a woman cast as sex object, that is, seen as sexually desirable and potentially available ("seductress" is a perception, and the woman herself may not be consciously behaving seductively), share her attention widely, she risks the debasement of the whore. Yet should she form a close alliance with any man in particular, she arouses resentment, particularly because she represents a scarce resource; there are just not enough women to go around.

In several situations observed, a high-status male allied himself with a seductress and acted as her "protector," not only because of his promise to rescue her from the sex-charged overtures of the rest of the men but also because of his high status per se. The powerful male (staff member, manager, sponsor, etc.) can easily become the protector of the still "virgin" seductress, gaining through masking his own sexual interest what other men could not gain by declaring theirs. However, the removal of the seductress from the sexual marketplace contains its own problems. Other men may resent a high-status male for winning the prize and resent the woman for her ability to get an in with the high-status male that they themselves could not obtain as men. While the seductress is rewarded for her femaleness and ensured attention from the group, then, she is also the source of considerable tension; and needless to say, her perceived sexuality blots out all other characteristics.

Men may adopt the role of protector toward an attractive woman, regardless of her collusion, and by implication cast her as a sex object, reminding her and the rest of the group of her sexual status. In the guise of helping her, protectors may actually put up further barriers to a solitary woman's full acceptance by inserting themselves, figuratively speaking, between the woman and the rest of a group. A male sales trainer typically offered token women in training groups extra help and sympathetically attended to the problems their male peers might cause, taking them out alone for drinks at the end of daily sessions.

Pet. The pet is adopted by the male group as a cute, amusing little thing and taken along on group events as symbolic mascot—a cheerleader for the shows of male prowess that follow. Humor is often a characteristic of the pet. She is expected to admire the male displays but not to enter into them; she cheers from the sidelines. Shows of competence on her part are treated as extraordinary and complimented just because they are unexpected (and the compliments themselves can be seen as reminders of the expected rarity of such behavior). One woman reported that, when she was alone in a group of men and spoke at length on an issue, comments to her by men after the meeting often referred to her speech-making ability rather than to what she said (e.g., "You talk so fluently"), whereas comments the men made to one another were almost invariably content or issue oriented. Competent acts that were taken for granted when performed by males were often unduly fussed over when performed by saleswomen, who were considered precocious or precious at such times. Such attitudes on the part of men in a group encourage self-effacing, girlish responses on the part of solitary women (who after all may be genuinely relieved to be included) and prevent them from realizing or demonstrating their own power and competence.

Iron maiden. The iron maiden is a contemporary variation of the stereotypical roles into which strong women are placed. Women who fail to fall into any of the first three roles and in fact resist overtures that would trap them in such roles (like flirtation) might consequently be responded to as though tough or dangerous. (One saleswoman developed just such a reputation in company branches throughout the country.) If a token insisted on full rights in the group, if she displayed competence in a forthright manner, or if she cut off sexual innuendos, she was typically asked, "You're not one of those women's libbers, are you?" Regardless of the answer, she was henceforth viewed with suspicion, treated with undue and exaggerated politeness (by references to women inserted into conversations, by elaborate rituals of *not* opening doors), and kept at a distance; for she was demanding treatment as an equal in a setting in which no person of her kind had previously been an equal. Women inducted into the iron maiden role are stereotyped as tougher than they are (hence the name) and trapped in a more militant stance than they might otherwise take.

Responses of Tokens to Role Entrapment

The dynamics of role entrapment tend to lead to a variety of conservative and low-risk responses on the part of tokens. The time and awkwardness involved in correcting mistaken impressions often lead them to a preference for already-established relationships, for minimizing change and stranger contact in the work situation. It is also often easier to accept stereotyped roles than to fight them, even if their acceptance means limiting a token's range of expressions or demonstrations of task competence, because acceptance offers a comfortable and certain position. The personal consequence for tokens, of course, is a certain degree of self-distortion. Athanassiades (1974), though not taking into account the effects of numerical representation, found that women, especially those with low risk-taking propensity, tended to distort upward communication more than men and argued that many observed work behaviors of women may be the result of such distortion and acceptance of organizational images. Submissiveness, frivolity, or other attributes may be feigned by people who feel these are prescribed for them by the dominant organizational culture. This suggests that accurate conclusions about work attitudes and behavior cannot be reached by studying people in the token position, since there may always be an element of compensation or distortion involved. Thus many studies of professional and managerial women should be reexamined in order to remove the effects of numbers from the effects of sex roles.

IMPLICATIONS

This paper has developed a framework for understanding the social perceptions and interaction dynamics that center on tokens, using the example of women in an industrial sales force dominated numerically by men. Visibility generates performance pressures, polarization generates group-boundary heightening, and assimilation generates role entrapment. All of the phenomena associated with tokens are exaggerated ones: the token stands out vividly, group culture is dramatized, boundaries become high-lighted, and token roles are larger-than-life caricatures.

REFERENCES

Aries, Elizabeth. "Interaction Patterns and Themes of Male, Female, and Mixed Groups." Ph.D. dissertation, Harvard University, 1973.

Athanassiades, John C. "An Investigation of Some Communication Patterns of Female Subordinates in Hierarchical Organizations." *Human Relations* 27 (March 1974): 195–209.

Coser, Rose Laub. "Laughter among Colleagues: A Study of the Social Functions of Humor among the Staff of a Mental Hospital." *Psychiatry* 23 (February 1960): 81–95.

Cussler, Margaret. *The Woman Executive.* New York: Harcourt Brace, 1958.

Epstein, Cynthia Fuchs. *Woman's Place: Options and Limits on Professional Careers.* Berkeley: University of California Press, 1970.

Ferber, Marianne Abeles, and Huber, Joan Althaus. "Sex of Student and Instructor: A Study of Student Bias." *American Journal of Sociology* 80 (January 1975): 949–63.

Greenbaum, Marcia. "Adding 'Kenntnis' to 'Kirche, Kuche, und Kinder.' " *Issues in Industrial Society* 2 (2, 1971): 61–68.

Hennig, Margaret. "Career Development for Women Executives." Ph.D. dissertation, Harvard University, 1970.

Hughes, Everett C. "Dilemmas and Contradictions of Status." *American Journal of Sociology* 50 (March 1944): 353–59.

_____. "Race Relations in Industry." In *Industry and Society,* edited by W. F. Whyte, pp. 107–22. New York: McGraw-Hill, 1946.

_____. *Men and Their Work.* Glencoe, Illinois: Free Press, 1958.

Kanter, Rosabeth Moss. *Commitment and Community.* Cambridge, Massachusetts: Harvard University Press, 1972.

_____. *Men and Women of the Corporation.* New York: Basic, forthcoming.

Laws, Judith Long. "The Psychology of Tokenism: An Analysis." *Sex Roles* 1 (March 1975): 51–67.

Levine, Adeline, and Crumrine, Janice. "Women and the Fear of Success: A Problem in Replication." *American Journal of Sociology* 80 (January 1975): 964–74.

Lorber, Judith. "Trust, Loyalty, and the Place of Women in the Informal Organization of Work." Paper presented at the annual meeting of the American Sociological Association, San Francisco, 1975.

Lynch, Edith M. *The Executive Suite: Feminine Style.* New York: AMACOM, 1973.

Megaree, Edwin I. "Influence of Sex Roles on the Manifestation of Leadership." *Journal of Applied Psychology* 53 (October 1969): 377–82.

O'Farrell, Brigid. "Affirmative Action and Skilled Craft Work." Mimeographed. Center for Research on Women, Wellesley College, 1973.

Rieff, Philip, ed. *Freud: Sexuality and the Psychology of Love.* New York: Collier, 1963.

Sarason, Seymour B. "Jewishness, Blackness, and the Nature-Nurture Controversy." *American Psychologist* 28 (November 1973): 961-71.

Segal, Bernard E. "Male Nurses: A Case Study in Status Contradiction and Prestige Loss." *Social Forces* 41 (October 1962): 31-38.

Strong, Bryan. "Toward a History of the Experiential Family: Sex and Incest in the Nineteenth Century Family." *Journal of Marriage and the Family* 35 (August 1973): 457-66.

Tiger, Lionel. *Men in Groups.* New York: Random House, 1969.

U.S. Council of Economic Advisers. *Annual Report of the Council of Economic Advisers.* Washington, D. C.: Government Printing Office, 1973.

Wolman, Carol, and Frank, Hal. "The Solo Woman in a Professional Peer Group." *American Journal of Orthopsychiatry* 45 (January 1975): 164-71.

ANTHONY R. HARRIS
Imprisonment and Criminal Choice

INTRODUCTION

This paper considers empirically the effects of imprisonment on youthful offenders' expectations concerning the possible payoff values of "going straight" and "going crooked." Our concern stems from the labeling perspective's more general theoretical interest in the relationship between official intervention in the life of an actor who has deviated behaviorally and consequent changes in his "motivational/decision-making" state.[1]

As argued in the early labeling-perspective statements of Tannenbaum (1938) and Lemert (1951), public identification and treatment of an actor as deviant—a contingency which faces many actors never actually identified and treated—creates conditions conducive, ironically, to further deviant behavior on the part of that actor. From this perspective, official intervention increases the chances of fostering commitment to deviance when

---

1. Concern with the social and psychological effects of intervention represents only one theme in the labeling perspective. Motivational issues, in turn, represent only one variant of this theme. (It is a vulgarization to represent the perspective as constituted simply by this theme, or this theme as constituted simply by the process of an actor accepting a label.)

Source: Harris, Anthony R. "Imprisonment and the Expected Value of Criminal Choice: A Specification and Test of Aspects of the Labeling Perspective." *American Sociological Review* 40 (1975): 71-78, 83-87. Permission granted by The American Sociological Association and the author.

the likelihood of such commitment before intervention might have been low—of making it more, rather than less, difficult for an actor to "turn back."

One of Lemert's major reasons (1951, 1967) for adopting this position involves consideration of the motivational system of an actor experiencing official intervention. Prior to such intervention an actor's deviant behavior might be characterized as lacking a well-developed motivational base (a feature of "primary deviance"). A presumably unintended function of intervention (with it its usual ancillary social processes[2]), however, is to help create in the individual an articulated motivational system appropriate to the particular deviant "label" (a feature of "secondary deviance"). In turn, this developed system is likely to become the basis for increased, rather than decreased, decision-making in favor of deviant behavior. Thus for Lemert and others in the labeling perspective, intervention becomes a major cutting edge between the "drift" (Matza, 1964) of "primary" deviance, and the psychologically well-organized basis of "secondary" deviance.

Despite the implicit clarity of these positions, the relevant literature offers little by way of expansion, propositionalization, or testing (for an exception, *see* Gove, 1970). In the following an attempt is made on all these counts.... In line with the labeling perspective ... we shall pursue the argument that criminal behavior, as a variable to be explained, is not a "special" kind of behavior. Analysis of data gathered from questionnaires administered to 234 inmates in a prison for youthful offenders in 1971 will be used to evaluate the usefulness of these positions....

The version of the general labeling model to be examined here involves the simple ... chain:

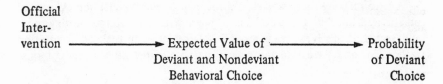

Official
Inter-
vention ————————▶ Expected Value of ————————▶ Probability
Deviant and Nondeviant   of Deviant
Behavioral Choice   Choice

Our specification of that part of the labeling perspective of concern in this paper leads us to expect: (a) a positive relation between official intervention ... with its corollary processes—and the expected value of deviant choice relative to that of nondeviant choice ..., and (b), a positive relation between the relative expected value of deviant choice ... and the probability of future deviant choice.... More concretely, we shall examine the

---

2. By "ancillary social processes" we mean the major processes of: degradation ceremonies, institutionalization, immersion in deviant subcultures, the creation of a dossier or record, the reduction of life-chances in the legitimate occupational sphere, and interpersonal rejection.

relationship between imprisonment ... and the relative expected value of criminal choice ... and between the latter and the probability of "going crooked." ...

METHODS

Questionnaires administered to 234 black and white male inmates in Yardville Youth Reception and Correction Center in Trenton, New Jersey, in 1971 provide the basis for evaluating our specification of the labeling perspective. Two basic hypotheses are to be considered: (a) the relative expected value of criminal choice is increased with increased imprisonment and (b) the probability of future criminal behavior is increased with increases in the relative expected value of criminal choice.

Setting

Yardville Center is one of the most modern components of New Jersey's correctional system and is considered by some to be its showcase. Opened in 1968, the Center's physical plant has a capacity of 904 beds. In that area of the Center where all of the data were collected, each individual remanded to Yardville is processed through a two- to three-week diagnostic profile. On the basis of his criminal dossier and diagnostic profile each inmate is assigned to one or another of the units in the state's correctional complex, one of which is Yardville itself.

A large meeting room was used throughout the data collection. At regular prearranged intervals groups of five to ten inmates entered the meeting room and seated themselves freely around a large table. In each administration session, inmates were told the general purpose of the study in these terms:

> What we're doing is a study of people's attitudes towards their careers, what they think of their futures. We have decided to come to Yardville because we think that what inmates think about this is very important. A lot of people these days are very aware of the problems inmates have in prison and when they get out.

It was then explained that we had no official connection with Yardville, that questionnaires would remain anonymous and leave Yardville with us, and that inmates were free not to take the questionnaire if they desired, but that if they stayed they would be "paid" a pack of cigarettes for their time. (Across forty-six administrations, two inmates chose to leave.) Questions were called for, then the questionnaire was read aloud, taking between sixty to seventy minutes to complete, including a five- to ten-minute break at midpoint. No guards were present in the room during any session. ...

Measures

Imprisonment. Initially, two simple measures indexed self-reported imprisonment prior to the measurement situation: number of prior times in prison, and total prior months spent in prison.[3] While not in themselves carrying special theoretical content, these measures were assumed to be generally indicative of more meaningful processes corollary to repeated incarceration: pressures by others to define self as criminal, forced immersion in criminal subcultures, anticipation of postrelease difficulties in finding a "straight" job or in going back to school, etc.[4] ... Preliminary analyses revealed that with reasonable empirical and theoretical justification a single measure of imprisonment could be defined as an additive combination of total prior months in prison + a weighted index of number of prior times in prison.[5] (In similar fashion, measures of probation and parole were constructed.) The resulting measure of imprisonment, then, was designed to assess summarily an inmate's degree of exposure to a variety of processes and experiences associated with imprisonment and well documented elsewhere. (cf. Schrag, 1961; Ohlin, 1956; Cressey, 1961; Sykes, 1958; Glaser, 1969; Irwin, 1970.)

Relative Expected Value of Criminal Choice. Of primary concern in the research was a measure attempting to capture inmates' evaluation of two

3. It is stressed that "imprisonment" refers to total prior prison experience. As such, the present sample is an alternative to a sample of those outside prison with comparable imprisonment histories and demographic characteristics (i.e., we would expect both the present and the hypothetical "outside" group to show similar imprisonment effects). It is stressed even more that the present data—cross-sectional with respect to imprisonment history—is not the equivalent of panel data.

4. We are not here thinking solely of "prisonization" or prison "socialization" processes. Strictly speaking, these terms have been used to refer to inmates' adaptations to prison per se (cf. Wheeler, 1961; Garabedian, 1963; Atchley and McCabe, 1968), and not to the anticipatory perceptions of postrelease success of concern here. Clemmer (1958, p. 301) states: "No suggestion is intended that a high correlation exists between ... prisonization and criminality." Clearly, this is not the position adopted in the labeling perspective.

5. The measure of "imprisonment" represents a combination of "times" and "months" and is comprised by the sum of total months of prior imprisonment plus the number of times imprisoned squared. This data-reduction technique appeared justified on several grounds. First, no fully clear theoretical distinction is to be gained by separating "times" and "months." While "times" might be understood as indexing, say, "number of times officially labeled criminal," and "months" as indexing, say, "criminal socialization processes," each process strongly implies the other. Second, there is collinearity between "times" and "months." The correlation is about .50 for both races. This r sums over each subsample, however, and increases with increasing imprisonment. To include both types of measures as independent variables is to attenuate the effects of each. Finally, analysis of the relevant partial correlations reveals that the effects of the "months" variable (controlling for "times") are greater than the effects of the "times" variable (controlling for "months"). Insofar as "times" has low but independent effects on the

major alternative kinds of behavioral choice: "going crooked" and "going straight." . . .

Following Strodtbeck and Short (1964), we assume, at a minimun, that actors are able to rank the payoff values of outcomes contingent on alternative, personal behavioral choices. We also assume that actors weight this value by the perceived likelihood of its occurring. Thus while the perceived value of being a bank president might represent the strongest preference in an actor's array of personal preferences, he might also perceive the likelihood of this payoff to be nil. If we express subjective expected utility as the joint product of value and probability, "trying to become a bank president" thus would have a very low expected utility.

We also want to take into account the perception of simultaneous "negative" payoffs (disutilities). We assume, that is, that a choice also contains a possible disincentive value (a subjectively expected disutility). . . .

Concrete outcomes associated with "going straight" and "going crooked" were generated in a series of pilot studies in Yardville through the use of open-ended questions. . . .

The Probability of Future Criminal Behavior.   A simple measure of the probability of future criminal behavior was obtained by asking inmates to indicate, on a scale from 0% to 100%, their chances of "going straight" after finishing their present prison terms. . . .

Hypotheses

1. The greater the imprisonment, (a) the lower the expected value of "going straight," (b) the higher the expected value of "going crooked," and (c) the higher the relative expected value of criminal choice.
2. The higher the . . . [relative expected value of criminal choice], the greater the probability of future criminal behavior. . . .

FINDINGS

The data indicate that blacks and whites are affected differentially by imprisonment. [(Table 1)] . . . The effects are of substantially greater magnitude

dependent variable, we decided to include "times" in the reduced measure as well. Values for "times" ranged from one to five (five or more times in prison). If these raw values were added to "months" the combined effects of the two measures would scarcely differ from the effects of "months" alone. An exponential weighting procedure for "times" was decided upon. The value of "times," now in combination with "months," varies by its raw value squared—perhaps the simplest and clearest exponential weighting—and thus ranges from one to twenty-five. This procedure tends to increase the effects of "months" on the dependent variable only marginally for both races (Harris, 1973).

Table 1: Comparable Levels of [Relative Expected Value of Criminal Choice] for Blacks and Whites at Various Imprisonment Intervals, Showing Resultant "t" from Difference of Mean Tests within Intervals

Imprisonment Interval	Mean REV$_C$ ($\bar{X}$), Standard Deviation (s.d.), and N	Blacks	Whites	"t"
1 - 6 months	X.:	.410	.345	2.795*
	s.d.:	.111	.129	
	N.:	(27)	(25)	
7-12 months	X.:	.400	.303	2.945*
	s.d.:	.116	.114	
	N.:	(29)	(24)	
13-24 months	X.:	.427	.215	3.213*
	s.d.:	.105	.119	
	N.:	(29)	(13)	
25-36 months	X.:	.440	.351	2.433*
	s.d.:	.102	.104	
	N.:	(19)	(15)	
37-48 months	X.:	.432	.363	2.796*
	s.d.:	.055	.064	
	N.:	(14)	(12)	
$\geq$ 49 months	X.:	.504	.456	1.324
	s.d.:	.064	.124	
	N.:	(15)	(16)	

*p $\leq$ .05

for whites with extended imprisonment than for comparable blacks. The assumption of imprisonment as a cause of "relative criminal rationality" seems more generally justifiable for whites than blacks.

... [The findings of the impact of length of imprisonment on relative expected value of criminal choice,] together with the findings on racial differences, in [this regard, suggest] the outlines of a more elaborate process model.... We might hypothesize that the effects of imprisonment are not unidimensional, but are comprised of a negative and decelerating rehabilitation or "treatment" (T) effect on [relative expected value of criminal choice (REV$_C$)] and a positively accelerating labeling or "criminalizing" (C) effect on ... [relative expected value of criminal choice].

Figure 1: Postulated "Treatment" and "Criminalizing" Effects on REV_C by I

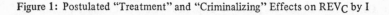

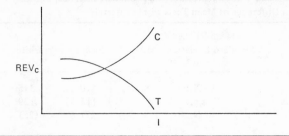

Figure 1 suggests that we find the treatment (T) effect to be strong during initial, limited imprisonment and the criminalizing (C) effect to be existent but weak during this time. Inmates experiencing the net trend of rehabilitation during initial imprisonment might be expected to "go straight" and not recidivate—though differentially so according to ... [relative expected value of criminal choice] levels ... Those inmates still (or back) in prison after the effects of ... [treatment] have attenuated and the effects of ... [criminalization] have started to accelerate (as depicted above) would be expected to find the choice of criminal behavior increasingly attractive. ...

CONCLUSIONS

From the point of view of the labeling perspective, the data are illuminating in three basic ways. First, curvilinear trends between imprisonment and the relative expected value of criminal choice suggest that a revision may be in order of simple linear expectations about the general relationship between labeling processes and responses to them. In related terms, the present research does not support the labeling viewpoint that the sequence of becoming deviant accelerates increasingly (Goffman, 1961). While for whites the relative expected value of criminal choice becomes increasingly governed by imprisonment with increasing imprisonment, the direction of the relationship appears to change over time. Thus the notion of the ever-increasing deviant "spiral" is not evidenced here.

Second, perhaps the most significant of the findings has to do with racial differences. While labeling theorists have been sensitive to the differential treatment of blacks and whites by agents and agencies of social control, it is not clear that such sensitivity has extended to the expectation of differential reactions of blacks and whites (or any other identifiable racial group) to official intervention. It is entirely reasonable to expect differential reactions to labeling processes on the basis of such characteristics in a population as race, ethnicity, SES, or even sex.

Third, however, the present research does support the fundamental labeling viewpoint that being deviant is (or becomes) a relatively rational state of affairs from the subjective standpoint of actors so defined. While only blacks with four or more years of prison experience (see Table 1) showed absolutely greater (i.e., $> .500$) levels of criminal than "straight" expected value, and hence a potentially more rational ground for the consistent choice of criminal behavior, with extended imprisonment both races showed relatively strong criminal expected value. The data also showed this expected value to be substantially associated with inmates' perceived probability of future criminal behavior.

REFERENCES

Atchley, Robert C., and McCabe, M. Patrick. "Socialization in correctional communities: a replication." *American Sociological Review* 33 (October 1968): 774-85.

Clemmer, Donald. *The Prison Community.* New York: Holt, Rinehart and Winston, 1958 (Reissue).

Cressey, Donald. *The Prison: Studies in Institutional Organization and Change.* New York: Holt, Rinehart and Winston, 1961.

Garabedian, Peter. "Social roles and processes of socialization in the prison community." *Social Problems* 11 (Fall 1963): 139-52.

Glaser, Daniel. *The Effectiveness of Prison and Parole Systems.* Indianapolis: Bobbs-Merrill, 1969.

Goffman, Erving. *Asylums.* New York: Doubleday Anchor, 1961.

Gove, Walter. "Societal reaction as an explanation of mental illness." *American Sociological Review* 35 (October 1970): 873-84.

Harris, Anthony. "Deviant identity, rational choice, and cognitive simplification." Unpublished Ph.D. dissertation. Princeton University, 1973.

Irwin, John. *The Felon.* New Jersey: Prentice-Hall, 1970.

Lemert, Edwin. *Social Pathology.* New York: McGraw-Hill, 1951.

———. *Human Deviance, Social Problems, and Social Control.* New Jersey: Prentice-Hall, 1967.

Matza, David. *Delinquency and Drift.* New York: John Wiley & Sons, 1964.

Ohlin, Lloyd. "Modification of the criminal value system." In *Sociology and the Field of Corrections.* New York: Russell Sage Foundation, 1956.

Schrag, Clarence. "Some foundations for a theory of correction in the prison." In *Studies in Institutional Organization and Change,* edited by Donald Cressey. New York: Holt, Rinehart, and Winston, 1961.

Strodtbeck, Fred, and Short, J., Jr. "Aleatory risks versus short-run hedonism in explanation of gang action." *Social Problems* 12 (Fall 1964): 127-140.

Sykes, Gresham. *The Society of Captives.* Princeton: Princeton University Press, 1958.

Tannenbaum, Frank. *Crime and the Community.* Boston: Ginn, 1938.

Wheeler, Stanton. "Social organization in correctional communities." *American Sociological Review* 26 (October 1961): 697-712.

THOMAS MORIARTY

Stigma in the Experience of Deviance

Deviancy, at least initially, is unpleasant for the individual. For Goffman (1963), the deviant's major problem is acceptance by nondeviants, and the tendency for unanimous majorities to reject and ridicule deviants has been experimentally demonstrated (Asch, 1952; Schachter, 1951). Individuals, therefore, may try to avoid being deviant or at least avoid being recognized by others as deviant. Becker (1963) suggests that "secret deviants" are quite numerous, and Goffman has many conjectures about the problems of "passing," techniques the deviant uses to control and conceal information that would signal his deviation and discredit him in the eyes of others.

In the event that neither change nor secrecy is possible or desirable, the individual may seek out others who share his deviancy. The new reference group may help the individual validate his deviant aspect as natural and good (Festinger, 1954) while satisying needs for acceptance and providing skills for dealing with the problems of being deviant. (In the case of racial and ethnic minorities, this is usually accomplished during socialization).

Membership in a deviant group has psychological consequences for the individual, especially in his relations with fellow deviants. On a simple level, one might assume that a deviant individual would like his fellow deviants more than he would nondeviants. Much psychological theory (e.g., Heider,

Source: Moriarty, Thomas. "Role of Stigma in the Experience of Deviance." *Journal of Personality and Social Psychology* 29, 6 (1974): 849–855. Copyright ©1974 by The American Psychological Association. Reprinted by permission.

1958) as well as research (e.g., Byrne, 1961) have been devoted to the simple proposition that interpersonal attraction is a function of similarity. On the other hand, it has occasionally been suggested that ambivalence is common among deviants, which in the extreme, becomes self-hatred. For Lewin (1948), self-hatred toward similar others stems from the fact that being identified with the group may limit the individual's opportunities, engendering frustration and aggression; the latter cannot be directed against the majority (which is highly valued because of the opportunities it offers), and so it is directed against the self and similar others.

Conformity (the tendency to be influenced in one's judgments by the judgments of others) is a fact of group life. As Festinger (1954) has suggested, the costs and difficulties involved in performing reality tests often necessitate reliance on group wisdom. Members of deviant groups are not exempt from this fact, although the majority may cease to function as the appropriate reference group. As Cooley (1902) pointed out, nonconformity to the majority may reflect conformity to a deviant reference group rather than independence on the part of the individual. It seems likely that an individual who has adopted a deviant reference group will conform more to fellow deviants than to nondeviants. In a study using a similar methodology, Darley, Moriarty, Darley, and Berscheid (in press) found support for this hypothesis.

The Present Study

Assuming a minority—majority situation arises, under what conditions will the minority individual *feel* deviant? It is assumed that feelings of deviance are revealed in the following way: (a) attempts to change the deviant aspect, thereby avoiding the unpleasantness of deviant status; (b) ambivalence toward similar others, that is, fellow deviants; (c) a change in reference group, indicated by greater reliance on the judgments of fellow deviants than on those of the majority; and (d) an attempt to pass as nondeviant when the individual's deviance is unknown to others.

In the present experiment, an attempt was made to create deviance in the laboratory, based on opinion divergence. Each subject discovered during the course of an opinion exchange that his opinions on important political and social issues were at variance with those of the majority of others present. One of the others in the group consistently agreed with his opinions, thereby providing social support. To assess the effects of stigma, the minority was derogated in half of the cases; to assess the consequences of secret deviance, the subject either announced his opinions publicly to the group or merely listened to the opinions of the others. The variables were manipulated orthogonally, giving rise to four conditions under which opinion divergence occurred. After indicating first impressions of each of the other members of the group, the subject was paired with one of them in a disguised test of susceptibility to social influence. Finally, after completing a questionnaire designed to elicit his feelings about the experience, the subject was fully debriefed and was thanked for his cooperation.

METHOD

Subjects

The subjects were white males, drawn from the Introductory Psychology courses at New York University and Fairleigh Dickinson. The original design called for 80 subjects (10 per cell), and the experiment continued until that quota was met.[1]

Procedure

Each subject received a telephone call inviting him to take part in a human relations study scheduled for the following day. He was told that the study would take about one hour of his time and, while providing information about how people work together, would enable him to fulfill part of the research requirement in the Introductory Psychology course. The subject was told to be on time since the study could not begin until all participants had arrived.

Upon arrival, the subject was ushered into one of a series of small rooms containing a desk and chair, a set of headphones, and wall sign that stated, "You are Subject No. 6." When seated, the subject was directed to fill out an opinion inventory that consisted of 10 attitudinal statements dealing with the war in Vietnam, the wisdom of capital punishment, freedom of the press, etc. After indicating agreement or disagreement with each item, the subject was directed to don the headphones through which he would receive all subsequent instructions. The experimenter then left, and the opinion exchange began.

Via the headphone set, the subject was told that the purpose of the experiment was to see how first impressions are formed. The experimenter

1. Actually, 90 subjects participated in the experiment. Ten subjects (11% of the total sample) expressed strong doubts about the true purpose of the auditory acuity test during the debriefing. Suspicious subjects were excluded prior to the data analysis, which was based on 80 subjects; however, subsequent analyses based on all 90 subjects revealed no major departures from the findings reported here.

would read each item and the subject, when his number was called, was to announce his opinion on the issue by reading the answer he had written on the opinion inventory, which he still had before him. During the exchange, the subject was to form an impression of each of the others in the group.

By the time the exchange had ended, the subject had learned that on 8 of the 10 issues, four of the five others (the majority) consistently disagreed with his views; one of the five (the fellow minority member) consistently agreed with him on those 8 issues.

Of course, each subject was "Subject No. 6." Following the suggestions of Blake and Brehm (1954), a tape recording was used to simulate the presence of the group. By means of a dual-track stereo tape recording, all subjects heard the identical pattern of disagreement, regardless of the opinions they held.[2]

Independent Variables

Stigma. Halfway through the opinion exchange, "Subject No. 1" (the voice of an experimental confederate) interrupted the proceedings:

> May I ask a question ... without spoiling anything? I've been thinking about what's been going on and ... it's hard to believe anybody would have answers different from ours—I mean they're *obvious,* a guy would have to be *weird!*

At that point, other voices joined in, muttering agreement with Subject No. 1. The experimenter then cautioned all subjects against talking out of turn and resumed the exchange.

Public versus secret status. All subjects were instructed to announce their opinions to the group; however, in the secret conditions, the subjects did not. On the very first item of the opinion exchange, the experimenter announced that Subject No. 6's reply was not audible and attributed it to a probable malfunction in the latter's microphone that would be corrected later. The experimenter resumed the exchange, suggesting that if Subject No. 6 could hear the proceedings, he was to try to form an impression of the others.

2. The technical details of the procedure are outlined in: J. Darley and T. Moriarty. Techniques for the experimental study of conformity. Unpublished manuscript, 1965. (Available from the author on request.)

Dependent Variables

Attraction. At the end of the exchange, the subject rated each of the others on a series of 20-point scales. The scale designed to measure attraction provided the subject with verbal anchors that corresponded to the scale values as follows: 17-20 points (extreme liking), 13-16 points (moderate liking), 9-12 points (neither like nor dislike), 5-8 points (moderate disliking), and 1-4 points (extreme disliking). The experimenter entered the subject's room briefly to make sure the rating instructions were clear. (In the secret conditions, the experimenter used this opportunity to replace the subject's "defective" microphone.)

Conformity. After completing the first-impressions inventory, the subject took part in a test allegedly designed to measure auditory acuity. The test (again conducted with headphones) involved judging the number of clicks over a series of 12 trials.[3] Subjects worked on the test in pairs, and after each trial the real subject (who was always preceded by a confederate of the experimenter) announced his judgment. The pairing of confederate and subject was made to appear as though determined by chance.[4] In fact, the subject was paired either with Subject No. 4 (the fellow minority member) or Subject No. 5 (one of the former majority). In either case, the auditory judgments of the confederates were identical, with confederates systematically overestimating on 11 of the 12 trials. (On the first trial, the confederate gave the correct answer.) Overestimates ranged from 1 to 15 points, and on 7 of the 11 trials the confederate's estimates were 10 points over the correct answer.

The test just described was intended as a measure of susceptibility to social influence, and the index of conformity was the number of times the subject overestimated on the 11 critical trials.

---

3. The clicks were produced by an electric metronome and recorded at a speed of 360 beats per minute. The average number of clicks per trial was 45, the range, from 31 to 65. The task was difficult, and correct judgments were infrequent. Baseline (no influence) data for an accidental sample of 10 male students indicated that errors of underestimation were most common; errors of overestimation occurred on 2.1 of the 11 critical trials. In this experiment, concern was not with accuracy but with errors of overestimation.

4. When the subject arrived for the experiment, he signed a form for the experimenter's records that had already been "signed" by the others in the group. The purpose of this procedure was twofold: it added credibility to the pretense that there really were others in the group and predetermined work pairs for the auditory acuity study. The pairing was pointed out to the subject as he signed the form.

RESULTS

Feelings of Deviance and Avoidance Behavior

It has been suggested that the feeling of deviance is unpleasant and that the individual tries to avoid deviant status when possible. The feeling of deviance should evidence itself in the desire to change one's deviant aspect and, in some cases, in actual change. Two sources of data are relevant to this issue:

1. On the postexperimental questionnaire (before debriefing), subjects were asked to reflect on the opinion exchange and to report whatever feelings they had experienced at that time. Specifically, they were asked: "On those occasions when there was disagreement did you experience, even for just a brief moment, a desire to change your opinion, to make it more like the others?"

Of the 80 subjects, 27 (34 percent) reported experiencing a desire to change. Thus, about one third of the subjects found minority status unpleasant enough to want to change. However, this tendency was not randomly distributed throughout conditions. While 20 percent of those in the nonstigma conditions reported this desire, 48 percent in the stigma conditions did so ($z = 2.77$, $p < .01$). Stated differently, 19 of the 27 subjects (70 percent) who reported wanting to change were in the stigma conditions.

2. The experimental instructions were designed to discourage the occurrence of opinion change during the exchange since the latter, if it occurred to any large extent, would weaken the opinion divergence manipulation. The subjects were told that during the exchange they were simply to read aloud the opinions they had indicated on the opinion inventory. Violation of this instruction was infrequent in the public conditions. Fortunately, when it did occur, subjects spontaneously "corrected" the opinion inventory to bring it up to date with their public statements. Of course, those in the secret conditions did not announce their opinions publicly, but an examination of the opinion inventories after the exchange indicated that they too changed some opinions during the exchange.

Of the 80 subjects, 13 (16 percent) made one or more changes on the opinion inventory after the exchange had begun, and 11 of the 13 were in the stigma conditions. Thus, when overt opinion change occurs in the minority situation, it does so primarily when the minority is derogated ($p = .04$).[5]

---

5. In manipulating opinion divergence, it was arranged that subjects hear disagreement from the majority on 8 of the 10 opinion items. It is unlikely that changes during the opinion exchange materially reduced the impact of the manipulation. There were only 20 instances of opinion change for the 13 subjects who did change; change typically involved only 1 of the 8 critical items.

Table 1: Liking Scores for the Fellow Minority Member

Condition	Nonstigma	Stigma
Public	16.7	14.5
Secret	15.0	12.9

Note. The higher the liking score, the more positive the rating.

Table 2: Analysis of Variance: Liking Scores for the Fellow Minority Member

Source	df	MS	F
Public (A)	1	54.50	6.00*
Stigma (B)	1	92.50	10.18**
A X B	1	.00	< 1
Within	76	9.09	

    * $p < .05.$
    ** $p < .01.$

Interpersonal Attraction

At the conclusion of the opinion exchange, each subject indicated his liking for the fellow minority member and the four majority members. For each subject, the rating given the fellow minority member was compared with the best rating given the majority members.

The overall rating assigned to the fellow minority member was 14.8, clearly in that range of the scale labeled moderate liking. For the majority, the overall rating was, on the average, 11.3, which corresponds to the neutral range on the scale. This difference was reliable (for paired observations, $t = 7.45, p < .01$) and large ($r = .64$), accounting for roughly 41 percent of the variance in ratings. Thus, the subject typically views the fellow minority member with warm regard, while the majority, at best, viewed with neutrality.

The analysis of variance (Winer, 1962) was performed on the ratings of the fellow minority member to assess the effects of stigma on liking. As can be seen in Tables 1 and 2, stigma had a pronounced effect on liking for the fellow minority member: when the minority members were derogated by the majority, attraction between them was significantly lowered, though still in the positive range. The public-secret variable also produced a main effect: liking for the fellow minority member was greater in the public than in the secret conditions. The absence of an interaction indicates that the two effects were additive, and the fellow minority member was liked least in the case in which difference was stigmatized and the subject's own position was unknown to others.

Table 3: Conformity to a Majority Member

Condition	Nonstigma	Stigma
Public	3.0	3.8
Secret	2.5	2.6

Table 4: Analysis of Variance: Conformity to a Majority Member

Source	df	MS	F
Public (A)	1	7.23	< 1
Stigma (B)	1	2.03	< 1
A X B	1	1.23	< 1
Within	36	8.79	

Susceptibility to Social Influence

After completing the first-impressions inventory, subjects were paired with one of the confederates in a disguised test of social influence. One half of the subjects in each condition were paired with the fellow minority member and the other half, with a former majority member. (At this point in the analysis, then, there are eight cells.) For subjects paired with the fellow minority member, the conformity rate was 5.1; for those paired with the former minority member, 3.0. The difference was reliable ($t = 3.09, p < .01$). Thus, it would appear that the fellow minority member is, in general, able to exert more influence than is a former majority member.[6]

As can be seen in Tables 3 and 4, conformity to the former majority member was relatively unaffected by either the public or the stigma variable. Conformity to the fellow minority member was, however, affected by the experimental factors: Conformity was more frequent in the stigma than in the nonstigma conditions and was more frequent in the public than in the secret conditions (*see* Tables 5 and 6). The presence of a significant interaction suggests that the obtained effects were largely due to the high rate of conformity in the public-stigma condition. Duncan's new multiple-range

6. A comparison between this data and data obtained in the no-influence situation reveals that the subject was relatively immune to influence emanating from a former majority member ($t = .92, p > .05$) but was quite open to influence from a fellow minority member ($t = 2.96, p < .01$).

Table 5: Conformity to the Fellow Minority Member

Condition	Nonstigma	Stigma
Public	3.4	8.8
Secret	3.8	4.2

Table 6: Analysis of Variance: Conformity to the Fellow Minority Member

Source	df	MS	F
Public (A)	1	44.10	4.63*
Stigma (B)	1	84.10	8.82**
A X B	1	62.50	6.56*
Within	36	9.53	

$* p < .05.$
$** p < .01.$

test, contrasting all eight groups, reveals that conformity to the fellow minority member was more frequent in the public-stigma condition than in all the other conditions ($p < .01$). The remaining seven conditions did not differ reliably from each other ($p > .05$, in all cases).

Thus, conformity to a fellow minority member was heightened only when the minority status of the subject was known to the group and when stigma was involved.

DISCUSSION

The major focus of the present study is on the role of stigma in the experience of deviance, and current beliefs about "real-world" deviant individuals serve as criteria for assessing the importance of this variable. Specifically, to the extent that stigma is important, the feelings and behavior usually attributed to deviant individuals should be present in the stigma conditions and absent (or weak) in the nonstigma conditions.

The discovery that one is deviant is unpleasant, and individuals try to avoid being deviant, or at least avoid appearing deviant to others. In the present experiment, there were two manifestations of this avoidance: the desire to change one's opinions during the change and actual change (in spite of instructions to the contrary). The opinion items were selected to insure a lack of novelty, and it was assumed that most subjects would have clear opinions on the issues. Therefore, instances of change are viewed as attempts to avoid appearing deviant by reducing the overt discrepancy between the subject and the majority. While minority status in this experiment was unpleasant enough to produce these effects, they occurred primarily in the stigma conditions and only to a trivial degree in the nonstigma conditions.

The expected relationship between opinion similarity and attraction was confirmed: Agreers (fellow minority members) were liked more than were disagreers (the majority). An exception to this well-established rule is that deviants, despite similarity on the deviance dimension, feel ambivalence toward fellow deviants. Data in the present study suggest that stigma is responsible for ambivalence: while subjects in the nonstigma conditions viewed the fellow minority member with warm regard, these feelings were considerably dampened by the occurrence of stigma.

The significant main effect of the public-secret variable on the attractiveness of the fellow minority member indicates that liking for the latter is less when the subject's status is unknown to the group. Perhaps this phenomenon may be understood in terms of Heider's (1958) suggestion that interaction leads to increased liking. In the public conditions the subject took part in the exchange, while in the secret conditions the subject was merely a passive observer. The absence of a significant interaction, however, indicates that stigma decreases the attractiveness of the fellow minority member, whether the subject's own minority status is known or unknown to the others in the group.

The conformity data are consistent with the notion that deviants conform more to fellow deviants than to the majority. As we have seen, this is true only in the public-stigma condition. In all other conditions there was no difference between conformity to the fellow minority member and conformity to the majority. Again, the importance of the stigma factor is evident.

It has been proposed that secret deviants feel deviant but generally try to pass as nondeviant in the eyes of others. The responses of subjects in the secret-stigma condition fit this pattern rather nicely: private feelings toward the fellow minority member are characterized by the ambivalence usually associated with deviants, while public behavior is marked by independence of others known to be deviant.

The implications of these findings for the study of social deviance should be clear. Freedman and Doob (1968) have suggested that "if someone is different enough on any dimension regardless of whether the difference is evaluated positively or negatively he will be considered and consider himself a deviant [p. 4]." The opinion divergence created in the present experiment is quite extreme, and the present data indicate that although there may be consequences of being different from others, the reaction of the others is a critical determinant of the experience of deviance.

REFERENCES

Asch, S. E. *Social psychology.* Englewood Cliffs, New Jersey: Prentice-Hall, 1952.

Becker, H. S. *Outsiders.* New York: Free Press, 1963.

Blake, R. R., and Brehm, J. W. "The use of tape recording to simulate a group atmosphere." *Journal of Abnormal and Social Psychology* 49 (1954): 311-313.

Byrne, D. "Interpersonal attraction and attitudinal similarity." *Journal of Abnormal and Social Psychology* 62 (1961): 713-715.

Cooley, C. H. *Human nature and the social order.* New York: Charles Scribner's Sons, 1902.

Darley, J.; Moriarty, T.; Darley, S.; and Berscheid, E. "Increased conformity to a fellow deviant as a function of prior deviation." *Journal of Experimental Social Psychology,* in press.

Festinger, L. "A theory of social comparison processes." *Human Relations* 7 (1954): 117-140.

Freedman, J. L., and Doab, A. N. *Deviancy.* New York: Academic Press, 1968.

Goffman, E. *Stigma.* Englewood Cliffs, New Jersey: Prentice-Hall, 1963.

Heider, F. *The psychology of interpersonal relations.* New York: John Wiley & Sons, 1958.

Lewin, K. *Resolving social conflicts.* New York: Harper & Row, 1948.

Schachter, S. "Deviation, rejection and communication." *Journal of Abnormal and Social Psychology* 46 (1951): 190-208.

Winer, B. J. *Statistical principles in experimental design.* New York: McGraw-Hill, 1962.

RONALD A. FARRELL AND JAMES F. NELSON

A Causal Model of Secondary Deviance

More than a decade ago Becker (1963:22–25) suggested the importance of developing a deviance model that "takes into account the fact that patterns of behavior develop in an orderly sequence ... [He explained that] each step requires explanation, and what may operate as a cause at one step in the sequence may be of negligible importance at another...." Following ... [this suggestion], an effort to put forth such a model has recently been offered by Farrell and Morrione (1975). The work that follows is an empirical exploration of this model.

THE THEORY

While having application to other forms of deviance, the approach as developed by Farrell and Morrione is related to homosexual behavior. Homosexuality was chosen because the general processes with which the model deals were thought to be most clearly represented in this case. The model suggests that if one perceives others identifying him as homosexual and reacting to him in accordance with the popular stereotype, his self-definition may incorporate the stereotype. These responses and accompanied feelings of stigma are likely

Source: Farrell, Ronald A., and Nelson, James F. "A Causal Model of Secondary Deviance: The Case of Homosexuality." *Sociological Quarterly* 17 (Winter 1976): 109–120. Permission granted by the Midwest Sociological Society.

Figure 1. . . . [A Theoretical] Model of Secondary Deviance

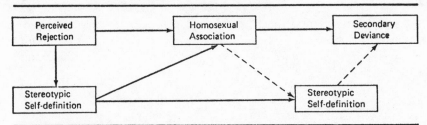

to be experienced with frustration. Bitterness, withdrawal to a homosexual group, and enculturation to a deviant role may be the outcome.[1] Implicit is the notion that much of the behavior generally associated with homosexuality may be conforming rather than deviant behavior. It conforms to both society's and the subculture's definition of homosexuality.

More specifically, the model states that the labeling process involves the creation of homosexuality as a salient and discrediting position prescribed in terms of a negative stereotype. Such a definition and the reactions that ensue restrict the alternative roles that the individual may assume, thereby limiting the nature and boundaries of his interaction. The effect is to become engulfed in the deviant role and to define one's self almost entirely in terms of its expectations.

Operating as a stigma, the societal reaction and self-definition then produce stress and the subsequent need for adaptation. In the case of the homosexual, a frequent adaptive outcome is to shift one's reference associations to other homosexuals, to a group whose members have experienced similar difficulties and wherein he is capable of conformity and the attainment of a more positive status.

As the individual receives input from the new associations and attaches meaning to it, he redefines his situation. The result is a form of behavior dependent upon his and other group members' conceptions of the homosexual role. Because those who form these associations are likely to be persons who have come to view themselves in terms of the stereotype, it is this role conception which serves as the basis for behavior. In that the group norms validate the homosexual role, a more positive personal identity is likely to evolve from the interaction.

1. "Secondary deviance," as a descriptive concept for the deviant roles which result from societal reaction, was first used by Lemert (1951, 1967). According to Lemert (1967:41) "the secondary deviant ... is a person whose life and identity are organized around the facts of deviance." "Deviations remain primary deviations or symptomatic and situational as long as they are rationalized or otherwise dealt with as functions of a socially acceptable role. . . . However, when a person begins to employ his deviant behavior or a role based upon it as a means of defense, attack, or adjustment to the overt and covert problems created by the consequent societal reaction to him, his deviation is secondary" (Lemert, 1951:75–76).

MAJOR PROPOSITIONS

In its simplest form, the model may be stated in terms of three major propositions . . . These interrelated propositions are diagramatically illustrated in Figure 1 (solid lines represent positive relations, while dashed lines represent negative relations). The propositions are as follows:

1. Incorporation of the homosexual stereotype into one's self-definition is a direct result of perceived societal rejection. . . . (This is indicated by the solid arrow from perceived rejection to stereotypic self-definition.)

2. As persons perceive societal rejection and incorporate a stereotypic self-definition, they adapt to their stress through association in homosexual groups. . . . (Shown by solid arrows from perceived rejection and stereotypic self-definition to homosexual association.)

3. Enculturation to secondary deviance occurs as persons associate in homosexual groups and come to redefine themselves in more positive terms. . . . (Shown by the solid arrow from homosexual association to secondary deviance; and by dashed arrows from homosexual association to stereotypic self-definition and from stereotypic self-definition to secondary deviance. The solid line from prior self-definition to self-definition [following homosexual association] indicates that prior self-definition [in addition to homosexual association] influences present self-definition.)

THE SAMPLE

The model was tested by using data collected from a sampling of 148 male homosexuals in and around a large midwestern city.[2] The data were obtained through the use of a questionnaire distributed through four homosexual bars and social clubs, two different organizations for homosexuals, and through individual contact with persons from various social class backgrounds. By tapping the homosexual community at various organizational and social class levels and taking whatever cases came to hand, we felt that we could obtain a sample that more nearly resembled the homosexual population. Furthermore, by distributing questionnaires through individual contacts, we attempted to reach persons who neither frequented gay bars and clubs nor were involved in the activities of homophile organizations. This made it possible to obtain subjects who, although possessing sufficient homosexual identity to participate in the study, had minimal involvement in the subculture.[3]

In the absence of true probability sampling, little can be said of the representativeness of the sample. A comparison with the urban male population,

2. In 1970 this standard metropolitan statistical area had a population in excess of one million inhabitants.

3. While females were also sampled, the apparent inappropriateness of the questionnaire items to their situation precluded a sufficient response for analysis.

however, showed them to be younger, disproportionately white, more educated, and consisting of more persons from the higher level occupations.

METHOD

Composite scales to tap the theory's concepts were developed from the
literature and from information obtained during an initial period of field
study. The items were revised after pretesting the questionnaire. Following
the return of the 148 questionnaires, each scale's items were tested for
internal consistency and those with low correlations and low discriminability
were omitted.[4] Scale scores were then computed for each person based on
his combined responses to a given scale's items. In each case the median was
used to dichotomize the variables. The operational definitions of the concepts
follow.

Perceived societal reactions refer to recurrent experiences of relative
acceptance or rejection in informal encounters, occurring either in fact or
in the minds of persons reporting them. Since stigma in the case of homosexuality seems to pertain prinicpally to secondary (as opposed to primary)
group relations (*see* Farrell and Morrione, 1974), perceived reactions were
operationally defined in terms of the stereotypic kind of responses that one
might experience in these more impersonal encounters. Adjectives from the
symbolic interaction literature that were thought to describe such reactions
were used to construct the scale items (*see* especially Cooley, 1902:258-260;
Thomas, 1923:49-50).

The measure of *self-definition* was also constructed from symbolic interactionism, particularly from Cooley's (1902:179-184) theory of the "looking
glass self." This perspective suggests that the person views himself as he
perceives others viewing him. We felt, therefore, that if perceived societal
reactions were to be considered in terms of stereotypic responses, the self-
definition should be considered in terms of its degree of concurrence with
the stereotype. Following this rationale and utilizing the results of a study
carried out by Simmons (1965:227), stereotypic self-definitions were tapped
by developing selected aspects of the homosexual stereotype into a composite scale.

Association in homosexual groups was conceptualized along the lines of
Sutherland's theory of "differential association" (1955:77-80). Questions
were asked to measure the frequency, duration, priority, and intensity of

4. Coefficient alpha was used to obtain a coefficient of equivalence for each composite
scale. This statistical procedure provides a measure of internal consistency by giving the
average split-half correlation for all possible ways of dividing a scale's items into two
parts (*see* Cronbach, 1951). The questions and alpha coefficient for each scale may be
obtained by writing the senior author.

this involvement. When the items were tested for internal consistency, however, it was found that persons who had been involved in homosexual groups for a long period of time were not necessarily those who were also high in the frequency, priority, and intensity of these associations.[5] On this basis, the time dimension was eliminated from the measure.

Finally, *secondary deviance* was operationally defined in terms of behaviors that appear to be aspects of enculturation to the homosexual subculture, and not behaviors that might incline the individual to associate with homosexuals in the first place. The items are based both on observations made during the initial period of field study and on descriptive material dealing with the homosexual community (the work of Leznoff and Westley, 1956, and Hooker, 1967, proved especially useful). Based on these sources, the variable was operationally defined as behaviors suggesting intense social and psychological involvement with one's deviance within the context of the homosexual subculture.

THE ANALYSIS

An ideal test of the model requires that the variables be measured at different points in time. While the data obtained for this study are not longitudinal, the following analysis treats them as such in that the propositions are sequentially analyzed. Those who may find this unacceptable may treat the variables as nonrecursive and replace all single-headed arrows by double-headed ones in the path diagrams that follow.[6]

The model was tested by the log-linear technique of causal inference. This method allows one to impose a causal ordering to nominal data and provides results that are easily interpreted.... (*See* Goodman, 1972, 1973a, 1973b.)

Unfortunately, the model in Figure 1 could not be completely tested because the data do not include a measure of self-definition prior to association in homosexual groups. Aside from this, the order in Figure 1 was used to fit causal models to the data....

Two somewhat different models seem to fit the data reasonably well.... Path diagrams for [these] models ... appear in Figures 2 and 3 respectively.

5. This may be because those who were high on these latter dimensions had recently "come out" into the "gay world" and felt the greatest need for their group. The immediate effects of socially and psychologically identifying oneself as homosexual, then, also may necessitate an intense involvement with other homosexuals.

6. The parameters in the double-headed arrow case are identical to those in the single-headed case for [the] model ... [in] ... Figure 3 and only slightly different for [the] model ... [in] Figure 2.

Figure 2. A Fitted Model of Secondary Deviance

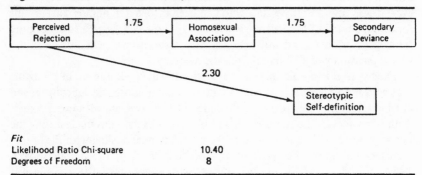

Fit	
Likelihood Ratio Chi-square	10.40
Degrees of Freedom	8

To keep interpretations simple, the path-like coefficients are presented in their multiplicative form. They show how each variable affects the odds that the other variables will be high or positive. For example, in Figure 2, if *perceived rejection* is high, then the odds that *homosexual association* is high is increased by the multiplication of 1.75. If *perceived rejection* is low, then the odds that *homosexual association* is high is decreased by the multiplication of 1/1.75 or .57.[7]

INTERPRETATION

While the ... [theoretical] model could not be tested in its entirety, the analysis nevertheless suggests several modifications of the scheme.

Looking at either Figure 2 or 3, we see that *only* homosexual association is related to secondary deviance. This both confirms and negates part of the model. The model is partially confirmed in that perceived rejection affects secondary deviance only indirectly through its relation to homosexual association. The model is partially negated, however, in that stereotypic self-definition does not appear to be directly (and perhaps not even indirectly) related to secondary deviance.

Making inferences about the relations between perceived rejection, homosexual association, and stereotypic self-definition is speculative because self-measures were not taken prior to homosexual association. Realizing that the following is speculation, there appear to be two plausible interpretations of the analysis, one supporting and one negating the theoretical scheme.

7. A similar interpretation applies for all coefficients, except the term labeled *perceived rejection* and *homosexual association* in Figure 3. This term represents a second order interaction between *perceived rejection*, *homosexual association*, and *stereotypic self-definition*.

Figure 3. A Fitted Model of Secondary Deviance

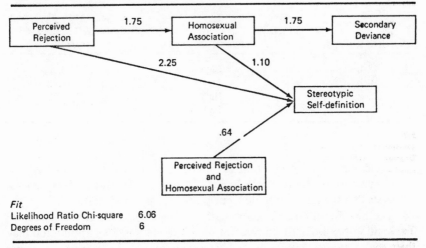

Fit
Likelihood Ratio Chi-square   6.06
Degrees of Freedom   6

The supporting interpretation is based on the premise that the relations shown in Figures 2 and 3 are quite influenced by the unmeasured variable, prior self-definition. The methodological basis of the argument comes from several observations made by Goodman (1972). He showed that if an unmeasured variable is related in the same manner (positively or negatively) to two measured variables, it will tend to induce a positive relation between these two variables. Further, if the actual relation between the two observed variables is negative, then the observed relation may appear to be independent. In a sense, the induced positive relation may cancel out the negative relation.

In the present case, the unmeasured variable is prior self-definition and the two measured variables are homosexual association and present self-definition. Theoretically (*see* Figure 1) these variables have the same relationships as the situation derived from Goodman's work. In this sense, [the] model [in Figure 2] can be viewed as being consistent with the theoretical relations between homosexual association and self-definition shown in Figure 1.

If one ignores the effect of prior self-definition, [the] model . . . in Figure 3 also offers support to the theoretical relation between homosexual association and self-definition following such association. Table 1 (derived from Figure 3) shows that the odds that stereotypic self-definition is high are affected by the joint level of perceived rejection and homosexual association. Notice that for persons who perceived rejection, the odds of developing a stereotypic self-definition are lower for those associating with homosexuals than for those not associating. This suggests that joining together with other homosexuals may improve the individual's self-definition and, therefore, the findings lend support to the theory. (Note, however, that for subjects

Table 1: Odds That Stereotypic Self-Definition Is High in . . . [Figure 3]

Variable And Its Level		Odds That Stereotypic Self-Definition Is High
Perceived Rejection	Homosexual Association	
High	High	2.22
High	Low	3.83
Low	High	.92
Low	Low	.36

who did not perceive rejection the converse is true; the odds of having a stereotypic self-definition are higher for those associating. This reversal suggests that the theoretical model may need further modification.)

The negating interpretation is based on the assumption that homosexual association has little (if any) effect on self-definition. This assumption may also be supported by both . . . [Figures 2 and 3]. . . . [Figure 2] shows independence between these variables and . . . [Figure 3] (*see* Table 1) shows that although both perceived rejection and homosexual association affect the self-definition, most of the effect seems to come from perceived rejection.

In summary, then, there appear to be two somewhat different models suggested by the analysis. The model most in agreement with the original theoretical formulations appears in Figure 4. The relationship of self-definition in this model needs further research. The model least in agreement with the original theoretical formulations appears in Figure 5.

DISCUSSION AND IMPLICATIONS

The analysis also has implications for the theories from which the model building originated.

Labeling theory and more generally the symbolic interactionist perspective postulate a relation between the perceived reactions of others and the development of self-definition. Research on homosexuality, however, has offered contradictory evidence for this relationship. We believe that this is largely because these studies have conceptualized societal reactions in very different terms, either as single formalized responses, or in terms of the recurrent perceived responses of others in informal encounters.

For example, a study by Williams and Weinberg (1971) considered "less than honorable discharge" from military service as a negative societal response. Partial replication of their work by Farrell and Hardin (1974) used arrest for homosexual behavior as the societal response. Both studies found no significant relationship between these formal labels and self-definition. On the other hand, a more recent study by Weinberg and Williams (1974)

Figure 4. [Empirical] Model Most in Agreement with the . . . [Theoretical] Model

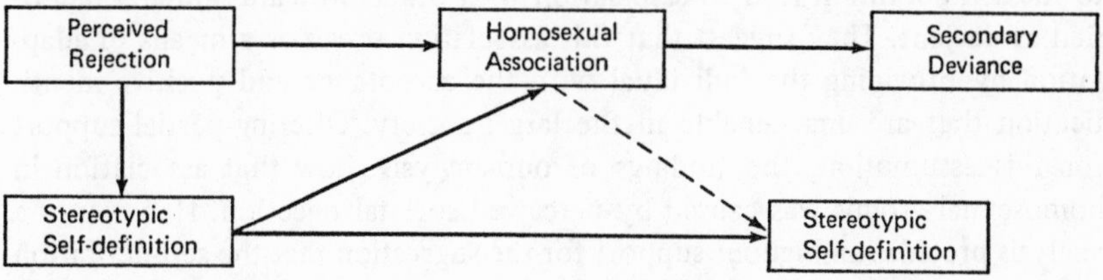

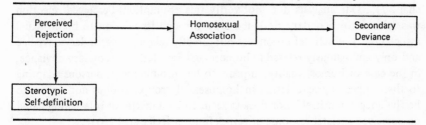

Figure 5. [Empirical] Model Lease in Agreement with the . . . [Theoretical] Model

found relationships between several indicators of self-definition and the perceived or anticipated responses of others in a more informal context.

The relationahip found in our work further confirms what is suggested by these studies. Labeling, at least for homosexuals, represents a more general interaction process than is found in the single or isolated events commonly associated with labeling theory. These latter events, while often traumatic, may have considerably less impact on the individual because they usually lack sufficient publicity to arouse a more general public reaction. (This point has also been made by Lemert, 1967:42 and 60; Schur, 1971:70-71; and Williams and Weinberg, 1971:183.)

The operational definition of societal responses used here also deviates from that normally derived from the symbolic interactionist approach. Whereas the traditional emphasis has been on the importance of primary group relations in the development of the self, the present study has dealt with societal responses that presumably occur in secondary group encounters. Our finding that the self is affected by such responses suggests that deviance, in the case of homosexuality, is indeed a highly salient position. Perceived actions of persons who would be otherwise insignificant to the individual take on importance, apparently due to the negative significance which society and eventually the homosexual give to the deviation. Because of the saliency of the position, the individual develops a heightened awareness of his deviation and a hypersensitivity to the responses of others, responding intensely to even the most subtle reactions of secondary encounters.

[Earlier theorists (e.g., Tannenbaum, 1938:16-21; Cohen, 1955; 1959) have suggested] . . . that perceived societal rejection and subsequent threat to the self-definition lead to association with others who are similarly identified as deviant. They suggest that this association serves as a means of adaptation by providing the individual with the acceptance and positive identification that are unattainable in the larger society. Offering partial support for this assumption, the findings of our analysis show that association in homosexual groups was caused by perceived societal rejection. However, the analysis provides ambiguous support for the suggestion that the self-definition also influenced (or was influenced by) such association.

[It has also been argued] . . . that perceived [social] response and self-definition directly affect deviant behavior [(Merton, 1938; Parsons, 1951, chap. 7)]. Our analysis does not verify this assumption. Perceived rejection was related to secondary deviance only through its relation to homosexual association. And self-definition was not directly related to secondary deviance and only ambiguously related to homosexual association. Secondary deviance, in the case of homosexuality, appears to be an outcome of persons adapting to their stigma by associating in homosexual groups. It does not appear to be the adaptation itself; nor does it seem to be a matter of role taking based on perceived societal response or self-definition [(Glaser, 1956)].

Finally, . . . the enactment of deviant behavior . . . [has been said to depend] on the individual's ability to validate his role (*see* Sutherland, 1955:78–80; and Sykes and Matza, 1957). Based on this assumption, the model in Figure 1 suggests that enculturation to secondary deviance likewise depends in part on a redefinition of the self in more positive terms, a redefinition that occurs as a result of the social and cultural support obtained from association in homosexual groups. The results of our analysis do not support this assumption. The findings show no significant relation between a more positive self-definition and secondary deviance. Persons who associated in homosexual groups engaged in secondary deviance regardless of the self-definitional changes that may (or may not) have resulted from such association.

CONCLUSION

In its simplest form, it appears that secondary deviance is caused by association in homosexual groups which results from perceived societal rejection. The role that self-definition plays in this process could not be clearly determined. However, the data suggest that it is not directly related to secondary deviance and may or may not be related to homosexual association. Implicit in the analysis is the need for a sensitive measure of self-definition, one that would tap its dynamic quality and, therefore, explain its importance (if any) in the development of secondary deviance.

REFERENCES

Becker, Howard S. *Outsiders.* New York: Free Press, 1963.

Cohen, Albert C. *Delinquent Boys.* New York: Free Press, 1955.

———. "The Study of Social Disorganization and Deviant Behavior." In *Sociology Today,* edited by Robert K. Merton, Leonard Broom and Leonard S. Cottrell, pp. 461–84. New York: Basic Books, 1959.

Cooley, Charles Horton. *Human Nature and the Social Order.* New York: Charles Scribner's Sons, 1902.

Cronbach, L. J. "Coefficient alpha and the internal structure of tests." *Psychometrika* 16 (1951): 297–334.

Farrell, Ronald A., and Hardin, Clay W. "Legal stigma and homosexual career deviance." In *Crime and Delinquency: Dimensions on Deviance,* edited by Marc Riedel and Terence Thornberry, pp. 128–40. New York: Praeger Publishers, 1974.

Farrell, Ronald A., and Morrione, Thomas J. "Social interaction and stereotypic responses to homosexuals." *Archives of Sexual Behavior* 3 (September 1974): 425–442.

———. "Conforming to deviance." In *Social Deviance,* edited by Ronald A. Farrell and Victoria Lynn Swigert, pp. 375–87. Philadelphia: J. B. Lippincott, 1975.

Glaser, Daniel. "Criminality theories and behavioral images." *American Journal of Sociology* 61 (March 1956): 433–44.

Goodman, L. A. "A general model for the analysis of surveys." *American Journal of Sociology* 77 (1972): 1035–1086.

———. "Causal analysis of data from panel studies and other kinds of surveys." *American Journal of Sociology* 78 (1973a): 1135–1191.

———. "The analysis of multidimensional contingency tables when some variables are posterior to others: a modified path analysis approach." *Biometrika* 60 (1973b): 179–192.

Hooker, Evelyn. "The homosexual community." In *Sexual Deviance,* edited by John H. Gagnon and William Simon, pp. 167–84. New York: Harper & Row, 1967.

Lemert, Edwin M. *Social Pathology: A Systematic Approach to the Theory of Sociopathic Behavior.* New York: McGraw-Hill, 1951.

———. *Human Deviance, Social Problems and Social Control.* Englewood Cliffs, New Jersey: Prentice-Hall, 1967.

Leznoff, M., and Westley, W. "The homosexual community." *Social Problems* 3 (April 1956): 257–263.

Merton, R. K. "Social structure and anomie." *American Sociological Review* 3 (October 1938): 672–682.

Parsons, Talcott. *The Social System.* New York: Free Press, 1951.

Schur, Edwin M. *Labeling Deviant Behavior: Its Sociological Implications.* New York: Harper & Row, 1971.

Simmons, J. L. "Public stereotypes of deviants." *Social Problems* 13 (Fall 1965): 223–232.

Sutherland, Edwin, and Creasey, Donald. *Principles of Criminology.* Chicago: J. B. Lippincott, 1955.

Sykes, G., and Matza, D. "Techniques of neutralization: a theory of delinquency." *American Sociological Review* 22 (December 1957): 664–670.

Tannenbaum, Frank. *Crime and the Community.* Boston: Ginn and Co., 1938.

Thomas, William I. *The Unadjusted Girl.* Boston: Little, Brown and Co., 1923.

Weinberg, Martin S., and Williams, Colin J. *Male Homosexuals: Their Problems and Adaptations.* New York: Oxford University Press, 1974.

Williams, Colin J. and Weinberg, Martin S. *Homosexuals and the Military.* New York: Harper & Row, 1971.

PART FOUR
Anomie and Adaptation to Strain

Central to the labeling perspective is the notion that societal reaction to nonconformity has consequences for self-concept. Rejection of persons for their possession of disvalued attributes or behavior constitutes a serious threat to self-esteem. The resolution of the stress that accompanies status loss is the subject of anomie theory.

Anomie theorists posit that deviant behavior is a consequence of frustrated access to internalized success goals. The expectations and needs of human beings are social in nature. Aspirations, therefore, must be regulated by forces external to the individual, that is, by standards and norms that are also socially derived. A well-ordered society not only defines goals commensurate with the ability of its members to achieve them, but provides the means necessary for their successful pursuit. It sometimes happens, however, that society experiences a disruption in its normative structure. Whether through sudden boon or large scale catastrophe, individuals become uncertain of the levels of achievement or standards for behavior that are expected of them. When this occurs, society is said to be normless, or anomic (Durkheim, 1897).

In modern, industrial society, social systems suffer a more chronic form of deregulation. Ever-expanding markets and consumption capabilities imply that success goals are increasingly distant and, therefore, never quite reachable. Similarly, imbalances in the cultural emphases on goals relative to the institutionalized means for their attainment constitute additional sources of normlessness. Robert K. Merton (1938) has argued, for example, that American society is characterized by a universal emphasis on pecuniary success. All persons, independent of their social status, are encouraged and, in fact, expected to strive for quite lofty achievement levels. Rags-to-riches heroes, as depicted in the media and educational system, diffuse and perpetuate this cultural emphasis. At the same time, however, the means for goal achievement are differentially distributed. Not all individuals have access to the performance opportunities essential for goal attainment. Class and race discrimination in education and employment mean that some may be denied the opportunities for success. If such persons have adopted the cultural goals as their own, social psychological stress and the need to adapt to that stress will be the likely outcome. This adaptation may involve the selection of behaviors that are deviant or criminal.

A most important contribution of anomie theory to the study of deviant behavior concerns the subculture. Given the stress that arises when status or achievement is blocked, individuals may turn to others sharing similar problems of adjustment (Cohen, 1955; 1959). The norms and values that emerge within subcultural associations define behaviors and goals which, while condemned by the larger society, are both accessible and rewarding to group members.

The pains of imprisonment, as discussed by Gresham Sykes in "The Society of Captives: Adaptation to the Pains of Imprisonment," demonstrates the applicability of the subcultural solution to stress. Prolonged confinement, with the frustrations and deprivations that accompany loss of liberty, constitutes a threat to an individual's sense of self-worth. At the same time, the possible adjustments to these pains are limited. Escape, whether physical or psychological, is difficult if not impossible. Open rebellion is precluded both by the probability of failure and the lack of cohesion essential for an organized confrontation, while there exists widespread belief that peaceful change is equally unlikely.

While the stresses of imprisonment are not capable of being removed, they may at least be mitigated by the development of a subculture consisting of norms and values that define the nature of prisoner relationships, the attitudes appropriate to prison life, and the rights and obligations that attend membership in the prison community. This society of captives allows the inmate to withstand the experience of confinement with some minimization of difficulty.

While blocked access to goals may affect all status levels, it is the lower classes that are most vulnerable to the differential distribution of means. The American educational system, for example, is an arena within which children from all social classes and races come together to compete for academic success. Since the schools are operated by middle-class personnel, status is awarded on the basis of their standards. Differences in prior socialization result in the failure of lower-status youth to compete successfully in terms of this middle-class measuring rod. If these children have internalized the norms governing the classroom situation and have adopted the middle-class referents as their own, stress will result and delinquency will be a probable adaptation (Cohen, 1955).

Delbert Elliott's investigation of delinquency rates among high-school-aged children, "Delinquency, School Attendance and Dropout," demonstrates that the educational system does operate as a source of status frustration. Findings that nonconformity is much higher for children in school than among those who have dropped out before graduation indicate that, by removing the frustration, delinquency can be avoided. In addition, Elliott reports that those lower socioeconomic children who are eventual dropouts have the highest frequency of delinquent involvement while in school, and the lowest rates when they leave. This pattern is considerably diminished for high-status youth. It appears that lower-class children can resolve the stress of status deprivation by retreating to a normative system more rewarding of the performance style of which they are capable. Higher-status children, on the other hand, cannot easily escape the middle-class standards that pervade so many other dimensions of their lives. Termination of a high school career does not appreciably relieve the status frustrations of blocked goals.

The importance of access to legitimate means to culturally valued goals is the focus of Brian Odell's research on delinquency and opportunity, "Accelerating Entry into the Opportunity Structure." Adjudicated delinquents were experimentally placed in treatment programs with varying emphases on legitimate opportunities. Those youths participating in educational and job placement programs were found subsequently to have dramatically lower recidivism rates than those in the more traditional casework settings. By facilitating entry into the means structure essential to goal attainment, the original motivation for nonconformity was effectively terminated.

If opportunities remain blocked, the experience of stress tends to produce a search for others who are similarly affected. Through continued interaction, norms and values may then emerge which support group members in their illegitimate adaptations. Relying on an observational analysis of the predelinquent careers of institutionalized juveniles, Martin Haskell specifies this process in "Toward a Reference Group Theory of Delinquency," by constructing a reference group theory of delinquent behavior.

The first reference group of the predelinquent is the family. Within this circle of intimate others, conformity to law-abiding norms is strongly motivated. In order to commit deviant acts, the juvenile must neutralize the controlling effects of family commitments and shift reference identification to those who are supportive of such behavior.

Among lower-class boys, exposure to middle-class standards may lead them to depreciate the successes of their parents. In addition, evaluations of self, using the same standards, produce feelings of inadequacy. With the effects of normative referents diminished and status achievement frustrated, the juvenile will search for supportive ties. This will result in nonconformity if the adopted referents espouse delinquent norms.

The subculture becomes a powerful medium for the diffusion and reinforcement of deviance. Elliott Liebow's "Tally's Corner: The Subculture of Black Streetcorner Men" addresses both the origins of the subculture and the impact of such associations on behavior.

The world of streetcorner men is a product of failure to conform to dominant achievement expectations. Disrupted family relationships and poor work histories confirm both the individual's sense of worthlessness and the inevitability of the pattern of failure that continues intergenerationally. The lower-class black male turns to the streetcorner group where situations can be redefined to maintain the integrity of its members. At the same time, however, these emergent norms further ensure additional failure. The behavior of the streetcorner male, therefore, is not the result of cultural values distinct from the larger society, but a response to an attempt to achieve dominant goals and, upon not being able to do so, "concealing his failure from others and from himself as best he can."

In sum, theory and research within the anomie tradition has contended that deviant behavior is an adaptation to frustrated achievement. When access to legitimate means is blocked or continuing efforts at conformity remain unsuccessful, persons may experience stress and the need for its resolution. Interaction with others whose adaptation to blocked goals includes reliance on illegitimate means will result in deviant or criminal behavior.

REFERENCES

Cohen, Albert K. *Delinquent Boys.* New York: Free Press, 1955.
_____. "The Study of Social Disorganization and Deviant Behavior." In *Sociology Today: Problems and Prospects,* edited by Robert K. Merton, Leonard Broom, and Leonard S. Cottrell. New York: Basic Books, 1959.
Durkheim, Emile. *Suicide.* 1897. Translated by John A. Spaulding and George Simpson. New York: Free Press, 1951.
Merton, Robert K. "Social Structure and Anomie." *American Sociological Review* 3 (1938): 672-82.

GRESHAM M. SYKES

The Society of Captives: Adaptation
to the Pains of Imprisonment

This study . . . concerns itself with a single system of total power—the social
system of the New Jersey State Maximum Security Prison. Here more than
300 custodial, clerical, and professional state employees are organized into
bureaucratic administrative staff charged with the duty of governing approximately 1,200 adult male criminals held in confinement for periods of time
ranging from one year to life. . . .

. . . [T]he ready cooperation and encouragement of the [prison] officials
. . . did much to eliminate the problem of administrative reticence: official
files, standard operating procedures, and other records were made freely
available. In addition, the open-handed support of the prison administration
made it possible to interview guards, civilian work supervisors, and inmates
under conditions making for a good deal of frankness. The anonymity of
those who provided information could be assured and men could be questioned on the job, in their cells, in the recreation hall, and so on. There
remained, of course, many barriers to easy communication between the
writer and both the custodians of the institution and their captives, for a
prison is founded in part on secrecy and the observer from the free community is inevitably defined as an intruder, at least initially. Gradually, however,
over a period of three years, it was possible to become redefined as a more or

Source: Sykes, Gresham M. *The Society of Captives: A Study of a Maximum Security
Prison*. New Jersey: Princeton University Press, 1958: xvi, xix-xx, 78-83. Copyright ©
1958 by Princeton University Press. Reprinted by permission.

less neutral figure in the schismatic struggles which split the prison and much of this reluctance to talk was overcome. . . .

Imprisonment . . . is painful. The pains of imprisonment, however, cannot be viewed as being limited to the loss of physical liberty. The significant hurts lie in the frustrations or deprivations which attend the withdrawal of freedom, such as the lack of heterosexual relationships, isolation from the free community, the withholding of goods and services, and so on. And however painful these frustrations or deprivations may be in the immediate terms of thwarted goals, discomfort, boredom, and loneliness, they carry a more profound hurt as a set of threats or attacks which are directed against the very foundations of the prisoner's being. The individual's picture of himself as a person of value—as a morally acceptable, adult male who can present some claim to merit in his material achievements and his inner strength—begins to waver and grow dim. Society did not plan this onslaught, it is true, and society may even "point with pride" to its humanity in the modern treatment of the criminal. But the pains of imprisonment remain and it is imperative that we recognize them, for they provide the energy for the society of captives as a system of action.

Before we examine how the inmate population actually sets about its task of relieving the pains of imprisonment, however, it is worthwhile to look at other reactions to the bitter frustrations and threats of confinement which do *not* occur or occur but seldom. By so doing we can better understand the strength of those reactions which do take place. The pains of imprisonment generate enormous pressure which is translated into behavior with all the greater vigor because, like a body of steam under heavy compression with only a few outlets, the body of prisoners is limited in modes of adaptation.[1]

Now if men are confronted with a painfully frustrating situation, they can of course attempt to solve their problem by literally escaping from the situation by means of physical withdrawal. In the case of the inmates of the maximum security prison, however, it is hardly necessary to point out that such a solution is diametrically opposed to the premise on which their world is founded. Perhaps for a few prisoners (the so-called *escape artists,* for example), dreams of flight, however impractical, mercifully disguise the harsh meaning of imprisonment. Their lives are plans for the future rather than present realities.[2] But for most of the inmates, the most obvious solution

1. Robert K. Merton's (1949) discussion of types of reaction to frustrating situations, i.e. conformity, innovation, ritualism, retreatism, and rebellion, provides an excellent starting point for our analysis. His typology, however, has been changed to meet the specific details of our study.

2. The accounts of soldiers captured during the last war vividly illustrate how planning to escape was used, sometimes quite deliberately, to divert the captive's attention from his existing plight. *See* also Philip, n. d.

to the pains of imprisonment is ruled out ... and the prisoner must solve his problems within the closely-guarded frontier that is the Wall, if he is to solve his problems at all.

Yet there is another kind of escape from the prison which is at least theoretically possible, i.e. psychological withdrawal. This can take the form of renouncing the goals, the drives, or the needs which are frustrated, either consciously or unconsciously, leaving the prisoner immune in apathy or seeking the gratifications of sublimation. Or it can take the form of a withdrawal into fantasy based on fondled memories of the past or imaginary dramas of life after release. There are a number of inmates in the New Jersey State Prison who have so managed to escape the rigors of their existence, but it is not the path of the majority of prisoners. Perhaps the goals which are frustrated are too important, too vital, to be relinquished by the majority of men. Perhaps the tendency toward a full-fledged retreat into a world of fantasy is reserved for the few who were but lightly linked with reality before their confinement. In any case, most inmates fail to escape the pains of imprisonment by means of these psychological mechanisms just as surely as they fail to escape by physically forcing a breach in the wall and the attacks on the self must be countered in other terms.

If men in prison cannot cure their ills by these modes of retreat, there still remains the possibility of rebellion or innovation. The inmates could try to overthrow or change the custodial regime to ease the frustrations and deprivations which plague them. It is true, of course, that in the event of an open battle, victory inevitably lies in the hands of the guards. Yet men will revolt in a desperate situation even though they know there is no chance of success; the certainty of failure is only one of the reasons why prisoners do not band together in open conflict against their rulers.[3] Of equal or greater importance is the fact that the inmate population is shot through with a variety of ethnic and social cleavages which sharply reduce the possibility of continued mass action called for by an uprising. The inmates lack an ideological commitment transcending their individual differences and the few riots which do occur are as likely to collapse from dissension among prisoners as from repression by the custodial force. One notable exception to this point is to be found in the passive resistance movements of conscientious objectors confined in federal prisons during World War II; but the inmates of the New Jersey State Prison have never achieved this degree of organization.

If forceful change is avoided as a solution to the pains of imprisonment

3. A revolt—a riot—may fail, of course, in the sense that prisoners do not permanently seize the reins of power, yet it may succeed by arousing public opinion so that the conditions of imprisonment are eased. Public outcries for "reforms," however, quickly die away when the status quo is reestablished.

in the ordinary course of events, attempts at peaceful change through the use of persuasion are no less rare. The prisoners are well aware that the custodians face a public which would not permit the removal of confinement's frustrations even if they—the custodians—desired to do so. Perhaps it would be more accurate to say that the public *might* allow conjugal visits, furloughs in the free community, a higher standard of living, and so on. But if such changes will come, they will probably come in the somewhat distant future and the persuasive arguments of imprisoned criminals will be a minor factor in bringing these innovations about. The inmate population has little hope of solving problems here and now by the gentle tactics of orderly political activity. Efforts at change from below remain in the form of an individual letter to the governor, an isolated complaint to the newspapers, or an occasional petition presented to the warden.

Unable to escape either physically or psychologically, lacking the cohesion to carry through an insurrection that is bound to fail in any case, and bereft of faith in peaceful innovation, the inmate population might seem to have no recourse but the simple endurance of the pains of imprisonment. The frustrations and deprivations of confinement, with their attendant attacks on the prisoner's self-image, would strike the prisoner with full force and the time spent in prison would have to be marked down as time spent in purgatory. And to a large extent this is what does happen in reality. There are no exits for the inmate in the sense of a device or series of devices which can completely eliminate the pains of imprisonment. *But if the rigors of confinement cannot be completely removed, they can at least be mitigated by the patterns of social interaction established among the inmates themselves.* In this apparently simple fact lies the key to our understanding of the prisoner's world.

Frustrated not as an individual but as one of many, the inmate finds two paths open. On the one hand, he can attempt to bind himself to his fellow captives with ties of mutual aid, loyalty, affection, and respect, firmly standing in opposition to the officials. On the other hand, he can enter into a war of all against all in which he seeks his own advantage without reference to the claims or needs of other prisoners. In the former case, the rigors of the environment are met with group cohesion or inmate solidarity. Toleration replaces "touchiness," fellow prisoners are persons to be helped rather than exploited, and group allegiance emerges as a dominant value. The inmate's orientation is "collectivistic." (cf. Parsons and Shils, 1951.) In the latter case, the rigors of the environment elicit an alienated response. Abhorrence or indifference feed the frictions of prison life. Fellow prisoners are persons to be exploited by every expedient that comes to hand; the officials are simply another hazard in the pursuit of the inmate's goals and he stands ready to betray his fellow captives if it advances his interests. The inmate's orientation can be termed "individualistic." (Parsons and Shils, 1951.)

In actuality, the patterns of social interaction among inmates are to be found scattered between these two theoretical extremes. The population of prisoners does not exhibit a perfect solidarity yet neither is the population of prisoners a warring aggregate. Rather, it is a mixture of both and the society of captives lies balanced in an uneasy compromise. . . .

REFERENCES

Merton, Robert K. "Social Structure and Anomie." In *Social Theory and Social Structure*. Glencoe, Illinois: Free Press, 1949.

Parsons, Talcott, and Shils, Edward A., eds. *Towards A General Theory of Action*. Cambridge, Massachusetts: Harvard University Press, 1951.

Philip, Alban M. *The Prison-Breakers*. New York: Henry Holt and Co., n.d.

DELBERT S. ELLIOTT
Delinquency, School Attendance, and Dropout

Theoretical explanations of delinquent behavior have come to place increasing emphasis upon some form of "status deprivation" as the motivational source of lower-class delinquency (Bordua, 1960; Cohen, 1955; Cloward and Ohlin, 1960). According to these views, the socialization of lower-class boys does not adequately prepare them to compete effectively for status rewards in middle-class-dominated institutions. The intense frustration experienced by these boys consequently motivates them toward delinquent patterns of behavior in an attempt to recoup their loss of self-esteem.

Albert Cohen in *Delinquent Boys* suggests that the school in particular awards status upon the basis of middle-class standards. Here, lower- and middle-class youths compete for status in terms of the same set of middle-class criteria, with the result that lower-class youths are relegated to the lowest status positions. As a result of the unequal competition, lower-class youths develop feelings of insecurity, become frustrated, and begin to search for some solution to their status problem (Cohen, 1955:112-19).

Delinquency is thus viewed as a by-product of the unequal competition at school. Youths who are denied opportunities to achieve higher status positions because of their lower-class socialization are consequently "provoked" to engage in delinquent behavior in an attempt to avail themselves

Source: Elliott, Delbert S. "Delinquency, School Attendance and Dropout." *Social Problems* 13 (1966): 307-309, 312-314. Permission granted by The Society for the Study of Social Problems and the author.

of illegitimate means to reach legitimate goals[1] or to express their rejection and disdain for middle-class goals which are not available to them.[2]

Delinquency is not the only alternative open to youths who experienced status deprivation in school. Dropping out of school also offers a solution to this problem and is not confined to those lacking intellectual ability. Studies of school dropouts suggest that capable youth are leaving school prior to graduation to escape a condition similar to that described by Cohen and Cloward and Ohlin. For example, Lichter (1962:247-48) and his associates concluded that the capable dropout leaves school because of his desire to escape frustrations encountered in the school milieu:

> The dropouts left school because they were motivated to *run away* from a disagreeable situation; they did not feel impelled to run toward a definite and positive goal. Although they discussed employment, their talk was vague, aimless, or unrealistic.... The decision to drop out was the outcome of an accumulation of school problems and the belief that it was too late to correct the difficulties. Dropping out was not only the easiest course to take, but a passive, not an active resolution of the educational problem.

One significant point regarding the decision to drop out of school as an alternative to the status frustration experienced in school is that it should reduce the motivational stimulus to engage in delinquent behavior. The individual who drops out is no longer involved in the competition with middle-class youth at school and the adjustment problem described by Cohen as the motivational source of delinquency is at least partially resolved.[3] If status deprivation experienced at school is causally related to delinquency, it follows that the probability of engaging in delinquent behavior is less for

1. Cloward and Ohlin maintain that some communities have both conventional and criminal opportunity structures. Boys in these communities who experience aspirational blockage in the legitimate opportunity system turn to the illegitimate opportunity system in an effort to achieve their aspirations. This solution is essentially that described by Merton (1957:141-49) as an innovating mode of adaptation.

2. Cohen, on the other hand, maintains that the delinquent subculture engages in behavior which expresses rejection and derogation of middle-class norms and goals. Vandalism, for example, is seen as an expression of the delinquent's disdain of the middle-class norm regarding private property.

3. It is possible, however, that the individual has merely traded the status frustrations encountered at school for those encountered in our economic institutions. The availability of satisfactory employment may well be a necessary condition for the effective resolution of the status deprivation problem.

out-of-school youth than for in-school youth.[4] This proposition is examined in this study in the form of two specific hypotheses:

    1. The rate of delinquency is greater for boys while in than while out of school.[5]

    2. Delinquents who drop out have a higher delinquency rate while in than while out of school.

THE STUDY DESIGN

The study population is composed of 743 tenth-grade boys who entered the two largest high schools in a large western city in September, 1959.[6] In this *ex post facto* design, data were gathered on this group of boys for a three-year period beginning with their entrance into high school in September, 1959 and ending with their class graduation in June of 1962.[7] The research design specified a comparison of the delinquency rates of these boys while in and out of school. The "in-school" and "out-of-school" distinction requires that each boy be classified as a graduate or dropout. Boys who graduated in

---

4. The hypothesis that delinquency is related to frustrations encountered in the school milieu and that leaving this milieu reduces the motivation for delinquent behavior appears consistent with the fact that offense rates in the U.S. drop significantly after 17, when most lower-class American youth leave school and enter the labor force. (Lunden, 1961:28; Bernard, 1957:421–44; McCord *et al.*, 1959:21; Dunham and Knaver, 1954.) In England, the rate of delinquency drops much earlier, at the age of 14 or 15; again, this is when most English youth *leave school* and enter the labor force.

5. It is recognized that leaving school may not reduce the likelihood of a boy who is already delinquent committing another delinquent act. The delinquent's identification and involvement with an existing delinquent group may lead him to continue his delinquent activities, as a requirement of group membership, even though the original motivational stimulus for this kind of behavior has been eliminated. However, if the dropout is not a member of a delinquent group prior to leaving school, the probability of his joining this kind of group or committing another delinquent act should be reduced.

6. The total number of males entering these two schools in 1959 was 821. Seventy-eight of this original group transferred out of the area during the three-year study period and were dropped from the analysis, leaving 743 subjects.

7. Police contacts during the summer months of 1960 and 1961 were not considered in this analysis. Almost all of the subjects were out of school during this period of time and there was no practical way of determining how many subjects left the area and for what periods of time. During the school year, all graduates were in school and only dropouts had to be contacted to determine their whereabouts. The official referral rate declines during the summer months. [San Diego Police Department—Juvenile Division, Monthly Reports, 1960, 1961, and 1962.] Had contacts reported during the summer months been included, the most probable effect would have been a decrease in the out-of-school referral rate. Since this works in favor of the hypothesis, it was decided to exclude summer time contacts from the analysis.

June, 1962 or were in school throughout the entire study period were classified as graduates. All those who left school (during the three years) were
classified as dropouts. The dropout category thus includes those who were
"pushed" out of school for disciplinary problems as well as those who left
voluntarily. Those who left to move to another geographical area were
excluded from the analysis.[8] All boys classified as graduates were in school
during the entire study period and consequently contributed *only* to the in-
school delinquency rate. Boys classified as dropouts were in-school for some
part of the study period and out of school for the remainder of the period,
contributing to *both* the in-school and out-of-school delinquency rates.[9] Of
the 743 boys in the study, 182 were classified as dropouts and 561 were
classified as graduates.

The comparison of in- and out-of-school delinquency rates also required
that these rates be calculated upon a common base. Consequently, it was
necessary to determine the actual number of days graduates and dropouts
were attending school and the number of days the dropouts were out of
school. The number of in-school days for graduates was constant. The number of in-school days for dropouts varied, depending upon the date they left
school. School records were examined to determine this date, and an attempt
was made to contact each dropout during September and October of 1962 to
determine the number of days he was out of school and in the study area.
This information was secured for 132 or 73 percent of the 182 dropouts. For
the remainder, an estimate of their out-of-school time in the area was made
after examining all available records. The latest date the subject was *known* to
be in the area was used to calculate the length of time this subject was out-of-
school and in the study area. The estimate of the number of out-of-school
days is therefore a conservative one.[10]

Official contact reports by police, sheriff, and other law enforcement
agencies constitute the measure of delinquency. The date and nature of
each offense, as stated on the contact report (referral), were recorded.[11] ...

8. This was determined by a "request for transcript" received by the school of origin.
In several cases boys indicated they were moving but no request for transcript was
received. In this event, they were classified as dropouts and an attempt was made to
locate them in the local area.

9. There were two boys who dropped out of school for a period of time and then
reentered school. The number of days they were out of school contributed to the
calculation of the out-of-school rate and *both* their in-school periods contributed to
the in-school rate. Neither boy had an official contact.

10. A conservative estimate works against the hypothesis in this case, since it max-
imized the out-of-school delinquency rate.

11. Kobrin (1951) asserts that police "complaint records" or contact reports are
probably the most inclusive measure of delinquency obtainable though he recognizes
that they are not an accurate measure of delinquent behavior. Since a comparison of

Table 1: Delinquent Referral Rate* Among Boys in and out of School

| SES Areas | In School | | | Out of school |
	Graduates	**Dropouts	Sub-total	**Dropouts
Lower	4.13	8.70	4.96	2.42
Higher	4.92	4.95	4.92	4.63
Total	4.34	8.03	4.95	2.75

    *   Number of referrals per 10,000 in- or out-of-school days.
   ** These are the same individuals during two different time periods.

FINDINGS

The comparison of the in- and out-of-school delinquency referral rates is presented in Table 1. The overall in-school referral rate is 4.95 compared to an out-of-school rate of 2.75. This difference is substantial and in the direction hypothesized. Table 1 also presents the in-school delinquency rates for both graduates and future dropouts and for those residing in lower and higher socioeconomic (SES) neighborhoods. The highest delinquency rate was observed among lower SES dropouts prior to their leaving school. It is quite possible that their involvement in this kind of activity was responsible for some of them being pushed out of school. What is surprising is that this same group of boys had the lowest referral rate after dropping out of school. Their out-of-school rate is less than one-third their in-school rate. These data clearly support the hypothesis.

Cohen's explanation of delinquency applies specifically to working-class boys and the status deprivation variable automatically incorporated the class variable. Since there was no attempt to obtain a measure of this independent variable in this study, it seemed important to calculate separate rates for those from lower and higher SES areas. While the in-school rate for boys from higher SES areas is greater than their out-of-school rate, the difference is quite small and may be of little substantive significance. In fact, there appears to be little difference in any of the rates shown for boys from higher SES areas. The in-school rates for dropouts and graduates are almost identical and are only slightly greater than the out-of-school rates. It would appear that leaving school does not have the same impact on boys from higher SES areas as it does on those from lower SES areas. One might expect

---

in- and out-of-school delinquent offense rates is made, truancy offenses were excluded. The calculation of the total number of in- and out-of-school days does not include any days after an individual's eighteenth birthday since an individual is generally not treated as a juvenile after his eighteenth birthday and only juvenile records were consulted.

Table 2: Offense Rates* for Delinquent Dropouts Before and After Leaving School

SES Areas	Before	After
Lower	64.96	34.52
Higher	40.12	23.75
Total	60.78	31.01

* Number of delinquent referrals per 10,000 student-days.

that leaving school would affect boys from these two SES areas differently. While leaving school should help to eliminate the status frustration of boys from lower-class areas, it would not necessarily solve the adjustment problem of those from middle- and upper-class areas. Boys from lower-class areas can retreat into the lower-class community where they may seek employment in the unskilled or semi-skilled occupations which are available to them. Their parents and other adult members of their community are willing to accept these occupations as legitimate endeavors for young men.

Boys from middle-class areas who leave school subsequently find themselves limited to lower-class occupations while their parents and other adult members of their community continue to hold middle-class expectations for them. They are unable or unwilling to meet the formal expectations of school and are equally unable to meet the expectations of their parents if they drop out of school.

A separate but related issue involves the effect of leaving school on the referral rate of boys who were known officially as delinquents while in school. Although the rate of delinquent referral is less for boys while out of school than while in school, it does not necessarily follow that those who have official referrals while in school will have fewer referrals after leaving school. To test the hypothesis that delinquents who drop out have a higher referral rate while in school, in- and out-of-school referral rates were calculated for this group. (Table 2)

The data in Table 2 support this hypothesis. The in-school referral rate for delinquents is almost twice their out-of-school referral rate. This relationship holds for delinquents from both lower and higher SES areas. The rates in Table 2 also suggest that delinquents from lower SES neighborhoods have a higher referral rate than do delinquents from higher SES neighborhoods. This is particularly interesting since there is little difference in the proportions (.112 and .118) of boys from each of these two areas who are delinquent, i.e., who had one or more official referrals on file. It appears that delinquents from lower SES neighborhoods are more frequent offenders than are those from higher SES areas.

CONCLUSION

Cohen suggests that delinquency on the part of lower-class boys is a response to the unequal competition encountered at school. Delinquency is thus associated with frustration and failure pratically experienced in school, for it is in this milieu that youth from disparate cultural backgrounds are forced to compete for middle-class success goals.

There are several alternatives available to those who experience frustration at school. They may remain in school and attempt to deal with their frustration by attacking the system of norms and values which they believe to be the source of their difficulties. Delinquent behavior may thus be viewed as an expression of their resentment toward this system and those who attempt to enforce its norms. On the other hand, those experiencing failure may leave school making a "retreatist" adaptation in an effort to escape from the situation which produces the frustrations. No longer frustrated by the unequal competition at school, there is little or no need to attack the school or the normative system it represents.

It was hypothesized, therefore, that 1) the rate of delinquency referral is greater for boys while in school than while out of school; and 2) delinquents who drop out have a higher referral rate while in school than while out of school. The data supported both hypotheses. The small difference between in- and out-of-school offense rates for boys from higher SES neighborhoods suggests that dropping out of school may not constitute a solution to problems of status deprivation for boys from higher SES areas. One might infer that dropout is a satisfactory solution for those from lower SES areas for the delinquency rate of such youth is lower after leaving school than it was while they were in school.

REFERENCES

Bernard, Jessie. *Social Problems at Midcentury.* New York: Dryden, 1957.

Bordua, David J. "Sociological Theories and Their Implications for Juvenile Delinquency: A Report of a Children's Bureau Conference." U.S. Department of Health, Education and Welfare, 1960.

Cloward, Richard, and Ohlin, Lloyd. *Delinquency and Opportunity.* Glencoe, Illinois: Free Press, 1960.

Cohen, Albert K. *Delinquent Boys.* Glencoe, Illinois: Free Press, 1955.

Dunham, W. H., and Knaver, M. E. "The Juvenile Court and Its Relationship to Adult Criminality." *Social Forces* (March 1954): 290-96.

Kobrin, Solomon. "The Conflict of Values in Delinquency Areas." *American Sociological Review* 16 (1951): 652-61.

Lichter, Solomon, et al. *The Dropouts.* New York: Free Press of Glencoe, 1962.
Lunden, Walter. *Statistics on Delinquents and Delinquency.* Iowa: Art Press, 1961.
McCord, William, et al. *Origins of Crime.* New York: Columbia University Press, 1959.
Mays, John Barron. *Growing Up in the City.* Liverpool: University Press, 1954.
Merton, Robert K. *Social Theory and Social Structure.* Glencoe, Illinois: Free Press, 1957.

BRIAN NEAL ODELL

Accelerating Entry into the Opportunity Structure

Traditionally, juvenile court treatment programs have been based upon psychological or psychiatric interpretations of behavior. In such programs, delinquency is viewed as a symptom of the client's emotional or personality problems; the social situation of the youth draws relatively little attention except as it contributes to the child's purported emotional problems.

In recent years, sociological explanations of delinquency have been advanced which argue that the delinquent's antisocial behavior results not from his personality problems and emotional inadequacies, but from failures within the social system.[1] Prominent among these formulations has been Cloward and Ohlin's (1960) theory of differential access to opportunity. Combining the anomie theory of Merton (1957:146) and the "Chicago school" concept of differentials in access to illegitimate means (Shaw, 1930 and 1931; Shaw and McKay, 1942; Shaw et al, 1929), Cloward and Ohlin conclude that individuals become delinquent because they are denied access to the legitimate opportunity structure. All people, Cloward and Ohlin argue, aspire initially toward the traditional indices of success (e.g., wealth and material possessions) but some people—particularly lower-class individuals—are denied access to the legitimate means to achieve such success (e.g., edu-

1. Matza (1964) provides a cogent assessment of both the individual and social structure causation theories.

Source: Odell, Brian Neal. "Accelerating Entry into the Opportunity Structure: A Sociologically—Based Treatment for Delinquent Youth." *Sociology and Social Research* 58, 3 (1974): 312–317. Permission granted by Sociology and Social Research.

cation and vocational training). Blocked from entry into the legitimate opportunity structure, they are forced to turn to illegal means to achieve their success-goals. It is at this point that they become delinquent.[2]

Cloward and Ohlin's opportunity theory introduces several concepts which are of critical importance in explaining lower-class delinquency. First, it is argued that the lower-class individual aspires to the same success-goals as the middle-class individual. Second, it is pointed out that the legitimate means to achieve these goals are less available to the lower-class individual. Third, the lack of importance attributed by lower-class persons to education is shown to represent not a devaluing of education, but rather a realistic perception of their lack of access to educational opportunity. And fourth, lower-class delinquency is depicted as a problem of the individual only to the extent that the individual is denied access to the means of legitimate success.

What are the implications of this theory for juvenile court treatment programs? Would not a program which prepares the individual to enter the opportunity structure be more effective than a program which ministers to emotional or personality problems? In an attempt to answer this question an analysis was made of an "opportunity theory" treatment program at a Midwestern juvenile court. This program prepares delinquents to enter the opportunity structure by providing both a high school equivalency diploma course and assistance in securing employment. It was hypothesized that completion of the program would lead to a position in the opportunity structure and that this position, in turn, would lead to a decrease in delinquency. The results indicate that: (1) Completion of the high school equivalency program did indeed permit the delinquent youth to enter the legitimate opportunity structure. (2) The opportunity theory treatment program was significantly more effective than the traditional psychologically-based "casework" programs in reducing recidivism. (3) The impressive drop in recidivism among the delinquents who entered the opportunity structure may have been due as much to their changed self-concepts and reference groups as it was to their new position in the opportunity structure.

THE RESEARCH DESIGN

Sixty boys under the jurisdiction of the St. Louis County juvenile court in Clayton and under the supervision of juvenile court caseworkers were included in the study. The youths were high school dropouts, ages 15 years

2. Empirical tests of Cloward and Ohlin's opportunity theory include Short et al (1965); Fredericks and Molnar (1969); Landis and Scarpitti (1965); Landis et al (1964); and Elliott (1962). Theoretical treatments of the opportunity theory include Bordua (1961) and Himelhoch (1965).

and 10 months to 16 years and 3 months, with "serious and persistent" patterns of juvenile offenses. The number of adjudicated offenses committed by each boy ranged from 6 to 19 with a mean of 10.7. All boys were lower-class when measured against the traditional indices; of the 60 boys, 44 were nonwhite and 16 white. The boys as a group evidenced massive educational retardation; demonstrated skill level was 4.1 years behind the last grade placement. The boys' case histories revealed sporadic and short-lived attempts to secure and retain employment. Most had held part-time jobs at some time, but none had a work pattern which yielded even a subsistence level of income.

Through a random process, the original sample of 60 boys was divided into four groups of 15; measurement of the boys' intelligence and level of educational impairment revealed no significant differences between the groups. Racial composition of the groups was controlled to ensure an equal white—nonwhite ratio. The groups were:

Group I, Traditional Casework: this was a control group. These boys continued under the supervision of their caseworkers and were entered in no experimental program. In this and all groups, both the subjects and their caseworkers were unaware of the nature of the research design. Throughout the duration of the project, caseworkers had complete latitude to take any action they felt necessary to serve the needs of the client and the community. This was true for all groups.

Group II, Intensive Casework: to control for the fact that the boys in the experimental groups might sense that they were participating in "something special" and thus respond to the special attention rather than the independent variable, Group II was provided with a "special" program. This group participated in a three-month program of intensive counseling involving both the boys and their parents. Group and individual sessions were held in addition to the boys' regular conferences with their caseworkers.

Group III, Education and Employment: this was an experimental group. Fifteen boys were enrolled in the juvenile court's high school equivalency diploma program. This program is based upon high interest subject matter, programmed learning, and a tutorial system in which each youth proceeds at his own pace. Tutors were area college students and community volunteers. The duration of the program ranged from four to twelve weeks during which time the youth was prepared to pass the Graduate Equivalency Test which yields the G.E.D. high school equivalency diploma.

After completion of the program, youths were placed by court personnel in jobs provided by local employers. Each job provided a minimum work week of thirty hours and an hourly pay rate of at least $1.40. Graduates of the program who desired further education were enrolled, with the assistance of court personnel, in local vocational schools or junior colleges.

Table 1: Participation in the Opportunity Structure (School or Employment)

Groups	3 months	6 months	9 months
I*	1 (n = 13)	2 (n = 12)	1 (n = 10)
II[a]	2 (n = 14)	3 (n = 13)	1 (n = 11)
III[b]	13 (n = 15)	13 (n = 15)	13 (n = 15)
IV[c]	7 (n = 14)	8 (n = 14)	9 (n = 14)
	$X^2 = 23.479$	$X^2 = 17.403$	$X^2 = 17.510$
	$p < .001$	$p < .011$	$p < .011$

* During the twelve-month program, contact was lost with five boys in this group. One moved out of town, and four were placed by their caseworkers in institutional settings.

a Communication was lost with four boys in this group. Two moved outside the court's jurisdiction, one could not be located, and one was placed in an institution.

b Communication was broken with no one in this group.

c One boy in this group was placed in an institution.

Group IV, Education Only: this group was also enrolled in the G.E.D. high school equivalency program. After completion of the program, however, they were not given assistance in securing jobs or further education. This group had its tutoring sessions at a different time than Group III and was unaware of the additional assistance provided that group.

RESULTS

Evaluations of the youths were made at three-month intervals for a period of nine months following the completion of the initial three-month experimental period. As expected, Groups III and IV, the two groups participating in the G.E.D. diploma program, demonstrated significantly greater entry into the opportunity structure (conceptualized as regular employment or participation in post-high school education or training programs): and, furthermore, these results were maintained throughout the period of evaluation. In Group III, 13 of the 15 youths completed their G.E.D. programs within three months: two youths dropped out after three weeks. In Group IV, again, 13 of the 15 boys completed the program within the allotted time; one dropped out after a month, and one was placed by his caseworker in an out-of-town institution a week before the inception of the program. Table 1 reveals the participation of the boys in jobs or training programs for a nine-month period following completion of the three-month experimental project.

In a second test of the boys' entry into the opportunity structure, the mean weekly income of those boys who secured jobs was computed. Table 2

Table 2:   Mean Weekly Income for Those Working (Gross Income)

Time Period	Group I r	Group II r	Group III r	Group IV r
3 mos.	$22.50(n=1) 1.0	$34.20(n=2) 3.5	$56.90(n=9) 29.0	$42.30(n=7) 13.0
6 mos.	$34.20(n=2) 3.5	$36.70(n=3) 8.0	$65.10(n=11) 46.0	$48.70(n=7) 21.0
9 mos.	$35.60(n=1) 6.0	$43.40(n=1)17.0	$86.00(n=11) 57.0	$60.90(n=7) 37.0

Mann - Whitney U
n_1 (10) = groups I and II
n_2 (52) = groups III and IV
a = .0001: c.v. = 3.76
z = 4.855, p < .0001

Table 3:   Recidivism by 3-month periods* (In Percentages. Noncumulative)

Groups	3 months	6 months	9 months
I	38.5%	33.4%	20.0%
II	35.7%	23.0%	27.3%
III	6.7%	0.0%	6.7%
IV	7.2%	0.0%	7.2%
	X^2 = 7.518	X^2 = 10.454	X^2 = 3.124
	p < .05	p < .02	p < .30

*   These percentages represent only adjudicated offenses.

depicts these findings. Apparently the G.E.D. high school equivalency program permitted a significant number of chronic juvenile offenders to enter the opportunity structure. The G.E.D. program participants (Groups III and IV) had more employment and higher income than either Group I, which received the standard counseling services of the court, or Group II, which participated in an intensive counseling program. Furthermore, the employment gained by Groups III and IV, especially Group III, was of a less menial nature and promised occupational advancement and some sense of security.

It was hypothesized earlier that juvenile offenses among lower-class youth represent the use of illegal means to secure societally-approved goals such as wealth and material possessions. Further, it was argued that youths who enter the legitimate opportunity structure through training and employment would be less likely to commit further delinquency. The results of this study support these conclusions.

Table 3 depicts the percentage of boys in each group who were rereferred to the juvenile court during each three-month period. Recidivism was markedly higher among Groups I and II, the casework groups, than among Groups III and IV, the G.E.D. groups.[3] Not only was the percentage of offenses lower among Groups III and IV, but the nature of their referrals differed from Groups I and II. Only one offense among Groups III and IV was a property offense (shoplifting), the remainder were minor authority offenses. Among Groups I and II, however, there were serious property offenses including two burglaries and three larcenies. The entry of Groups III and IV into the opportunity structure appears to have led to a decrease in their adjudicated delinquency. Thus, Cloward and Ohlin's hypotheses is tentatively supported.

Interviews were conducted with the boys in the four groups at the inception and the completion of the project. The interview procedures were loosely structured and the results not subject to empirical verification. However, it was our impression that the boys in Groups I and II retained their negative self-images and antisocial reference groups while Groups III and IV developed more positive self-images and more "traditional" reference groups. Indeed, the boys in the G.E.D. high school equivalency groups seemed to identify with their former tutors, court personnel, and their employers. They defined themselves as on the way to a "good life." . . .

CONCLUSIONS

It is acknowledged that this study was restricted by a small sample and a limited period of evaluation. Nevertheless, several general conclusions may be offered:

1. Juvenile court treatment programs based upon sociological (opportunity structure) or social-psychological (self-image and reference group) constructs seem to decrease recidivism among lower-class, persistently-offending boys more dramatically than do more traditional treatment programs based upon psychiatric or psychological formulations of behavior.
2. A high school equivalency program coupled with a job placement program is effective in curtailing delinquency among lower-class boys who have dropped out of school. Such a program is more effective than a high school equivalency program unsupported by a job-placement program. Either program is more effective than a traditional casework approach.
3. Cloward and Ohlin's theory of differential access to the opportunity structure is tentatively supported.

3. The poor performance of the casework groups confirms previous studies of casework ineffectiveness. *See,* for example, Powers and Witmer (1951); Meyer et al (1965); and Fischer (1973).

4. Increased access to the opportunity structure seems accompanied by a more positive self-image and allegiance to more 'approved' reference groups.
5. Additional research is necessary to define the independent and/or dependent effects of these factors in controlling delinquency.

REFERENCES

Bordua, D. J. "A Critique of Sociological Interpretations of Gang Delinquency." *The Annals of the American Academy of Political and Social Science* 338 (November (1961): 120-36.

Cloward, Richard A., and Ohlin, Lloyd E. *Delinquency and Opportunity: A Theory of Delinquent Gangs.* New York: Free Press, 1960.

Elliott, D. S. "Delinquency and Perceived Opportunity." *Sociological Inquiry* 32 (Spring 1962): 216-27.

Fischer, J. "Is Casework Effective? A Review." *Social Work* 18 (January 1973): 5-20.

Fredericks, Marcel A., and Molnar, Martin. "Relative Occupational Anticipations and Aspirations of Delinquents and Non-delinquents." *Journal of Research in Crime and Delinquency* 6 (1969): 1-7.

Himelhoch, J. "Delinquency and Opportunity: An End and a Beginning of Theory." In *Applied Sociology,* edited by Alvin Gouldner and S.M. Miller, pp. 189-207. New York: Free Press, 1965.

Landis, Judson R., and Scarpitti, Frank R. "Perceptions Regarding Value Orientation and Legitimate Opportunity: Delinquents and Non-Delinquents." *Social Forces* 44 (1965): 83-91.

Landis, Judson R.; Dinitz, Simon; and Reckless, Walter C. "Differential Perceptions of Life Chances: A Research Note." *Sociological Inquiry* 34 (Winter 1964): 60-66.

Matza, D. *Delinquency and Drift.* New York: John Wiley & Sons, 1964.

Merton, R. K. *Social Theory and Social Structure.* Glencoe, Illinois: Free Press, 1957. Revised and enlarged edition.

Meyer, Henry J.; Borgatta, Edgar; and Jones, Wyatt. *Girls at Vocational High: An Experiment in Social Work Intervention.* New York: Russell Sage Foundation, 1965.

Powers, Edwin, and Witmer, Helen. *An Experiment in the Prevention of Delinquency: The Cambridge-Somerville Youth Study.* New York: Columbia University Press, 1951.

Shaw, C. R. *The Jack-Roller.* Chicago: University of Chicago Press, 1930.

———. *The Natural History of a Delinquent Career.* Chicago: University of Chicago Press, 1931.

Shaw, Clifford R., and McKay, Henry D. *Juvenile Delinquency and Urban Areas.* Chicago: University of Chicago Press, 1942.

Shaw, Clifford R.; Zorbaugh, Frederick M.; McKay, Henry D.; and Cottrell, Leonard S. *Delinquency Areas.* Chicago: University of Chicago Press, 1929.

Short, James F., Jr.; Rivera, Ramon; and Tennyson, Ray A. "Perceived Opportunities, Gang Membership and Delinquency." *American Sociological Review* 30 (February 1965): 56-67.

MARTIN R. HASKELL

Toward a Reference Group Theory
of Delinquency

Merton's (1957) typology of modes of individual adaptation ... [furnishes]
us with a comprehensive outline of the forms that deviant behavior can take.
Cloward (1959) contributes toward an extension of the theory of social
structure and anomie by emphasizing the existence of differential systems
of opportunity and of variations in access to them.

Shaw and McKay (1942), reporting on a study which covered twenty
cities and tens of thousands of juvenile delinquents found that delinquency
rates were highest in the slum areas of every city studied. Cohen (1955)
provides a partial explanation of this phenomenon by demonstrating the
existence of a delinquent subculture in the slum areas of a big city. In his
more recent work on deviant-behavior as interaction process, Cohen (1959)
makes a further contribution toward a general theory of deviance-conformity
by analyzing the choices available to the individual confronted with socially
structured strain.

We know, then, that the highest delinquency rates are found in the slums
of our big cities and that a delinquent subculture is found in the same slums.
The probability is, however, that a majority of the boys in those areas do
not participate in delinquent acts. In most families of delinquent boys in
these areas there are nondelinquent siblings. How can we account for this
differential response? Furthermore, juvenile delinquency occurs in middle-

Source: Haskell, Martin R. "Toward a Reference Group Theory of Juvenile Delinquency."
Social Problems 8, 3 (Winter 1960-61): 220–226, 230. Permission granted by The
Society for the Study of Social Problems and the author.

class areas relatively free of the delinquent subculture described by Cohen and on occasion sons of middle-class parents participate in delinquent behavior. How can we account for delinquency in middle-class areas? How can we account for differential response in middle-class families?

In this paper an attempt will be made to formulate a reference group theory which will provide answers to these questions. The participation in a delinquent act will be explained in terms of the identification of the actor with some group and the application of the norms of that group in a given situation. . . .

The author of this paper was placement director of Berkshire Farm for Boys, a residential treatment school for adolescent delinquent boys for three years ending July 1, 1960. In charge of the after-care program in New York City, he had access to case histories including data obtained prior to institutionalization, institutional history, and experiences upon return to New York City. His duties involved him in group therapy and role training sessions with boys and members of their families (1959). There were seventy boys given after-care supervision during the three-year period.

Observations and insights derived from working with these boys and their families provide support for a reference group theory of delinquent behavior. . . . The . . . theory . . . will be stated as a series of seven statements or propositions in an effort to answer the question: how does the individual become committed to delinquency?

Proposition 1. The family is the first personal reference group of the child. The concept personal reference group is borrowed from Jennings (1953). In her terms, a psyche group is one in which the individual as a person receives sustenance, recognition, approval, and appreciation for just being "himself." It consists of those persons with whom the individual wants to associate in a person to person way and with whom he values emotional relationships. A socio group is one in which the individual's efforts and ideals are focused toward objectives which are not his alone. Concerns must be shared and obligations held in common. It is a psyche group that is the personal reference group of the individual. The family is the first such group of which he is a member. How long it remains his personal reference group may depend on how well it performs the functions referred to above.

Proposition 2. The family is a normative reference group. By normative group we mean one whose norms conform to those of the larger society. A reference group is a group in which the individual is motivated to gain or maintain membership. The individual therefore holds attitudes to conform with his perception of consensus. When a membership group becomes a reference group it performs a normative function and may also perform a comparison function (Kelley, 1952).

A normative reference group as used in this paper is a reference group whose norms conform to those of the larger society. The family is such a group. It is generally ranged on the side of order and the parents function as agents of society in transmitting the culture to the child. Even in families with criminal parents the child is encouraged by the parents to conform to the norms of the society and is punished for deviation.

Many writers have discussed the relationship between social class and delinquency. Delinquency rates in lower-class families are found to be higher than those in middle-class families and the following explanations are usually offered to account for this fact:

1. Differences in family structure. There are more one-parent families in the lower class because there are more unmarried mothers, more divorces, and more separations. Such families often have a woman at the head of them and lack a father image. In those families that are not on relief, the mother goes to work leaving the children with an aged grandmother, other relatives, or neighbors. The families are for large parts of the day, "no parent" families.
2. Differences in values. Middle-class families place greater emphasis on educational and occupational goals and reward achievement in these areas. Differences in sex norms, attitudes toward property, and fighting are also frequently mentioned.

Less than twenty-five percent of the Berkshire Farm boys on after-care in New York City were members of families which included a father. All but one or two of the families would be classified as lower-class, applying the ususal objective criteria. Depth interviews with parents of Berkshire Farm boys on after-care revealed that unpleasant contacts with police, truant officers, schools, and courts were commonly experienced. Parents repeatedly referred to the inconveniences and hardships they suffered as a result of the delinquency of their sons. Disciplinary action they had taken to get boys to go to school, stay away from gangs, and obey various laws including beatings, withholding of privileges, restriction of movement, and complaints to police and children's court. In only one instance did a parent express approval of a delinquent act of a boy or defend his delinquent behavior.

In group and individual sessions boys spontaneously identified the views of parents as opposed to truancy, fighting, stealing, destruction and other forms of delinquent behavior. Each reported some punitive action taken by parents when delinquent behavior came to their attention. Diagnoses of family difficulties led to the therapeutic objective of making parents less punitive.

It is generally recognized that in the middle-class family parents exert pressure on their children to conform to the norms of the larger society. With respect to the legal norms of the larger society the lower-class families of

Berkshire Farm boys also apply sanctions to enforce conformity. The difference, if any, is probably one of degree. The family, middle-class or lower-class is a normative group and as long as it remains a reference group of the boy it is a normative reference group.

Proposition 3. Prior to his participation in a delinquent act a street group has become a personal reference group of the delinquent boy. The term "street group" is used instead of "gang" to indicate amorphous character, lack of structure, and the fact that the group need *not* be committed to a delinquent subculture. Berkshire Farm boys trace their earliest meaningful peer group relationships to street groups, ranging from three to 12 in number, with which they identified from the time they were nine to 11 years of age. It was in concert with one or more boys from such a street group that each participated in his first delinquent act. . . .

Proposition 4. The street group that becomes the personal reference group of the lower-class boy in New York City has a delinquent subculture. The lower-class boys in the Berkshire Farm after-care program expressed attitudes and values similar to those described by Cohen in *Delinquent Boys.* Two boys from middle-class neighborhoods, while associated with street groups, did not express such attitudes toward property, stealing, or truancy.

Proposition 5. A boy, for whom a street group is a personal reference group is likely, in the dynamic assessment preceding a delinquent act, to decide in favor of the delinquent act. The street group, whether or not it has a delinquent subculture, has no clearly defined objectives and engages in a considerable amount of experimental behavior, some of which is delinquent. Once the street group has become his personal reference group a boy needs the approval of the others. The boys in his personal reference group who are with him at the time of the act will exercise an important influence upon the outcome of his assessment. He cannot afford to have them regard him as "punking out" or "chicken." In all probability he will participate in the delinquent act.

Proposition 6. The individual tends as a member of a personal reference group to import into its context attitudes and ways of behaving which he is currently holding in socio-group life. Important studies in intergenerational conflict in families of immigrants illustrate the fact that children acquire attitudes and ways of behaving in school and in other socio groups and bring these attitudes into the home. The result in immigrant families has been the rejection of parental norms and values (Thomas and Znaniecki, 1927). The same process appears to be operating in our lower-class families. Applying the standards learned in school the lower-class boy will find his parents on the low end of the scale in education, occupation, and morals. Importing these attitudes into the home leads him to reject his parents and tends to neutralize the normative influence which they exercise.

An illustration in terms of Merton's modes of individual adaptation may clarify the process. In our society money and success are culture goals. Institutionalized means for attaining them are education, work, and thrift. In the family, a normative group, the boy will learn both the culture goals and the institutionalized means. The family is his personal reference group and his initial adaptation is conformity. If, in socio groups, he learns that the culture goals are unattainable and the institutionalized means available to him are unacceptable he may choose the adaptation of "rebellion." Delinquent boys who chose this form of adaptation are probably the core members and leaders of gangs. If, in socio groups the culture goals are reinforced and the institutionalized means are found to be unacceptable, the boy may choose the adaptation of "innovation." Delinquent boys who chose this form of adaptation are probably peripheral members of gangs.

Innovators and rebels bring attitudes and ways of behaving into the home which cause conflict with normative members of their families. Their newly acquired attitudes cause them to reject the goals and means advocated by their parents and their deviations meet with disapproval. We can see how this can lead the boy to the street and to delinquency.

The same process may lead away from delinquency. The gang member who is an "innovator" accepts the culture goals of money and success. He rejects the institutionalized means of the larger society and substitutes means institutionalized in his delinquent personal reference group, the gang. These approved means may include stealing, gambling, and fighting. Satisfying relationships in a work group, a normative socio group, may influence the development of new attitudes and ways of behaving. As he desires acceptance in the work group he tends to assimilate the sentiments and values of the prestigeful stratum. These sentiments and values oppose stealing, gambling, and fighting, the means approved in his gang. He may carry back to the gang the new attitudes and ways of behaving.

Thomas and Znaniecki (1927) and others have demonstrated that this process operates when the family is the personal reference group and the school is the normative socio group. Case histories of Berkshire Farm boys on after-care indicate that this process operates when a street group is the personal reference group and a work group or some other group is the normative socio group. Boys who were successful in such socio groups as work or school groups resisted participation in delinquent acts even when in the company of members of their street groups. They tended more and more to apply attitudes developed in the work group. Although virtually every boy had a truancy record before being sent to Berkshire Farm for Boys, 14 of the 39 boys on after-care who were employed attended evening high schools. School was accepted as a means of upward mobility and attitudes favorable to school attendance had been reinforced in the work group. Attitudes unfavorable to stealing were also carried from the work group to the street group. The cases of Jerry and Lefty following illustrate the application of this proposition.

Proposition 7. In a situation where the individual is a member of a norma-tive personal reference group and of a delinquent personal reference group satisfying relationships in normative socio groups will exercise a decisive influence against participation in a delinquent act. Forty-six of the Berkshire Farm boys on after-care in New York City were living with their immediate families. The families for these boys are here considered normative personal reference groups. Twenty-two of these boys were known to be members of gangs, street groups with delinquent subcultures. These boys will be con-sidered members of both delinquent personal reference groups and normative personal reference groups.

Defining a failure as a boy who has been reinstitutionalized by a court, Berkshire Farm has had ten failures in New York City during the three-year period from July, 1957 to July, 1960. Nine of the ten failures were members of both normative personal reference groups (families) and delinquent per-sonal reference groups (gangs). A comparison of the functioning in some normative socio groups of the nine gang boys who were failures with the thirteen who were not follows:

1A. Not one of the nine failures was employed at the time of his offense. Seven of them were unemployed more than half the year preceding the offenses and were not attending school.

1B. Of the 13 nonfailures, 11 expressed satisfaction with their jobs and had excellent work records. None of the 11 had been unemployed more than two months of the year and six of them had been on the same jobs for more than a year.

2A. Two of the nine failures were attending school and were subjects of repeated disciplinary action for truancy and bad conduct at school.

2B. One of the two nonfailures who attended school had an excellent school record and was working part time. The other had a poor record and was a frequent truant. Three of those working were attending evening school.

3A. None of the nine failures reported attendance at church or member-ship in a church group.

3B. Four of the nonfailures reported church attendance and two reported membership in church groups.

4A. Four of the nine failures were repeatedly running away from home. Parents of the other five complained about them for staying out late at night, stealing from other members of the family, and negativism.

4B. Parents of three of the nonfailures complained about them for staying out late and negativism. There were no complaints alleging theft. The parents of seven of the nonfailures praised them for honesty, cleanliness, material contributions to the family, and exerting a positive influence on younger siblings.

One may conclude from the above that the nonfailures had more satisfying relationships in work groups than the failures. They expressed greater job satisfaction and had far better work records. The number involved in school and church groups was too small for generalization; however, more non-failures than failures participated in these groups. The more favorable attitudes of parents may reflect the fact that behavioral norms were carried from the work group to the home and were reflected in behavioral changes that met with parental approval.

An examination of the case histories of the nine failures and the 13 nonfailures compared above reveals no significant differences in race, age, intelligence, family composition, or offenses leading to institutionalization. Two of the nonfailures and one of the failures were core members of gangs. The membership of the others was peripheral, involving limited identification and occasional participation in gang activities. Members of both groups had countless opportunities to participate in delinquent acts. An important difference between the failures and nonfailures is found in the more satisfying relationships in normative socio groups experienced by the nonfailures. This would indicate that satisying relationships in normative socio groups exercised the decisive influence against participation in delinquent acts. The cases of Teddy and Pedro cited below illustrate the application of this proposition.

Jerry—talking about a projected purse snatching.

I looked around for a week and couldn't find another job. I was ashamed to come and tell you because I promised not to quit the other job you got me. I had no money and I had nothing to eat that day. I waited for Phil and asked him for two dollars. We were walking along the park on 59th street. Phil said: "Two dollars are not going to help you. Look at those two handbags on the bench. Let's grab them and run for it. The two old ladies won't know what happened." I said no—I don't know why. It just didn't make sense. Here I have only two more years to finish high school. Things are "cool." I like things the way they are. I liked my old job. Maybe I'll get another one like it.

I went to see Jimmy. He bought me a meal and sent me down to see you this morning.

Teddy, who had been a war lord of a Brooklyn gang, discussing plans for a robbery.

The four of us were walking down the street and we started talking about robbing the candy store. Joe thought it was a good idea and they started to make plans. I told them I had to go and left. I knew they were going to rob the store and I wanted no part of it. I like my job—things are much better at home since I'm working. Why should I take a chance on something like that?

Pedro—describing a projected robbery.

We were just talking—when someone said: "This bookie that lives here has a lot of dough—a thousand dollars maybe. We can knock him over as he comes out of the house." I didn't like the idea. I'm working and doing all right. What would happen if I get caught. What would my girl say? I was scared. The cops were sure to pick me up for questioning if the robbery happened. I couldn't just take off and let them pull it. I said: "This guy won't have more than a few dollars. There are too many of us." My friend Louis took my side. We started to argue. There were 7 of us arguing. This bookie walked out, right between us and no one laid a hand on him.

Lefty—discussing the projected stealing of a car.

They wanted a car to go to Rockaway. Whenever they used to ask me if I was with them on something I always said yes. This time I said count me out. I'm doing all right on my job. I've only got two years to finish evening high school. Taking a car is crazy. If they get sore at me over this, the hell with them. I've got other friends.

In each of the situations described above, association with the street group had become less important to the boy. He was reluctant to jeopardize satisying relationships in normative socio groups. Attitudes and behaviors developed in those groups were carried over to the street group.

The family is almost universally opposed to a boy's affiliation with a street group. How then does a boy who is a member of a normative personal reference group, his family, become a member of a delinquent personal reference group, a street group with a delinquent subculture?

The following constitutes an attempt to explain this phenomenon:

1. The lower-class boy, a few years after he enters the school system, usually before he is ten years of age, becomes aware of the fact that, applying the standards of the educational system, his parents are failures. Their occupations are rated low, education considered poor, residence depreciated, and habits of dress, eating, and personal cleanliness portrayed as subnormal. The boy's resentment toward his parents grows. A father of one of the boys, a steamfitter, stated that his sons are ashamed of him. They consider his work dirty. Where and why, he asked, have they been taught to look down upon him? And by whom? It is no coincidence that virtually every boy in the program looks down upon the occupation of his father or mother. The two exceptions are from middle-class families.

2. The lower-class boy perceives of himself as unlikely to succeed at school. This confirms his feelings of inferiority and inadequacy. He accepts

the vague success goal imparted to him at school and correctly appraises the likelihood of his failure.

3. Other than the "success" goal, the lower-class boy acquires no realistic goal of any kind. It is amazing how many will reply "I don't know" to the question, "What do you want to be?" Each boy knows that he is not likely to become president, governor, an industrialist, or a member of any of the professions or occupations viewed with favor in his classroom or in his text books. He knows that he can become a worker of some sort, but finds this sort of endeavor viewed as inferior by his middle-class school system.

4. The boy in the lower-class family perceives of himself as viewed with disfavor at home because he consumes without contributing. Time and again boys say that they are accused of eating too much, being too hard on clothes, spending too much, etc.

5. The boy, whether in a lower-class or middle-class family, is objectively inferior to the adults in the family in earnings, skills, and prestige. As a result he tends to perceive himself as generally inferior. He acquires feelings of social competence only as a result of experiences in which he has produced intended effects on other people: making them respond, obtaining expressions of affection, having expressions of affection, and giving advice which is accepted. Failing to experience feelings of social competence in the family confirms feelings of inferiority and leads the individual to seek other groups in which he can succeed.

6. The boy, lower-class or middle-class, who fails to acquire feelings of social competence in the family and does not derive satisfactions in normative socio groups such as work or school groups, gravitates to the street for a great deal of his social life.

7. On the street he finds others who, like himself, have been unsuccessful in experiencing social competence in the family or anywhere else. These boys usually lack any relationships in normative socio groups. If a street group is already in existence the boy we have described tries to join it. If he is accepted; if he wins recognition, approval, and appreciation; if here he can make others respond and occasionally have his advice accepted; the group becomes his personal reference group. If the group has a delinquent subculture he has become a member of a delinquent personal reference group....

REFERENCES

Cloward, Richard A. "Illegitimate Means, Anomie, and Deviant Behavior." *American Sociological Review* 24 (April 1959): 164–176.

Cohen, Albert K. *Delinquent Boys: The Culture of the Gang*. Glencoe, Illinois: Free Press, 1955.

_____. "The Study of Social Disorganization and Deviant Behavior." In *Sociology Today*, edited by R. K. Merton, L. Broom, and L. S. Cottrell, pp. 461–84. New York: Basic Books, 1959.

Haskell, Martin R. "Role Training and Job Placement of Adolescent Delinquents: The Berkshire Farm After-Care Program." *Group Psychotherapy* (September 1959): 250–257.

Jennings, Helen H. "Sociometric Structure in Personality and Group Formation." In *Group Relation at the Crossroads,* edited by Muzafer Sherif and M. O. Wilson, pp. 332–63. New York: Harper & Row, 1953.

Kelley, Harold H. "Two Functions of Reference Groups." In *Readings in Social Psychology,* edited by G. E. Swanson, T. M. Newcomb and E. L. Hartley, pp. 410–14. New York: Henry Holt, 1952.

Merton, Robert K. *Social Theory and Social Structure.* Glencoe, Illinois: Free Press, 1957.

Shaw, Clifford R., and McKay, Henry D. *Juvenile Delinquency and Urban Areas.* Chicago: University of Chicago Press, 1942.

Thomas, William I., and Znaniecki, Florian. *The Polish Peasant in Europe and America.* New York: Knopf, 1927.

ELLIOT LIEBOW

Talley's Corner: The Subculture
of Black Streetcorner Men

This study . . . [is] primarily concerned with the inside world of the streetcorner Negro man, the world of daily, face-to-face relationships with wives,
children, friends, lovers, kinsmen, and neighbors. An attempt . . . [is] made
to see the man as he sees himself, to compare what he says with what he does,
and to explain his behavior as a direct response to the conditions of lower-
class Negro life rather than as mute compliance with historical or cultural
imperatives. . . .

The data were collected during twelve months of intensive participant
observation in 1962 and on a more intermittent basis through the first six
months of 1963. They span the four seasons of the year and all hours of
the day and night.

The great bulk of the material is drawn from two dozen Negro men who
share a corner in Washington's Second Precinct as a base of operations. These
men are unskilled construction workers, casual day laborers, menial workers
in retailing or in the service trades, or are unemployed. They range in age
from the early twenties to the middle forties. Some are single, some married
men; some of the latter are living with their wives and children, some not. . . .

[The] inside world [of streetcorner men] does not appear as a self-
contained, self-generating, self-sustaining system or even subsystem with clear

boundaries marking it off from the larger world around it. It is in continuous, intimate contact with the larger society—indeed, is an integral part of it—and is no more impervious to the values, sentiments, and beliefs of the larger society than it is to the blue welfare checks or to the agents of the larger society, such as the policeman, the police informer, the case worker, the landlord, the dope pusher, the Tupperware demonstrator, the numbers backer, or the anthropologist.

One of the major points of articulation between the inside world and the larger society surrounding it is in the area of employment. The way in which the man makes a living and the kind of living he makes have important consequences for how the man sees himself and is seen by others; and these, in turn, importantly shape his relationships with family members, lovers, friends, and neighbors.

Making a living takes on an overriding importance at marriage. The young, lower-class Negro gets married in his early twenties, at approximately the same time and in part for the same reason as his white or Negro working- or middle-class counterpart. He has no special motive for getting married; sex is there for the taking, with or without marriage, and he can also live with a woman or have children—if he has not done this already—without getting married. He wants to be publicly, legally married, to support a family and be the head of it, because this is what it is to be a man in our society, whether one lives in a room near the Carry-out or in an elegant house in the suburbs.

Although he wants to get married, he hedges on his commitment from the very beginning because he is afraid, not of marriage itself, but of his own ability to carry out his responsibilities as husband and father. His own father failed and had to "cut out," and the men he knows who have been or are married have also failed or are in the process of doing so. He has no evidence that he will fare better than they and much evidence that he will not. However far he has gone in school he is illiterate or almost so; however many jobs he has had or hard he has worked, he is essentially unskilled.[1] Armed with models who have failed, convinced of his own worthlessness, illiterate and unskilled, he enters marriage and the job market with the smell of failure all around him. Jobs are only intermittently available. They are almost always menial, sometimes hard, and never pay enough to support a family.

In general, the menial job lies outside the job hierarchy and promises to offer no more tomorrow than it does today. The Negro menial worker remains a menial worker so that, after one or two or three years of marriage and as many children, the man who could not support his family from the very beginning is even less able to support it as time goes on. The longer he works, the longer he is unable to live on what he makes. He has little

---

1. And he is black. Together, these make a deadly combination and relegate him to the very bottom of our society.

vested interest in such a job and learns to treat it with the same contempt held for it by the employer and society at large. From his point of view, the job is expendable; from the employer's point of view, he is. For reasons real or imagined, perhaps so slight as to go unnoticed by others, he frequently quits or is fired. Other times, he is jobless simply because he cannot find a job.

He carries this failure home where his family life is undergoing a parallel deterioration. His wife's adult male models also failed as husbands and fathers and she expects no less from him. She hopes but does not expect him to be a good provider, to make of them a family and be head of it, to be "the man of the house." But his failure to do these things does not make him easier to live with because it was expected. She keys her demands to her wants, to her hopes, not to her expectations. Her demands mirror the man both as society says he should be and as he really is, enlarging his failure in both their eyes.

Sometimes he sits down and cries at the humiliation of it all. Sometimes he strikes out at her or the children with his fists, perhaps to lay hollow claim to being man of the house in the one way left open to him, or perhaps simply to inflict pain on this woman who bears witness to his failure as a husband and father and therefore as a man. Increasingly he turns to the streetcorner where a shadow system of values constructed out of public fictions serves to accommodate just such men as he, permitting them to be men once again provided they do not look too closely at one another's credentials.[2]

At the moment his streetcorner relationships take precedence over his wife and children he comes into his full inheritance bequeathed him by his parents, teachers, employers, and society at large. This is the step into failure from which few if any return, and it is at this point that the rest of society can wring its hands or rejoice in the certain knowledge that he has

2. This "shadow system" of values is very close to Hyman Rodman's "value stretch." Members of the lower-class, he says, "share the general values of the society with members of other classes, but in addition they have stretched these values, or developed alternative values, which help them adjust to their deprived circumstances" (Rodman, 1963:209).

I would add at least two qualifications to Rodman's and other formulations that posit an alternate system of lower-class values. The first is that the stretched or alternative value systems are not the same order of values, either phenomenologically or operationally, as the parent or general system of values: they are derivative, subsidiary in nature, thinner and less weighty, less completely internalized, and seem to be value images reflected by forced or adaptive behavior rather than real values with a positive determining influence on behavior of choice. The second qualification is that the alternative value system is not a distinct value system which can be separately invoked by its users. It appears only in association with the parent system and is separable from it only analytically. Derivative, insubstantial, and co-occurring with the parent system, it is as if the alternative value system is a shadow cast by the common value system in the distorting lower-class setting. Together, the two systems lie behind much that seems paradoxical and inconsistent, familiar and alien, to the middle-class observer from his one-system perspective.

ended up precisely as they had predicted he would.

The streetcorner is, among other things, a sanctuary for those who can no longer endure the experience or prospect of failure. There, on the streetcorner, public fictions support a system of values which, together with the value system of society at large, make for a world of ambivalence, contradiction and paradox, where failures are rationalized into phantom successes and weaknesses magically transformed into strengths. On the streetcorner, the man chooses to forget he got married because he wanted to get married and assume the duties, responsibilities and status of manhood; instead, he sees himself as the "put-upon" male who got married because his girl was pregnant or because he was tricked, cajoled, or otherwise persuaded into doing so. He explains the failure of his marriage by the "theory of manly flaws." Conceding that to be head of a family and to support it is a principal measure of a man, he claims he was too much of a man to be a man. He says his marriage did not fail because he failed as breadwinner and head of the family but because his wife refused to put up with his manly appetite for whiskey and other women, appetites which rank high in the scale of shadow values on the streetcorner. . . .[3]

[The] . . . streetcorner world does not at all fit the traditional characterization of the lower-class neighborhood as a tightly knit community whose members share the feeling that "we are all in this together." Nor does it seem profitable . . . to look at it as a self-supporting, on-going social system with its own distinctive "design for living," principles of organization, and system of values.

. . . Marriage among lower-class Negroes, for example, has been described as "serial monogamy," a pattern in which the woman of childbearing age has a succession of mates during her procreative years. The label "serial monogamy" clearly has a cultural referent, deriving as it does from the traditional nomenclature used to designate culturally distinctive patterns of marriage, such as polygyny, polyandry, monogamy, and so on. "Serial monogamy," then, as against the unqualified monogamous ideal of American society at large, refers to and *is used as evidence for* the cultural separateness and distinctiveness of the urban, lower-class Negro.

When these same phenomena are examined directly in the larger context of American life, both "serial monogamy" and cultural distinctiveness tend to disappear. In their place is the same pattern of monogamous marriage found elsewhere in our society but one that is characterized by failure. The woman does not have a simple "succession of mates during her procreative years." She has a husband and he a wife, and their hopes and their intentions—if not their expectations—are that this will be a durable, per-

3. "The behaviors of lower-class persons which are considered deviant, either by the members of their own groups or by the larger society, can be regarded as efforts to attain some sense of valid identity, as efforts to gratify the prompting of needs from inside and to elicit a response of recognition as valid persons from those around them" (Rainwater, 1965).

manent union. More often, however, it is their fears rather than their hopes which materialize. The marriage fails and they part, he to become one of a "succession of mates" taken by another woman whose husband has left her, and she to accept one or more men. While these secondary and subsequent liaisons are, for the most part, somewhat pale reflections of the formal marriage relationship, each is modeled after it and fails for much the same reasons as does marriage itself. From this perspective, then, the succession of mates which characterizes marriage among lower-class Negroes does not constitute a distinctive cultural pattern "with an integrity of its own." It is rather the cultural model of the larger society as seen through the prism of repeated failure. Indeed, it might be more profitable ... to look on marriage here as a succession of failures rather than as a succession of mates.[4]

... From this perspective, the streetcorner man does not appear as a carrier of an independent cultural tradition. His behavior appears not so much as a way of realizing the distinctive goals and values of his own subculture, or of conforming to its models, but rather as his way of trying to achieve many of the goals and values of the larger society, of failing to do this, and of concealing his failure from others and from himself as best he can.[5]

... [Thus,] many similarities between the lower-class Negro father and son (or mother and daughter) do not result from "cultural transmission" but from the fact that the son goes out and independently experiences the same failures, in the same areas, and for much the same reasons as his father. What appears as a dynamic, self-sustaining cultural process is, in part at least, a relatively simple piece of social machinery which turns out, in rather mechanical fashion, independently produced look-alikes.

4. "It is important that we not confuse basic life chances and actual behavior with basic cultural values and preferences.... The focus of efforts to change should be on background conditions and on precipitants of the deviant behaviors rather than on presumably different class or cultural values" (Lewis, 1963:43).

5. "... concealment and ego-protection are of the essence of social intercourse" (Hughes, 1958:43).

REFERENCES

Hughes, Everett C. *Men and Their Work*. Glencoe, Illinois: Free Press, 1958.

Lewis, Hylan. "Culture, Class and the Behavior of Low Income Families." Paper prepared for Conference on Views of Lower-Class Culture. New York: June 27-19, 1963 (Mineo)

Rainwater, Lee. "Work and Identity in the Lower Class." Paper prepared for Washington University Conference on Planning for the Quality of Human Life, April, 1965 (Mineo)

Rodman, Hyman. "The Lower-Class Value Stretch." *Social Forces* 42 (December 1963): 205–15.

PART FIVE

Social and Cultural Support in Learning Deviant Behavior

The selection of a reference group sympathetic to the problems of adjustment that attend frustrated achievement is a concept that is central to anomie theory. Social and cultural support theorists focus on the learning processes that occur in such associations. According to this perspective, deviant and conforming behavior alike is learned in intimate interaction within groups characterized by an excess of definitions either favorable or unfavorable to violation of the law (Sutherland, 1947). By differentially associating with those demonstrating a preponderance of deviant norms, individuals acquire the techniques, drives, motives, attitudes, and rationalizations conducive to nonconformity. Depending upon the frequency, duration, and the priority of these associations in an individual's life cycle, along with the intensity of associational ties, persons will develop varying levels of commitment to deviant careers.

One of the most basic forms of learning is imitation. Children's play, mob violence, and even procreation are exemplary of the imitative nature of human action (Tarde, 1928). David Phillips investigates the role of imitation in "The Influence of Suggestion on Suicide." Immediately following newspaper reports of self-inflicted death, the incidence of suicide increases. In imitation of the behavior of others, therefore, persons will construct their own lines of action.

"The Professional Thief," as depicted by Edwin Sutherland, illustrates succinctly the process of associational learning in the case of crime. Professional theft is a group way of life. As such, it includes the relevant techniques for committing the crime, behavioral codes, the award of status, traditions, normative consensus, and organization. Becoming a thief necessitates association with and recognition by other thieves. Through selection and tutelage, individuals acquire the norms, values, and behavior patterns essential for a career as a professional.

The importance of a supportive learning environment in the development and maintenance of deviant behavior is also the focus of Howard Becker's study, "Becoming a Marihuana User." The regular use of marihuana must be preceded by interaction with others more familiar with the drug. As a result of this participation, the novice acquires the proper techniques for smoking the substance and an ability to recognize its intoxicating effects. More importantly, the initiate learns to define these new experiences as pleasurable. Intense thirst, hunger, dizziness, and nausea, as well as fear of insanity, are sensations that, under most circumstances, individuals would seek to avoid. Through association with veteran users, however, these states are redefined as enjoyable and, therefore, worthy of cultivation. Curiosity or peer pressure may have led to the initial experiment with majihuana. Continued use requires both familiarity with the proper methods and internalization of the appropriate attitudes. These are secured only through the processes of social interaction.

While persons may be associating in groups where deviant or delinquent norms prevail, they are also members of a larger society. As such, they are aware of the stigma attached to nonconformity. Before they can engage in a deviant act, therefore, they must be able to redefine the behavior in more acceptable terms. An important element of differential association concerns the acquisition of verbalized rationalizations that neutralize societal condemnation (Sutherland, 1947; Sykes and Matza, 1957). Donald Cressey's study of the violation of trust, "Other People's Money: Violators' Vocabularies of Adjustment," demonstrates the effects of such rationalization techniques in facilitating criminal behavior.

Violation of trust, or embezzlement, occurs when an employee perceives a financial problem that can only be solved through illegitimate means. In order to do so, the eventual offender must be able to view the behavior as essentially noncriminal, justifiable under the circumstances, or as part of a general irresponsibility. Such rationalizations are readily available in the social environment of the employee. Tales of the situations of previous trust violators provide the vocabulary necessary for the present offense. In this manner, the embezzler becomes capable of illegitimate action.

Cressey has argued that prior to engaging in deviant behavior, persons must be able to neutralize the threat to self-concept posed by deliberate nonconformity. When deviance is accidental or ascribed, neutralization techniques are employed to de-discredit an already stigmatized status. This is the focus of Zachary Gussow and George Tracy's "Status, Ideology, and Adaptation to Stigmatized Illness: A Study of Leprosy."

Individuals diagnosed as having this disease are required to maintain residence in or near the one leprosarium or several out-patient clinics nation-wide. Given the physical proximity of these patients and the frequency of interaction, there has emerged a subculture wherein is found an ideology designed to attenuate the stigma attached to the disease.

Popular conceptions of leprosy include notions of maximal physical disability and extreme contagion. In addition, it is a disease typically associated with unsanitary conditions and biblical warnings concerning the wages of sin. The diagnosis, therefore, constitutes a serious assault upon the self. While an individual may believe that he has not changed as a person, he knows that others regard him as totally different. To defend against self- and other-stigmatization, patients have developed a stigma theory, a system of explanations that permit the patient to minimize the seriousness of the illness and mitigate, therefore, the consequences of the label.

The search for positive self-evaluation is continuous. Conformer and deviant alike require interaction with significant others who satisfy this need. This assumption lies at the heart of social and cultural support theory and has been central to several of the selections discussed thus far. Studies of professional theft, marihuana smoking, trust violation, and even physical disability point to the salience of the reference group in redefining the disvalued behavior in more positive terms. It is conceivable, then, that association in deviant or criminal groups not only provides the skills but, through its effects on self-concept, the motivation necessary for sustained nonconformity. If individuals perceive rejection from the larger society, they may turn to those who are more rewarding of the behavior or attributes in question. In this supportive learning environment, the maintenance of deviance is virtually assured.

The relationships among commitment to nonconformity, psychological adjustment, and the support of significant others are addressed in Sue Hammersmith and Martin Weinberg's "Homosexual Identity: Commitment, Adjustment, and Significant Others." Commitment to homosexuality is an important determinant of psychological well-being. This commitment may either produce a tendency to seek out the support of significant others or is a product of such support. Most likely, both processes operate simultaneously. The support one receives from referent others shapes the level of homosexual commitment, while at the same time, increased commitment influences the selection of particular referents and the importance attached to their evaluations.

As indicated earlier, persons are not only members of deviant groups, but occupy statuses and roles in the larger society as well. The nature of this social bond is such that the greater the attachment to conforming others, commitment to conventional lines of action, and involvement with legitimate activities (Hirschi, 1969), the less likely it is that deviant associations will produce nonconformity. Conversely, when normative ties are weakened, the behavioral impact of deviant associations will increase.

In "Affective Ties and Delinquency," Eric Linden and James Hackler explore this issue in an analysis of deviant and conforming ties in the case of delinquency. Juveniles with diminished attachments to conventional others and strong ties to deviant peers are most likely to be involved in delinquent behavior. Those whose social ties are exclusively normative, on the other hand, are least often delinquent. Association in deviant groups, therefore, is not in itself a determinant of nonconformity. Rather, such associations will produce deviant behavior to the extent that bonds to conventional society have been weakened or truncated.

Human behavior develops in reference to one's network of significant others. Individuals, that is, will adopt as their own those norms and values that earn them the acceptance of persons to whom they look for reward. If the behaviors prescribed by one's associations are defined as illegitimate in the dominant social order, deviance or criminality will be the outcome.

Since society is heterogeneous, it is inevitable that the standards of some groups will be censured by others. In this instance, nonconformity is a product of the learning opportunities available to the numerous substrata in the population. In addition, however, deviant associations may be the only support system available to those whose characteristics or behaviors have elicited rejection from the more respectable segments of society. Isolated from conventional ties, the socially stigmatized may turn to those similarly rejected for the support that is essential for positive self-evaluation. It is at this point that the social and cultural support approach expands anomie theory's treatment of the subculture. Through association with others whose adaptation to status loss is a subcultural one, persons will acquire the skills, values, and rationalizations that further confirm them in their illegitimate activities.

REFERENCES

Hirschi, Travis. *Causes of Delinquency.* Los Angeles: University of California Press, 1969.
Sutherland, Edwin H. *Principles of Criminology.* Philadelphia: J. B. Lippincott, 1947.
Sykes, Gresham M. and Matza, David. "Techniques of Neutralization: A Theory of Delinquency." *American Sociological Review* 22 (1957): 664-70.
Tarde, Gabriel. *Penal Philosophy.* Boston: Little, Brown and Co., 1928.

DAVID PHILLIPS

The Influence of Suggestion on Suicide

Two hundred years ago, Goethe wrote a novel called *The Sorrows of the Young Werther,* in which the hero committed suicide. Goethe's novel was read widely in Europe, and it was said that people in many countries imitated Werther's manner of death. According to Goethe, "My friends . . . thought that they must transform poetry into reality, imitate a novel like this in real life and, in any case, shoot themselves; and what occurred at first among a few took place later among the general public. . . ." (Goethe, quoted in Rose, 1929:24.) Widespread imitation of Werther's suicide was never conclusively demonstrated, but authorities were sufficiently apprehensive to ban the book in several areas, including Italy (Gray, 1967), Leipzig, and Copenhagen (Rose, 1929). . . .

The dearth of studies linking suicide and suggestion is somewhat puzzling, in view of the general importance ascribed to contagion and suggestion in other areas of sociology (Blumer, 1955; Cantril, 1963; Toch, 1965; Klapp, 1969; Lang and Lang, 1961). . . . In this paper, I will use American and British statistics to show that the number of suicides increases after the story of a suicide is publicized in the newspapers.[1] It seems appropriate to call

1. Some authors (for example, Meerloo, 1968:82–90; Motto, 1967) have noted in passing that suicides increased after Marilyn Monroe's death, but they were not prompted by this observation to examine systematically the suicide level after many publicized suicides.

Source: Phillips, David. "The Influence of Suggestion on Suicide: Substantive and Theoretical Implications of the Werther Effect." *American Sociological Review* 39, 3 (1974): 340–347, 353–354. Permission granted by The American Sociological Association and the author.

this increase in suicides "the Werther effect," after Goethe's hero. I will show that this effect is probably due to the influence of suggestion on suicide. . . .

INCREASE IN NATIONAL SUICIDES AFTER A PUBLICIZED SUICIDE

A list of postwar suicides publicized in the newspapers was generated from *Facts on File,* a general index to world news. The *New York Times Index* was then used to determine a subset of particularly publicized suicides, namely, those appearing on the front page of the *New York Times.* The *New York Times,* was used because it is the only U. S. daily newspaper with a large circulation (averaging about 700,000, 1950-1970) and an index covering the entire postwar period. Later in this investigation, the *New York Daily News* (the most popular U. S. newspaper), the *Chicago Tribune,* and the *London Daily Mirror* will also be examined.

National postwar suicide statistics are available for each month during the period 1946-1968. These statistics can be used to determine the effect of front-page suicides during the period 1947-1967. If front-page suicides stimulate a rise in national suicides, this increase can be detected by a technique developed in an earlier paper (Phillips and Feldman, 1973). The use of this technique can be illustrated in the case of Daniel Burros, a leader of the Ku Klux Klan who committed suicide on November 1, 1965 when the newspapers revealed that he was Jewish. In the month after Burros' death, November of 1965, 1,710 suicides were recorded. There were 1,639 suicides in November of the previous year (1964) and 1,665 suicides in November of the subsequent year (1966). The average, $(1,639 + 1,665)/2 = 1,652$ can be taken as an estimate of the number of suicides expected in November of 1965, under the null hypothesis that Burros' death had no effect on national suicides. It can be seen that this method of estimating the expected number of suicides controls for the effects of the seasons on suicide and for the existence of linear trends over time in the level of suicide. Because the observed number of suicides in November 1965 (1,710) is greater than the number expected (1,652) there was a rise in suicides just after Daniel Burros killed himself.[2]

In general, the above procedure was used to estimate the effect of front-page suicides. However, in some instances, the following modifications were required.

1) Burros' suicide occurred in November of 1965, and November of 1964 and 1966 were used as control months to estimate the effect of Burros'

2. One might wish to examine the increase in the suicide rate in the month after the story, rather than the increase in the number of suicides. Unfortunately, one cannot indulge this wish because the necessary data are lacking. To calculate the suicide rate in the month after a story, one would need monthly population figures; and these are generally unknown, or estimated only.

death. However, if another front-page suicide had occurred in November of 1966 it would be inappropriate to use this as one of the control months. Instead, November of 1967 would be a more appropriate choice.

2) If Burros' suicide had been discussed on November 30, 1965 instead of on November 1, it would be inappropriate to seek the effects of Burros' death in November; instead, December would be a more appropriate choice. In general, if the *Times* discussed a front-page suicide late in a month (after the 23rd), the month after the *Times* story was examined. The 23rd was chosen as a cut-off point because it was arbitrarily assumed that the effect of a front-page story would last only two weeks. This implies that a front-page story will have its major effect primarily in the month of the story, if the story appears on or before the 23rd of the month. Otherwise, the greatest effect of the front-page story will be in the month after the story....

Table 1 gives the number of U. S. suicides observed after a front-page suicide, and the number expected under the null hypothesis that front-page suicides have no effect on the level of national suicides. It can be seen that suicides increase after twenty-six front-page stories, and decrease after seven of them. Given the null hypothesis the probability of twenty-six or more suicide peaks out of thirty-three is .00066 (binomial test, p = .5; n = 33; $X \geqslant 26$).[3]

In the next section, I will show that the Werther effect is probably caused by the effect of suggestion on suicide.

3. This probability, calculated from the binomial distributions (p = .5; $X \geqslant 26$; n = 33), holds only if one assumes independence among the thirty-three successive suicide rises. Because of the logic of statistical testing, one can never prove that these thirty-three rises are mutually independent. The most one can do is test for dependence amongst the thirty-three observations and, if one finds none, assume independence amongst them. Accordingly, the Von Neumann test for serial correlation (Von Neumann et at., 1941) was used to test for dependence; no evidence of dependence was found and independence was assumed. The Von Neumann test was originally designed for observations drawn from an underlying normal distribution, and one cannot assume that my observations are drawn from such a distribution. However, Phillips and Chase (1969) have shown statistically that the Von Neumann test can be used for other distributions as well. For a more detailed discussion of the problem of dependence, see Phillips (1970).

Another, related problem must also be considered before the binomial test can be applied meaningfully to the results in Table 1. Exactly the same suicide data are used to determine whether suicides rise after Burros' death and to determine whether they rise after Morrison's death. Obviously, it would be inappropriate to count the same suicide rise twice in determining the statistical significance of my findings, because this would make the statistical significance artificially high. Hence, for the purposes of significance testing, the Burros and Morrison suicide stories have been treated as one story; and the rise in suicides after Burros and Morrison killed themselves has been counted only once. For similar reasons, the Graham and Ward suicide stories, which occurred on the same date, have been treated as one story only. Thus, although there are thirty-five suicide stories described in Table 1, they have been treated as thirty-three stories to ensure that the statistical significance of the results in Table 1 is not artificially high.

CAUSES OF THE WERTHER EFFECT

In attempting to determine the causes of the Werther effect, I will ... show that the available evidence is consistent with the effect of suggestion on suicide. . . .

Timing of the Werther Effect with Respect to
Newspaper Stories on Suicide.

If the Werther effect is caused by the publicizing of suicide stories, then the rise in the national suicide level should occur only *after* each suicide story appears. One cannot check this prediction as precisely as one would wish because U. S. suicide statistics are not tabulated by day of occurrence, only by month. Nonetheless, these monthly suicide statistics allow us to determine approximately whether suicide levels rise before or after suicide stories.

Figure 1 gives the rise in suicides in the month *before* the suicide story appears, in the month *when* it appears,[4] and in the months *thereafter*. As predicted, suicide levels are not higher than expected in the month before the stories appear; but they are considerably higher than expected in the month of the story and in the month thereafter. In these two months, the number of excess suicides is 2,034 (1275 + 759). This is an average of 58.1 (2,034/35) excess suicides per suicide story.

Of course, it is conceivable that some excess suicides in the month of the suicide story occur before that story appears. It is possible that suicides increase early in the month of a suicide story even though that story appears later in the month. This is unlikely, however, because of the following evidence. If suicides rise only *after* a story appears, then stories appearing late in the month should elicit a relatively small rise in suicides in the month *of* the story, and a relatively larger rise in suicides in the month *after* the story. Conversely, stories appearing early in the month should elicit a relatively large rise in suicides in the month of the story, and a relatively smaller rise in suicides in the month after the story.

These predictions are consistent with the available data: stories appearing on or before the 15th of the month elicit a total rise of 636 suicides in the month of the story and in the month thereafter. Ninety-eight percent of this rise (624/636) occurs in the month of the story. In contrast, stories

---

4. The total number of excess suicides in the month of the suicide story (1,275) is not equal to the sum of the excess suicides listed in Table 1 (1,298.5). This is because, in Table 1, the number of excess suicides was calculated sometimes for the month after the suicide story, and sometimes for the month of the story, depending on whether the story appeared late or early in the month.

Figure 1. Fluctuation in the Number of Suicides, Before, During and After the Month of the Suicide Story

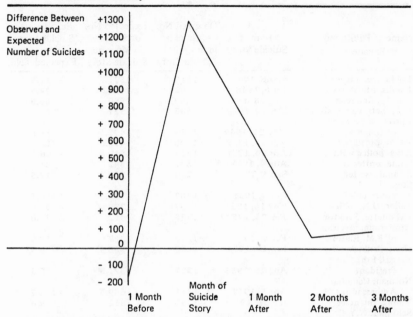

appearing after the 15th of the month elicit a rise of 1,398 suicides in the month of the story and in the month thereafter. Only forty-seven percent of this rise (651/1398) occurs in the month of the story.

Variation in the Size of the Werther Effect According to Amount of Newspaper Publicity

If the Werther effect is due to the influence of newspaper publicity on suggestible potential suicides, then the more publicity given to a story of suicide, the larger should be the rise in suicides after the appearance of that story. Thus, for example, the more days a suicide story appears on the front-page, the larger should be the rise in suicides after that story appears. Unfortunately, it is difficult to check this prediction with *New York Times* stories because the *Times* devoted more than one day of front-page space to only three suicides.[5] However, the *New York Daily News,* the most

5. These were Ward, Forrestal, and Schupler, who received two, three, and three days of coverage, respectively. On the average, the number of national suicides increased 100.3 in the month after each of these three committed suicide; while suicides increased by 33.2 after each of the remaining front page suicides listed in Table 1. One would expect this result if the Werther effect is caused by suggestion.

Table 1. Rise in the Number of U. S. Suicides after Suicide Stories Publicized on Page 1 of the *New York Times*

Name of Publicized Suicide	Date of Suicide Story	Observed No. of Suicides in Mo.[a] after Suicide Story	Expected No. of Suicides in Mo. after Suicide Story	Rise in U.S. Suicides after Suicide Story: Observed– Expected No.
Lockridge, author	Mar 8, 1948	1510	1521.5	- 11.5
Landis, filmstar	Jul 6, 1948	1482	1457.5	24.5
Brooks, financier	Aug 28, 1948	1250	1350	- 100.0
Holt, betrayed husband	Mar 10, 1949	1583	1521.5	61.5
Forrestal, Ex-Secretary of Defense	May 22, 1949	1549	1493.5	55.5
Baker, professor	Apr 26, 1950	1600	1493.5	106.5
Lang, police witness	Apr 20, 1951	1423	1519.5	- 96.5
Soule, professor	Aug 4, 1951	1321	1342	- 21.0
Adamic, writer	Sep 5, 1951	1276	1258.5	17.5
Stengel, N.J. police chief	Oct 7, 1951	1407	1296.5	110.5
Feller, U.N. official	Nov 14, 1952	1207	1229	- 22.0
LaFollette, Senator	Feb 25, 1953[b]	1435	1412	23.0
Armstrong, inventor of F.M. Radio	Feb 2, 1954	1240	1227	13.0
Hunt, Senator	Jun 20, 1954	1458	1368.5	89.5
Vargas, Brazilian President	Aug 25, 1954	1357	1321.5	35.5
Norman, Canadian Ambassador	Apr 5, 1957	1511	1649.5	- 138.5
Young, financier	Jan 26, 1958	1361	1352	9.0
Schupler, N.Y.C. councilman	May 3, 1958	1672	1587	85.0
Quiggle, Admiral	Jul 25, 1958	1519	1451	68.0
Zwillman, Underworld leader	Feb 27, 1959	1707	1609	98.0
Bang-Jensen, U.N. diplomat	Nov 27, 1959	1477	1423	54.0
Smith, police chief	Mar 20, 1960	1669	1609	60.0
Gedik, Turkish Minister	May 31, 1960	1568	1628.5	- 60.5
Monroe, filmstar	Aug 6, 1962	1838	1640.5	197.5
Graham, publisher Ward, implicated in Profumo Affair	Aug 4, 1963	1801	1640.5	160.5
Heyde & Tillman,[c] Nazi officials	Feb 14, 1964	1647	1584.5	62.5
Lord, N.J. Party chief	Jun 17, 1965	1801	1743	58.0
Burros, KKK Leader Morrison, war critic	Nov 1, 1965 Nov 3, 1965	1710	1652	58.0
Mott, American in Russian jail	Jan 22, 1966	1757	1717	40.0
Pike, son of Bishop Pike	Feb 5, 1966	1620	1567.5	52.5
Kravchenko, Russian defector	Feb 26, 1966	1921	1853	68.0
Lo Jui-Ching, Chinese Army leader	Jan 21, 1967	1821	1717	104.0
Amer, Egyptian Field Marshall	Sep 16, 1967	1770	1733.5	36.5
				1298.5

[a] For rules determining the month to be examined, see text.
[b] All February statistics have been normed for a month of 28 days.
[c] The suicides of Heyde and Tillman were discussed in the same suicide story.

Note: Source of Suicide statistics: U.S. Department of Health, Education, and Welfare, Public Health Service, *Vital Statistics of the U.S.*, Yearly Volumes, 1947–1968.

Table 2: Size of the Suicide Rise after a Suicide Story by Number of Days Devoted to the Story on the Front Page of the *New York Daily News*

Number of Days on Page 1 of the *News*	0[a]	1[b]	2[c]	3[d]	4[e]
Average rise in U.S. Suicides after each suicide story[f]	25.26	28.54	35.25	82.63	197.5

[a] The following suicide stories carried in the *New York Times* fall in this category: Lockridge, Baker, Lang, Soule, Armstrong, Hunt, Vargas, Norman, Zwillman, Gedik, Smith, Graham, Heyde, Tillman, Morrison, Kravchenko, Amer, Lo Jui-Ching.

[b] This category includes: Landis, Brooks, Forrestal, Stengel, Adamic, Feller, LaFollette, Bang-Jensen, Lord, Burros, Mott, Pike.

[c] This category includes Holt and Young.

[d] This category includes Schupler and Ward.

[e] This category includes Monroe.

[f] Ward and Graham died on the same date, August 4, 1963. Half the rise in suicides in August, 1963, has been credited to Ward, and half to Graham. A similar procedure has been followed for Heyde and Tillman, who died on February 14, 1964, and for Burros and Morrison, who died on November 1 and November 3, 1965.

Note: Source of suicide statistics: U.S. Department of Health, Education, and Welfare, Public Health Service, *Vital Statistics of the U.S.*, Yearly Volumes, 1947–1968.

popular daily newspaper in the U. S., can be used for this purpose. The thirty-five suicide stories on page one of the *New York Times* can be divided into five categories, according to the number of days they appear on the front-page of the *New York Daily News*. Table 2 shows that, as predicted, the more days a story appears on the front-page of the *News,* the larger the average rise in suicides after that story appears. The five categories in this table (0 day, 1 day, etc.) would be ranked in the predicted order by chance .0083 (1/120) of the time.

Table 2 implies that suicides increase more after stories publicized in the *Times* and in the *News* than they do after stories publicized in the *Times* alone. On the average, suicides rise by 22.03 in the month after stories publicized by the *Times* alone (those in category 0). Suicides increase an average of 51.3 after stories publicized in both the *Times* and the *News* (stories in categories 1–4). Of course, this result would be expected if the Werther effect is related to newspaper publicity.

Coverage in the *Times* and in the *News* might also be related to the size of the Werther effect in another way. If this effect is caused by the suggestive influences of newspaper publicity, then suicides that receive a great deal of

Table 3: The Percentage Rise in Suicides in New York City and in the Rest of the Country after Suicide Stories Publicized Mainly in New York City

Suicide Story	Percentage Rise in Suicides	$\dfrac{\text{Observed-Expected}}{\text{Expected}}$ x100
	In New York City	In Remainder of U.S.
Adamic	8.62	1.04
Stengel	13.33	7.97
Schupler	25.58	4.50
Lord	4.58	3.27

Note: Source of New York City suicides statistics: New York City, Department of Health, *Vital Statistics.*

Source of U.S. suicides statistics: U.S. Department of Health, Education, and Welfare, Public Health Service, *Vital Statistics of the U.S.*

publicity in New York City, but very little elsewhere, should elicit large increases in New York City suicide levels, and smaller increases in other parts of the United States. Unfortunately, suicide stories which grip the imagination of the New York public almost always interest the rest of the country as well. Only four suicides were publicized on page one of the *Times* and the *News* but were not publicized on the front-page of the *Chicago Tribune,* one of the largest U. S. newspapers outside New York City.[6]

Table 3 shows that after each of these four publicized suicides, the proportional rise in New York City suicides is greater than the proportional rise in the rest of the country. This result would occur by chance .062 of the time (Wilcoxon's matched pairs signed rank one-tailed test). This result is not statistically significant at the .05 level but is very nearly so. Consequently, one might find it instructive to collect additional data to examine the problem more extensively. If suicide stories generate a rise in suicides mainly in the area where they are most publicized, then two predictions can be made:

　　1) Suicide stories publicized in the U. S. but not in Great Britain should elicit larger rises in American suicides than in British suicides.

　　2) Suicide stories publicized in Britain should elicit larger rises in British suicides than stories not publicized in Britain.

6. The assumption that these four suicide stories were relatively unpublicized outside of New York City becomes even more plausible when we learn that all four suicides died in the New York City area and that three of the four were minor local political figures (Stengel, Lord, Schupler) unlikely to excite national interest. However, the fourth suicide (Adamic) did have some national reputation as a writer.

Table 4. Percentage Rise in Suicides in the U. S. and in Britain (England and Wales) after Suicide Stories always Publicized in the U. S. and Occasionally in Britain, 1956-1967

Suicide Story	Publi-cized in Britain	Percentage Rise in U.S. Suicides: Observed-Expected Expected	Percentage Rise in British Suicides: Observed-Expected Expected	Difference between Percentage Rise in U.S. & Percentage Rise in Britain, after Suicide Stories not Publicized in Britain
Norman	No	-8.40	- 2.63	- 5.77
Young	No	.66	-11.77	12.43
Schupler	No	5.36	.11	5.47
Quiggle	No	4.69	- 1.09	5.78
Zwillman	No	6.09	- 5.52	11.61
Bang-Jensen	No	3.79	-10.03	13.82
Smith	No	3.73	- 8.59	12.32
Gedik	No	-3.72	-13.23	9.51
Monroe	Yes	12.04	9.83	
Ward	Yes	9.78	17.26	
Heyde and Tillman	No	3.94	6.60	- 2.66
Lord	No	3.33	- 9.88	13.21
Burros and Morrison	No	3.51	- 6.75	10.26
Mott	No	2.33	- .85	3.18
Pike	No	3.35	12.04	- 8.69
Kravchenko	No	3.67	8.67	- 5.00
Lo Jui-Ching	No	6.06	- 2.06	8.12
Amer	No	2.11	- 3.96	6.07

Note: Source of U.S. suicide statistics: U.S. Department of Health, Education, and Welfare, Public Health Service, *Vital Statistics of the U.S.*

Source of British suicide statistics: Great Britain, General Register Office, *The Registrar General's Statistical Report for England and Wales.*

The most popular British daily newspaper, *The London Daily Mirror* (Newspaper Press Directory), was used as an indicator of the publicity given to a suicide story in Britain. It was assumed that a story covered by the *Mirror* received wide publicity in Britain, and that a story not covered by the *Mirror* received little or no publicity in Britain. Copies of the *Mirror* are available from 1956 in the Library of Congress. Table 4 indicates which of the suicide stories on the front-page of the *New York Times* (1956-1967) were also on the front-page of the *Mirror*. Table 4 also gives the size of the proportional rise in suicides after each suicide story, in the United States and in England and Wales.

As predicted, American suicides generally rise more than British suicides after a suicide story publicized in the U. S. but not in Britain. This result is significant at .005 (Wilcoxon matched pairs signed ranks test, one-tail). On the average, British suicides decreased by 2.72 percent after suicide stories not publicized in Britain. In contrast, suicides increased an average of 13.54 percent after the two stories that did appear on the front-page of the *Mirror*. These two, which are the most heavily publicized of all the stories in Table 4, produce the first and third largest rises in British suicide in that table. A result as extreme as this one would occur less than .025 of the time by chance (Mann-Whitney two sample U-Test). Thus, as predicted, the stories publicized in Britain produce significantly larger rises in British suicides than stories not publicized there.[7]

---

7. In this study, I have found no conclusive evidence that the means used by the publicized against the "suggestion hypothesis." However, failure to imitate one aspect of the front-page suicide need not imply that the front-page suicide is imitated in no respect whatever.

REFERENCES

Blumer, H. "Collective behavior." In *Principles of Sociology,* edited by A. M. Lee, pp. 167–222. New York: Barnes and Noble, 1955.

Cantril, H. *The Psychology of Social Movements.* New York: John Wiley & Sons, Inc., 1963.

Gray, R. *Goethe: A Critical Introduction.* Cambridge: Cambridge University Press, 1967.

Klapp, O. E. *Collective Search for Identity.* New York: Holt, Rinehart & Winston, Inc., 1969.

Lang, K., and Lang, G. E. *Collective Dynamics.* New York: Thomas Y. Crowell Co., 1961.

Meerloo, J. A. M. "Hidden suicide." In *Suicidal Behaviors,* edited by H. L. P. Resnik, pp. 82–9. Boston: Little Brown and Co., 1968.

Motto, J. A. "Suicide and suggestibility." *American Journal of Psychiatry* 124 (August 1967): 252–6.

Phillips, D. P., and Chase, G. A. "On the robustness of the Von Neumann test." Technical Report Number 115. Johns Hopkins University, Department of Statistics, 1969.

Phillips, D. P. Dying as a Form of Social Behavior. Unpublished doctoral dissertation. Princeton University, 1970.

Phillips, D. P., and Feldman, K. A. "A dip in deaths before ceremonial occasions: some new relationships between social integration and mortality." *American Sociological Review* 38 (December 1973): 678–96.

Rose, W. "Introduction." In *The Sorrows of Young Werther,* by J. W. von Goethe, pp. I–XXIX, translated by W. Rose. London: Scholastic Press, 1929.

Stengel, E. *Suicide and Attempted Suicide.* Baltimore: Penguin Books, 1964.

Toch, H. *The Social Psychology of Social Movements.* Indianapolis: Bobbs-Merrill Co., 1965.

United States Public Health Service. *Vital Statistics of the United States.* Yearly volumes, 1937-1968. Washington: Government Printing Office.

Von Neumann, J., et al. "The mean square successive difference." *Annals of Mathematical Statistics* 12 (1941): 153–62.

EDWIN H. SUTHERLAND

The Professional Thief

The principal part of this ... [work] is a description of the profession of
theft by a person who had been engaged almost continuously for more
than twenty years in that profession. . . .

His experiences were necessarily limited, and his point of view may have
been biased. In order to supplement his experiences and to correct a possible
bias, I submitted the manuscript to four other professional thieves and to two
former detectives. Without submitting the manuscript, I discussed the ideas
and problems with several other professional thieves, with several other
representatives of municipal and private police systems, and with clerks in
stores. From all these sources I secured oral or written comments. Furthermore, I have brought to bear on these problems all the available published
literature regarding professional thieves. . . .

The professional thief who described his profession was known as Chic
Conwell. He was born in Philadelphia about fifty years ago. His family was
in comfortable circumstances. In adolescence he was ushering in a theater,
formed an attachment for a chorus girl, married her, began to use narcotic
drugs occasionally in association with her, left home, and became a pimp. In
that occupation he became acquainted with thieves and through them learned
to steal. He worked during subsequent years as a pickpocket, shoplifter, and

Source: Sutherland, Edwin H. *The Professional Thief.* Chicago: University of Chicago
Press, 1937: v–viii, 197–198, 200–207, 209–214. Copyright © by The University of
Chicago Press. Permission granted.

confidence man. He stole in practically all of the American cities and many of the European cities. He lived in the underworld for twenty years and was thoroughly acquainted with it and with the techniques of many types of professional thieves.

In addition to several short terms in houses of correction, he served three terms in state and federal penitentiaries, with a total of about five years. The first term occurred soon after he became a professional thief and before he had perfected the techniques and connections which give relative immunity to professional thieves. The second imprisonment was a compromise required by the fact that a public official, who was indirectly involved in the same theft, had a more powerful claim for protection than did this thief. The third imprisonment was on a narcotic-drug charge. During the years between these prison terms, he was stealing almost continuously. Subsequent to his release after the third term he worked regularly at legitimate occupations, when he could find work, until his death in 1933, and during this time he did not use narcotic drugs.

Chic Conwell was an attractive person. A friend made the comment: "Chic was a confidence man and a good one. A good confidence man must have something lovable about him." He could have passed readily as a lawyer, a banker, or a merchant so far as personal appearance and casual conversation were concerned. He had the initiative, ingenuity, and abilities that are characteristic of leaders. He was near the top of his profession.

The profession of theft is more than isolated acts of theft frequently and skillfully performed. It is a group-way of life and a social institution. It has techniques, codes, status, traditions, consensus, and organization. It has an existence as real as that of the English language. It can be studied with relatively little attention to any particular thief. The profession can be understood by a description of the functions and relationships involved in this way of life. In fact, an understanding of this culture is a prerequisite to the understanding of the behavior of a particular professional thief....

THE PROFESSION OF THEFT AS A COMPLEX OF TECHNIQUES

The professional thief has a complex of abilities and skills, just as do physicians, lawyers, or bricklayers. The abilities and skills of the professional thief are directed to the planning and execution of crimes, the disposal of stolen goods, the fixing of cases in which arrests occur, and the control of other situations which may arise in the course of the occupation. Manual dexterity and physical force are a minor element in these techniques. The principal elements in these techniques are wits, "front," and talking ability. The thieves who lack these general abilities or the specific skills which are based on the general abilities are regarded as amateurs, even though they may steal habitually.[1] Also, burglars, robbers, kidnapers, and others who engage in the "heavy rackets" are generally not regarded as professional thieves, for they depend primarily on manual dexterity or force. A few criminals in the "heavy rackets" use their wits, "front," and talking ability, and these are regarded by the professional thieves as belonging to the profession.

The division between professional and nonprofessional thieves in regard to this complex of techniques is relatively sharp. This is because these techniques are developed to a high point only by education, and the education can be secured only in association with professional thieves; thieves do not have formal educational institutions for the training of recruits.[2] Also, these techniques generally call for cooperation which can be secured only in association with professional thieves. Finally, this complex of techniques represents a unified preparation for all professional problems in the life of the thief. . . .

THE PROFESSION OF THEFT AS STATUS

The professional thief, like any other professional man, has status. The status is based upon his technical skill, financial standing, connections, power, dress, manners, and wide knowledge acquired in his migratory life. His status is seen in the attitudes of other criminals, the police, the court officials, newspapers, and others. The term "thief" is regarded as honorific and is used regularly without qualifying adjectives to refer to the professional thief. It is so defined in a recent dictionary of criminal slang (Ersine, 1935): "Thief, *n.* A member of the underworld who steals often and successfully. This term is applied with reserve and only to habitual criminals. It is considered a high compliment."

Professional thieves are contemptuous of amateur thieves and have many epithets which they apply to the amateurs. These epithets include "snatch-and-grab thief," "boot-and-shoe thief," and "best-hold cannon." Professional thieves may use "raw-jaw" methods when operating under excellent protection, but they are ashamed of these methods and console themselves with the knowledge that they could do their work in a more artistic manner if necessary. They will have no dealings with thieves who are unable to use the correct methods of stealing. . . .

1. Several statistical studies of habitual thieves, defined in terms of repeated arrests, have been published. Some of these are excellent from the point of view of the problems with which they deal, but they throw little light on professional thieves because they do not differentiate professional thieves from other habitual thieves. *See* Grassberger, 1933; Beger, 1929; John, 1929.

2. Stories circulate at intervals regarding schools for pickpockets, confidence men, and other professional thieves. If formal schools of this nature have ever existed, they have probably been ephemeral.

THE PROFESSION OF THEFT AS CONSENSUS

The profession of theft is a complex of common and shared feelings, sentiments, and overt acts. Pickpockets have similar reactions to prospective victims and to the particular situations in which victims are found. This similarity of reactions is due to the common background of experiences and the similarity of points of attention. These reactions are like the "clinical intuitions" which different physicians form of a patient or different lawyers form of a juryman on quick inspection. Thieves can work together without serious disagreements because they have these common and similar attitudes. This consensus extends throughout the activities and lives of the thieves, culminating in similar and common reactions to the law, which is regarded as the common enemy. Out of this consensus, moreover, develop the codes, the attitudes of helpfulness, and the loyalties of the underworld.

The following explanation of the emphasis which thieves place on punctuality is an illustration of the way consensus has developed:

It is a cardinal principle among partners in crime that appointments shall be kept promptly. When you "make a meet" you are there on the dot or you do not expect your partner to wait for you. The reason why is obvious. Always in danger of arrest, the danger to one man is increased by the arrest of the other; and arrest is the only legitimate excuse for failing to keep an appointment. Thus, if the appointment is not kept on time, the other may assume arrest and his best procedure is to get away as quickly as possible and save his own skin. (Benton, 1936:269.)

One of the most heinous offenses that a thief can commit against another thief is to inform, "squeal," or "squawk." This principle is generally respected even when it is occasionally violated. Professional thieves probably violate the principle less frequently than other criminals for the reason that they are more completely immune from punishment, which is the pressure that compels an offender to inform on others. Many thieves will submit to severe punishment rather than inform. Two factors enter into this behavior. One is the injury which would result to himself in the form of loss of prestige, inability to find companions among thieves in the future, and reprisals if he should inform. The other is loyalty and identification of self with other thieves. The spontaneous reactions of offenders who are in no way affected by the behavior of the squealer, as by putting him in coventry, are expressions of genuine disgust, fear, and hatred. (Van Cise, 1936:321; Willard, 1899:23–24; 1908: 331–40.) Consensus is the basis of both of these reactions, and the two together explain how the rule against informing grows out of the common experiences of the thieves.

Consensus means, also, that thieves have a system of values and an *esprit de corps* which support the individual thief in his criminal career. The distress of the solitary thief who is not a member of the underworld society of criminals is illustrated in the following statement by Roger Benton (1936:62, 66-67, 80-81) at the time when he was an habitual but not a professional forger:

> I had no home, no place to which I could return for sanctuary, no friend in the world to whom I could talk freely.... I was a lone man, my face set away from those of my fellows. But I didn't mind—at least I didn't think I minded. [A little later he became acquainted in St. Louis with Nero's place, which was a rendezvous for theatrical people.] I liked Nero. I liked the crowd that gathered in his place and I wanted my evening entertainment there to continue. And I found that I was hungrier for human companionship than I had known. Here I found it.... It was a gay interlude and I enjoyed it thoroughly, and neglected my own work [forgery] while I played and enjoyed the simple, honest friendships of these children of the stage. [Still later.] I could not rid myself of the crying need for the sense of security which social recognition and contact with one's fellows and their approval furnishes. I was lonely and frightened and wanted to be where there was someone who knew me as I had been before I had become a social outcast.

Among the criminal tribes of India the individual was immersed almost completely in a consistent culture and felt no distress in attacking an outsider because this did not make him an enemy in any group which had significance for him. Nowhere in America, probably, is a criminal so completely immersed in a group that he does not feel his position as an enemy of the larger society. Even after Roger Benton became a member of the underworld as a professional forger, he felt lonely and ill at ease: "I was sick of the whole furtive business, of the constant need to be a fugitive among my fellows, of the impossibility of settling down and making a home for myself, and of the fear of imprisonment." (1936:242.)

The professional thief in America feels that he is a social outcast. This is especially true of the professional thieves who originated in middle-class society, as many of them did. He feels that he is a renegade when he becomes a thief. Chic Conwell states that the thief is looking for arguments to ease his conscience and that he blocks off considerations about the effects of his crimes upon the victims and about the ultimate end of his career. When he is alone in prison, he cannot refrain from thought about such things, and then he shudders at the prospect of returning to his professional activities. Once he is back in his group, he assumes the "bravado" attitudes of the other thieves, his shuddering ceases, and everything seems to be all right. Under the circumstances he cannot develop an integrated personality, but the distress is mitigated, his isolation reduced, and his professional life made possible because he has a group of his own in which he carries on a social existence as a thief, with a culture and values held in common by many thieves. In this sense, also, professional theft means consensus.

THE PROFESSION OF THEFT AS DIFFERENTIAL ASSOCIATION

Differential association is characteristic of the professional thieves, as of all other groups. The thief is a part of the underworld and in certain respects is segregated from the rest of society. His place of residence is frequently in the slums or in the "white-light" districts where commercial recreations flourish. Even when he lives in a residential hotel or in a suburban home, he must remain aloof from his neighbors more than is customary for city dwellers who need not keep their occupations secret. . . .

The final definition of the professional thief is found within this differential association. The group defines its own membership. A person who is received in the group and recognized as a professional thief is a professional thief. One who is not so received and recognized is not a professional thief, regardless of his methods of making a living.

Though professional thieves are defined by their differential association, they are also a part of the general social order. It would be a decided mistake to think of professional thieves as absolutely segregated from the rest of society. . . . The professional thief has the fundamental values of the social order in the midst of which he lives. The public patterns of behavior come to his attention as frequently as to the attention of others. He reads the newspapers, listens to the radio, attends the picture shows and ball games, and sees the new styles in store windows. He is affected just as are others by the advertisements of dentifrices, cigarettes, and automobiles. His interest in money and in the things that money will buy and his efforts to secure "easy money" fit nicely into the pattern of modern life. Though he has consensus within his own profession in regard to his professional activities, he also has consensus with the larger society in regard to many of the values of the larger society.

THE PROFESSION OF THEFT AS ORGANIZATION

Professional theft is organized crime. It is not organized in the journalistic sense, for no dictator or central office directs the work of the members of the profession. Rather it is organized in the sense that it is a system in which informal unity and reciprocity may be found. This is expressed in the *Report of the* [Chicago] *City. Council Committee on Crime* (p. 164) as follows:

While this criminal group is not by any means completely organized, it has many of the characteristics of a system. It has its own language; it has its own laws; its own history; its traditions and customs; its own methods and techniques; its highly specialized machinery for attack upon persons and particularly upon property; its own highly specialized modes of defense. These professional criminals have interurban, interstate, and sometimes international connections.

The complex of techniques, status, consensus, and differential association which have been described previously may be regarded as organization. More specifically, the organization of professional thieves consists in part of the knowledge which becomes the common property of the profession. Every thief becomes an information bureau. For instance, each professional thief is known personally to a large proportion of the other thieves, as a result of their migratory habits and common hangouts. Any thief may be appraised by those who know him, in a terse phrase, such as "He is O.K.," "He is a no-good bastard," or "Never heard of him." The residue of such appraisals is available when a troupe wishes to add a new member, or when a thief asks for assistance in escaping from jail.

Similarly, the knowledge regarding methods and situations becomes common property of the profession. "Toledo is a good town," "The lunch hour is the best time to work that spot," "Look out for the red-haired saleslady—she is double-smart," "See Skid if you should get a tumble in Chicago," "Never grift on the way out," and similar mandates and injunctions are transmitted from thief to thief until everyone in the profession knows them. The discussions in the hangouts keep this knowledge adjusted to changing situations. The activities of the professional thieves are organized in terms of this common knowledge.

Informal social services are similarly organized. Any thief will assist any other thief in a dangerous situation. He does this both by positive actions, such as warning, and by refraining from behavior that would increase the danger, such as staring at a thief who is working. Also, collections are taken in the hangouts and elsewhere to assist a thief who may be in jail or the wife of a thief who may be in prison. In these services reciprocity is assumed, but there is no insistence on immediate or specific return to the one who performs the service.

The preceding description of the characteristics of the profession of theft suggests that a person can be a professional thief only if he is recognized and received as such by other professional thieves. Professional theft is a group-way of life. One can get into the group and remain in it only by the consent of those previously in the group. Recognition as a professional thief by other professional thieves is the absolutely necessary, universal, and

definitive characteristic of the professional thief. This recognition is a combination of two of the characteristics previously described, namely, status and
differential association. A professional thief is a person who has the status of
a professional thief in the differential association of professional thieves.

Selection and tutelage are the two necessary elements in the process of
acquiring recognition as a professional thief. These are the universal factors
in an explanation of the genesis of the professional thief. A person cannot
acquire recognition as a professional thief until he has had tutelage in professional theft, and tutelage is given only to a few persons selected from the
total population.

Selection and tutelage are continuous processes. The person who is not a
professional thief becomes a professional thief as a result of contact with
professional thieves, reciprocal confidence and appreciation, a crisis situation,
and tutelage. In the course of this process a person who is not a professional
thief may become first a neophyte and then a recognized professional thief.
A very small percentage of those who start on this process ever reach the
stage of professional theft, and the process may be interrupted at any point
by action of either party.

Selection is a reciprocal process, involving action by those who are professional thieves and by those who are not professional thieves. Contact is
the first requisite, and selection doubtless lies back of the contacts. They may
be pimps, amateur thieves, burglars, or they may be engaged in legitimate
occupations as clerks in hotels or stores. Contacts may be made in jail or in
the places where professional thieves are working or are spending their leisure
time. If the other person is to become a professional thief, the contact must
develop into appreciation of the professional thieves. This is not difficult,
for professional thieves in general are very attractive. They have had wide
experience, are interesting conversationalists, know human nature, spend
money lavishly, and have great power. Since some persons are not attracted
even by these characteristics, there is doubtless a selective process involved
in this, also.

The selective action of the professional thieves is probably more significant
than the selective action of the potential thief. An inclination to steal is not
a sufficient explanation of the genesis of the professional thief. Everyone
has an inclination to steal and expresses this inclination with more or less
frequency and with more or less finesse. The person must be appreciated
by the professional thieves. He must be appraised as having an adequate
equipment of wits, front, talking ability, honesty, reliability, nerve, and
determination. The comparative importance of these several characteristics
cannot be determined at present, but it is highly probable that no characteristic is valued more highly than honesty. It is probably regarded as more
essential than mental ability. This, of course, means honesty in dealings
within their own group.

An emergency or crisis is likely to be the occasion on which tutelage begins. A person may lose a job, get caught in amateur stealing, or may need additional money. If he has developed a friendly relationship with professional thieves, he may request or they may suggest that he be given a minor part in some act of theft. He would, if accepted, be given verbal instructions in regard to the theory of the racket and the specific part he is to play. In his first efforts in this minor capacity he may be assisted by the professional thieves, although such assistance would be regarded as an affront by one who was already a professional. If he performs these minor duties satisfactorily, he is promoted to more important duties. During this proba- tionary period the neophyte is assimilating the general standards of morality, propriety, etiquette, and rights which characterize the profession, and he is acquiring "larceny sense." He is learning the general methods of disposing of stolen goods and of fixing cases. He is building up a personal acquaintance with other thieves, and with lawyers, policemen, court officials, and fixers. This more general knowledge is seldom transmitted to the neophyte as formal verbal instructions but is assimilated by him without being recognized as instruction. However, he is quite as likely to be dropped from participation in further professional activities for failure to assimilate and use this more general culture as for failure to acquire the specific details of the techniques of theft.

As a result of this tutelage during the probationary period, he acquires the techniques of theft and consensus with the thieves. He is gradually permitted into differential association with thieves and given tentative status as a professional thief. This tentative status under probation becomes fixed as a definite recognition as a professional thief. Thereby he enters into the systematic organization which constitutes professional theft.

REFERENCES

Beger, Fritz. *Die rückfälligen Betrüger.* Leipzig: E. Wiegandt, 1929.

Benton, Roger. *Where Do I Go From Here?* New York: Lee Furman, 1936.

Ersine, Noel. *Underworld and Prison Slang.* Upland, Indiana: A. D. Freese and Sons, 1935.

Grassberger, Roland. *Gewerbs—und Berufsverbrechertum in den Vereinigten Staaten von Amerika.* Vienna: J. Springer, 1933.

John, Alfred. *Die Rückfallsdiebe.* Leipzig: E. Wiegandt, 1929.

Report of the City Council Committee on Crime. Chicago.

Van Cise, Philip S. *Fighting the Underworld.* Boston: Houghton Mifflin, 1936.

Willard, Josiah Flynt. *Tramping with Tramps.* New York: Century, 1899.

———. *My Life.* New York: Baker, 1908.

HOWARD S. BECKER

Becoming a Marihuana User

The use of marihuana is and has been the focus of a good deal of attention on the part of both scientists and laymen. One of the major problems students of the practice have addressed themselves to has been the identification of those individual psychological traits which differentiate marihuana users from nonusers and which are assumed to account for the use of the drug. That approach, common in the study of behavior categorized as deviant, is based on the premise that the presence of a given kind of behavior in an individual can best be explained as the result of some trait which predisposes or motivates him to engage in the behavior (Marcovitz and Meyers, 1944; Gaskill, 1945; Charen and Perelman, 1946).

This study is likewise concerned with accounting for the presence or absence of marihuana use in an individual's behavior. It starts, however, from a different premise: that the presence of a given kind of behavior is the result of a sequence of social experiences during which the person acquires a conception of the meaning of the behavior, and perceptions and judgments of objects and situations, all of which make the activity possible and desirable. Thus, the motivation or disposition to engage in the activity is built up in the course of learning to engage in it and does not antedate this learning process. For such a view it is not necessary to identify those "traits" which "cause" the behavior. Instead, the problem becomes one of describing the

Source: Becker, Howard S. "Becoming a Marihuana User." *American Journal of Sociology* 59 (1953): 235–242. Copyright ©1953 by The University of Chicago Press. Permission granted.

set of changes in the person's conception of the activity and of the experience it provides for him (Mead, 1934:277-80).

This paper seeks to describe the sequence of changes in attitudes and experience which lead to *the use of marihuana for pleasure.* Marihuana does not produce addiction, as do alcohol and the opiate drugs; there is no withdrawal sickness and no ineradicable craving for the drug (cf. Adams, 1942). The most frequent pattern of use might be termed "recreational." The drug is used occasionally for the pleasure the user finds in it, a relatively casual kind of behavior in comparison with that connected with the use of addicting drugs. The term "use for pleasure" is meant to emphasize the noncompulsive and casual character of the behavior. It is also meant to eliminate from consideration here those few cases in which marihuana is used for its prestige value only, as a symbol that one is a certain kind of person, with no pleasure at all being derived from its use.

The analysis presented here is conceived of as demonstrating the greater explanatory usefulness of the kind of theory outlined above as opposed to the predispositional theories now current. This may be seen in two ways: (1) predispositional theories cannot account for that group of users (whose existence is admitted) (cf. Kolb, 1938; Bromberg, 1939) who do not exhibit the trait or traits considered to cause the behavior and (2) such theories cannot account for the great variability over time of a given individual's behavior with reference to the drug. The same person will at one stage be unable to use the drug for pleasure, at a later stage be able and willing to do so, and, still later, again be unable to use it in this way. These changes, difficult to explain from a predispositional or motivational theory, are readily understandable in terms of changes in the individual's conception of the drug as is the existence of "normal" users.

The study attempted to arrive at a general statement of the sequence of changes in individual attitude and experience which have always occurred when the individual has become willing and able to use marihuana for pleasure and which have not occurred or not been permanently maintained when this is not the case. This generalization is stated in universal terms in order that negative cases may be discovered and used to revise the explanatory hypothesis (Lindesmith, 1947:chap. 1).

Fifty interviews with marihuana users from a variety of social backgrounds and present positions in society constitute the data from which the generalization was constructed and against which it was tested. The interviews focused on the history of the person's experience with the drug, seeking major changes in his attitude toward it and in his actual use of it and the reasons for these changes. The final generalization is a statement of that sequence of changes in attitude which occurred in every case known to me in which the person came to use marihuana for pleasure. Until a negative case is found, it may be considered as an explanation of all cases of marihuana use for pleasure. In addition, changes from use to nonuse are shown to be related to similar changes in conception, and in each case it is possible to explain variations in the individual's behavior in these terms.

This paper covers only a portion of the natural history of an individual's use of marihuana, starting with the person having arrived at the point of willingness to try marihuana. He knows that others use it to "get high," but he does not know what this means in concrete terms. He is curious about the experience, ignorant of what it may turn out to be, and afraid that it may be more than he has bargained for. The steps outlined below, if he undergoes them all and maintains the attitudes developed in them, leave him willing and able to use the drug for pleasure when the opportunity presents itself.

I

The novice does not ordinarily get high the first time he smokes marihuana, and several attempts are usually necessary to induce this state. One explanation of this may be that the drug is not smoked "properly," that is, in a way that ensures sufficient dosage to produce real symptoms of intoxication. Most users agree that it cannot be smoked like tobacco if one is to get high:

> Take in a lot of air, you know, and . . . I don't know how to describe it, you don't smoke it like a cigarette, you draw in a lot of air and get it down in your system and then keep it there. Keep it there as long as you can.

Without the use of some such technique[1] the drug will produce no effects, and the user will be unable to get high:

> The trouble with people like that [who are not able to get high] is that they're just not smoking it right, that's all there is to it. Either they're not holding it down long enough, or they're getting too much air and not enough smoke, or the other way around or something like that. A lot of people just don't smoke it right, so naturally nothing's gonna happen.

If nothing happens, it is manifestly impossible for the user to develop a conception of the drug as an object which can be used for pleasure, and use will therefore not continue. The first step in the sequence of events that must occur if the person is to become a user is that he must learn to use the proper smoking technique in order that his use of the drug will produce some effects in terms of which his conception of it can change.

1. A pharmacologist notes that this ritual is in fact an extremely efficient way of getting the drug into the blood stream (Walton, 1938:48).

Such a change is, as might be expected, a result of the individual's participation in groups in which marihuana is used. In them the individual learns the
proper way to smoke the drug. This may occur through direct teaching:

> I was smoking like I did an ordinary cigarette. He said, "No, don't do it
> like that." He said, "Suck it, you know, draw in and hold it in your
> lungs till you . . . for a period of time."
> I said, "Is there any limit of time to hold it?"
> He said, "No, just till you feel that you want to let it out." So I did
> that three or four times.

Many new users are ashamed to admit ignorance and, pretending to know
already, must learn through the more indirect means of observation and
imitation:

> I came on like I had turned on [smoked marihuana] many times before,
> you know. I didn't want to seem like a punk to this cat. See, like I didn't
> know the first thing about it—how to smoke it, or what was going to
> happen, or what. I just watched him like a hawk—I didn't take my eyes
> off him for a second, because I wanted to do everything just as he did it.
> I watched how he held it, how he smoked it, and everything. Then when
> he gave it to me I just came on cool, as though I knew exactly what the
> score was. I held it like he did and took a poke just the way he did.

No person continued marihuana use for pleasure without learning a
technique that supplied sufficient dosage for the effects of the drug to
appear. Only when this was learned was it possible for a conception of the
drug as an object which could be used for pleasure to emerge. Without such a
conception marihuana use was considered meaningless and did not continue.

II

Even after he learns the proper smoking technique, the new user may not
get high and thus not form a conception of the drug as something which can
be used for pleasure. A remark made by a user suggested the reason for this
difficulty in getting high and pointed to the next necessary step on the
road to being a user:

> I was told during an interview, "As a matter of fact, I've seen a guy who
> was high out of his mind and didn't know it."
> I expressed disbelief: "How can that be, man?"
> The interviewee said, "Well, it's pretty strange, I'll grant you that, but
> I've seen it. This guy got on with me, claiming that he'd never got high,

one of those guys, and he got completely stoned. And he kept insisting that he wasn't high. So I had to prove to him that he was."

What does this mean? It suggests that being high consists of two elements: the presence of symptoms caused by marihuana use and the recognition of these symptoms and their connection by the user with his use of the drug. It is not enough, that is, that the effects be present; they alone do not automatically provide the experience of being high. The user must be able to point them out to himself and consciously connect them with his having smoked marihuana before he can have this experience. Otherwise, regardless of the actual effects produced, he considers that the drug has had no effect on him: "I figured it either had no effect on me or other people were exaggerating its effect on them, you know. I thought it was probably psychological, see." Such persons believe that the whole thing is an illusion and that the wish to be high leads the user to deceive himself into believing that something is happening when, in fact, nothing is. They do not continue marihuana use, feeling that "it does nothing" for them.

Typically, however, the novice has faith (developed from his observation of users who do get high) that the drug actually will produce some new experience and continues to experiment with it until it does. His failure to get high worries him, and he is likely to ask more experienced users or provoke comments from them about it. In such conversations he is made aware of specific details of his experience which he may not have noticed or may have noticed but failed to identify as symptoms of being high:

I didn't get high the first time. . . . I don't think I held it in long enough. I probably let it out, you know, you're a little afraid. The second time I wasn't sure, and he [smoking companion] told me, like I asked him for some of the symptoms or something, how would I know, you know. . . . So he told me to sit on a stool. I sat on—I think I sat on a bar stool—and he said, "Let your feet hang," and then when I got down my feet were real cold, you know.

And I started feeling it, you know. That was the first time. And then about a week after that, sometime pretty close to it, I really got on. That was the first time I got on a big laughing kick, you know. Then I really knew I was on.

One symptom of being high is an intense hunger. In the next case the novice becomes aware of this and gets high for the first time:

They were just laughing the hell out of me because like I was eating so much. I just scoffed [ate] so much food, and they were just laughing at me, you know. Sometimes I'd be looking at them, you know, wondering why they're laughing, you know, not knowing what I was doing. [Well, did they tell you why they were laughing eventually?] Yeah, yeah, I come back, "Hey, man, what's happening?" Like, you know, like I'd ask, "What's happening?" and all of a sudden I feel weird, you know. "Man, you're on, you know. You're on pot [high on marihuana]." I said, "No, am I?" Like I don't know what's happening.

The learning may occur in more indirect ways:

I heard little remarks that were made by other people. Somebody said, "My legs are rubbery," and I can't remember all the remarks that were made because I was very attentively listening for all these cues for what I was supposed to feel like.

The novice, then, eager to have this feeling, picks up from other users some concrete referents of the term "high" and applies these notions to his own experience. The new concepts make it possible for him to locate these symptoms among his own sensations and to point out to himself a "something different" in his experience that he connects with drug use. It is only when he can do this that he is high. In the next case, the contrast between two successive experiences of a user makes clear the crucial importance of the awareness of the symptoms in being high and reemphasizes the important role of interaction with other users in acquiring the concepts that make this awareness possible:

[Did you get high the first time you turned on?] Yeah, sure. Although, come to think of it, I guess I really didn't. I mean, like that first time it was more or less of a mild drunk. I was happy, I guess, you know what I mean. But I didn't really know I was high, you know what I mean. It was only after the second time I got high that I realized I was high the first time. Then I knew that something different was happening.
[How did you know that?] How did I know? If what happened to to me that night would of happened to you, you would've known, believe me. We played the first tune for almost two hours—one tune! Imagine, man! We got on the stand and played this one tune, we started at nine o'clock. When we got finished I looked at my watch, it's a quarter to eleven. Almost two hours on one tune. And it didn't seem like anything.
I mean, you know, it does that to you. It's like you have much more time or something. Anyway, when I saw that, man, it was too much. I knew I must really be high or something if anything like that could happen. See, and then they explained to me that that's what it did to you, you had a different sense of time and everything. So I realized that that's what it was. I knew then. Like the first time, I probably felt that way, you know, but I didn't know what's happening.

It is only when the novice becomes able to get high in this sense that he will continue to use marihuana for pleasure. In every case in which use continued, the user had acquired the necessary concepts with which to express to himself the fact that he was experiencing new sensations caused by the drug. That is, for use to continue, it is necessary not only to use the drug so as to produce effects but also to learn to perceive these effects when they occur. In this way marihuana acquires meaning for the user as an object which can be used for pleasure.

With increasing experience the user develops a greater appreciation of the drug's effects; he continues to learn to get high. He examines succeeding experiences closely, looking for new effects, making sure the old ones are still there. Out of this there grows a stable set of categories for experiencing the drug's effects whose presence enables the user to get high with ease.

The ability to perceive the drug's effects must be maintained if use is to continue; if it is lost, marihuana use ceases. Two kinds of evidence support this statement. First, people who become heavy users of alcohol, barbiturates, or opiates do not continue to smoke marihuana, largely because they lose the ability to distinguish between its effects and those of the other drugs.[2] They no longer know whether the marihuana gets them high. Second, in those few cases in which an individual uses marihuana in such quantities that he is always high, he is apt to get this same feeling that the drug has no effect on him, since the essential element of a noticeable difference between feeling high and feeling normal is missing. In such a situation, use is likely to be given up completely, but temporarily, in order that the user may once again be able to perceive the difference.

III

One more step is necessary if the user who has now learned to get high is to continue use. He must learn to enjoy the effects he has just learned to experience. Marihuana-produced sensations are not automatically or necessarily pleasurable. The taste for such experience is a socially acquired one, not different in kind from acquired tastes for oysters or dry martinis. The user feels dizzy; thirsty; his scalp tingles; he misjudges time and distances; and so on. Are these things pleasurable? He isn't sure. If he is to continue marihuana use, he must decide that they are. Otherwise, getting high, while a real enough experience, will be an unpleasant one he would rather avoid.

---

2. "Smokers have repeatedly stated that the consumption of whiskey while smoking negates the potency of the drug. They find it very difficult to get 'high' while drinking whiskey and because of that smokers will not drink while using the 'weed' " (cf. New York City Mayor's Committee on Marihuana, 1944:13).

The effects of the drug, when first perceived, may be physically unpleasant or at least ambiguous:

It started taking effect, and I didn't know what was happening, you know, what it was, and I was very sick. I walked around the room, walking around the room trying to get off, you know; it just scared me at first, you know. I wasn't used to that kind of feeling.

In addition, the novice's naïve interpretation of what is happening to him may further confuse and frighten him, particularly if he decides, as many do, that he is going insane:

I felt I was insane, you know. Everything people done to me just wigged me. I couldn't hold a conversation, and my mind would be wandering, and I was always thinking, oh, I don't know, weird things, like hearing music different. . . . I get the feeling that I can't talk to anyone. I'll goof completely.

Given these typically frightening and unpleasant first experiences, the beginner will not continue use unless he learns to redefine the sensations as pleasurable:

It was offered to me, and I tried it. I'll tell you one thing. I never did enjoy it at all. I mean it was just nothing that I could enjoy. [Well, did you get high when you turned on?] Oh, yeah, I got definite feelings from it. But I didn't enjoy them. I mean I got plenty of reactions, but they were mostly reactions of fear. [You were frightened?] Yes. I didn't enjoy it. I couldn't seem to relax with it, you know. If you can't relax with a thing, you can't enjoy it, I don't think.

In other cases the first experiences were also definitely unpleasant, but the person did become a marihuana user. This occurred, however, only after a later experience enabled him to redefine the sensations as pleasurable:

[This man's first experience was extremely unpleasant, involving distortion of spatial relationships and sounds, violent thirst, and panic produced by these symptoms.] After the first time I didn't turn on for about, I'd say, ten months to a year. . . . It wasn't a moral thing; it was because I'd gotten so frightened, bein' so high. An' I didn't want to go through that again, I mean, my reaction was, "Well, if this is what they call bein' high, I don't dig [like] it." . . . So I didn't turn on for a year almost, accounta that. . . .
Well, my friends started, an' consequently I started again. But I didn't have any more, I didn't have that same initial reaction, after I started turning on again.

[In interaction with his friends he became able to find pleasure in the effects of the drug and eventually became a regular user.]

In no case will use continue without such a redefinition of the effects as enjoyable.

This redefinition occurs, typically, in interaction with more experienced users who, in a number of ways, teach the novice to find pleasure in this experience which is at first so frightening (Charen and Perelman, 1946:679). They may reassure him as to the temporary character of the unpleasant sensations and minimize their seriousness, at the same time calling attention to the more enjoyable aspects. An experienced user describes how he handles newcomers to marihuana use:

Well, they get pretty high sometimes. The average person isn't ready for that, and it is a little frightening to them sometimes. I mean, they've been high on lush [alcohol], and they get higher that way than they've ever been before, and they don't know what's happening to them. Because they think they're going to keep going up, up, up till they lose their minds or begin doing weird things or something. You have to like reassure them, explain to them that they're not really flipping or anything, that they're gonna be all right. You have to just talk them out of being afraid. Keep talking to them, reassuring, telling them it's all right. And come on with your own story, you know: "The same thing happened to me. You'll get to like that after awhile." Keep coming on like that; pretty soon you talk them out of being scared. And besides they see you doing it and nothing horrible is happening to you, so that gives them more confidence.

The more experienced user may also teach the novice to regulate the amount he smokes more carefully, so as to avoid any severely uncomfortable symptoms while retaining the pleasant ones. Finally, he teaches the new user that he can "get to like it after awhile." He teaches him to regard those ambiguous experiences formerly defined as unpleasant as enjoyable. The older user in the following incident is a person whose tastes have shifted in this way, and his remarks have the effect of helping others to make a similar redefinition:

A new user had her first experience of the effects of marihuana and became frightened and hysterical. She "felt like she was half in and half out of the room" and experienced a number of alarming physical symptoms. One of the more experienced users present said, "She's dragged because she's high like that. I'd give anything to get that high myself. I haven't been that high in years."

In short, what was once frightening and distasteful becomes, after a taste for it is built up, pleasant, desired, and sought after. Enjoyment is introduced by the favorable definition of the experience that one acquires from others. Without this, use will not continue, for marihuana will not be for the user an object he can use for pleasure.

In addition to being a necessary step in becoming a user, this represents an important condition for continued use. It is quite common for experienced users suddenly to have an unpleasant or frightening experience, which they cannot define as pleasurable, either because they have used a larger amount of marihuana than usual or because it turns out to be a higher-quality marihuana than they expected. The user has sensations which go beyond any conception he has of what being high is and is in much the same situation as the novice, uncomfortable and frightened. He may blame it on an overdose and simply be more careful in the future. But he may make this the occasion for a rethinking of his attitude toward the drug and decide that it no longer can give him pleasure. When this occurs and is not followed by a redefinition of the drug as capable of producing pleasure, use will cease.

The likelihood of such a redefinition occurring depends on the degree of the individual's participation with other users. Where this participation is intensive, the individual is quickly talked out of his feeling against marihuana use. In the next case, on the other hand, the experience was very disturbing, and the aftermath of the incident cut the person's participation with other users to almost zero. Use stopped for three years and began again only when a combination of circumstances, important among which was a resumption of ties with users, made possible a redefinition of the nature of the drug:

It was too much, like I only made about four pokes, and I couldn't even get it out of my mouth, I was so high, and I got real flipped. In the basement, you know, I just couldn't stay in there anymore. My heart was pounding real hard, you know, and I was going out of my mind; I thought I was losing my mind completely. So I cut out of this basement, and this other guy, he's out of his mind, told me, "Don't, don't leave me, man. Stay here." And I couldn't.

I walked outside, and it was five below zero, and I thought I was dying, and I had my coat open; I was sweating, I was perspiring. My whole insides were all . . . , and I walked about two blocks away, and I fainted behind a bush. I don't know how long I laid there. I woke up, and I was feeling the worst, I can't describe it at all, so I made it to a bowling alley, man, and I was trying to act normal, I was trying to shoot pool, you know, trying to act real normal, and I couldn't lay and I couldn't stand up and I couldn't sit down, and I went up and laid down where some guys that spot pins lay down, and that didn't help me, and I went down to a doctor's office. I was going to go in there and tell the doctor to put me out of my misery . . . because my heart was pounding so hard, you know. . . . So then all weekend I started flipping, seeing things there and going through hell, you know, all kinds of abnormal things. . . . I just quit for a long time then.

[He went to a doctor who defined the symptoms for him as those of a nervous breakdown caused by "nerves" and "worries." Although he was no longer using marihuana, he had some recurrences of the symptoms which led him to suspect that "it was all his nerves."] So I just stopped worrying, you know; so it was about thirty-six months later I started making it again. I'd just take a few pokes, you know. [He first resumed use in the company of the same user-friend with whom he had been involved in the original incident.]

A person, then, cannot begin to use marihuana for pleasure, or continue its use for pleasure, unless he learns to define its effects as enjoyable, unless it becomes and remains an object which he conceives of as capable of producing pleasure.

IV

In summary, an individual will be able to use marihuana for pleasure only when he goes through a process of learning to conceive of it as an object which can be used in this way. No one becomes a user without (1) learning to smoke the drug in a way which will produce real effects; (2) learning to recognize the effects and connect them with drug use (learning, in other words, to get high); and (3) learning to enjoy the sensations he perceives. In the course of this process he develops a disposition or motivation to use marihuana which was not and could not have been present when he began use, for it involves and depends on conceptions of the drug which could only grow out of the kind of actual experience detailed above. On completion of this process he is willing and able to use marihuana for pleasure.

He has learned, in short, to answer "Yes" to the question: "Is it fun?" The direction his further use of the drug takes depends on his being able to continue to answer "Yes" to this question and, in addition, on his being able to answer "Yes" to other questions which arise as he becomes aware of the implications of the fact that the society as a whole disapproves of the practice: "Is it expedient?" "Is it moral?"[3] Once he has acquired the ability to get enjoyment out of the drug, use will continue to be possible for him. Considerations of morality and expediency, occasioned by the reactions of society, may interfere and inhibit use, but use continues to be a possibility

3. Another paper will discuss the series of developments in attitude that occurs as the individual begins to take account of these matters and adjust his use to them.

in terms of his conception of the drug. The act becomes impossible only when the ability to enjoy the experience of being high is lost, through a change in the user's conception of the drug occasioned by certain kinds of experience with it.

In comparing this theory with those which ascribe marihuana use to motives or predispositions rooted deep in individual behavior, the evidence makes it clear that marihuana use for pleasure can occur only when the process described above is undergone and cannot occur without it. This is apparently so without reference to the nature of the individual's personal makeup or psychic problems. Such theories assume that people have stable modes of response which predetermine the way they will act in relation to any particular situation or object and that, when they come in contact with the given object or situation, they act in the way in which their makeup predisposes them.

This analysis of the genesis of marihuana use shows that the individuals who come in contact with a given object may respond to it at first in a great variety of ways. If a stable form of new behavior toward the object is to emerge, a transformation of meanings must occur, in which the person develops a new conception of the nature of the object (cf. Strauss, 1952). This happens in a series of communicative acts in which others point out new aspects of his experience to him, present him with new interpretations of events, and help him achieve a new conceptual organization of his world, without which the new behavior is not possible. Persons who do not achieve the proper kind of conceptualization are unable to engage in the given behavior and turn off in the direction of some other relationship to the object or activity.

This suggests that behavior of any kind might fruitfully be studied developmentally, in terms of changes in meanings and concepts, their organization and reorganization, and the way they channel behavior, making some acts possible while excluding others.

REFERENCES

Adams, Roger. "Marihuana." *Bulletin of the New York Academy of Medicine* 18 (November 1942): 705-30.

Bromberg, Walter. "Marihuana: A Psychiatric Study." *Journal of the American Medical Association* 113 (July 1939): 11.

Charen, Sol., and Perelman, Luis. "Personality Studies of Marihuana Addicts." *American Journal of Psychiatry* 102 (March 1946): 674-82.

Gaskill, Herbert S. "Marihuana, an Intoxicant." *American Journal of Psychiatry* 102 (September 1945): 202-4.

Kolb, Lawrence. "Marihuana." *Federal Probation* 11 (July 1938): 22-25.

Lindesmith, Alfred R. *Opiate Addiction.* Bloomington: Principia Press, 1947.

Marcovitz, Eli, and Meyers, Henry J. "The Marihuana Addict in the Army." *War Medicine* 4 (December 1944): 382-91.

Mead, George Herbert. *Mind, Self and Society.* Chicago: University of Chicago Press, 1934.

New York City Mayor's Committee on Marihuana. *The Marihuana Problem in the City of New York.* Lancaster, Pennsylvania: Jacques Cattrell Press, 1944.

Strauss, Anselm. "The Development and Transformation of Monetary Meanings in the Child." *American Sociological Review* 17 (June 1952): 275-86.

Walton, R. P. *Marihuana: America's New Drug Problem.* Philadelphia: J. B. Lippincott, 1938.

DONALD R. CRESSEY

Other People's Money:
Violators' Vocabularies of Adjustment

[Two criteria for inclusion of cases in this investigation of embezzlement were established.] First, the person must have accepted a position of trust in good faith. This is almost identical with the requirement of the legal definition that the "felonious intent" in embezzlement must be formulated *after* the time of taking possession. All legal definitions are in agreement in this respect. Second, the person must have violated that trust by committing a crime. These criteria permit the inclusion of almost all persons convicted of embezzlement and larceny by bailee and, in addition, a proportion of those convicted of confidence game, forgery, and other offenses. Some of the offenses in each category are violations of positions of trust which were accepted in good faith. The phenomenon under investigation was therefore defined as "criminal violation of financial trust." . . .

The main source of direct information in regard to the behavior under scrutiny, now called "the criminal violation of financial trust," was interview material obtained in informal contacts with all prisoners whose behavior met the criteria and who were confined at the Illinois State Penitentiary at Joliet (April-September, 1949), the California Institution for Men at Chino (October-May, 1950-51), and the United States Penitentiary at Terre Haute, Indiana (June-August, 1951). In each institution the names of all inmates confined for offenses such as embezzlement, larceny by bailee, confidence game, forgery, uttering fictitious checks, conspiracy, grand theft (California),

Source: Cressey, Donald R. *Other People's Money*. Glencoe, Illinois: The Free Press, 1953:20, 22-25, 93-99, 174-77. Permission granted by the author.

theft of government property, falsification of a bill of lading used in interstate shipment, and theft of goods in interstate shipment was obtained. The personal file of each of 503 inmates was examined with the aim of screening out those cases which obviously did not meet the criteria. Official documents such as the "State's Attorney's Report," "The Attorney General's Report," presentence investigation reports, the prosecuting agency's report, and official commitment papers were heavily relied upon, but other documents, such as letters from former employers and from relatives and friends, newspaper clippings, and the prisoner's statement upon admission to the institution also were consulted. These documents revealed, as expected, that many cases did not meet the first criterion—acceptance of a position of trust in good faith—and these cases were not considered further. Whenever there was doubt, however, the case was kept in the list of eligible cases and later the subject was interviewed. . . .

In the interviews the subjects were never asked the question, "Did you accept your position of trust in good faith?" Instead, the interviewer prompted each subject to talk about the circumstances surrounding acceptance of the position of trust and the term of incumbency before violation, then waited for the subject to give the desired information spontaneously. The subjects did not know what the criteria were, and it was not until later that they learned that trust violators were the subject of the study. . . .

[Central to this study is the finding that those who engaged in violations of trust did so because of what they perceived to be a nonshareable financial problem, that is a problem which could not be dealt with through legitimate means. The focus of what follows is on the adjustive mechanisms that such persons employed in the application of illegitimate solutions to these problems.]

After a trusted person has defined a problem as nonshareable, the total pertinent situation consists of a problem which must be solved by an independent, secret, and relatively safe means by virtue of general and technical information about trust violation. In this situation the potential trust violator identifies the possibilities for resolving the problem by violating his position of trust and defines the relationship between the nonshareable problem and the illegal solution in language which enables him to look upon trust violation (a) as essentially noncriminal, (b) as justified, or (c) as a part of a general irresponsibility for which he is not completely accountable. . . .

We began using the "rationalization" terminology when it was discovered that the application of certain key verbalizations to his conduct enables the trusted person to "adjust" his conceptions of himself as a trusted person with his conceptions of himself as a user of entrusted funds for solving a nonshareable problem, but the use of the term in this way is not in keeping with popular usage or with usage by some sociologists, psychologists, and psychiatrists. An ordinary definition of the term indicates that rationalization takes place *after* the specific behavioral item in question has occurred. One buys an automobile and then "rationalizes" that he needs it because his health is poor. The notion here is that of an *ex post facto* justification for behavior which "has really been prompted by deeply hidden motives and unconscious tendencies." (Noyes, 1940:49; cf. Woodworth, 1940:537; Ruch, 1941:181.) But the term is also used to refer to a process of finding some logical excuse for questionable behavior tendencies (Richards, 1946:84), for thoughts as well as acts (Young, 1946:122), and for decisions to perform an act (LaPiere and Farnsworth, 1949:13).

In addition, a rationalization has been considered as a verbalization which purports to make the person's behavior more intelligible to others in terms of symbols currently employed by his group (Lindesmith and Strauss, 1949: 308). It follows from this kind of definition that the person may prepare his rationalization before he acts, or he may act first and rationalize afterward. In the cases of trust violation encountered, significant rationalizations were always present *before* the criminal act took place, or at least at the time it took place, and, in fact, after the act had taken place the rationalization often was abandoned. If this observation were generalized to other behavior we would not say that an individual "buys an automobile and then rationalizes," as in the example above, but that he buys the car because he is able to rationalize. The rationalization is his motivation (cf. Mills, 1940), and it not only makes his behavior intelligible to others, but it makes it intelligible to *himself.* . . .

[O]ne phase of the process which results in trust violation is the application, to the trusted person's own conduct, of language categories which enable him to adjust two rather conflicting sets of values and behavior patterns. But such verbalizations necessarily are impressed upon the person by other persons who have had prior experience with situations involving positions of trust and trust violation. Before they are internalized by the individual they exist as group definitions of situations in which crime is "appropriate." Contacts with such definitions obviously are necessary prior to their internalization as rationalizations. The following propositions, for example, are ideal-type definitions of situations in which trust violation is called for and which, hence, amount to ideologies which sanction the crime: "Some of our most respectable citizens got their start in life by using other people's money temporarily";[1] "In the real estate business there is nothing wrong about using deposits before the deal is closed"; "All people steal when they get in a tight spot."

The following propositions are the personalized versions of those definitions after they have been assimilated and internalized by an individual: "My intent is only to use this money temporarily so I am 'borrowing,' not

1. cf. Dumas, 1915:129–227, especially Act II: "What is business? That's easy. It's other people's money, of course."

'stealing' "; "My immediate use of real estate deposits is 'ordinary business' ";
"I have been trying to live an honest life but I have had nothing but troubles
so 'to hell with it.' " The individual in a specific, present, situation uses such
rationalizations in the adjustment of personal conflicting values, but the
use of the verbalization in this way is necessarily preceded by observation
of rather general criminal ideologies.

This point may be illustrated by citation.... [The case] demonstrates
well the significance of applying to one's own nonshareable problem situation
a rationalization which has been learned from others since in this case the
verbalization which made criminality seem somehow justified in his situation
apparently did not become available to the person until immediately prior
to the crime. A young drug addict accepted a porter's job in a retail concern,
was liked and admired by his employer, and soon was given the additional
duty of carrying the daily receipts to the bank for deposit. After some
prodding and encouragement by two associates, one of whom also was an
addict, he delivered the day's receipts to one of them, smeared his clothing
with mud, and reported to the police that he had been kidnapped and robbed.
When asked to explain his offense he said:

> Power of suggestion I guess. A couple of fellows suggested that it would
> be a good idea. If it hadn't been for the coaxing and reminding I don't
> think I would have done it. I didn't want to do it myself; I would have
> just forgot it if it was left up to me. I really don't want to say I was
> influenced because I have a mind of my own, but I know I wouldn't have
> attempted it alone because I thought a lot of my employer. *I had con-*
> *sidered it before but had never thought about how to get it or anything,*
> *so it didn't take much talking or persuasion.* Maybe my resistance was
> low because of my greed or something. It sounded so easy, and he ex-
> plained it so clearly that there wouldn't be much chance involved. I
> would be much better off. They presented it to me in such a form that it
> would be just like a gift. It was there. I knew it was a possibility and could
> be done. And then when I told X he wondered why I hadn't done it long
> before that. I had thought of it before, but I thought a lot of the man I
> worked for, so I didn't do anything about it, and didn't even think about
> it much. *He said I wouldn't lose my job and that my boss would think as*
> *much of me, and that it was the company's money and not the boss's,*
> *and that no one would know the difference. That sounded pretty good to*
> *me at the time, so I said that I would do it.*

We see then that, having general information about trust violation and
about the conditions under which trust violation occurs, the trust violator,
upon the appearance of the nonshareable problem, applies to his own situation
a rationalization which the groups in which he has had membership have

applied to the behavior of others, and which he himself has applied to the behavior of others. He perceives that the general rule applies to his specific case. Such an application to himself of the symbols held by the members of his groups has been described by Mead (1922:157-63; 1934:135-226) as taking the role of the "generalized other." Thus, the imagination of how he appears to others, and of how he would appear if his nonshareable problem were revealed to others is a controlling "force" in the behavior of the trusted person.

In a "non-shareable-problem—position-of-trust" situation trusted persons "objectify" their own actions to the extent that they place themselves in the place of another person or group of persons with the status of "trustee" and hypothesize their reactions. The hypothesized reactions to "borrowing" in order to solve a nonshareable problem, for example, are much different from hypothesized reactions to "stealing," and the trusted person behaves accordingly. Similarly, the hypothesized reactions to a conception of self as an "ill" person or as a "pressed" person have different implications for behavior than hypothesized reactions to a conception of self as a "criminal."[2]

It is because of hypothesized reactions which do not consistently and severely condemn his criminal behavior that the trusted person takes the role of what *we* have called the "trust violator."[3] *He* often does not think of

---

2. Although it was not in any way checked by her research, Redden offers the following hypothesis, based on Mead's distinction between the "I" and the "me," about the role-taking behavior of embezzlers. "In his rehearsal of consequences in the process of taking the role of another he [the embezzler] fails to integrate himself with the organized pattern of approved social behavior. He fails or refuses to try to devise a plan by reflective thinking which will increase his value to the organization and call forth recognition in terms of increased income. Thwarted in his attempt or impatient of the duration of time necessary to fulfill his wish on the socially desirable level, his mental activity is centered on a plan of borrowing, converting his employer's goods or money to his own use, to fulfill the wish for a margin above the equilibrium of income and cost of living to satisfy some latent desire in a minimum of time. He completes the act hypothetically, taking the role of another but contrary to the common organized pattern of social behavior in business relationships and in the social group. His hypothetical solution may be a new technique or method which if discovered by the employer would mean dismissal from his employ and community disapproval. His mental activity is in opposition to the organized sets of attitudes of the social group. The two aspects of the self of the embezzler are in conflict, the social or impersonal self integrates the hypothetical act with the organized social behavior of the group by naming the act resulting from the proposed plan borrowing, with intent to replace or repay; the other aspect of self, the personal or a-social, views his plan as opposed to organized social behavior, independent of the group and unknown to the group." (Redden, 1939:27-29)

3. In this connection, we shall see later that when the long-term violator who has convinced himself that he is a "borrower" decides that he is "in too deep" the attitudes of his group toward "embezzlement" and "crime" can no longer be avoided, and his behavior takes on the characteristics of the role which he *then* conceives of himself as playing. Similarly, we shall see that while there exists in most groups in our culture a

himself as playing that role, but often thinks of himself as playing a role
such as that of a special kind of "borrower," "businessman," or even "thief."
In order to do so, he necessarily must have come into contact with a culture
which defined those roles for him. If the roles were defined differently in
his culture, or if he had not come into contact with the group definitions,
he would behave differently.

The rationalizations used by trust violators, then, reflect contacts with
cultural ideologies which themselves are contradictory to the theme that
honesty is expected in all situations of trust.[4] When used by the individual,
such ideologies adjust contradictory personal values in regard to criminality
on the one hand and integrity, honesty, and morality on the other.[5]

rather general condemnation of "trust violation" or "stealing" this condemnation is
not as general when the "mitigating circumstances" are known. That is, some categories
of criminal behavior are not as severely or consistently condemned as others. The trust
violator behaves according to the cultural definitions of those categories.

4. "When rationalizations are extensively developed and systematized as group doctrines
and beliefs, they are known as ideologies. As such, they acquire unusual prestige and
authority. The person who uses them has the sense of conforming to group expectations,
of doing the 'right thing.' . . . Unscrupulous and sometimes criminal behavior in business
and industry is justified in terms of an argument which begins and ends with the assertion
that 'business is business.' . . . The principal advantage of group rationalizations or
ideologies, from the individual's standpoint, is that they give him a sense of support and
sanction. They help him to view himself and his activities in a favorable light and to
maintain his self-esteem and self-respect." (Lindesmith and Strauss, 1949:309-310.)

5. In a letter to the author even an official of a bonding company differentiated between "embezzlers" and "crooks" by saying: "Actually the average embezzler is no
more crook than you or I. As a result of circumstances, he finds himself in some position
where, with no criminal intent, he 'borrows' from his employer. One circumstance leads
to another and it is only a matter of time before he is discovered and discharged with
or without prosecution."

REFERENCES

Dumas, Alexander. *The Money Question*. Translation in *Poet Lore* 26 (March-April
        1915): 129-227.
LaPiere, R. T., and Farnsworth, P. R. *Social Psychology*. New York: McGraw-Hill, 1949.
Lindesmith, A. R., and Strauss, A. L. *Social Psychology*. New York: Dryden Press, 1949.
Mead, George H. "A Behavioristic Account of the Significant Symbol." *Journal of
        Philosophy* 19 (March 1922): 157-63.
_____. *Mind, Self and Society*. Chicago: University of Chicago Press, 1934.
Mills, C. Wright. "Situated Actions and Vocabularies of Motive." *American Sociological
        Review* 5 (December 1940): 904-13.
Noyes, A. P. *Modern Clinical Psychiatry*. Philadelphia: W. B. Saunders, 1940.

Redden, Elizabeth. "Embezzlement, A Study of One Kind of Criminal Behavior With Prediction Tables Based on Fidelity Insurance Records." Ph.D. Dissertation, University of Chicago, 1939.

Richards, T. W. *Modern Clinical Psychology.* New York: McGraw-Hill, 1946.

Ruch, F. L. *Psychology and Life.* New York: Scott, Foresman and Co., 1941.

Woodworth, R. S. *Psychology.* New York: Henry Holt and Co., 1940.

Young, K. *Personality and Problems of Adjustment.* New York: F. S. Crofts and Co., 1946.

ZACHARY GUSSOW AND GEORGE S. TRACY

Status, Ideology, and Adaptation to Stigmatized Illness: A Study of Leprosy

[E]fforts toward destigmatization [by discredited persons is most often found] in more permanent groupings, especially in social settings where they live together in more or less continuous interaction, where they are able to develop their own subculture, norms, and ideology, and where they possess some measure of control over penetrating dissonant and discrediting views from without.

It is precisely these circumstances under which a *group* of "stigmatized" evolve their own stigma theory that interest us here. We are concerned with the meaning of this more or less consciously constructed perspective to their lives and its function in facilitating a linkage with the wider society. To this end, we conceptualize the *career patient status* as a mode of adaptation to chronic stigmatizing conditions and elucidate its ideological base in a stigma theory.

The argument is developed in terms of problems faced and strategies employed by leprosy patients at the USPHS Hospital, Carville, Louisiana, in their efforts to delineate a viable social and psychological explanation for the widespread prejudice toward leprosy patients. The ideology and strategy presented following serve to provide patients with a means of attenuating self-stigma and altering other-stigma. From a description of this particular

Source: Gussow, Zachary and Tracy, George S. "Status, Ideology, and Adaptation to Stigmatized Illness: A Study of Leprosy." *Human Organization* 27, 4 (Winter 1968): 317–325. Reprinted by permission of The Society of Applied Sociology.

system of adjustment it is possible to suggest in the final section some general characteristics of the career patient status and the conditions contributing to its development.

GENERAL BACKGROUND AND METHODOLOGY

Leprosy has been little studied sociologically as either disease or stigma in the United States and is scarcely known to the American public. Prior to 1961, when the senior author first undertook to study the illness and the hospital-colony at Carville, Louisiana (Gussow, 1964; Gussow and Tracy, 1965), there had been only a few local psychological and epidemiological studies (Dimaya, 1963; Belknap and Haynes, 1960; Lowinger, 1959; Johnwick, 1961) and no general sociological or social psychological research.

The USPHS Hospital at Carville is the only leprosarium in the continental United States. It was established in 1894 as the Louisiana Home for Lepers and came under PHS jurisdiction in 1921. The resident patient population at Carville is relatively stable at slightly more than 300. In addition to the Carville hospital, there are at present four PHS leprosy out-patient clinics: one each in New Orleans; San Francisco; San Pedro, California; and Staten Island, New York. At San Francisco, the largest leprosy out-patient clinic, 166 cases of leprosy were seen between the years 1960 and 1967 (Fasal, Fasal and Levy, 1967). The total number of cases of leprosy in the United States is simply not known. The standardized estimate of 2,000 to 2,500 has been used for some time, but experienced workers in the field believe this is somewhat low and variously estimate the number at approximately two to three times the supposed figure. On a worldwide basis the prevalence is estimated at anywhere from 12 to 16 million cases.

In the present study, over 100 patients, Carville residents plus New Orleans and San Francisco out-patients, were interviewed intensively in interviews that ranged from one hour to, in some cases, over twelve hours, with the average between two and three hours. The patients interviewed for this study equal about one-third of the stable Carville in-patient population and approximately four percent of the estimated leprosy cases in the United States. In addition to patient interviews, the study included patient group discussions, individual psychotherapy sessions, interviews with Carville staff members, recordings of staff meetings, and participant observation of hospital and colony life.

SOME MEDICAL AND BEHAVIORAL CHARACTERISTICS
OF THE DISEASE

Leprosy is a chronic communicable disease of the skin, eyes, internal organs, peripheral nerves, and mucous membranes. It can produce severe physical handicaps and disfigurement, especially when untreated. There are also a number of significant uncertainties regarding basic epidemiological questions of etiology, susceptibility, contagion, resistance, treatment, and societal reactions which limit treatment and rehabilitation. Five of these are especially relevant here.

(1) The mode of transmission is not thoroughly understood. Prolonged and intensive skin-to-skin contact with an active case is believed necessary for infection to take place. However, respiratory transmission has not been completely ruled out nor has the role of insect vectors. The idea that genetic factors may play a crucial role, particularly with respect to susceptibility, is becoming increasingly popular. The incubation period is prolonged and undetermined, apparently anywhere from a few months, to many years (Badger, 1964; USPHS Hospital, 1963, 1964).

(2) The mycobacterium *(Mycobacterium leprae)* thought to be responsible has not been successfully cultivated *in vitro*. The disease resists experimental transmission in humans, leaving doubt about the identified organism, in addition to raising questions about the relationship of host to organism (Carpenter and Miller, 1964; USPHS Hospital, 1963, 1964).

(3) Success of treatment is also uncertain. Medical authorities are reluctant to use the term "cure." Current drugs such as the sulfones introduced in the early 1940s are more effective in general than earlier drugs but are useless with some patients and induce strong reactions in others. As a result, individuals do not know and cannot readily learn what disabilities may occur, or how long they may remain a potential communicable risk (Bushby, 1964; USPHS Hospital, 1963, 1964).

(4) Leprosy, in the United States at least, is rarely suspected as a likely diagnosis. Even today diagnosis based on a clinical examination alone, without the aid of a biopsy, is difficult. The disease is therefore frequently mistaken for other conditions, and patients may be treated for long periods for the wrong disease (USPHS Hospital, 1960, 1961).

(5) The legal status of patients is also unclear. Aliens are usually constrained to seek treatment at Carville or face the possibility of deportation. State laws applying to U.S. citizens are varied and differentially enforced (Doull, 1950; USPHS Hospital, 1960, 1961). Criteria for "discharge" from Carville vary with disease classification, clinical judgment, rehabilitation potential, and assessment of patients' responsibleness. Indefinite out-patient treatment may be advised.

Additional insight into the nature of leprosy is provided by Olaf Skinsnes (1964:13-15), a pathologist who recently constructed a hypothetical disease expressing the ultimate in physical disablement and in eliciting extreme negative social and emotional responses. This hypothetical disease would: (1) be externally manifest; (2) be progressively crippling and deforming; (3) be nonfatal and chronic, running an unusually long course; (4) have an insidious onset; (5) have a fairly high endemicity, but not be epidemic;

(6) be associated with low standards of living; (7) appear to be incurable; and (8) as a master-stroke, it would have a long incubation period. (Trautman et al., 1965:927-29.) This illness would expose the individual to long and protracted experience with pain, suffering, and deformity, as well as social ostracism. Death alone would not be the frightening element; the major threat would be bodily deterioration and assault on the body-ego. Skinsnes (1964:15) notes the resemblance of leprosy to his hypothetical disease and concludes that "it appears reasonable to postulate that it is this complex and its uniqueness which is responsible for the unique social reactions to leprosy."

The popular view of leprosy of course portrays the disease in just such black terms. The very name evokes an image of a maximally ravaged, untreated victim. In addition to its depiction in fiction and film, this view is typically found in the fantasies and expectations of newly diagnosed patients. Like others in the general population, they usually possess little real information about the disease and have had little or no previous contact with persons known to have it. In fantasy and expectation leprosy is considered "highly" contagious, horribly deforming, extremely painful, and eventually fatal. The stereotypic belief is widely held that toes, ears, noses, and other bodily appendages literally fall off. Many individuals also think of it as a legendary disease or one associated only with tropical "jungle" life, and are astonished to learn that leprosy actually exists in industrial nations.

Perhaps best epitomizing the bleakness of the popular view is the fact that it excludes the idea of amelioration. New patients anticipate being banished "for life." Importantly, they rarely have to be told or have to learn from experience the advisability of concealing their disease. Even when they know little about leprosy or profess never even to have heard the name they invariably realize its stigma and begin to develop strategies for keeping this information from others. However, the notion of "high" contagion is usually strong. New patients are apt to take precautionary measures far in excess of anything suggested by medical authorities. The urgency with which some of them consent to immediate hospitalization even when there is no compelling medical or public health pressure in that direction further indicates their perception of the situation as "extreme" and requiring immediate treatment or confinement.

The popular or "folk" view of leprosy seems to represent two levels of experience. In terms of deformity, pain, and societal reactions, though not in terms of contagion or fatality, the image comes close to describing actual leprosy in untreated cases of advanced deterioration, though not what it must be nor is in all or most cases. At another level the "folk" view represents a fantasy of the worst that can happen to one's body—a *fantasy of total maximal illness* (Gussow, Knight and Muler, 1964). In fantasy the two darkest fates are to "lose one's mind" as in lunacy or to "lose one's body" as in leprosy. Both involve a loss of self, either psychic identity or body image. Given the unique combination of disease characteristics and the associated medical and social limitations and uncertainties, it is readily apparent that neither the fantasy of leprosy as total maximal physical illness nor extreme cases of the real disease is conducive to an optimistic or hopeful outlook for patients.

LEPROSY AS AN IDENTITY CRISIS

Diagnosis of leprosy with or without concomitant hospitalization, signals a sudden, radical, undesired, and unanticipated transformation of the patient's life program. Many activities and relationships formerly engaged in must be modified or given up. The situation is further compounded by the chronicity of the disease and the need for continued prophylactic actions to prevent exacerbation of symptoms. The disease becomes the nucleus around which the patient's life program is transformed. The disease also sets boundaries which, for many patients, impose a severe truncation of their normal status and role activities. In this complex, self- and other-stigmatization are but two facets contributing to a major identity crisis.[1]

A further complication in the crisis comes with the patient's realization that (1) while he has a serious condition (serious either as disease or stigma or both), he has not changed as a person, yet (2) society would now regard him as totally different. The patient fears that his condition will engender not only a discontinuity between his past and previously expected future, but also will create an incongruity between his self-identity and his social identity. As long as he can conceal his condition, he can, within limits, engage normally in behavior open to him on the basis of a social identity in which others do not know of his stigma. But once the condition is known, the patient is faced with the problem of "building a world," to use Goffman's phrase. He has to learn what from the past must be discarded and what is salvageable, which past activities and roles will facilitate adaptation, which will not, and what new behaviors need to be added.

Patients handle the discontinuity and dissonance between self and social identities in a variety of ways, and the kind and quality of their adjustment can be expected to vary according to their relation to others who hold different views about leprosy. In Goffman's treatment of single stigmatized individuals interacting with normals in everyday encounters, the penetrating social norms remain continually in effect. Under these circumstances it is

1. We are using the term self-identity in the same sense as Erikson has used "identity"— "that is, as a well-organized ego acting in an appropriate environment with a sense of confidence in the persistence of both itself and the environment." (Quoted from Cumming and Cumming, 1966:42). When the identity is threatened or drastically changed, a crisis ensues which forces the individual to reevaluate himself, the world about him, or both (op. cit.:chap. 3).

difficult for the stigmatized person to see himself differently than others see him for he continues to live, work, and play in social contexts that affirm the conventional standards.

We are concerned here, however, with situations in which the stigmatized develop and implement an ideology counter to the dominant one that stigmatizes them. They formulate a theory of their own to account for their predicament, to de-discredit themselves, to challenge the norms that disadvantage them and supplant these with others that provide a base for reducing or removing self-stigma and other-stigma. The most significant element for this to take place, it would seem, is a mutually reenforcing collectivity of like-stigmatized people, a subculture capable of maintaining effective immunity from the dominant code. Such collectivities may be of the urban homosexual variety or the rash of "hippie" movements which, although located physically within the larger society, nevertheless manage to set themselves apart, reenforcing each other's actions while setting some degree of social, emotional, and cognitive distance between themselves and their critics.

Another such collectivity is that formed by the leprosy patients at the USPHS Hospital in Carville. Originally (in its presulfone days) an asylum, it is now a "quasi-open residential treatment community" (Nichols, 1966), with a well-developed patient culture which has evolved a distinctive and coherent stigma theory of its own in isolation from the mainstream of American social routines.

THE PATIENTS' THEORY OF STIGMA

A diagnosis of leprosy, followed by hospitalization or out-patient treatment, introduces the new patient to the known medical facts and to many of the misconceptions and uncertainties related to the disease. It is a common fact of our observation that new patients hold expectations which compare leprosy with Biblical notions and include the fantasy of "total maximal physical illness." Early in the introduction to their new career, patients learn that Biblical references and contemporary leprosy are associated only in historical myth and misconception. This aspect of the stigma theory attempts to demythologize leprosy by emphasizing the historical, social, and medical errors and confusions which surround it. The theory further argues that leprosy as now known is wholly undeserving of the social prejudice it arouses and elaborates the view that society's negative image arises not from the medical and physiological facts but from faulty Biblical exegesis based at best on poorly substantiated historical evidence and reasoning. Scientific and medical data are adduced to show that leprosy historically has been mistakenly identified with a wide variety of other skin and nerve conditions and that for centuries it has been a general catch-all category

for any number of horrible aspects of innumerable and unexplained deforming illnesses that have afflicted mankind.

The theory also attempts to deal with contagion. Since there are a number
of medical and scientific uncertainties relating to contagion, the theory
understandably encounters certain difficulties. Much is made of leprosy as
a "mildly contagious" disease, but the epidemiology is uncertain; and the
question is commonly raised that if it is only "mildly" contagious, how come
so many people have it? At Carville it is routine to relate that in nearly
three-quarters of a century of operation only one employee ever contracted
the disease and this man, it is pointedly added, was reared in the leprosy
endemic area of Southern Louisiana. At times, the theory goes further and
declares that in some regions leprosy may be considered a "noncommuni-
cable" disease.

In line with the theory, serious proposals are advanced by patients and
leprosy workers alike to change the name of the illness to Hansen's Disease.
The term "leper" in particular, but also the term "leprosy," is considered
opprobrious and inappropriate except in the ancient, Biblical context. The
present-day condition is termed "Hansen's Disease" or "so-called leprosy"
in order to clarify the distinction between present reality and past symbol
and myth.

The stigma or perhaps more correctly, the destigmatizing theory is advanced
in various ways. Almost without exception it plays a part in all printed or
verbal presentations to the public by patients or their representatives. It
appears in its most explicit form in the pages of The Star, a bimonthly journal
published by the patients and distributed internationally. The theory is less
a "line" in Goffman's sense than an ideological position. Unlike "codes"
or "lines," it does not emphasize or elaborate rules of conduct by which the
stigmatized should guide themselves in their relations with normals so much
as it provides a "world view." As ideology the theory is a highly formal
explanation of the stigmatic nature of their illness which permits patients
to minimize the notion that they are severely afflicted and also provides
them with readily available and, to them, provable evidence that society
has wrongly labeled them.

The theory is thus a nativistic effort to redefine the disease and remove
it from its hitherto eminent position as the idealized maximal horrible illness.
It also importantly supplies some measure of hope, optimism, and certainty
through the suggestion that the social and psychological problems patients
face are due substantially to society's defective view of the disease. The
basic assumption is that ostracism and rejection will appreciably diminish
and perhaps even totally disappear when social misconceptions are corrected.
In this respect, the USPHS Hospital itself actively functions as a disseminator
of the stigma theory by encouraging visitors through an established routine
of tours, seminars, and planned programs utilizing local groups and the mass
media. An average of 13,000 visitors annually tour the hospital.

Since the new patient usually had a somewhat nihilistic view of leprosy
before his own socialization into the world of patients, the position that
society is wrong about the disease is one he can convincingly endorse. Psychologically, the theory functions to drain energy, and very often hostility,
away from physical and medical aspects of the disease that are realistically
distressing, about which little is presently known, and for which little or
nothing can be done. Instead, the theory focuses attention on a punitive and
misunderstanding society whose views, it contends, can be altered if sufficient
effort is made to bring the "real" facts before the public and if the public
makes an honest effort to replace their erroneous views with the idea that
leprosy is "just like any other illness."

The theory understandably heavily emphasizes a social and historical
perspective rather than the medical and physiological aspects of the disease
since it is an attempt to introduce a measure of certainty and optimism into
an area of experience that is for many markedly uncertain, and for some
considerably less than hopeful. There is, however, a germ of truth in the
theory. Leprosy is not of course, except in extreme conditions, the ultimate
disease it is fantasied to be; nor is it the Biblical "disease."

Although incomplete as a social or historical explanation for the prejudices
encountered, the theory has important value for patient adaptation and
de-discreditation. Psychologically, leprosy patients typically exhibit a sense
of total rejection by society and initially even by themselves. Interestingly,
this sense of initial self-rejection sometimes offers the patient an opportunity
to work out, or at least, work on intrapsychic conflicts that may have ante-
dated the illness. For some patients with a premorbid, diffuse self-identity,
leprosy may ultimately have an integrating effect. For regardless of the
discrediting nature of the disease, as an identity mark it cannot but impress
upon the individual an acute awareness that if he did not know who he was
before, there can be no question as to who he is now. In not wishing to
accept this "who he is now" which might result in considerable apathy and
hopelessness, the stigma theory provides patients with an available rationale
for reevaluating their discredited status and, additionally, for engaging in
ego-satisfying and socially syntonic assertive actions.

The following selection from a patient interview illustrates the way elements of the stigma theory may be used to explain the nonspecialness of
leprosy and to account for public prejudice:

This patient has been at Carville for 15 years and is now married to another
patient. She reports the disease has never given her much trouble. Her
bacteriological status is close to negative at this time. She believes both
cancer and heart disease are worse illnesses than leprosy. Yet, to this
day "my family don't know nothing about my having this disease. My
brothers and sisters they just know I'm sick and in a hospital, that's all."

Interviewer: What do you think there is about leprosy that makes people afraid of it?

Patient: Actually, because they don't know anything about it. When you say leprosy everybody gets so scared. It's so contagious they think, and it has always been in the Bible that it was so contagious that they naturally connect the two and think you had better get away from it.

Interviewer: How realistically afraid of the disease do you think people should be?

Patient: Well, I don't think they should be afraid of it no more than you would be afraid of tuberculosis. You're not afraid to go out there among people with tuberculosis. The name itself makes people afraid because they don't know anything about it. But, I don't think people would be afraid if they knew more about it.

Compare the above with the way this same patient reports her feelings and views on first learning she had leprosy, and note the connection in her mind between leprosy as the fantasy of maximal illness and leprosy as a real disease:

Interviewer: Had you ever heard the name leprosy before you were diagnosed?

Patient: No, I never heard it before not even though my sister was sick with it. In fact, she was never diagnosed for leprosy. The doctors could never find out what was wrong with her. They learned it at the time when she died. But I never connected the word until they told me about it. It was a big shock.

Interviewer: How did you feel when they told you that you had leprosy?

Patient: It was just unbelievable. I never did think that I could have something like this disease. I didn't know it existed either. I thought maybe in India or perhaps out there in the jungles, but then I never thought about it.

Interviewer: Why do you think you were so shocked when you didn't know anything about the disease or never heard the name before?

Patient: Just like I say, the name. You measure it with something out of the Bible and imagine that's what it is. I think everybody who has had this disease experiences the same thing when they are told. They think it is impossible. What kind of a disease is it when we don't know anything about it?

Interviewer: What did you think was going to happen to you after being told you had leprosy?

Patient: Well, at that time when they told me I had to come over here I thought I had come to the end of the world. I had never been out of [another state] all my life and when they told me I had to come all the way to Louisiana I thought I would probably go and never come back again, that I'd die or something. Those were my thoughts, that I'd probably die out here somewheres.

Most patients, as the patient cited above, elect to conceal their leprosy identity from society. Many take up permanent residence at the hospital where they live, work, and sometimes marry. They protect themselves by "colonizing." They maintain the notion of society's ignorance and misconceptions about leprosy as a means of reconciling their own lowered self-esteem. Through exposure to and socialization by other patients they incorporate the stigma theory into their own world view. Each patient, however, utilizes the theory in whatever way his own psychodynamics and life situation permits and/or requires.

THE THEORY AS LEGITIMATION FOR CAREER PATIENT STATUS

A number of patients, apparently independently of severity or visibility of symptoms, reveal their condition to society in quite open ways. In the interest of altering the public image of leprosy, which they hold as bearing the major responsibility for their discredited status and predicament in life, these patients assume the stance of educators bringing specialized information about leprosy to the public. Such *career patients* engage in a number of activities which are legitimized through the elements of the stigma theory and carry the approval of the majority of other patients.

The following case history, abstracted from extensive interviews with one such patient, illustrates some of the ways attitudes toward leprosy are reformulated and basic problems of revealing and educating are handled by those who are career patients.

The patient has been a fairly regular Carville resident since his first admission more than five years ago. He has a more benign and less contagious form of the disease. He has no visible symptoms and the disease seems dormant at present. The patient is below middle age and his general health is good. His present wife—they married since his admission to Carville—is a Carville patient with a severe form of the disease and requires continuous medical care. Both live together at the hospital, visiting outside for varying periods. He works sporadically both at Carville and at various jobs outside. He does not use an alias.

The patient's view of the disease has been modified considerably since his diagnosis. At that time he believed leprosy to be highly contagious, extremely painful, even fatal and that he would soon lose various body parts—nose, ears, toes, etc. He continuously tested for signs of atrophy and also experienced depressive moods including rumination about suicide. He carefully concealed knowledge of his disease from others, passing his symptoms off as due to a nonstigmatized condition. He was upset when the Carville staff did not endorse his fantasy for total and immediate confinement. Now he believes leprosy is a minimal disease, especially when treatment is begun early. He ranks cancer, heart disease, tuberculosis, arthritis, and rheumatism as worse than leprosy. He views genetic susceptibility as a prime factor in contagion. Now he never denies having leprosy and pointedly informs others of his true condition.

This patient is an active "educator" of the public and keeps himself informed about leprosy. He frequently talks to various groups as a leprosy patient and appears on television and radio. He is committed to generating more public interest in the disease and welcomes all questions and opportunities to discuss it. He acknowledges the existence of public fear, has personally experienced it, and feels that continuous efforts are necessary to overcome intractable public disinterest and fear. In order to correct erroneous public views and minimize the contagion factor, he paradoxically cites prevalence figures higher than those usually given by medical authorities.

Selective disclosing of information about leprosy is acknowledged by this patient: "There are many ways of telling people." When addressing the public, he sidesteps questions about and minimizes the problems of deformity to avoid reinforcing existing fantasies and misconceptions. In talking to Carville visitors, he feels the matter of deformity can be placed in perspective by pointing to the many patients who are not disfigured and by relating deformity to inadequacy of the older drugs, to the "oldtimers," and to those whose treatment was begun late. He links the maximal illness fantasy of leprosy and the stigma to the teachings of the churches and to writers and film makers who continue to hold erroneous ideas.

The patient cites his own experiences and marked shift in viewpoint as an example of the "conversion" anticipated in the public once an interest in and an understanding of the disease is created. He believes he has avoided developing a discredited self-identity through his education activities and the opportunities they have provided him in disclosing his leprosy identity. Concealers, he notes, have denied themselves this opportunity; their fear of exposure has altered their self-conception to that of an "outsider."

At present he is working outside Carville where his employer and his coemployees know all about him. He would not have it otherwise, he says. Informally he reveals his identity in almost all appropriate situations with only minor reservations.

In functioning as educational specialists the relationship of such patients to society undergoes an important shift. For some it furnishes them with a clear identity perhaps for the first time in their lives, providing them with altruistic service roles which, considering the fact the majority of patients at Carville are lower-class and rural, would not ordinarily be open to them. Some write articles and books, speak on the radio, appear on television or before community groups of various types both out in the community and on patient-panels to Carville visitors. Two prominent examples of career patients are Gertrude Hornbostel and Joey Guerrero, whose brief biographies appear in Stanley Stein's book *Alone No Longer* (1963). Stein himself is probably the most prominent current career patient. All who reveal themselves are potential educators. However, the decision to reveal is usually made only after much thought and weighing of consequences. Only when the patient believes he can cope with the reactions he anticipates is he likely to decide on this alternative.

Some career patients, like the one cited in the above case history, bear little evidence of their condition. This may seem logical insofar as such patients present the best case for leprosy in face-to-face encounters with the public, serving as examples to contradict the "erroneous" public view of the disease, and lending credence to the patients' special stigma theory of leprosy. At the same time, there is a paradox in that these individuals are the very ones who could most easily "pass" and thereby minimize social rejection. That they do not choose this path is a comment on the fact that stigma may provide the basis for a total self-conception.

An important limitation of the patient educator relates to the kind and amount of information he may freely impart to the public. His function decrees he present leprosy in a favorable light. To emphasize the medical and social uncertainties or elaborate on the pathological picture of the disease might intensify reactions rather than temper them. The picture of the disease he presents must be carefully designed not to alarm. Thus, in the case history above, the patient mentioned "there are many ways of telling people" and many ways of dealing with difficult and embarrassing questions about deformity. The managment of information has its own pitfalls, however. To reveal too much may be self-defeating. At the same time what is presented cannot be so out of tune with reality that it is dismissed as an obvious effort to paint an overly optimistic picture. The situation is especially precarious in view of public ideas of the disease as "extreme." Emphasis is thus placed on correcting errors and misconceptions rather than on fully elaborating all the factual details of leprosy. By no means is this position accepted by all. Dr. Skinsnes, for example, opposes changing the designation of the illness to Hansen's Disease and argues that "lasting returns from efforts to change society's unreasoning dread of leprosy will come from dissemination of facts regarding the true nature of the disease together with information about the hope now found in available effective treatment." (1964:16.)

Career patients, when not engaged in public education activities outside of Carville, require a place to which they may retreat. Refuge is most readily available at the hospital itself. Individuals who have attempted to maintain the dual statuses of career patient and private citizen in outside communities often, though not always, experience severe role conflicts. While "accepted" as public educators about leprosy, they find that this limited acceptance does not always qualify them for general social acceptance. Patient educators on tour often find it expedient to use an alias so that adverse publicity will not precede or follow them when they wish to settle down.

There are probably few individuals who can permanently tolerate feeling discredited without making efforts to alleviate or restructure their definition of self. Insofar as the career patient status is viable, it assists in this task. From discredited concealers whose safety lies in hiding their identity, such individuals take on a new and laudable, though somewhat marginal, position as educational specialists. Their self-esteem and social prestige is elevated. Their actions receive the approval of the hospital and others within the leprosy community and ultimately may be deemed worthy by society in general. Many patients are thus motivated to energetic and outgoing lives, and the public attitudes to which they address themselves are undoubtedly moved toward some increasing understanding and tolerance. However, it must be pointed out that *at the present time this status appears to be the only legitimate one the leprosy patient has available to him for life in open society.*

FURTHER PERSPECTIVE ON STIGMA THEORIES AND CAREER PATIENTS

Though the destigmatizing ideology and the concept of career patient have been elaborated here in relation to leprosy, such statuses and ideologies are not limited to this illness alone. In mental illness, also, there is a stigma theory operating. Cumming and Cumming (1965:1) note that

[one] mechanism is redefinition of the situation so that the 'public' is held to be ignorant and prejudiced about those who must go to mental hospitals. In this mechanism, only the initiated know that such people are not crazy at all, but only temporarily ill, or in need of a rest.

The entire mental health movement is in a sense directed toward attenuating the stigma of mental illness and reducing the public's horror of it. Such ideologies are present also in a number of other conditions, although in a more diffuse form. In alcoholism, for example, there is an attempt to shift public belief in "weakness of character" as a main component to a more acceptable emotional illness model. Similarly, urban homosexuals are active and vocal in their attempts to alter public views and stereotypes.

We offer the generalization that stigma theories tend to develop and achieve a more articulate, coherent, and viable form to the extent that four conditions obtain: (1) there is a basic inadequacy of the existing social model to deal with the many and complex dimensions of the total problem; (2) persons involved in the stigmatized condition are engaged in close and sufficiently prolonged interaction so that a subculture, with ideology and norms, may develop; (3) the stigmatized are sufficiently free of daily encroachment on their lives by dissonant public views; and (4) there are a few (or at least one thoroughly dedicated) of the "discredited" able to enunciate and disseminate a coherent "stigma theory" and willing to risk the concomitant exposure. These few can then, as "career patients," legitimately use the theory for their own adaptation and, more significantly, to effect a transformation in society's attitudes toward their deviant groups.

REFERENCES

Badger, L. F. "Epidemiology." In *Leprosy in Theory and Practice*, edited by Robert G. Cochrane and T. F. Davey, chap. 6. Baltimore: Williams and Wilkins Co., 1964.

Belknap, Harold R., and Haynes, W. G. "A Genetic Analysis of Families in Which Leprosy Occurs." M. D. thesis, Tulane University School of Medicine, New Orleans, 1960.

Bushby, S. R. M. "Chemotherapy." In *Leprosy in Theory and Practice*, edited by Robert G. Cochrane and T. F. Davey, chap. 20. Baltimore: Williams and Wilkins Co., 1964.

Carpenter, Charles M., and Miller, J. N. "The Bacteriology of Leprosy." In *Leprosy in Theory and Practice*, edited by Robert G. Cochrane and T. F. Davey, chap. 2. Baltimore: Williams and Wilkins Co., 1964.

Cumming, John, and Cumming, E. "On the Stigma of Mental Illness." *The Community Mental Health Journal* 1, 1 (1965): 1.

Dimaya, Natividad. "An Analytical Study of the Self-Concept of Hospital Patients with Hansen's Disease." Doctoral dissertation, Wayne State University, School of Social Welfare, Detroit, 1963.

Doull, James A. "Laws and Regulations Relating to Leprosy in the United States of America." *International Journal of Leprosy* 18, 2 (April-June 1950): 145-54.

Fasal, Paul; Fasal, E., and Levy, L. "Leprosy Prophylaxis." *Journal of the American Medical Association* 199 (March 1967): 905.

Gussow, Zachary. "Behavioral Research in Chronic Disease: A Study of Leprosy." *Journal of Chronic Diseases* 17 (1964): 179-89.

Gussow, Zachary; Knight, E. H.; and Miller, M. F. "Stigma—Theory and the Genesis of the Patient—Professional: Patient Adaptation to Leprosy." Paper presented at the 131st Annual Meeting, American Psychiatric Association, New York. Mimeographed. 1964.

Gussow, Zachary, and Tracy, G. S. "Strategies in the Management of Stigma: Concealing and Revealing by Leprosy Patients in the United States." Mimeographed. 1965.

Johnwick, Edgar. "A Reply to Lowinger's Article on Leprosy and Psychosis." *International Journal of Leprosy* 29, 1 (January-March 1961): 110-11.

Lowinger, Paul. "Leprosy and Psychosis." *American Journal of Psychiatry* 116 (July 1959): 32-37.

Nichols, Dorothy S. "The Function of Patient Employment in the Rehabilitation of the Leprosy Patient." M.A. thesis, Department of Sociology, Louisiana State University, 1966: 109.

Skinsnes, Olaf K. *Leprosy Rationale.* New York: American Leprosy Missions, December 1964.

Stein, Stanley. *Alone No Longer.* New York: Funk and Wagnalls, 1963.

Trautman, John R.; Johnwick, E. B.; Hasselblad, O. W.; and Crowther, C. I. "Social and Educational Aspects of Leprosy in the Continental United States." *Military Medicine* 130, 9 (September 1965).

USPHS Hospital. Annual Reports. Carville, Louisiana. Mimeographed. 1960, 1961.

——— . "Syllabus of Lecture Notes." 4th and 4th Seminar on Leprosy in Collaboration with American Leprosy Missions, Carville, Louisiana. Mimeographed. 1963, 1964.

SUE KIEFER HAMMERSMITH AND MARTIN S. WEINBERG

Homosexual Identity: Commitment, Adjustment, and Significant Others

Central to the symbolic interactionist perspective is the notion that through the social interaction in which they engage, people seek to establish and maintain stable identities and to evaluate them positively (Schwartz and Stryker, 1971). It has also been pointed out that a person accomplishes this by commitment to "socially recognized and meaningful categories" and that one's identity may be attained by commitment not only to "non-deviant" categories but to "deviant" ones as well (Cohen, 1965).

With regard to this conception of "deviant identity," several points become salient. The deviant, like the so-called conformist, is seen as engaged in establishing his identity and receiving validation through social interaction. Thus, deviant identities may reflect not personal disintegration or failure, as is often supposed, but rather success in establishing an identity. We would also expect that the more committed one is to any socially meaningful category, even if it is generally evaluated as deviant, the more "settled" the questions of identity will be and thus the more stable his self-conception.

Symbolic interactionism also suggests that one seeks to evaluate himself positively and that one derives his self-evaluation from incorporating the perceived evaluations of "significant others" (Schwartz and Stryker, 1971). We would further expect, then, that the more committed a person is to any

Source: Hammersmith, Sue Kiefer, and Weinberg, Martin S. "Homosexual Identity: Commitment, Adjustment, and Significant Others." *Sociometry* 36, 1 (1973): 56-57, 59-63, 69-73, 75-79. Permission granted by The American Sociological Association and the authors.

category of identity (compared to those not so committed), the more his significant others will support such an identity. Thus, the easier it will be for him to incorporate a positive self-conception and to attain psychological well-being. . . .

We are proposing, then, that commitment to a deviant identity indicates self-affirmation, hence adjustment, on the part of the deviant, and that it is associated with social validation, or support, of that identity by others. Thus we hypothesized that commitment to homosexuality would be:

1. positively related to stability of self-concept.
2. positively related to self-esteem.
3. negatively related to symptoms of maladjustment (such as anxiety symptoms or depression).
4. positively related to perceived support of significant others.

These hypotheses, it must be noted, suggest correlational rather than causal relationships. Indeed, many different causal relationships could produce the hypothesized correlations between psychological adjustment, homosexual commitment, and support. (While *perceived* support is not to be considered equivalent to *actual* support, the former is hereafter referred to as "support" for the sake of brevity. In other words, we recognize that perceptions of support can be inaccurate due to misreadings, projecting one's own increased acceptance of homosexuality, etc.) A number of models underlying the hypothesized correlations are suggested by the symbolic interactionist perspective.[1] In presenting and discussing these models, the term "adjustment" is used to refer to high stability of self-concept, . . . [high] self-esteem, and . . . low anxiety symptoms and depression.

$$(M1) \quad X_1: \text{Commitment} \xrightarrow{\quad + \quad} X_2: \text{Adjustment} \xrightarrow{\quad + \quad} X_3: \text{Support}$$

It may be suggested that commitment to an identity positively influences adjustment and that adjustment influences the choice of significant others who are supportive. The logic producing this model is roughly as follows.

1. In this paper we deal exclusively with recursive models, i.e., models which do not contain feedback loops or reciprocal relations between two variables. We do not deal with nonrecursive models for two reasons.

First, the path coefficients in a nonrecursive model can be identified only if one includes enough exogenous variables that have no direct effect on at least some of the endogenous variables. We do not have additional variables which meet this criterion. (For a technical statement of the criterion, *see* Blalock, 1969:65.)

In addition, there is some justification in terms of simplicity for employing a recursive model, even when one suspects some reciprocal influence between two variables. (For a discussion of this issue, *see* Blalock, 1969:46.)

The search for a socially meaningful, continuing identity is basic to the human process. Until or unless one settles upon such an identity, one suffers anxiety and uncertainty. This anxiety is motivational in the person's continuing search for an identity.

As one becomes committed to a deviant identity (i.e., as one settles upon that identity as the present and future foundation for self-regard and relating to others), anxiety about identity decreases. Having found a socially meaningful identity, the deviant's self-concept stabilizes; he finds it intrinscially rewarding to have an established identity, and his self-esteem and psychological adjustment increase.

As part of this "settling in" process, the deviant, now more sure of himself, elicits validation from his social environment. This is accomplished by devaluating the opinions of those who do not support the deviant identity and by attaching importance to the opinions of those who do support it.

According to the first model, the less committed deviant, by contrast, is socially and psychologically less sure of himself and his worth. Anxious about and unstable in his identity, he reaches in many directions for social validation, including evaluating as significant the opinions of those who do not support the deviant identity.

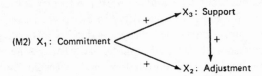

Again emphasizing the independence of the person's commitment to a deviant identity, the second model suggests that commitment increases psychological adjustment—i.e., that it increases self-esteem and stability of self-concept, and decreases anxiety and depression. The rationale for this assertion was explored in the discussion of Model 1.

Likewise, the highly committed homosexual is seen to focus on those who most support that identity, consequently increasing psychological adjustment by finding validation. Thus, for the highly committed deviant an improvement in adjustment is obtained both by his commitment and by his success in finding support from others.

$$\text{(M3)} \quad X_3 : \text{Support} \xrightarrow{\quad + \quad} X_2 : \text{Adjustment} \xrightarrow{\quad + \quad} X_1 : \text{Commitment}$$

The third model highlights the importance of social validation in making an identity rewarding or not, suggesting that support of significant others influences psychological adjustment, which in turn influences commitment. This model . . . suggests that the person derives his self-concept from others' reactions to him.[2] If others support the deviant identity, then the deviant's adjustment improves as he (a) is relieved of the anxiety accruing from an "unsettled" identity and (b) experiences the pleasure intrinsic to an identity and its validation. Through such positive reinforcement he becomes highly committed to the deviant identity.

If, however, he perceives the people he considers important as questioning the validity and worth of the identity, the deviant is likely to remain in an identification limbo, unstable in his self-concept, unsure of his worth, [and] not highly committed to that identity.

Thus, whereas the first, voluntaristic model suggests that the significance a person attaches to another's evaluation of him *follows from* commitment, this model suggests that the significance one attaches to various others' opinions is largely given *before* he settles into an identity, and that significant others' opinions, as the person perceives them, influence the degree of commitment to that identity. Thus, commitment to a deviant identity, which in the first model is the social psychological determinant of electing significant others who are supportive, is, in this model, the product of significant others.

$$\text{(M4)} \quad X_3: \text{Support} \xrightarrow{\quad + \quad} X_1: \text{Commitment} \xrightarrow{\quad + \quad} X_2: \text{Adjustment}$$

It also could be argued that support of significant others directly influences commitment. If significant others support one's deviant identity as it develops, or if he can find new supportive others whose opinions are respected, the deviant is likely to become highly committed to his deviant

---

2. [An explicit statement of this model appears in an article by Schwartz, Fearn, and Stryker (1966) on emotionally disturbed children.] ... "Given rewards for disturbed behavior [support], that disturbed behavior may become integral to a role-making process out of which an identity as a disturbed child may be reinforced. Such reinforcement may, then, lead the child to form a coherent, stable identity as a disturbed child, and to value that identity positively [stability of self-concept and self-esteem]. This in turn implies a high degree of commitment to a disturbed role [commitment]" (p. 300).

The authors do not, however, employ this model throughout. In the following quotation, they indicate that commitment determines rather than derives from adjustment and support: "... as one becomes more committed to the deviant role of being emotionally disturbed, the better and more stable will be one's self-meanings. ... [T]hose least committed to the deviant role are more open to influence on their own self-meanings from a variety of others ... while those most committed to their deviant roles are least influenced by others save those most supportive of their role behavior. ..." (p. 300). Schwartz *et al.* also provide different models for the committed and uncommitted: among the uncommitted, self-anxiety causes them to have significant others who do not support the deviant identity (p. 304); among the committed, however, supportive significant others relieve "whatever little anxiety in self existed" (p. 305).

identity. Thus, he settles into that identity, which in turn produces higher self-esteem, stability of self-concept, and psychological well-being. If significant others do not support the identity, the deviant regrets that identity, has low commitment to it, and consequently suffers with feelings of maladjustment. In Model 4, then, deviant commitment intervenes between support of significant others and psychological adjustment.

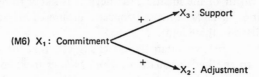

One could argue, quite simply, that support of the deviant's significant others determines both his level of commitment to homosexuality and, independently, his adjustment. This is to say, the deviant's perception of significant others as supportive influences positively the degree of satisfaction with, and commitment to, the identity. Independently, Model 5 proposes, the deviant's perception of his significant others as supportive also increases his adjustment. This model indicates that neither is commitment the result of adjustment, nor adjustment the result of commitment. Rather, it suggests that one's adjustment and commitment both follow, somewhat deterministically, from support by significant others.

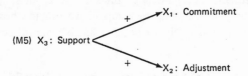

Finally, it could be suggested that commitment is the crucial factor that influences, independently, both the validation one elicits from one's social environment—i.e., significant others who are supportive—and one's adjustment. This suggests, again, that as a person becomes more committed to his homosexual identity, he tends to attach more importance to the opinions of those who are supportive of him in that identity and less [importance to the opinions of] those who are not.

Model 6 also proposes that the more committed homosexual is better adjusted because he has settled into an identity with which he is satisfied; it suggests, however, that support of his significant others does not directly affect the homosexual's psychological adjustment or his homosexual commitment.

[These models were tested with questionnaire data from a larger study of 2,497 male homosexuals in the United States, the Netherlands, and Denmark (Weinberg and Williams, 1974). Respondents were contacted through homophile organizations, homosexual bars, and private social clubs. Question-

Table 4: Zero-order Correlation between Commitment (c) and Adjustment (a)

Measure of adjustment	r_{ca}		
	United States	Netherlands	Denmark
Stability of self-concept	.30***	.21***	.14
Self-esteen	.35***	.32***	.29***
Anxiety symptoms	- .18***	- .13***	- .12
Depression	- .36***	- .39***	- 32***

Note: *indicates statistical significance at the .05 level, **at the .01 level, and ***at the .001 level.

naires were returned by 1,117 respondents in the United States, 1,077 in the Netherlands, and 303 in Denmark, representing 38.7, 45.1, and 24.2 percent response rates respectively.] ...

RESULTS

As hypothesized, commitment to homosexuality is found to be positively related to stability of self-concept and to self-esteem, and negatively related to measures of psychological maladjustment (Table 1).[3]

[T]he association which ... [others have found] between commitment to a deviant role and a stable, positive self-concept (Schwartz, Fearn, and Stryker, 1966) is replicated among adult male homosexuals in the United

3. Observed correlations can be corrected for attenuation according to the formula

$$r_{x'y'} = \frac{r_{xy}}{\sqrt{r_{xx}r_{yy}}}$$

Where r_{xy} is the observed correlation, r_{xx} is the reliability of x, r_{yy} is the reliability of y, and $r_{x'y'}$ is the "true" correlation between variables x and y, which presumably would be obtained if they were measured without error (Nunnally, 1967:217-219). Since the reliabilities of x and y are less than one, the "true" correlations are larger than those observed.

Since we do not have an estimate of the reliability of the support measure, however, we cannot make this correction for all correlations. Thus, we present the observed correlations.

[4. Scales of stability of self-concept, self-esteem, anxiety symptoms, and depression consist of the items used by Rosenberg (1965). (For descriptions of all the measures used in this paper, see the original article from which this excerpt was taken—Eds.)

Alpha coefficients for these scales are .78 for homosexual commitment, .79 for stability of self-concept, .86 for self-esteem, .85 for anxiety symptoms, and .88 for depression. There was no theoretical rationale for computing alpha for our measure of support.]

Figure 1: Composite of Tested Models

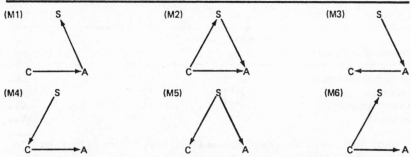

Graphic summary of the models tested where C indicates homosexual commitment; S, support of significant others; A, psychological adjustment ... high self-esteem and stability of self-concept and low anxiety symptoms and depression.

States and the Netherlands. (For Denmark, the correlations were in the predicted direction; due to the weaker correlations and smaller sample size for Denmark, however, statistical significance was obtained only for self-esteem and depression.) ...

If adjustment is a direct product of commitment only, as specified by Models 1, 4, and 6, then we would expect the correlation between commitment and adjustment not to be affected by controlling for the support of others.[5] (Figure 1 contains a composite of the models.) If, alternatively, commitment and adjustment are both independent products of support of significant others (M5), then the correlation between commitment and adjustment should disappear or substantially decrease when support is controlled. Likewise, if the relationship between commitment and adjustment in any way involves the support of others as an intervening variable (as in M2), then the relationship between commitment and adjustment should disappear or substantially decrease when support is controlled.

Referring to Table 2, we see that the partial r's between commitment and the various measures of adjustment, controlling for support of significant others, do not differ significantly from the zero-order ones.[6] Thus we see

5. If commitment and support are very highly intercorrelated, then controlling for support can decrease the correlation between commitment and adjustment, even when support is directly related only to commitment. This occurs because the control removes a large portion of the variance in commitment. Our data show, however, that r_{cs} is not high.

6. The only situation in which controlling for support of significant others could fail to affect the correlation between commitment and adjustment with support of significant others directly related to adjustment would be one in which support of significant others is *negatively* related to either commitment or adjustment. This is not possible since we obtain neither negative partial r's nor negative partial b's between support of significant others and either commitment or adjustment, controlling for the third variable.

Table 2: Zero-order and Partial Correlations between Commitment (c) and Adjustment (a), Controlling for Support of Significant Ohters (s)

Measure of adjustment	United States	
	r_{ca}	$r_{ca \cdot s}$
Stability of self-concept	.30***	.31***
Self-esteem	.35***	.34***
Anxiety symptoms	− .18***	− .17***
Depression	− .36***	− .35***

Measure of adjustment	Netherlands	
	r_{ca}	$r_{ca \cdot s}$
Stability of self-concept	.21***	.20***
Self-esteem	.32***	.30***
Anxiety symptoms	− .13***	− .12***
Depression	− .39***	− .37***

Measure of adjustment	Denmark	
	r_{ca}	$r_{ca \cdot s}$
Stability of self-concept	.14	.13
Self-esteem	.29***	.32***
Anxiety symptoms	− .12	− .10
Depression	− .32***	− .38***

Note: *indicates statistical significance at the .05 level, **at the .01 level, and ***at the .001 level.

that the models which hold support of significant others to be the determining background variable of commitment and adjustment, or an intervening variable between them (... M5 and M2) are not supported. Rather, commitment and adjustment are related directly, positively, and independently of support of significant others (as suggested by Models 1, 3, 4, and 6).

A number of models (M2, M3, [and] M5) contain the common-sense assumption that persons with more supportive significant others will be more psychologically adjusted because of it, but this assumption is not given much support by our data. For such a direct relationship, the partial correlation between adjustment and support, controlling for commitment, would have to meet two criteria. (1) It would have to be statistically significant (a probability level of .05 was used). (2) The actual value of the correlation coefficient would have to be large enough to be substantively important (any coefficient less than .10 was considered negligible). ... [I]n general, the partial correlations in Table 3 show the relationship between adjustment

Table 3:   Zero-order and Partial Correlations between Support of Significant Others (s)
and Adjustment (a), Controlling for Commitment (c)

	United States	
Measure of adjustment	r_{sa}	$r_{sa \cdot c}$
Stability of self-concept	.05	.02
Self-esteem	.15***	.08**
Anxiety symptoms	− .07*	− .03
Depression	− .15***	− .08*

	Netherlands	
Measure of adjustment	r_{sa}	$r_{sa \cdot c}$
Stability of self-concept	.07*	.03
Self-esteem	.22***	.07*
Anxiety symptoms	− .08*	− .05
Depression	− .17***	− .11**

	Denmark	
Measure of adjustment	r_{sa}	$r_{sa \cdot c}$
Stability of self-concept	.04	− .07
Self-esteem	.17*	.11
Anxiety symptoms	− .11	.13
Depression	− .27***	− .22**

Note: *indicates statistical significance at the .05 level, **at the .01 level, and ***at
the .001 level.

and support, controlling for commitment, to be negligible among homosexual males in each country.[7]
    . . . [This indicates that generally, among male homosexuals, support of
significant others does not directly affect psychological adjustment (as proposed by M2, M3, and M5). Thus the commonsense assumption that support
promotes adjustment is shown in this instance to be incorrect. Moreover,
the negligible partial correlations between support and adjustment also
disconfirm M1, which proposes that adjustment determines the selective
evaluation of others as significant.] This indicates that, for our sample at

7. An exception to be noted, however, is that for both the Netherlands and Denmark, a
statistically significant partial correlation between support and depression remains after
commitment is controlled. (The partial correlations between self-esteem and support
and between depression and support in the United States, and between self-esteem and
support in the Netherlands are dismissed because, although they are statistically significant, they are below the magnitude of .10 which we chose as the lower limit of substantive, as distinguished from statistical, significance.)

Table 4: Zero-order and Partial Correlations between Commitment (c) and Support of Significant Others (s), Controlling for Adjustment (a)

Measure of adjustment	United States	
	r_{cs}	$r_{cs \cdot a}$
Stability of self-concept	.22***	.21***
Self-esteem	.22***	.17***
Anxiety symptoms	.22***	.21***
Depression	.22***	.18***

Measure of adjustment	Netherlands	
	r_{cs}	$r_{cs \cdot a}$
Stability of self-concept	.21***	.20***
Self-esteem	.21***	.18***
Anxiety symptoms	.21***	.20***
Depression	.21***	.15***

Measure of adjustment	Denmark	
	r_{cs}	$r_{cs \cdot a}$
Stability of self-concept	.21**	.22**
Self-esteem	.21**	.17*
Anxiety symptoms	.21**	.23**
Depression	.21**	.13

Note: *indicates statistical significance at the .05 level, **at the .01 level, and ***at the .001 level.

least, support and adjustment are both related to commitment, but are not directly related to each other—i.e., that commitment is either an intervening variable or a background variable affecting both support and adjustment, as suggested by M4 and M6.

As hypothesized, commitment to homosexuality is positively related to support of significant others, with a zero-order r of .22 in the United States and .21 in the Netherlands and Denmark. All the models predict that commitment and support of significant others will be positively related. Some models (M1 and M3) suggest, however, that adjustment is an important intervening variable. The deterministic version of such a model (M3) suggests that if support of significant others is high, psychological comfort in the deviant role is high, and therefore, there will be high commitment to that role.... The more voluntaristic version (M1) suggests that once a person has chosen an identity, psychological comfort increases, and that in order to reinforce his certainty in this identity, the person thereafter evaluates more highly the opinions of those who support, and less highly the opinions of those who do not support, that identity.

We can again test the adequacy of models M1 and M3 by seeing if the

Figure 2: Models Supported Which Relate Support of Significant Others for the Deviant Identity (S), Commitment to that Identity (C), and Psychological Adjustment (A).

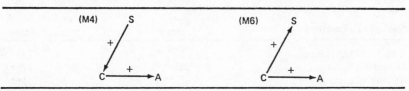

relationship between commitment and support is significantly affected when we control for adjustment, as it would be if adjustment were an intervening variable (Table 4).

In none of the three countries does the relationship between commitment and support of significant others disappear or significantly decrease when we control for adjustment. Again, rejection of M1 and M3 is indicated, along with the conclusion that as far as the variables included in this study are concerned, commitment is related to support of significant others directly, and only directly.

In sum, then, commitment is directly related to both adjustment and support but the latter variables do not directly affect each other in any significant way. Thus, based on data from three countries, it appears that, among the models proposed, the Support of Significant Others-Commitment-Adjustment Model (M4) and the Voluntaristic Independent Effects Model (M6) best represent the probable relationships between homosexual commitment, adjustment, and support of significant others (Figure 2).

Our data provide no basis for preferring one of these models over the other, i.e., we cannot determine the direction of the relationship between commitment and support (cf. Blalock, 1972:445–448). It may be that each model best represents a particular type of homosexual. Indeed, although we could not deal with nonrecursive models in this paper (*see* footnote 1), it seems likely that both processes are at work—that the level of homosexual commitment is determined in part by perceived support of one's significant others, while the evaluation of various others as being significant or not depends in part on one's commitment. It is, in fact, just such feedback mechanisms that are suggested by symbolic interactionism. . . .

SUMMARY

A number of models suggested by the symbolic interactionist perspective relating deviant commitment, psychological adjustment, and perceived support of the deviant identity by significant others were tested with data gathered from a large sample of male homosexuals from the United States, the Netherlands, and Denmark. Homosexual commitment was found to be positively related to psychological adjustment and support of significant others. Adjustment and support were not found to be directly related to each other and were found to be only weakly related through commitment.

Of the six models tested, two were supported. Both of these models propose that, for homosexuals, commitment—i.e., having "settled into" a homosexual identity—leads to better psychological adjustment as indicated by a more stable, positive self-image, fewer anxiety symptoms, and less depression. In addition, one model proposes that support of his homosexual identity by significant others positively influences the homosexual's commitment to that identity. Alternatively, the other supported model suggests that the homosexual's commitment influences his selective evaluation of the importance he attaches to others' opinions of him.

REFERENCES

Blalock, Hubert M., Jr. *Theory Construction: From Verbal to Mathematical Formulations.* Englewood Cliffs, New Jersey: Prentice-Hall, 1969.

——. *Social Statistics, Second Edition.* New York: McGraw-Hill, 1972.

Cohen, Albert K. "The sociology of the deviant act." *American Sociological Review* 30 (February 1965): 5-14.

Nunnally, Jum C. *Psychometric Theory.* New York: McGraw-Hill, 1967.

Rosenberg, Morris. *Society and the Adolescent Self-Image.* Princeton: Princeton University Press, 1965.

Schwartz, M.; Fearn, G. F. N.; and Stryker, S. "A note on self conception and the emotionally disturbed role." *Sociometry* 29 (September 1966): 300-305.

Schwartz, Michael, and Stryker, Sheldon. *Deviance, Selves and Others.* Washington: American Sociological Association, 1971.

Weinberg, Martin S., and Williams, Colin J. *Male Homosexuals: Their Problems and Adaptations.* New York: Oxford University Press, 1974.

ERIC LINDEN AND JAMES C. HACKLER

Affective Ties and Delinquency

DIFFERENTIAL ASSOCIATION THEORY

Perhaps the most widely known theory of criminal and delinquent behavior is Sutherland's theory of differential association. The theory views delinquency as the product of group influences by which the individual learns both the techniques and the motives and drives involved in committing deviant acts. This learning takes place in a process of socialization within a group context. Thus, an act which may be deviant within the context of the larger society may conform to the normative standards of particular groups within the society.

As Sutherland presented it, differential association stresses ties to normative definitions which may be favorable or unfavorable to violation of the law. When we look at studies which claim to have tested differential association . . . we see instead an emphasis on ties to persons—specifically, on ties to deviant peers. For example, Short (1958:21), whose research has served as a model for a good deal of the empirical work on differential association, has stated, "We wish to focus attention on a particular type of differential association— interaction with friends who are defined by adolescents as delinquent."

Source: Linden, Eric, and Hackler, James C. "Affective Ties and Delinquency." *Pacific Sociological Review* 16, 1 (January 1973): 27-29, 31-32, 35-46. Permission granted by Sage Publications, Inc.

This focus on ties to persons rather than on ties to normative "definitions" is compatible with Sutherland's perspective; he evidently assumed that ties to persons are just the means by which these normative definitions are learned. However, it is no less compatible with the view that it is ties to persons—with or without the kind of normative commitment that Sutherland suggested go along with it—that is the crucial explanatory variable. The second interpretation of differential association, then, appears to view the theory as a kind of reference group theory, more concerned with who is taken into account in making decisions about how to behave than with the way one learns certain moral rules that then guide his behavior. This second view has the advantage of being supported by a good deal of empirical research. . . . Judging from the sorts of data which have been called relevant to differential association theory, it may be the case that this reference group conception was the way people read the theory regardless of Sutherland's intentions.

As mentioned above, most of the studies designed to test differential association were concerned only with ties to deviant peers. This approach does not do justice to Sutherland's theory which is obviously concerned with more than just association with delinquent friends no matter which interpretation we give it. The affective ties model has been developed from the second view of differential association and goes beyond just looking at a boy's ties to deviant peers to examine ties to conventional peers and parents as well. In so doing, the model seems to be consistent with control theories of delinquency, though the differential association framework attaches greater importance to the influence of deviant peers than is the case with control theory.

CONTROL THEORY

In contrast to differential association theory, which emphasizes the importance of attachment to persons sharing criminal value patterns, control theory "sees in the delinquent a person relatively free of the intimate attachments, the aspirations, and the moral beliefs that bind most people to a life within the law" (Hirschi, 1969:preface). Thus, the delinquent is not viewed as being tied to a different value system or even to deviant peers, but is seen as being relatively free of ties to society. "If a person does not care about the wishes and expectations of other people—that is, if he is insensitive to the opinion of others—then he is to that extent not bound by the norms. He is free to deviate" (Hirschi, 1969:18). It is his lack of ties to society, then, that frees the individual to commit delinquent acts (see also Matza, 1964; Nye, 1958; and Reiss, 1951).

THE AFFECTIVE TIES MODEL

... The model discussed here looks at the connection between involvement in delinquency and affective ties to parents and to both deviant and conventional peers. ... [T]he model [is based] on the assumption that an actor is motivated to maximize the approval and esteem of his close associates by acting in ways the actor believes they will approve and admire, and by avoiding action the actor believes they will know about and disapprove. Working from this assumption, we can look at four variables in the relationship between an actor and his associates which should be taken into account in order to explain the actor's behavior:

1. The *closeness* of the actor to each of his associates. How much is he concerned about their approval or esteem?
2. The *visibility* of his action to each of his associates. How likely are they to know about his actions?
3. The *responsiveness* to his action of each of his associates.[1] How much would a given action affect their general esteem for him? (These three variables determine the strength of the influence.)
4. The *behavioral preferences* of each of his associates. (This variable determines the direction of that influence.)

If a particular associate is very close, very likely to know of the actor's behavior, and very likely to change his opinion about the actor on the basis of this knowledge, then that associate would have maximum influence. That influence would be a deterrent against delinquency involvement if the associate is believed to approve of nondelinquency. However, if the associate is believed to approve of delinquency, then this relationship should encourage delinquency involvement. In contrast, if an associate is so remote from the actor that there is no concern for that associate's good opinion, *or* if an associate would be very unlikely to know about a particular act that is contemplated, *or* if an associate is already so strongly positive or so strongly negative toward the actor that knowledge of a particular act would be unlikely to change that associate's opinion, then this relationship would be of little or no consequence regardless of whether the associate approved or disapproved of delinquency. ...

1. In the data used for this study, only inadequate indicators were available for visibility and responsiveness of others, and their addition to the model resulted in only very slight predictive gains. In order to show fully the reasoning underlying the model, all four variables will be discussed, although empirical analysis will be limited to closeness and behavioral preferences—which are the most theoretically important variables. Preliminary analysis of a further test done on other data indicates that visibility and responsiveness of others add significantly to the variance in delinquency explained by the model (Linden, 1972).

AFFECTIVE TIES, CONTROL THEORY, AND
DIFFERENTIAL ASSOCIATION

In extending the usual focus on ties to deviant peers to include ties to conventional peers and parents, the affective ties model might be seen as linking the reference group interpretation of differential association (with its emphasis on ties to deviant peers) with control theory (with its emphasis on ties to the conventional order).

The most recent statement of a control theory of delinquency is that of Hirschi (1969). The utility of linking differential association with control theory can be illustrated with reference to his study. In Hirschi's initial discussion of control theory, he does not differentiate between attachments to conventional and to deviant peers. For example, in analyzing data bearing on attachment to parents and peers, he concludes that "the hypothesis that attachment to adolescent friends is conducive to delinquency is difficult to justify on theoretical grounds" (Hirschi, 1969:145). With the affective ties perspective in mind, we might argue that, while attachment to adolescent friends is not necessarily conducive to delinquency, it may be the case that attachment—not just contact, but affective ties—to deviant peers will be conducive to delinquency, especially in the absence of ties to conventional peers or adults. This notion is not contradicted by Hirschi's data. In fact, he concludes that "the theory [control theory] underestimated the importance of delinquent friends" (Hirschi, 1969:230).

While the inclusion of ties to parents and conventional peers is consistent with our interpretation of differential association, their use in the model is more in keeping with control theory than with differential association theory. According to Sutherland and Cressey (1966:226-228), for example, a boy may be isolated from his family or his family may fail to present him with nondelinquent patterns of behavior, but, in either case, the boy's associations outside the home are important with regard to delinquency involvement. They say that "these two processes [isolation and socialization failure] are important because they increase the probability that a child will come into intimate contact with delinquents and will be attracted by delinquent behavior" (Sutherland and Cressey, 1966:227). Thus, as Hirschi (1969:98) points out, according to differential association theory, "lack of attachment to the parents merely increases the probability that the child will be exposed to criminal influences." From the point of view of control theory, however, "lack of attachment to the parents is directly conducive to delinquency because the unattached child does not have to consider the consequences of his actions for his relations with his parents" (Hirschi, 1969:98).

Hirschi (1969) and Jensen (1969) have both examined the relation between attachment to parents and delinquency. They found that, as expected by control theory, attachment to parents has an independent effect on delinquency when the delinquency of friends is held constant. Thus, in looking at affective ties to conventional others as independent variables, we have a model which takes into account this particular empirical criticism of differential association.

METHOD

The respondents investigated in this study were subjects chosen to take part in Opportunities For Youth, a delinquency prevention program (Hackler, 1966). During this program, data were obtained on 200 boys, ranging in age from 13-15, who resided in four low-cost housing projects in Seattle. These boys were divided into experimental and control groups for the program, but in the present study both groups will be used. In selecting subjects, an attempt was made to get a total sample of all the boys in this age group who lived in the four public housing projects in which the study took place.

Two questionnaires were administered to each of the boys, the first at the beginning of the project and the second at its conclusion. In addition to these questionnaires, data were obtained from the boys' teachers and from police records.

Closeness of ties to parents was measured by 23 questions dealing with closeness within the family. An average of these 23 responses was used as an indicator of the closeness of the boy and his parents. Closeness of ties to peers was measured by asking respondents how they felt about deviant and conventional peers, respectively. The questions asked:

Now think of three or four kids you know who sometimes (almost never) get into trouble. Adults would say these kids are "wild" ("O.K.") or maybe even "bad" ("nice"). If these kids were your close friends, would they be just the way you want them to be?

Delinquency involvement was measured by a nine-item self-report index.

RESULTS

A test was made of the predictive ability of the model which indicated moderate success in predicting those boys involved in delinquency[2] (Linden, 1970). The discussion here will focus on a comparison of affective ties, control theory, and differential association theory. Tables 1-5 give the results of this test.

2. This test utilized eight measures of delinquency including both self-report and official measures.

Table 1: Percentage Delinquent (self-report) Looking at Closeness of Ties to Each of Deviant Peers, Conventional Peers, and Parents

	Closeness of Affective Ties	
Behavioral Preferences	Moderate or Strong (% Delinquent)	Weak or None (% Delinquent)
Deviant Peers	26.6 (21 of 79)	24.0 (29 of 121)
Conventional Peers	19.3 (27 of 140)	38.3 (23 of 60)
Conventional Adults (Parents)	18.8 (24 of 128)	36.1 (26 of 72)

Table 2: Percentage Delinquent (self-report) Looking at Closeness of Ties to Conventional Peers and Parents

	Closeness of Ties to Conventional Peers	
Closeness of Ties to Parents	Moderate or Strong (% Delinquent)	Weak or None (% Delinquent)
Moderate or strong	16.8 (17 of 101)	25.9 7 of 27)
Weak or none	25.6 (10 of 39)	48.5 (16 of 33)

In Table 1, the self-reported delinquency rates are compared for those with strong and weak ties to each of deviant peers, conventional peers, and parents. Ties to both sets of conventional associates discriminated fairly well between delinquents and nondelinquents but, rather surprisingly, ties to deviant peers did rather poorly as a predictor of delinquency involvement. While 24 percent of those with weak or nonexistent ties to deviant peers were delinquent, only 26.6 percent of those boys having moderate or strong ties to deviant peers were delinquent. Not only is this finding inconsistent with much of the research that has been done based on differential association theory, it also conflicts with findings obtained from a study done using another group of boys involved in the Opportunities For Youth project (Hackler et al., 1971). The effects of this upon the present study will be briefly discussed below.

While Table 1 looked at each group of associates individually, in Tables 2-4 we are concerned with combinations of two groups of associates. Table 2, which shows the relationship between ties to parents and to conventional

Table 3: Percentage Delinquent (self-report) Looking at Closeness of Ties to Deviant
Peers and Parents

Closeness of Ties to Parents	Closeness of Ties to Deviant Peers	
	Moderate or Strong (% Delinquent)	Weak or None (% Delinquent)
Moderate or strong	18.8 (9 of 48)	18.8 (15 of 80)
Weak or none	38.7 (12 of 31)	34.2 (14 of 41)

Table 4: Percentage Delinquent (self-report) Looking at Closeness of Ties to Deviant
Peers and Conventional Peers

Closeness of Ties to Conventional Peers	Closeness of Ties to Deviant Peers	
	Moderate or Strong (% Delinquent)	Weak or None (% Delinquent)
Moderate or strong	22.2 (12 of 54)	17.4 (15 of 86)
Weak or none	36.0 (9 of 25)	40.0 (14 of 35)

peers and involvement in delinquency, provides strong support for control
theory perspective. As would be predicted on the basis of control theory,
48.5 percent of those boys having weak or nonexistent ties with both conventional peers and parents were delinquent while only 16.8 percent of
those boys having moderate or strong ties with both conventional peers and
parents were delinquent. For the two groups of boys having moderate or
strong ties to one set of associates and weak ties to the other, the percentage
involved in delinquency was almost identical—25.6 percent and 25.9 percent.
This table indicates rather clearly the impact on delinquency involvement
of the lack of ties to conventional others.

Tables 3 and 4 do not show the same sort of interaction between strengths
of ties to each of two groups of associates and delinquency involvement that
is found in Table 2. This is due, at least in part, to the very small difference
accounted for by ties to deviant peers.

Table 5, which looks simultaneously at ties to parents and to both conventional and deviant peers, allows us to compare the affective ties model

Table 5: Percentage Delinquent (self-report) Looking at Closeness of Ties to Conventional Adults, Conventional Peers, and Deviant Peers

Ties to Deviant Peers	Weak or Nonexistent Ties to Parents (% Delinquent)	Moderate or Strong Ties to Parents (% Delinquent)
Moderate or Strong		
Weak or nonexistent ties to conventional peers	58.3 (7 of 12)	15.4 (2 of 13)
Moderate or strong ties to conventional peers	26.3 (5 of 19)	20 (7 of 35)
Weak or Nonexistent		
Weak or nonexistent ties to conventional peers	42.9 (9 of 21)	35.7 (5 of 14)
Moderate or strong ties to conventional peers	25 (5 of 20)	15.2 (10 of 66)

with control theory. According to control theory, boys who have *no* strong ties to any group of associates are the most likely to become delinquent.[3] Thus, if we could show that ties to deviant peers increase the likelihood of involvement in delinquency among those with weak or nonexistent ties to conventional others, the value of modifying control theory to take into account the preferences of a boy's associates would be indicated.

Looking at Table 5, we would predict from control theory that involvement in delinquency would be greatest among those boys with no ties to any of the three groups of associates. This prediction is *not* supported by the data. Instead, the prediction made by the affective ties model—that boys with weak or nonexistent ties to conventional associates who have moderate or strong ties to deviant peers would be most involved in delinquency—is supported. We see in Table 5 that 42.9 percent of those with weak or nonexistent ties to any of the three groups of associates report themselves as delinquent. Of those boys with weak ties to conventional associates but with moderate or strong ties to deviant peers, 58.3 percent are delinquent. This finding was anticipated by Hirschi (1969:230) who concluded after his own research that his original formulation of control theory had "underestimated the importance of delinquent friends."

In most tests of differential association theory, attachment to deviant

3. Note, in this regard, the quotation from Hirschi (1969:145) cited earlier: "The hypothesis that attachment to adolescent friends is conducive to delinquency is difficult to justify on theoretical grounds." In its pure form, control theory asserts that it is the isolate, *not* the boy who has strong ties to deviant peers, who will be most likely to become involved in delinquency.

peers has been seen as the crucial variable in predicting delinquency involvement. By looking at Tables 1 and 5, we can determine if the extension of
this perspective provided by the affective ties model allows us to better
predict delinquency involvement. Cells a and b of Table 1 compare the
self-reported delinquency of those boys who have moderate or strong ties
to deviant peers with that of boys having weak or nonexistent ties. The
results show very little difference—only 2.6 percent between the two groups.[4]
When we turn to Table 5, however, we see that those individuals who have
ties to deviant peers but not to conventional peers or adults are the most
delinquent (58.3 percent) while those who have ties to conventional peers
and adults but not to deviant peers are the *least* delinquent (15.2 percent—a
difference of 43.1 percent). Thus, for the present data at least, ties to deviant
peers are not in themselves good predictors of delinquency, though in the
absence of ties to conventional adults and peers, ties to deviant peers seem
to be quite conducive to delinquency involvement.[5]

DISCUSSION

The data show that neither of the more traditional approaches was as successful as the affective ties model, which simply utilizes elements of both,
in predicting delinquency involvement. Thus, the present study demonstrates
the value of linking differential association and control theory so that the
effects of closeness of ties to each of deviant peers, conventional peers, and
conventional adults and the behavioral preferences of each of these groups
are all taken into account.

The data also indicate the necessity of integrating the control theory
perspective more fully into the model. For example, the findings presented
in Table 5 show that 42.9 percent of those with no strong ties to any set of
associates are delinquent, and that ties to parents have an impact regardless
of ties to other associates. These findings, which would have been predicted
by control theory, suggest that the lack of close ties to any associates is
productive of delinquency and that, even in the absence of close ties to
delinquent associates, weak parental ties are also productive of delinquency.

4. As mentioned above, this small difference is inconsistent with much of the research
on the influence of deviant peers on delinquent behavior. However, even if the results
had shown a greater difference between the two groups, the substantive conclusions
of this study would probably have been the same, as we would expect that the difference
in delinquency involvement between those who have ties to deviant peers and not to
conventional associates and those who have ties to conventional associates and not to
deviant peers would also be greater.

5. We must, of course, be cautious of interpretations based on cell sizes as small as
some of those in Table 5. However, these results are consistent with those of Hirschi
(1969) and Jensen (1969), who both used a much larger sample size.

Thus, we must revise our initial assumption that, if all associates preferred and approved of the same kind of behavior, other kinds of variation in the relationship between the actor and his associates would be irrelevant.

Hirschi found in his sample that there was no subculture of delinquency with strong bonds between the members and that relationships between delinquents are relatively hostile and distrustful. The data reported here give no reason to question this and, even though Hirschi's findings call into question some interpretations of differential association, they do not conflict with the model developed here. Rather than postulating a strong moral community which pressures the boy into committing delinquent acts, we might suggest, in keeping with control theory, that delinquents may have the same beliefs as do conventional adolescents, but that contact with deviant peers might make delinquency involvement more likely among those who have only weak ties to the conventional order. That is, once an adolescent has been set "adrift" because of the loosening of ties to conventional others (*see* Matza, 1964), one of the factors conducive to delinquency involvement is attachment to deviant peers. For example, in the case of a delinquent activity such as heroin use, it may be that those who engage in such activities do not have ties (or bonds, to use the language of control theory) to conventional society. However, because of the need to learn the techniques of using the drug and in order to obtain the drug, some ties to deviant peers are required. In this example, and in the case of other sorts of delinquent acts, it is not necessary to view the adolescent as being pushed into delinquency by a group of delinquent peers, but merely that, for an adolescent who does not have strong ties to the conventional order, ties to deviant peers may facilitate involvement in delinquency.[6]

6. Labelling theorists would suggest that a boy's involvement in delinquency would be likely to cause his alienation from conventional others and his attachment to delinquent peers. No test of causal ordering was attempted here. While there is almost certainly some degree of feedback between affective ties and delinquent behavior, research by Thrasher (1963), Karacki and Toby (1962), and Hirschi (1969) generally supports the ordering postulated here.

REFERENCES

Hackler, James C.; Linden, Eric; and Costner, Herbert. "Affective ties of youth, oppor- *Delinquency* (July 1966): 155–164.

Hackler, James C.; Linden, Eric and Costner, Herbert. "Affective ties of youth, opportunity structure, and delinquency." Presented to the Seventh World Congress of Sociology, Varna, Bulgaria, 1971.

Hirschi, Travis. *Causes of Delinquency.* Berkeley: University of California Press, 1969.

Jensen, Gary. "The family and delinquency: differential association as an intervening process." University of North Carolina Department of Sociology (unpublished), 1969.

Karacki, Larry, and Toby, Jackson. "The uncommitted adolescent: candidate for gang socialization." *Sociological Inquiry* (Spring 1962): 203-215.

Linden, Eric. "Affective ties and delinquency." M.A. thesis. University of Alberta, 1970.

―――. "Affective ties, control theory, and differential association: a sequential theory of delinquency." Presented at the annual meetings of the Pacific Sociological Association, Portland, Oregon, 1972.

Matza, David. *Delinquency and Drift*. New York: John Wiley & Sons, 1958.

Nye, F. Ivan. *Family Relationships and Delinquent Behavior*. New York: John Wiley and Sons, 1958.

Reiss, Albert J. "Delinquency as the failure of personal and social controls." *American Sociological Review* 16 (April 1951): 196-207.

Short, James F., Jr. "Differential association with delinquent friends and delinquent behavior." *Pacific Sociological Review* (Spring 1958): 20-25.

Sutherland, Edwin H., and Cressey, Donald R. *Principles of Criminology*. Philadelphia: J. B. Lippincott, 1966.

Thrasher, Frederic M. *The Gang*. Chicago: University of Chicago Press, 1963.

PART SIX
Group/Culture Conflict and Deviant Behavior

Modern, industrial society is highly pluralistic. Variations in class, race, ethnicity, geographical location, age, and sex are reflected in the many cultural distinctions that characterize each group. The implications of normative diversity for the development of deviant and conforming behavior was the subject of social and cultural support theory. If individuals participate in groups where there is an excess of definitions favoring norm violation, their behavior will follow accordingly.

Conflict theory is similarly concerned with the behavioral effects of social pluralism (Wirth, 1931; Sellin, 1938). In addition, however, the approach emphasizes the political nature of social organization (Chambliss and Seidman, 1971; Spitzer, 1975). Cultural diversity implies competition. That is, groups will compete with one another to assert their norms and values as the legitimate ones (Vold, 1958). By gaining access to the law-making and law-enforcing machinery of the State, the standards of some groups are defined as meritorious, while those of the defeated become deviant or criminal.

This process is illustrated in Joseph Gusfield's investigation of Prohibition, "Drinking as a Changing Form of Deviance." By the middle of the nineteenth century, the dominant morality of the land was that of abstinence. The norm required no legislative reinforcement, since drinker and nondrinker alike agreed on its validity. Through the repentance of those who lapsed from sobriety, the legitimacy of the temperance norm was further strengthened.

Abstinence became a legislative issue when the diffusion of norms unsympathetic to rigid sobriety threatened the traditional consensus. Unrepentant in the use of alcohol, the new "enemy" drinker was associated with the immigration of Irish Catholics and German Lutherans. Making up a large portion of the urban poor in the 1840s and 1850s, these groups brought with them a far more accepting attitude toward the consumption of alcohol.

The Temperance Movement of the late nineteenth and early twentieth centuries, therefore, was reflective of a distinct clash over cultural values. On the one side were the native born, rural, middle-class Protestants; on the other, the immigrant European Catholic or Lutheran, urban lower-class. Victory or defeat in the legislature became symbolic of moral dominance.

From a conflict perspective, the law is an institutionalized representative of the more powerful interests in society. Agents of social control, therefore, are primarily responsible for protecting the dominant order. This is the theme of the selection by Daniel Swett, "Cultural Bias in the American Legal System" which examines how the recruitment and training of the police ensure a personal commitment to the maintenance of the society as it is presently structured. American institutions and their symbols, the sanctity of human life, public and private property, authority, and social order are, by definition, good and must be preserved. Transgressions upon these focal values are attributed to those who depart from the middle-class ideal. The culturally different, therefore, insofar as they conform to stereotypic images of criminality in dress, demeanor, skin color, and behavior, become the targets of suspicion. This tendency to regard certain groups as prone to violation of the law has a self-fulfilling effect. Increased surveillance of cultural minorities results in inflated arrest rates that serve to confirm the original suspicion.

The criminal court is also characterized by a cultural homogeneity that disadvantages lower-status groups. The professional socialization of judges, prosecutors, and defenders; the selection of jurors and the middle-class value system they ultimately represent; problems of shared communication between the culturally diverse; and reliance on unsympathetic class and race stereotypes have consequences for legal treatment. Prosecutors may be more willing to prosecute, counsel less willing to defend, and judges and juries more likely to find guilty those whose characteristics and situation are seen as a threat to the middle-class way of life.

William Chambliss's observational study of two groups of adolescent boys, "The Saints and the Roughnecks," specifies the factors that lead to differential selection. The Saints, children of middle-class families, were as actively involved in delinquency as their lower-class counterparts, the Roughnecks. Yet, the former were, without exception, free from official arrest, while the latter were constantly in trouble with the police. In addition, the community, the school, and law enforcement agents thought of the Saints as essentially good boys and the Roughnecks as tough, young criminals.

The differential response to the two gangs is attributable to a number of class related characteristics. Easy access to automobiles allowed the middle-class youth to commit their delinquencies far from the watchful eye of the community. The restricted mobility of the lower-class boys, on the other hand, rendered their delinquencies more readily observable. The Saints were also proficient at presenting a respectful demeanor when confronted by authority. This ability to manipulate the system by feigning compliance was unshared by the Roughnecks. Overt hostility and disdain merited them the more negative reactions. Finally, the interpretation accorded the behavior of the two groups was affected by a cultural bias that imputes trouble potential to the lower classes. Even when the activities in question are equally visible and serious, the definition persists that the misbehavior of the more powerful are harmless pranks, while those of the powerless are criminal.

Public reaction to nonconformity, and the expectations upon which it is based, has a reinforcing effect. Upon entering adulthood, the Saints assumed roles as respectable members of the community. The Roughnecks, too, performed in the manner anticipated of them. With deviance reinforced by repeated sanction, their lives also became channeled into careers that were consistent with earlier predictions.

The creation of law and its enforcement are contingent upon relationships of dominance and subordination. Those groups whose interests are best represented by the social order define the range of behavior that will be tolerated and influence the selection and processing of law violators. Society and its institutions are mobilized, therefore, in terms of the norms and values of its more powerful segments. The distinction between this form of institutionalized bias and overt discrimination is an important one. Penalization of persons for reasons of class and race is not only illegal but calls into question the democratic commitment to full equality before the law. Rather, the class nature of American society is expressed in a far more covert manner. In this regard, popular conceptions of criminality may play a particularly important role in determining legal outcomes.

Our own study of the adjudication of persons charged with homicide, "Normal Homicides and the Law," surfaced the operation of one such conception in the case of violent behavior. The "normal primitive," a diagnostic category coined by a court-attached psychiatric clinic, represents a more popular stereotype of criminality that includes both class and race characteristics. Coming largely from the foreign born and black populations, such persons are said to have life-styles and innate attributes that predispose them to interpersonal aggression.

While part of a widely diffused conception of violent criminality, the normal primitive has become an institutionalized imagery within which legal decisions are made. Once individuals are defined in its terms, the presumption of innocence becomes inapplicable. Incapable of retaining private counsel, denied bail, and encouraged to enter a plea of guilt, such persons are further confirmed in the stereotype of their crime. For, without the resources essential for successful defense, the original prediction is ultimately fulfilled—

award of criminal conviction. In this way, beliefs and practices regarding the control of the powerless are affirmed without jeopardizing the collective myth.

According to the radical conflict approach, the origins of institutionalized bias are located in the economic relationships that comprise the infrastructure, or foundation, of society. The history of civilization has seen a progressive movement from slavery and feudalism to capitalism. Each of these economies is associated with an appropriate set of institutions, the superstructure, that supports the infrastructure and reflects the needs of the relevant interest groups. The capitalist mode of production characterizes American society. Through such institutions as the family, religion, education, government, and law, attitudes and values that preserve the hierarchy of status and wealth attending the capitalist order are diffused (Marx, 1936).

Because the infrastructure is predicated on inequality, problems of social control inevitably emerge. To deal with these problems are the various treatment and correctional agencies. Once again, as part of the superstructure, these agencies are designed to protect the relationships of production at the expense of the less powerful segments of the population (Spitzer, 1975).

Andrew Scull's "Madness and Segregative Control: The Rise of the Insane Asylum" exemplifies the role of social control in a capitalist economy. The development of capitalism destroyed the sense of social obligation to the poor. At the same time, increasing industrialization meant growing numbers of people living in poverty. The erection of factory-like workhouses allowed representatives of the new economy to oversee the distribution of relief while filtering out those able-bodied but unemployed who could then be coerced back into the labor force.

The heterogeneity of the workhouses, however, soon created problems of management. The insane, in particular, were not tractable to the routine upon which these institutions depended. Their segregation into asylums and the development of psychiatry both helped to create a new occupational group and, with its emphasis on cure through work, reaffirm basic capitalist values.

Richard Quinney, in "The Political Economy of Crime," points out that as capitalism progresses so does the incidence of conflict-related crime. The replacement of human labor by machines means that more and more people share less and less in the benefits of the economy. To control the revolutionary potential of this surplus population, greater expenditures for criminal justice are required.

The relationship between law and capitalism becomes most visible during periods of economic crisis. As unemployment rates increase, so do the numbers of admissions to state and federal prisons. For, unemployment makes actions of survival and frustration necessary on the part of the surplus population, while, at the same time, it necessitates some method of controlling that population on the part of the State.

From a conflict perspective, then, deviance is an outcome of the political organization of a culturally diverse society. Groups occupy various positions within the economic and power structures. Nonconformity is intimately related to the social and cultural conditions associated with these positions and with the processes by which laws are made and enforced to protect certain groups at the expense of others. In this view, crime and deviance lie not within the individual offender but in the institutions and agencies empowered to designate behavior as offensive.

This defining process and its self-fulfilling effects may be seen as a critical element in the maintenance of dominant group interests. By officially derogating the behaviors of social and cultural minorities, powerful segments of society are able to reaffirm the superiority of the norms and behaviors to which they stand committed.

REFERENCES

Chambliss, William J., and Seidman, Robert B. *Law, Order, and Power.* Reading, Massachusetts: Addison-Wesley, 1971.

Marx, Karl. *Capital.* New York: Modern Library, 1936.

Sellin, Thorsten. "Culture Conflict and Crime." *Bulletin 41.* New York: Social Science Research Council, 1938.

Spitzer, Steven. "Toward a Marxian Theory of Deviance." *Social Problems* 22 (1975): 638-51.

Vold, George. *Theoretical Criminology.* New York: Oxford University Press, 1958.

Wirth, Louis. "Culture Conflict and Misconduct." *Social Forces* 9 (1931): 484-92.

JOSEPH R. GUSFIELD

Drinking as a Changing Form of Deviance

The legal embodiment of attitudes toward drinking shows how cultural conflicts find their expression in the symbolic functions of law. . . .

The movement to limit and control personal consumption of alcohol began in the early nineteenth century, although some scattered attempts were made earlier (Krout, 1925). Colonial legislation was aimed mainly at controlling the inn through licensing systems. While drunkenness occurred, and drinking was frequent, the rigid nature of the Colonial society, in both North and South, kept drinking from becoming an important social issue (Krout, 1925:chap. 1 and 2; Earle, 1937:148-49, 156-65).

THE REPENTANT DRINKER

The definition of the drinker as an object of social shame begins in the early nineteenth century and reaches full development in the late 1820s and early 1830s. A wave of growth in Temperance organizations in this period was sparked by the conversion of drinking men to abstinence under the stimulus of evangelical revivalism (Gusfield, 1963:44-51). Through drinking men joining together to take the pledge, a norm of abstinence and sobriety

Source: Gusfield, Joseph R. "Moral Passage: The Symbolic Process in Public Designations of Deviance." *Social Problems* 15 (1967): 182-85. Permission granted by The Society for the Study of Social Problems and the author.

emerged as a definition of conventional respectability. They sought to control themselves and their neighbors.

The norm of abstinence and sobriety replaced the accepted patterns of heavy drinking countenanced in the late eighteenth and early nineteenth century. By the 1870s rural and small-town America had defined middle-class morals to include the Dry attitude. This definition had little need for legal embodiment. It could be enunciated in attacks on the drunkard which assumed that he shared the normative pattern of those who exhorted him to be better and to do better. He was a repentant deviant, someone to be brought back into the fold by moral persuasion and the techniques of religious revivalism (Gusfield, 1963:69–86). His error was the sin of lapse from a shared standard of virtue. "The Holy Spirit will not visit, much less will He dwell within he who is under the polluting, debasing effects of intoxicating drink. The state of heart and mind which this occasions to him is loathsome and an abomination" (Temperance Manual, 1836:46).

Moral persuasion thus rests on the conviction of a consensus between the deviant and the designators. As long as the object of attack and conversion is isolated in individual terms, rather than perceived as a group, there is no sense of his deviant act as part of a shared culture. What is shared is the norm of conventionality; the appeal to the drinker and the chronic alcoholic is to repent. When the Woman's Anti-Whiskey Crusade of 1873-1874 broke out in Ohio, church women placed their attention on the taverns. In many Ohio towns these respectable ladies set up vigils in front of the tavern and attempted to prevent men from entering just by the fear that they would be observed.[1] In keeping with the evangelical motif in the Temperance movement, the Washingtonians, founded in 1848, appealed to drinkers and chronic alcoholics with the emotional trappings and oratory of religious meetings, even though devoid of pastors (Krout, 1925:chap. 9).

Moral persuasion, rather than legislation, has been one persistent theme in the designation of the drinker as deviant and the alcoholic as depraved. Even in the depictions of the miseries and poverty of the chronic alcoholic, there is a decided moral condemnation which has been the hallmark of the American Temperance movement. Moral persuasion was ineffective as a device to wipe out drinking and drunkenness. Heavy drinking persisted through the nineteenth century and the organized attempts to convert the drunkard experienced much backsliding.[2] Nevertheless, defections from the

1. See the typical account by Mother Stewart, one of the leaders in the 1873-74 Woman's War on Whiskey, in Steward, 1889: 139–43; also see *Standard Encyclopedia of the Alcohol Problem,* 1930: 2902–05.

2. See the table of consumption of alcoholic beverages, 1850-1957, in Keller and Efron, 1959: 180.

standard did not threaten the standard. The public definition of respectability matched the ideals of the sober and abstaining people who dominated those parts of the society where moral suasion was effective. In the late nineteenth century those areas in which temperance sentiment was strongest were also those in which legislation was most easily enforceable.[3]

THE ENEMY DRINKER

The demand for laws to limit alcoholic consumption appears to arise from situations in which the drinkers possess power as a definitive social and political group and, in their customary habits and beliefs, deny the validity of abstinence norms. The persistence of areas in which Temperance norms were least controlling led to the emergence of attempts to embody control in legal measures. The drinker as enemy seems to be the greatest stimulus to efforts to designate his act as publicly defined deviance.

In its early phase the American Temperance movement was committed chiefly to moral persuasion. Efforts to achieve legislation governing the sale and use of alcohol do not appear until the 1840s. This legislative movement had a close relationship to the immigration of Irish Catholics and German Lutherans into the United States in this period. These nonevangelical and/or non-Protestant peoples made up a large proportion of the urban poor in the 1840s and 1850s. They brought with them a far more accepting evaluation of drinking than had yet existed in the United States. The tavern and the beer parlor had a distinct place in the leisure of the Germans and the Irish. The prominence of this place was intensified by the stark character of the developing American slum (Handlin, 1941:191–92, 201–09; Hansen, 1940). These immigrant cultures did not contain a strong tradition of Temperance norms which might have made an effective appeal to a sense of sin. To be sure, excessive drunkenness was scorned, but neither abstinence nor constant sobriety were supported by the cultural codes.

Between these two groups—the native American, middle-class, evangelical Protestant and the immigrant European Catholic or Lutheran occupying the urban lower-class—there was little room for repentance. By the 1850s the issue of drinking reflected a general clash over cultural values. The Temperance movement found allies in its political efforts among the nativist movements (Billington, 1938:chap. 15; Gusfield, 1963:55–57). The force and power of the antialcohol movements, however, were limited greatly by the political composition of the urban electorate, with its high proportion

---

3. Rowntree and Sherwell, 1900, using both systematic observation and analysis of Federal tax payments, concluded (p. 253) that ". . . local veto in America has only been found operative outside the larger towns and cities."

of immigrants. Thus the movement to develop legislation emerged in reaction to the appearance of cultural groups least responsive to the norms of abstinence and sobriety. The very effort to turn such informal norms into legal standards polarized the opposing forces and accentuated the symbolic import of the movement. Now that the issue had been joined, defeat or victory was a clear-cut statement of public dominance.

It is a paradox that the most successful move to eradicate alcohol emerged in a period when America was shifting from a heavy-drinking society in which whiskey was the leading form of alcohol, to a moderate one, in which beer was replacing whiskey. Prohibition came as the culmination of the movement to reform the immigrant cultures and at the height of the immigrant influx into the United States.

Following the Civil War, moral persuasion and legislative goals were both parts of the movement against alcohol. By the 1880s an appeal was made to the urban, immigrant lower-classes to repent and to imitate the habits of the American middle-class as a route to economic and social mobility. Norms of abstinence were presented to the nonabstainer both as virtue and as expedi[1] This effort failed. The new, and larger, immigration of 1890-1915 increased still further the threat of the urban lower-class to the native American.

... While the urban middle-class did provide much of the organizational leadership to the Temperance and Prohibition movements, the political strength of the movement in its legislative drives was in the rural areas of the United States. Here, where the problems of drinking were most under control, where the norm was relatively intact, the appeal to a struggle against foreign invasion was the most potent. In these areas, passage of legislation was likely to make small difference in behavior. The continuing polarization of political forces into those of cultural opposition and cultural acceptance during the Prohibition campaigns (1906-1919), and during the drive for Repeal (1926-1933), greatly intensified the symbolic significance of victory and defeat.[5] Even if the Prohibition measures were limited in their enforceability in the metropolis there was no doubt about whose law was public and what way of life was being labelled as opprobrious.

After Repeal, as Dry power in American politics subsided, the designation of the drinker as deviant also receded. Public affirmation of the temperance norm had changed and with it the definition of the deviant had changed. Abstinence was itself less acceptable. In the 1950s the Temperance movement,

4. William F. Whyte (1955: 99) has shown this as a major attitude of social work and the settlement house toward slum-dwellers he studied in the 1930s. "The community was expected to adapt itself to the standards of the settlement house." The rationale for adaptation lay in its effects in promoting social mobility.

5. Although a well-organized Temperance movement existed among Catholics, it was weakened by the Protestant drive for Prohibition: See Bland, 1951.

faced with this change in public norms, even introduced a series of placards with the slogan, "It's Smart *Not* to Drink."

Despite this normative change in the public designation of drinking deviance, there has not been much change in American drinking patterns. Following the Prohibition period the consumption of alcohol has not returned to its pre-1915 high. Beer has continued to occupy a more important place as a source of alcohol consumption. "Hard drinkers" are not as common in America today as they were in the nineteenth century. While there has been some increase in moderate drinking, the percentage of adults who are abstainers has remained approximately the same (one-third) for the past 30 years. Similarly, Dry sentiment has remained stable, as measured by local opinion results (Gusfield, forthcoming). In short, the argument over deviance designation has been largely one of normative dominance, not of instrumental social control. The process of deviance designation in drinking needs to be understood in terms of symbols of cultural dominance rather than in the activities of social control.

REFERENCES

Billington, Ray. *The Protestant Crusade, 1800-1860.* New York: Macmillan, 1938.

Bland, Joan. *Hibernian Crusade.* Washington, D. C.: Catholic University Press, 1951.

Earle, Alice. *Home Life in Colonial Days.* New York: Macmillan, 1937.

Gusfield, Joseph R. *Symbolic Crusade: Status Politics and the American Temperance Movement.* Urbana: University of Illinois Press, 1963.

———. "Prohibition: The Impact of Political Utopianism." In *The 1920s Revisited,* edited by John Braeman. Columbus: Ohio State University Press, forthcoming.

Handlin, Oscar. *Boston's Immigrants.* Cambridge, Massachusetts: Harvard University Press, 1941.

Hansen, Marcus. *The Immigrant in American History.* Cambridge, Massachusetts: Harvard University Press, 1940.

Keller, Mark, and Efron, Vera. "Selected Statistics on Alcoholic Beverage." In *Drinking and Intoxication,* edited by Raymond McCarthy. Glencoe, Illinois: Free Press, 1959.

Krout, John. *The Origins of Prohibition.* New York: Knopf, 1925.

Rowntree, Joseph, and Sherwell, Arthur. *State Prohibition and Local Option.* London: Hodder and Stoughton, 1900.

Standard Encyclopedia of the Alcohol Problem 6. Westerville, Ohio: American Issue Publishing Co., 1930.

Steward, Eliza D. *Memories of the Crusade.* 2nd ed. Columbus, Ohio: W. G. Hibbard, 1889.

Temperance Manual. N.p., 1836.

Whyte, William F. *Street Corner Society.* 2nd ed. Chicago: University of Chicago Press, 1955.

DANIEL H. SWETT

Cultural Bias
in the American Legal System

As a universal cultural institution, law may be considered as having the broad manifest function of maintaining social control by providing regularized procedures for conflict resolution. Within the broad framework of this manifest function, a wide variety of choices exists as to the ideal principles that may be emphasized either in formulation of the rules governing conflict resolution (leges) or in their procedural administration (ius). This range of choices may include such principles as reason, fairness, justice, individual freedom, equality, kinship, collective security, male superiority, physical or mental prowess, or any others compatible with the ethos of the society. While several such ideal principles may be incorporated into the legal system of any society, there appears to be a tendency to select one particular principle for emphasis over the others in the ius aspect of the system. The American legal system in which litigants contend against each other in court as adversaries provides a case in point. In the trial process, the validity of the litigants' positions, as indicated by whatever evidence may be introduced, is ideally determined on the basis of the law as written in accordance with applicable precedents. This concept of the trial function rests on two premises: first, that any lex is equally applicable to, understood, and concurred in by all within its spatial field; and second, that its temporal field is capable

Source: Swett, Daniel H. "Cultural Bias in the American Legal System." *Law and Society Review* 4, 1 (1969): 80-81, 83-84, 87-101. Permission granted by the Law and Society Association.

of infinite forward extension, and that it is just as pertinent to situations at any time subsequent to its enactment as it was to situations in the cultural past of its enactment.

These two premises—the first involves cultural homogeneity and the second, cultural stasis—will, if reflected in the ius, result in the system as a whole functioning to ensure maintenance of the existing sociocultural order. The premises will also result in a consequent built-in bias,[1] in the operating agencies of the ius against departures from the cultural ideal of the spatial and temporal fields. Testing of this hypothesis will be accomplished by ethnographic examination of the two cultures of the ius—the police, and the criminal court.

THE POLICE CULTURE

... Data-gathering on which this examination of the police culture is based took place over a period of nine years, from 1959 to the present, during which I served as an active reserve officer in two police agencies. Four years of this service were with a municipal police department in Coast County, one of the nine counties comprising the San Francisco Bay region; the last five years were with the sheriff's department of that county.[2] ...

Recruitment into the Police Culture

... Observation indicates that recruitment of personnel into Coast County law enforcement agencies is primarily from the lower-middle and upper-lower

1. The term "bias" is used herein to imply a proclivity, bent, or leaning in a certain general direction, with less harsher connotations than the rigid, unreasoning, performed judgments that are implied by the term "prejudice."

2. Regular participation in two-man beat patrolling provides an ethnographer with an ideal unstructured depth interview situation. Although there are occasional incidents of intensive activity, more than 90 percent of the average eight-hour shift is taken up with the dull, boring inactivity of routine patrolling. The continuous, monotonous, low-speed driving in an aimless pattern over the beat generates ennui. Darkness and the confines of the patrol car cause a feeling of isolation that is relieved only by the occasional radio transmissions. The only way for beat partners to combat this boredom and isolation and keep up their observational alertness is to converse with each other. This, coupled with the fact that the very real life dependence of each partner on the other inspires confidences, results in beat partners developing a close relationship, with intimate knowledge of each other's lives, in a short time. Because of the rather high degree of informal interaction and the frequent changes in beats and shifts, the life history, personal characteristics, attitudes, hobbies, financial status, and family problems of every officer, regular or reserve, speedily become common knowledge throughout the force. The author's beat patrolling on a full-time, paid basis during summer months thus facilitated data gathering pertaining to the police culture of Coast County.

classes on Warner's fivefold scale (1949:70).[3] Successful middle-class applicants are generally from "police families"; i.e., young men who are emulating
their fathers' or elder brothers' careers, or young men who aspired to a profession but were unable to complete their training. Many would-be-lawyers,
for example, may be found in the Coast County police ranks. Successful
applicants from the upper-lower-class group are generally young men who
have achieved apprentice-skilled, journeyman, or semiskilled artisan status
but who have aspirations of upward mobility, and young men who have
completed a satisfactory military service experience but without acquiring a readily marketable civilian skill. To both of the latter types, a law
enforcement career offers a salary in the white-collar bracket (entry level
ranges from about $8,000 to $10,000 per year), status, stability, security,
and possibility of advancement....

The requirements and selection procedures for entry and the potential
benefits of a law enforcement career in Coast County ... combine to encourage recruitment of men who are fairly homogeneous as to acceptance of
and respect for authority and emotional stability, and as to their approval
of the existing sociocultural order of American society. All, regardless of
ethnic origin, have a personal stake in the preservation and maintenance of
the latter, either because of what they consider to be their middle-class status
or because of their upward mobility to such status.

Concerning ethnic origin, it should be noted that about 95 percent of
all police personnel in the county, both regular and reserve, are whites of
European descent. Of the remainder, about 2 percent are Latin-American,
1 percent Oriental, and 2 percent Negro. In all jurisdictions, the Negro
officers are comparatively recent appointees, procured through a deliberate
but not too successful campaign to encourage Negro applicants....

The Police Value System

The congruence of several factors ... tends to produce a homogeneity of
values and attitudinal characteristics among law enforcement officers. These
factors (i.e., the type of individual attracted to law enforcement as a career,
selection procedures, enculturation into the police culture, and the personal
life-style of the officer) engender an operating value system that can most
readily be explained by using the model suggested by DuBois (1955). In this
model, the basic value premises of any culture are considered as resting upon

3. This is consistent with Niederhoffer's (1967:36) finding that for the past 15 years
the bulk of police candidates in New York City has been from the upper-lower class,
with a sprinkling from the lower-middle class. McNamara (1967:193), however, notes
that newly appointed patrolmen in New York tend to be primarily from the lower-
middle class. The latter also finds that, in the public view, police work is assigned more
prestige in the western regions of the nation than in the eastern (1967:163).

that culture's cognitive view of its environment, man's relationship to that environment and to other men. These premises then yield focal values or generalized behavioral directives, around each of which specific values or behavioral directives are clustered.

To the police culture, the environment is American society as presently structured. The cognitive view of this environment is positive, since entry into law enforcement work in itself constitutes commitment to the present structure of American society. This commitment is intensified by the officer's own self-concept, in which he is not only part of the official structure of that society but the visible representative to the public of its sovereign authority. Man's relationship to that environment is viewed as reciprocally supportive, so that the individual is obliged to contribute to the maintenance of the society and is in return entitled to the protection thereof. Man's relationships to other men must thus be in accordance with the prescriptions and proscriptions, or laws, of the society.

From these cognitive views, it is possible to postulate four premises on which the value system of the police culture is based. These are:

1. American society, as presently structured, is good and should be preserved.
2. The well-being of American society is dependent upon the security of the lives and property of its citizenry.
3. Crime, i.e., violations of law that threaten the lives and property of the citizenry, is in and of itself bad. This is analogous to the assumption of medical practitioners that health is good, illness bad.
4. Public peace, order, and regularity are requisite to the maintenance of American society. In consequence, individuals, situations, or events that are an actual or potential threat to public peace, order, and regularity are bad.

From these basic premises, five focal values may be drawn. These focal values are:

1. The institutions of American society must be respected and preserved. This includes the symbols of those institutions, such as the national flag.
2. Human life generally, and the lives of Americans in particular, must be respected and preserved.
3. Property, both public and private, must be respected and preserved.
4. Authority must be respected and preserved.
5. Order must be respected and preserved.

Clustering around each of these focal values are a variety of subsidiary, specific values. The subsidiary values, however, are recognized only to the extent that they do not conflict with the focal values and the basic premises underlying them. Thus individual freedom is an important subsidiary value and positively viewed so long as it does not encroach upon any of the focal values.

The police value system thus recognizes the right of the individual to live as he pleases just so long as the exercise of this right does not interfere with the integrity of American institutions, human life, property, authority, and order. Draft card burning, flag desecration, reckless driving, murder, theft, malicious mischief, extortion, sharp business practices, child neglect, overt homosexuality, and resisting arrest are all acts of individual freedom, but are negatively viewed as encroaching on the focal values. Related to the value of individual freedom is the concept of individual responsibility, so that welfare dependence, except when justified by age or physical condition, is also negatively viewed.

This police value system gives rise to a set of attitudinal characteristics that are reflected in police operations and thus incorporated into the ius. Behavior that transgresses upon the focal values of the police culture most often involves the unusual, i.e., some departures from the predictable range of behavior shared by the majority of the members of the American cultural system. Departures from this range of behavior are, in the officer's experience, associated with departures from the American cultural ideal and are thus an attribute of the culturally different. In consequence, the culturally different represent a threat to the existing sociocultural order and, by extension, to the person of the officer as well. The degree to which any individual is perceived as culturally different by the officer is the degree to which such an individual is considered a threat. Perceived cultural difference is thus the effective determinant of the degree of suspicion and caution the officer will exert in dealing with any given subject.

Perception of Cultural Difference

Perception of cultural difference by the police officer is both ethnocentric and stereotypical. The officer, having internalized the motivations and goals of middle-class America and incorporated the value profile of middle-class America as subsidiary to his focal values, measures cultural difference against the yardstick of this internalized cultural ideal. This measurement begins with the externals of physical appearance, dress, bearing, and speech and then proceeds to a determination, based on behavior, of adherence to or deviation from the focal and subsidiary values of the police culture.

Any member of an ethnic minority may be perceived, initially, as culturally different on the basis of physical appearance, such as skin color, alone. If, however, the subject's dress, bearing, and speech are in general conformance with the middle-class American norm for the circumstances, the perception is revised to one more nearly approaching cultural similarity than cultural difference. Another revision of the perception takes place as the subject's behavior is considered. If the behavior indicates transgression of any of the police culture's focal values, the perception of cultural differences immediately grows stronger. The officer's ultimate action in any given situation will, if all other factors are neutral, be governed primarily by this perception of cultural similarity or difference.

The handling of routine vehicular stops by Coast County deputy sheriffs provides an illustration.... Beat patrol deputies have ... developed what they refer to as the "attitude test." In applying the attitude test, the deputy explains the violation to the driver, the degree to which the violation constitutes a threat to lives and property of the driver, passengers, other motorists or pedestrians, and the fact that the violation is ground for citation or arrest. If, during this explanation, the driver appears properly impressed, the deputy will further explain that he is loathe to issue a citation and burden the driver with a fine or court appearance, and will then suggest corrective measures. These may range from a promise not to do it again, in the case of speeding, to parking and locking the car and radioing for a taxi in the case of inebriation.[4]

The driver who, after the usual protestations of innocence, evidences recognition and appreciation of the focal values of the police culture and agrees to the corrective measures suggested by the deputy is considered as having passed the attitude test and is released with a warning not to repeat the violation. Failure to pass the attitude test, i.e., evidence of rejection of the police culture's focal values of respect for life, property, authority, and order, invariably results in issuance of a citation and, in extreme cases, arrest and jailing.

Observation of deputies' behavior in administering the attitude test provided illustration of the manner in which cultural difference was perceived and the influence of this perception on deputies' attitudes. When physical appearance and dress of the subject indicated conformity to middle-class standards, suspicion decreased. However, if the subject's responses failed to indicate recognition and appreciation of the police culture's focal values, suspicion increased, attaining a peak if belligerence (failure to respect authority) or bribery (failure to respect an institution of American society) were involved. Similarly, if physical appearance and dress indicated nonconformity to middle-class standards, such as the long hair and exotic garb of the hippie, the African styles of the black nationalist, or the slick hair and "sharp"

---

4. Most motorists are successful in passing the attitude test. Fifty sets of citation blanks are contained in a book. A check of citation book issuance revealed that patrol deputies drew from two to four books per year. One patrol deputy was still using the same book drawn almost two years ago.

apparel of the Chicano, suspicion would be high initially, then decrease or increase according to evidence of recognition or rejection of the police culture's focal values.[5]

The propensity for police suspicion to increase according to ethnocentric perception of cultural difference is reinforced by stereotypes. As James (1961:731-34) has noted, stereotypes are not always made up out of whole cloth as the products of imagination and bigotry but do have some, though often far-fetched, empirical referents. The empirical referents of police stereotypes of the culturally different are, to them, hard, statistical facts. The FBI's *Uniform Crime Reports for the United States* (1966) shows disproportionately large numbers of arrest of Negroes and Indians for certain types of offenses (*see* Table 1); the California Bureau of Criminal Statistics calls attention to high proportions of convictions of Mexican-Americans and Negroes for three types of offenses;[6] as insurance rates indicate, persons under 25 years of age are disproportionately involved in vehicular offenses. Also, most law enforcement agencies maintain geographical offense-incidence maps which usually show a higher incidence of offenses in areas of predominantly Negro or Latin occupancy. These stereotypes are reflected in the increased suspicion with which the police regard the culturally different and are usually reciprocated by an equal degree of suspicion and distrust on the part of the culturally different, based on their own stereotype (for which some empirical referents do exist) of the police as bigoted bullies.

The effect of this reciprocal stereotyping on police relations with culturally different minorities is obvious. A culturally different minority, convinced that their vocabulary, values, and behavior will be misunderstood and misinterpreted by the police, shuns contact with them. Officers investigating cases within minority communities thus come up against a solid wall of silence and noncooperation, increasing suspicion and intensifying distrust of the minority on the part of the officers. The mutual distrust becomes cumulatively self-reinforcing, so that ultimately the officers and the minority regard each other as enemies. The disastrous turmoil in the United States today is probably as much or more a consequence of these impersonal cultural

---

5. The sheriff's department stresses maintenance of social distance between deputies and the public. Deputies are required to use conventional titles of respect in addressing adult citizens, and to insist that they be addressed as "deputy" or "officer." This discouragement of familiarity contributes to the effectiveness of the attitude test.

6. The following is an extract from State of California, Bureau of Criminal Statistics (1966):108.

As might be expected, the highest proportion of convictions for those persons of Mexican descent occurred in drug law violations. Bookmaking and assault violations were highest for those of Negro descent.

factors of ethnocentrism and stereotyping as it is of the manifest ill-will of one group toward another.[7] ...

The police's propensity to regard the culturally different with suspicion fosters sharper and increased surveillance of cultural minorities and minority communities. Police stereotyping of cultural minorities not only increases the suspicion and surveillance, but also serves as a self-fulfilling prophecy (Merton, 1957:421-423). Thus when police note, in statistical reports, that the arrest incidence of Indians for offenses involving drunkenness is several times that for the United States as a whole (Stewart, 1964; Swett, 1965), they are more prone to look for evidence of drunkenness in cases involving Indians and to see sufficient evidence to warrant arrest. ...

Table 1: Arrests By Race in the United States for Selected Offenses (1966)[a]

| Offense | Total | Arrests | | | |
		Caucasian	Negro	Indian	Other
Murder (nonnegligent manslaughter)	7,114	2,911 (41%)	4,068 (57%)	66 (1%)	69 (1%)
Forcible rape	10,235	5,249 (51%)	4,806 (47%)	68 (1%)	112 (1%)
Aggravated assault	75,040	37,060 (49%)	36,723 (49%)	650 (1%)	607 (1%)
Robbery	40,671	16,505 (40%)	23,451 (58%)	336 (1%)	379 (1%)
Weapons (carrying, etc.)	54,591	25,648 (47%)	28,092 (51%)	258	593 (1%)
Prostitution (commercialized vice)	29,661	11,751 (40%)	17,487 (59%)	156	264 (1%)
Gambling	80,483	18,815 (23%)	57,734 (72%)	23	3,911 (5%)
Drunkenness	1,465,295	1,059,254 (72%)	320,305 (22%)	77,203 (5%)	8,533 (1%)

Source: Uniform Crime Reports for the United States, 1966, Federal Bureau of Investigation, U.S. Department of Justice, Washington, D.C.

[a] Racial breakdown of U.S. population, as of July 1, 1967, was estimated in the U.S. Department of Commerce *Current Population Report*, Series p-25, No. 385, 14 February 1968, as follows: Caucasian, 175,055,000 (88%); Negro, 21,983,000 (11%); other, 2,079,000 (1%). No current figures are available for the Indian population. Census figures for 1960, however, showed an Indian population in the continental United States of 545,000, or 0.3% of the total population for that year.

THE CULTURE OF THE CRIMINAL COURT

For the purpose of this study, a criminal court is considered to be one in which misdemeanor or felony cases are tried or reviewed, so that no distinction need be made among the various levels of the judiciary. Although both professionals (judge, prosecutor, defense counsel) and nonprofessionals (jury, defendant, witnesses) participate in the courtroom trial process, the cultural characteristics of the court are in the main established by the professionals, though influenced to some degree by the nonprofessionals.

Regardless of their origins, members of the legal profession as a group must by reason of their professional status be considered part of the upper-middle-class stratum of American society.[8] As such, they have an even greater personal stake than the police in the preservation and maintenance of the existing sociocultural order.

The direction in which this stake motivates an individual member of the legal profession may vary, however, according to the role he plays in the courtroom culture. As holders of elective or appointive offices, judges and prosecutors may be motivated to view this stake from the frame of reference of a particular political or ethnic group (Riesman, 1954:442). Although the defense counsel who aspires to elective or appointive office may also hold this view, he is more of a free agent in that he may or may not espouse any cause, and can view his stake in the preservation and maintenance of the existing sociocultural order more in the light of his own personal inclinations. Thus while a small minority among the free agents of the legal profession may, because of personal conviction, strive for disruption and destruction of the existing sociocultural order rather than its preservation and maintenance, they are considered deviants by their colleagues.

7. Hostility to law enforcement officers within ethnic minority communities is often manifested in the most trivial incidents. On one "graveyard" patrol shift in the unincorporated black community in the southeastern portion of the county, in response to a neighbor's complaint, my partner and I asked a householder to do what he could to control his dog's incessant barking. Despite our polite phrasing of this request, the householder's aversion to police was so obvious that I could almost feel his hatred. This inspired a reciprocal hostility in me that required considerable effort to curb. Had my partner and I indulged our own feelings by relaxing the stiff facade of social distance, the householder would have been provoked to a physical assault, thus providing grounds for a felony arrest.

8. Mayer (1966:100) notes that two-thirds of all law students are from professional, proprietorial or managerial families, while Schmidhauser (1961:59) finds the Supreme Court as representing "the conscience of the American upper-middle-class . . . conditioned by the conservative impact of legal training and professional legal attitudes and associations."

Since the entry requirements into the legal profession include graduation from an accredited school of law and passing of a state bar examination, the professional members of the courtroom culture all undergo a similar enculturational experience regardless of their courtroom role. All thus acquire the same basic skill to manipulate the leges and accordingly influence the ius.

A full appreciation of the influence of the enculturational experience of members of the legal profession and a definitive establishment of their real, as distinguished from ideal, value system would require an extensive ethnographic examination that could best be accomplished by an anthropologist with legal training. However, limited observation of members of the legal profession and their behavior in a variety of professional situations enables some postulates. The particular situations observed included the client-defense counsel relationship during police interrogation of the client; the client-defense counsel relationship in the counsel's office and in the jail consultation room; the prosecutor-witness relationship outside of the courtroom; the judge-defense counsel-prosecutor relationship in consultation in the judge's chambers; and judge-defense counsel-prosecutor behavior in the courtroom during the trial process. Informal conversations with judges, prosecutors, and defense counsels provided additional data and insights.

All litigation, as members of the legal profession are prone to remark, is an adversary procedure. In this sense, the criminal trial is analogous to the gladiatorial contest, in which opposing principals may be represented by champions chosen for their skill in the manipulation of arms within the ground rules of the contest field.[9] In the criminal trial, the champions are the prosecutor and defense counsel; the arms they manipulate are the leges and the contest field is the court with the ground rules administered by the judge. This concept of litigation as an adversary procedure is apparent in all professional behavior of members of the legal profession and in their attitudes, and is consequently essential to understanding of the legal profession's value system.

Value System of the Criminal Court Culture

With all of the foregoing in mind, the legal profession's value system may be considered, again in terms of the DuBois model, as having the same first two basic premises as that of the police culture. For the remainder, however, the following are substituted:

3. The security of the lives and property of the citizenry, the public peace, and order are dependent upon the rule of the law. This requires

---

9. Bohannon (1964:195) considers gladiatorial contests and ordeals in the same light as courts in regard to defining legal situations.

that all conflict be settled by the adversary procedure of litigation.
4. No act is in and of itself bad. The sanctioning of any act can only
    be determined by the adversary procedure of litigation.

Among the focal values that may be drawn from these basic premises
are:

1. Any individual involved in conflict is entitled to the best legal pro-
    fessional representation that he can obtain.
2. Once committed to representation of an individual involved in con-
    flict, a member of the legal profession is obligated to serve the interests
    of that individual only and must not be distracted from this obligation
    by regard for the interests of any other individual or group.
3. In serving the interests of the individual he represents, a member of
    the legal profession is not concerned with absolutes such as guilt or
    innocence, right or wrong, and justice or injustice except as they
    may redound to the advantage of his client.
4. In serving the interests of the individual he represents, a member of
    the legal profession is obligated to exert maximum effort in manip-
    ulating the leges and the ground rules of the court to his client's
    advantage.

As in the case of the police, a variety of subsidiary, specific values cluster
around each of the focal values. The subsidiary values are, in the main, those
of the upper-middle-class, but influenced by such factors as the origin and
ideological convictions of the individual. Here, too, it is important to remember that the subsidiary values are recognized only to the extent that they
do not conflict with the focal values and the basic premises from which
these are drawn.

Since the criminal court is composed of both professionals and nonprofessionals, the effect of the nonprofessionals on the value system of the
culture of the criminal court must be considered. While influence of the
nonprofessionals on the courtroom culture is largely passive, it is nonetheless real, and ranges in degree of effectiveness from high for the jurors
to low for the witnesses and defendant. Cultural characteristics of jurors
are thus important.

Jury panels, in the jurisdictions comprising the San Francisco Bay region,
are drawn from rolls of registered voters. Ideally this practice should result
in any given jury panel containing a list of names representing an ethnic,
economic and sociocultural cross-section of the population in the court's
jurisdiction. In actuality, this is far from the case.

First, registered voters are either property owners or persons with a high
degree of residence stability. Transients, or those whose work involves frequent change of residence, are automatically excluded. Second, ethnic

minorities with a low tendency to exercise suffrage, such as Indians, Mexican-Americans and Negroes, are underrepresented on the voter rolls. Third, certain occupational categories are either excluded from jury panels automatically or usually excused from service, such as members of the legal profession, law enforcement officers, holders of elective public office, active medical practitioners, clergymen, and public school teachers.

Because of these factors, the middle-aged to elderly, middle-class, ethnic and cultural majority tend to predominate on any jury panel. This central tendency is intensified if prospective jurors who do not have these characteristics are challenged and excused for cause. The right to exercise a limited number of peremptory challenges by both prosecution and defense further increases the probability of the jury's adhering to this central tendency, since each challenge of a member of an underrepresented group by the prosecution decreases the relative representation of that group on the panel to a greater degree than does challenge of a member of the overrepresented group.[10]

Since the jurors bring into the courtroom culture their own value systems, normal jury selection procedures render the probability high that this will be the value system of the middle-aged, middle-class culture sympathetic to the political and economic power structure of the community. This value system tempers or adulterates to some degree that of the professionals in the courtroom culture, particularly insofar as the absolutes of guilt or innocence, right or wrong, justice or injustice are concerned.

The combination of professional and nonprofessional elements in the

---

10. In a controversial Bay region trial of a member of an ethnic minority accused of the murder of a police officer, jury selection took 14 court days. Although at least 40 percent of the population of the municipality in which the offense occurred was black, the jury panel was drawn from the county roll of registered voters, and consisted of 160 persons, of whom 27 were nonwhite. Of these, 22 were black. After excuses for cause and peremptory challenges, the ethnic composition of the jury and four alternates was one Negro, one Japanese-American, one Latin American and 13 Caucasians of European descent. Occupationally, the jury and alternates were composed of three salespersons, two bankers, one secretary, one bank secretary, one laboratory technician, one surveyor, one aircraft instrument technician, one machinist, one paper company employee, one aircraft catering service employee, and three housewives. Of the latter, one was married to a member of a municipal fire department and one to a forklift driver. The following table shows the disparity between the ethnic composition of the jury panel and the jury (including alternates):

	European-descent Caucasian	*Negro*	*Other*
Panel	83.1%	13.8%	8.1%
Jury and alternates	81.25%	6.25%	12.5%

courtroom culture materially affects adjudication in that the trial process is conducted in accordance with the value system of the legal profession, but the ultimate verdict, in a jury case, is determined largely in accordance with the value system of the jury. Because the basis for any jury verdict is the evidence adduced in court and the jurors' assessment of the defendant, professional manipulation of the leges within the ground rules of the court may so becloud the issue that the jury is left with no basis for judgment other than their assessment of the defendant.

Lack of Cultural Articulation

When there is a marked cultural difference between the defendant and judge, prosecutor, defense counsel, and jurors, there is a consequent lack of articulation in communication and understanding that is often intensified by professional manipulation of the leges. Cultural differences in speech, dress, bearing, and behavior then assume paramount importance, as illustrated in the following two cases:

The People v. *Young Beartracks.* Young Beartracks was accused of the first-degree murder of Chicago Eddie, which was alleged to have taken place following a poolroom argument. Though Beartracks admitted to shooting and killing Eddie, his plea of not guilty was based on his contention that Eddie was the aggressor and had been about to attack him with a razor. The incident occurred in the unincorporated black community in the southeastern portion of Coast County. Beartracks, Eddie, and all witnesses other than the deputy sheriffs who investigated the case were black. Since the deputies had not witnessed the shooting or events leading thereto, their testimony was limited to after-the-fact matters.

Cultural processes in the United States have encouraged development in black communities of a unique vocabulary, the meanings of which are not shared by the rest of the English language community. Testimony of witnesses concerning the events leading up to the actual homicide was phrased in this vocabulary. As a consequence, both judge and jury were left completely in the dark on at least one crucial point in this case.

The witnesses' testimony brought out that prior to the actual homicide, the deceased has "put him [the defendant] in the dozens."[11] Effort of

11. The "dozens," a cultural phenomenon of lower-class urban Negro communities, is a verbal contest in which the participants each try to out-insult the other. There are no limits to the range of insults, so that appearance, food habits, sexual behavior, mental ability, and physical characteristics of the participants, their siblings, parents, and other kin all become the subject of extreme vituperation—the more profane and obscene, the better. The loser in the contest is the one who is either provoked to violence or runs away.

defense counsel to procure a clarification of the word "dozens" was objected to by the prosecution on the grounds that the witness was not qualified as an expert in semantics. The objection was sustained by the court, so both judge and jury were denied knowledge of the fact that the homicide was a consequence of an extreme form of verbal aggression initiated by the deceased against the defendant.

The inability of both defense counsel and prosecutor to communicate with the witnesses in terms understandable to the judge and jury further beclouded the issues. Questions put to witnesses were responded to by blank stares, noncommittal monosyllables or completely irrelevant verbiage. Communications were so difficult that during one court recess the prosecutor remarked that it would have been easier to bring out the facts of the case if the witnesses were unable to speak English, so that competent interpreters could have been used.

The prosecutor's remark points up the fact that, though all participants in this trial were ostensibly speaking English, they were using two different vocabularies with two different sets of meanings. Witnesses did not understand or share the meanings of the vocabulary used by the professionals in the courtroom culture, and neither these gentlemen nor the jury understood nor shared the meanings of the vocabulary used by the witnesses.

When questioned on the stand, witnesses were faced with responding by silence, by admitting they did not understand the vocabulary words of the question, or by guessing (usually wrongly) at the meaning of the question. Either the first or third choice reflected on their credibility, as in the case of the witness who, after denying having had felony and misdemeanor convictions, was asked if he had ever served time in a correctional institution and responded, "No sir, but I was a steward in the merchant marine for twenty years."

This witness' credibility was destroyed when evidence was introduced showing that he had had both misdemeanor and felony convictions and had served time in prison. The witness was not taken aback by this revelation and admitted readily to the specific convictions and the prison sentence. What was not brought out, however, was that the words "felony," "misdemeanor," and "correctional institution" were unknown and unintelligible to him. His answers to questions using these words were based on a wrong guess as to their meanings.

Following the trial, several members of the jury were asked their opinion of the testimony and how they arrived at a verdict of guilty of murder in the second degree, with a sentence of five years to life. They indicated that the greater portion of the testimony had been incomprehensible to them, and that the witnesses appeared to be either morons who could not·

understand nor speak plain English or unconscionable liars.[12] For these reasons, their verdict had been based solely on the fact that Young Beartracks had admitted to shooting Chicago Eddie.

Because, in their estimation, Young Beartracks' contention that the shooting had been in self-defense (which if true would have warranted a verdict of not guilty) was neither proven nor disproven, the jury felt that a finding of guilty as charged (murder in the first degree with a mandatory death penalty) would be too harsh. Manipulation of the leges and lack of cultural articulation had precluded an understanding of the case, so that their verdict was a compromise based on standards of their own value system.

The People v. *Basher.* Basher's trial for assault and battery took place in Hill County, another of the nine counties comprising the San Francisco Bay region. The 18-year-old Basher, black, a high-school dropout and resident of an unincorporated black community, was serving a jail sentence for car theft when he was involved in a brawl with another inmate (also black) and several jail deputies.

As is often the case in a brawl involving several people, the circumstances were unclear. Eyewitness testimony was conflicting. On the witness stand, one deputy sheriff stated that Basher had acted solely to defend his person in the general melee, while another stated that Basher had taken advantage of the brawl to attempt infliction of serious bodily injury. The jury deliberated for a little more than six hours, during the course of which further instructions were requested from the judge, before reaching a verdict of guilty of assault only, a lesser offense, with a sentence of two years. Basher's trial was observed by a researcher, who reported:

[Basher's] way of life, demeanor, attitudes, manner of speaking, and many other things are different [from those of the jury] . For example, if Basher had had his hair cut shorter, if he would have shaved closer and been aware of the effect of his speech on the jury, he might have gotten off entirely.

On the stand, Basher slipped into slang and jive talk ... and had a certain air that could easily be mistaken for arrogance ... among his own peers this was the natural way.... His mannerisms, according to the D.A. bespoke his guilt. [Donald Hill, field notes]

12. Sapir (1921:4) has termed thought as "silent speech," since thinking is impossible without words in which to conceptualize and frame thoughts. This is borne out by the fact that psychologists now generally recognize the mysterious entity they term "intelligence" as measurable by the extent of an individual's vocabulary. The witnesses appeared unintelligent to the jurors because of their unfamiliarity with the vocabulary of the courtroom, although their own vocabulary was adequate for their normal functioning within their cultural environment.

In this case, Basher exemplified in almost every detail the negative stereo-type of the antisocial (to the white community) young Negro male. Not only did his hairstyle, dress, bearing, vocabulary, and pronunciation stress his cultural differences, but his tone and manner of speech were such as to create an impression of hostile belligerence on anyone not familiar with his cultural background. Had he been able to assume the protective camouflage of the jury's culture, i.e., had he had conventional dress, haircut, and speech, a quiet, composed manner, and circumspect bearing, the probability, in view of the conflicting evidence, of acquittal or a much lighter sentence would have been high.

Built-in Bias in the Courtroom Culture

The illustrations provided by these two cases are relatively obvious. There are, however, other and more subtle factors that tend to place the culturally different at a disadvantage in the courtroom. Not the least of these are negative stereotypes of cultural minorities. Shepardson (1968), for example, has noted that Indians are considered by the legal professionals to make poor witnesses with little concept of perjury, apt to make a statement in pretrial discussion, and then change their testimony completely on the witness stand.

The implications of such an attitude are far-reaching. All legal professionals, whether defending or prosecuting, like to win their cases. Too, all are familiar with criminal statistics. Prosecutors may thus be more willing to prosecute a member of a cultural minority than the actual evidence may warrant, if the offense is one that criminal statistics indicate to be "typical" of that minority. Defense counsel, on the other hand, may be reluctant to take a case in which the client's cultural characteristics constitute a handicap in the cultural environment of the courtroom. If persuaded to take the case, a defense counsel may feel that his client's best interests will be served by an out-of-court deal with the prosecutor to plead guilty to a lesser offense in a nonjury trial, regardless of actual guilt or innocence.[13] Many Indian informants, interviewed while serving jail sentences, claim to have received such advice. The member of a cultural minority, by reason of his lesser access to expert counsel and lesser understanding of the system, is more likely to be intimidated into accepting whatever deal is proffered than the member of the cultural majority.

Examination of the courtroom culture thus indicates that several factors work to the disadvantage of the culturally different in the trial process. These factors are: the value system of the legal profession, the procedures

13. Mayer (1966:46) estimates that four-fifths of the criminal cases in the United States end as guilty pleas bargained out against reduced sentences or reduced charges.

by which juries are selected, the value system of the jurors, the lack of articulation in communication between the culturally different and the professionals and nonprofessionals composing the court, and the negative stereotypes of cultural minorities held by the professionals. To this must be added the lesser, though significant, effect of similar negative stereotypes held by the nonprofessionals. As the adjudication arm of the ius, the courts are by reason of their cultural characteristics automatically biased against the culturally different.

REFERENCES

Bohannon, P. "Anthropology and the law." In *Horizons of Anthropology,* edited by S. Tax. Chicago: Aldine, 1964.

California, State of, Bureau of Criminal Statistics. *Crime and Delinquency in California.* Sacramento: Department of Justice, Division of Law Enforcement, 1966.

DuBois, C. "The dominant value profile of American culture." *American Anthropologist* 57 (December 1955): 1232-39.

James, B. L. "Social-psychological dimensions of Ojibwa acculturation." *American Anthropologist* 63 (August 1961): 721-46.

McNamara, J. H. "Uncertainties in police work." In *The Police,* edited by D. J. Bordua. New York: John Wiley & Sons, 1967.

Mayer, M. *The Lawyers.* New York: Harper & Row, 1966.

Merton, R. K. *Social Theory and Social Structure.* Glencoe, Illinois: Free Press, 1957.

Niederhoffer, A. *Behind the Shield.* Garden City, New York: Doubleday, 1967.

Reisman, D. *Individualism Reconsidered and Other Essays.* Glencoe, Illinois: Free Press, 1954.

Sapir, E. *Language.* New York: Harcourt, Brace and World, 1921.

Schmidhauser, J. R. *The Supreme Court.* New York: Holt, Rinehart & Winston, 1961.

Shepardson, M. "Navajo Indians and the Eleven Major Crimes." Paper presented to the Southwestern Anthropological Conference, San Diego, 1968.

Stewart, O. "Questions regarding American Indian criminality." *Human Organization* 23 (Spring 1964): 61-66.

Swett, D. H. "Deviant Behavior and Urban Adjustment: The American Indian Case in San Francisco and Oakland." Master's thesis. San Francisco: San Francisco State College, 1965.

Warner, W. L.; Meeker, M.; and Ellis, K. *Social Class in America.* New York: Harper & Row, 1949.

WILLIAM J. CHAMBLISS

The Saints and the Roughnecks

Eight promising young men—children of good, stable, white upper-middle-class families, active in school affairs, good precollege students—were some of the most delinquent boys at Hanibal High School. While community residents and parents knew that these boys occasionally sowed a few wild oats, they were totally unaware that sowing wild oats completely occupied the daily routine of these young men. The Saints were constantly occupied with truancy, drinking, wild driving, petty theft, and vandalism. Yet not one was officially arrested for any misdeed during the two years I observed them.

This record was particularly surprising in light of my observations during the same two years of another gang of Hanibal High School students, six lower-class white boys known as the Roughnecks. The Roughnecks were constantly in trouble with police and community even though their rate of delinquency was about equal with that of the Saints. What was the cause of this disparity? The result? The following consideration of the activities, social class and community perceptions of both gangs may provide some answers.

THE SAINTS FROM MONDAY TO FRIDAY

The Saints' principal daily concern was with getting out of school as early as possible. The boys managed to get out of school with minimum danger

Source: Chambliss, William J. "The Saints and the Roughnecks." *Society* 11 (1973): 24-31. Permission granted by Transaction, Inc.

that they would be accused of playing hookey through an elaborate procedure for obtaining "legitimate" release from class. The most common
procedure was for one boy to obtain the release of another by fabricating a
meeting of some committee, program, or recognized club. Charles might raise
his hand in his 9:00 chemistry class and asked to be excused—a euphemism
for going to the bathroom. Charles would go to Ed's math class and inform
the teacher that Ed was needed for a 9:30 rehearsal of the drama club play.
The math teacher would recognize Ed and Charles as "good students" involved in numerous school activities and would permit Ed to leave at 9:30.
Charles would return to his class, and Ed would go to Tom's English class
to obtain his release. Tom would engineer Charles' escape. The strategy
would continue until as many of the Saints as possible were freed. After
a stealthy trip to the car (which had been parked in a strategic spot), the
boys were off for a day of fun.

Over the two years I observed the Saints, this pattern was repeated nearly
every day. There were variations on the theme, but in one form or another,
the boys used this procedure for getting out of class and then off the school
grounds. Rarely did all eight of the Saints manage to leave school at the
same time. The average number avoiding school on the days I observed
them was five.

Having escaped from the concrete corridors the boys usually went either
to a pool hall on the other (lower-class) side of town or to a cafe in the
suburbs. Both places were out of the way of people the boys were likely
to know (family or school officials), and both provided a source of entertainment. The pool hall entertainment was the generally rough atmosphere,
the occasional hustler, the sometimes drunk proprietor and, of course, the
game of pool. The cafe's entertainment was provided by the owner. The
boys would "accidentally" knock a glass on the floor or spill cola on the
counter—not all the time, but enough to be sporting. They would also bend
spoons, put salt in sugar bowls, and generally tease whoever was working
in the cafe. The owner had opened the cafe recently and was dependent on
the boys' business which was, in fact, substantial since between the horsing
around and the teasing they bought food and drinks.

THE SAINTS ON WEEKENDS

On weekends the automobile was even more critical than during the week,
for on weekends the Saints went to Big Town—a large city with a population
of over a million 25 miles from Hanibal. Every Friday and Saturday night
most of the Saints would meet between 8:00 and 8:30 and would go into
Big Town. Big Town activities included drinking heavily in taverns or night-
clubs, driving drunkenly through the streets, and committing acts of vandalism and playing pranks.

By midnight on Fridays and Saturdays the Saints were usually thoroughly high, and one or two of them were often so drunk they had to be carried to the cars. Then the boys drove around town, calling obscenities to women and girls; occasionally trying (unsuccessfully so far as I could tell) to pick girls up; and driving recklessly through red lights and at high speeds with their lights out. Occasionally they played "chicken." One boy would climb out the back window of the car and across the roof to the driver's side of the car while the car was moving at high speed (between 40 and 50 miles an hour); then the driver would move over and the boy who had just crawled across the car roof would take the driver's seat.

Searching for "fair game" for a prank was the boys' principal activity after they left the tavern. The boys would drive alongside a foot patrolman and ask directions to some street. If the policeman leaned on the car in the course of answering the question, the driver would speed away, causing him to lose his balance. The Saints were careful to play this prank only in an area where they were not going to spend much time and where they could quickly disappear around a corner to avoid having their license plate number taken.

Construction sites and road repair areas were the special province of the Saints' mischief. A soon-to-be-repaired hole in the road inevitably invited the Saints to remove lanterns and wooden barricades and put them in the car, leaving the hole unprotected. The boys would find a safe vantage point and wait for an unsuspecting motorist to drive into the hole. Often, though not always, the boys would go up to the motorist and commiserate with him about the dreadful way the city protected its citizenry.

Leaving the scene of the open hole and the motorist, the boys would then go searching for an appropriate place to erect the stolen barricade. An "appropriate place" was often a spot on a highway near a curve in the road where the barricade would not be seen by an oncoming motorist. The boys would wait to watch an unsuspecting motorist attempt to stop and (usually) crash into the wooden barricade. With saintly bearing the boys might offer help and understanding.

A stolen lantern might well find its way onto the back of a police car or hang from a street lamp. Once a lantern served as a prop for a reenact- ment of the "midnight ride of Paul Revere" until the "play," which was taking place at 2:00 AM in the center of a main street of Big Town, was interrupted by a police car several blocks away. The boys ran, leaving the lantern on the street, and managed to avoid being apprehended.

Abandoned houses, especially if they were located in out-of-the-way places, were fair game for destruction and spontaneous vandalism. The boys would break windows, remove furniture to the yard and tear it apart, urinate on the walls, and scrawl obscenities inside.

Through all the pranks, drinking, and reckless driving the boys managed miraculously to avoid being stopped by police. Only twice in two years was I aware that they had been stopped by a Big City policeman. Once was for speeding (which they did every time they drove whether they were drunk or sober), and the driver managed to convince the policeman that it was simply an error. The second time they were stopped they had just left a nightclub and were walking through an alley. Aaron stopped to urinate and the boys began making obscene remarks. A foot patrolman came into the alley, lectured the boys, and sent them home. Before the boys got to the car one began talking in a loud voice again. The policeman, who had followed them down the alley, arrested this boy for disturbing the peace and took him to the police station where the other Saints gathered. After paying a $5.00 fine, and with the assurance that there would be no permanent record of the arrest, the boy was released.

The boys had a spirit of frivolity and fun about their escapades. They did not view what they were engaged in as "delinquency," though it surely was by any reasonable definition of that word. They simply viewed themselves as having a little fun and who, they would ask, was really hurt by it? The answer had to be no one, although this fact remains one of the most difficult things to explain about the gang's behavior. Unlikely though it seems, in two years of drinking, driving, carousing, and vandalism no one was seriously injured as a result of the Saints' activities.

THE SAINTS IN SCHOOL

The Saints were highly successful in school. The average grade for the group was "B," with two of the boys having close to a straight "A" average. Almost all of the boys were popular and many of them held offices in the school. One of the boys was vice-president of the student body one year. Six of the boys played on athletic teams.

At the end of their senior year, the student body selected ten seniors for special recognition as the "school wheels"; four of the ten were Saints. Teachers and school officials saw no problem with any of these boys and anticipated that they would all "make something of themselves."

How the boys managed to maintain this impression is surprising in view of their actual behavior while in school. Their technique for covering truancy was so successful that teachers did not even realize that the boys were absent from school much of the time. Occasionally, of course, the system would backfire and then the boy was on his own. A boy who was caught would be most contrite, would plead guilty, and ask for mercy. He inevitably got the mercy he sought.

Cheating on examinations was rampant, even to the point of orally communicating answers to exams as well as looking at one another's papers. Since none of the group studied, and since they were primarily dependent on one another for help, it is surprising that grades were so high. Teachers contributed to the deception in their admitted inclination to give these boys (and presumably others like them) the benefit of the doubt. When asked how the boys did in school, and when pressed on specific examinations, teachers might admit that they were disappointed in John's performance, but would quickly add that they "knew that he was capable of doing better," so John was given a higher grade than he had actually earned. How often this happened is impossible to know. During the time that I observed the group, I never saw any of the boys take homework home. Teachers may have been "understanding" very regularly.

One exception to the gang's generally good performance was Jerry, who had a "C" average in his junior year, experienced disaster the next year, and failed to graduate. Jerry had always been a little more nonchalant than the others about the liberties he took in school. Rather than wait for someone to come get him from class, he would offer his own excuse and leave. Although he probably did not miss any more classes than most of the others in the group, he did not take the requisite pains to cover his absences. Jerry was the only Saint whom I ever heard talk back to a teacher. Although teachers often called him a "cut up" or a "smart kid," they never referred to him as a troublemaker or as a kid headed for trouble. It seems likely, then, that Jerry's failure his senior year and his mediocre performance his junior year were consequences of his not playing the game the proper way (possibly because he was disturbed by his parents' divorce). His teachers regarded him as "immature" and not quite ready to get out of high school.

THE POLICE AND THE SAINTS

The local police saw the Saints as good boys who were among the leaders of the youth in the community. Rarely, the boys might be stopped in town for speeding or for running a stop sign. When this happened the boys were always polite, contrite, and pled for mercy. As in school, they received the mercy they asked for. None ever received a ticket or was taken into the precinct by the local police.

The situation in Big City, where the boys engaged in most of their delinquency, was only slightly different. The police there did not know the boys at all, although occasionally the boys were stopped by a patrolman. Once they were caught taking a lantern from a construction site. Another time they were stopped for running a stop sign, and on several occasions they were stopped for speeding. Their behavior was as before: contrite, polite, and penitent. The urban police, like the local police, accepted their demeanor as sincere. More important, the urban police were convinced that these were good boys just out for a lark.

THE ROUGHNECKS

Hanibal townspeople never perceived the Saints' high level of delinquency. The Saints were good boys who just went in for an occasional prank. After all, they were well dressed, well mannered, and had nice cars. The Roughnecks were a different story. Although the two gangs of boys were the same age, and both groups engaged in an equal amount of wild-oat sowing, everyone agreed that the not-so-well-dressed, not-so-well-mannered, not-so-rich boys were heading for trouble. Townspeople would say, "You can see the gang members at the drugstore, night after night, leaning against the storefront (sometimes drunk) or slouching around inside buying cokes, reading magazines, and probably stealing old Mr. Wall blind. When they are outside and girls walk by, even respectable girls, these boys make suggestive remarks. Sometimes their remarks are downright lewd."

From the community's viewpoint, the real indication that these kids were in for trouble was that they were constantly involved with the police. Some of them had been picked up for stealing, mostly small stuff, of course, "but still it's stealing small stuff that leads to big time crimes." "Too bad," people said. "Too bad that these boys couldn't behave like the other kids in town; stay out of trouble, be polite to adults, and look to their future."

The community's impression of the degree to which this group of six boys (ranging in age from 16 to 19) engaged in delinquency was somewhat distorted. In some ways the gang was more delinquent than the community thought; in other ways they were less.

The fighting activities of the group were fairly readily and accurately perceived by almost everyone. At least once a month, the boys would get into some sort of fight, although most fights were scraps between members of the group or involved only one member of the group and some peripheral hanger-on. Only three times in the period of observation did the group fight together: once against a gang from across town, once against two blacks, and once against a group of boys from another school. For the first two fights the group went out "looking for trouble"—and they found it both times. The third fight followed a football game and began spontaneously with an argument on the football field between one of the Roughnecks and a member of the opposition's football team.

Jack had a particular propensity for fighting and was involved in most of the brawls. He was a prime mover of the escalation of arguments into fights.

More serious than fighting, had the community been aware of it, was theft. Although almost everyone was aware that the boys occasionally stole things, they did not realize the extent of the activity. Petty stealing was a frequent event for the Roughnecks. Sometimes they stole as a group and coordinated their efforts; other times they stole in pairs. Rarely did they steal alone.

The thefts ranged from very small things like paperback books, comics, and ballpoint pens to expensive items like watches. The nature of the thefts varied from time to time. The gang would go through a period of systematically shoplifting items from automobiles or school lockers. Types of thievery varied with the whim of the gang. Some forms of thievery were more profitable than others, but all thefts were for profit, not just thrills.

Roughnecks siphoned gasoline from cars as often as they had access to an automobile, which was not very often. Unlike the Saints, who owned their own cars, the Roughnecks would have to borrow their parents' cars, an event which occurred only eight or nine times a year. The boys claimed to have stolen cars for joy rides from time to time.

Ron committed the most serious of the group's offenses. With an unidentified associate the boy attempted to burglarize a gasoline station. Although this station had been robbed twice previously in the same month, Ron denied any involvement in either of the other thefts. When Ron and his accomplice approached the station, the owner was hiding in the bushes beside the station. He fired both barrels of a double-barreled shotgun at the boys. Ron was severely injured; the other boy ran away and was never caught. Though he remained in critical condition for several months, Ron finally recovered and served six months of the following year in reform school. Upon release from reform school, Ron was put back a grade in school, and began running around with a different gang of boys. The Roughnecks considered the new gang less delinquent than themselves, and during the following year Ron had no more trouble with the police.

The Roughnecks, then, engaged mainly in three types of delinquency: theft, drinking, and fighting. Although community members perceived that this gang of kids was delinquent, they mistakenly believed that their illegal activities were primarily drinking, fighting, and being a nuisance to passersby. Drinking was limited among the gang members, although it did occur, and theft was much more prevalent than anyone realized.

Drinking would doubtless have been more prevalent had the boys had ready access to liquor. Since they rarely had automobiles at their disposal, they could not travel very far, and the bars in town would not serve them. Most of the boys had little money, and this, too, inhibited their purchase of alcohol. Their major source of liquor was a local drunk who would buy them a fifth if they would give him enough extra to buy himself a pint of whiskey or a bottle of wine.

The community's perception of drinking as prevalent stemmed from the fact that it was the most obvious delinquency the boys engaged in. When one of the boys had been drinking, even a casual observer seeing him on the corner would suspect that he was high.

There was a high level of mutual distrust and dislike between the Roughnecks and the police. The boys felt very strongly that the police were unfair and corrupt. Some evidence existed that the boys were correct in their perception.

The main source of the boys' dislike for the police undoubtedly stemmed from the fact that the police would sporadically harass the group. From the standpoint of the boys, these acts of occasional enforcement of the law were whimsical and uncalled for. It made no sense to them, for example, that the police would come to the corner occasionally and threaten them with arrest for loitering when the night before the boys had been out siphoning gasoline from cars and the police had been nowhere in sight. To the boys, the police were stupid on the one hand, for not being where they should have been and catching the boys in a serious offense, and unfair on the other hand, for trumping up "loitering" charges against them.

From the viewpoint of the police, the situation was quite different. They knew, with all the confidence necessary to be a policeman, that these boys were engaged in criminal activities. They knew this partly from occasionally catching them, mostly from circumstantial evidence ("the boys were around when those tires were slashed"), and partly because the police shared the view of the community in general that this was a bad bunch of boys. The best the police could hope to do was to be sensitive to the fact that these boys were engaged in illegal acts and arrest them whenever there was some evidence that they had been involved. Whether or not the boys had in fact committed a particular act in a particular way was not especially important. The police had a broader view: their job was to stamp out these kids' crimes; the tactics were not as important as the end result.

Over the period that the group was under observation, each member was arrested at least once. Several of the boys were arrested a number of times and spent at least one night in jail. While most were never taken to court, two of the boys were sentenced to six months' incarceration in boys' schools.

THE ROUGHNECKS IN SCHOOL

The Roughnecks' behavior in school was not particularly disruptive. During school hours they did not all hang around together, but tended instead to spend most of their time with one or two other members of the gang who were their special buddies. Although every member of the gang attempted to avoid school as much as possible, they were not particularly successful and most of them attended school with surprising regularity. They considered school a burden—something to be gotten through with a minimum of conflict. If they were "bugged" by a particular teacher, it could lead to trouble. One of the boys, Al, once threatened to beat up a teacher and, according to the other boys, the teacher hid under a desk to escape him.

Teachers saw the boys the way the general community did, as heading for trouble, as being uninterested in making something of themselves. Some were also seen as being incapable of meeting the academic standards of the school. Most of the teachers expressed concern for this group of boys and were willing to pass them despite poor performance, in the belief that failing them would only aggravate the problem.

The group of boys had a grade point average just slightly above "C." No one in the group failed either grade, and no one had better than a "C" average. They were very consistent in their achievement or, at least, the teachers were consistent in their perception of the boys' achievement.

Two of the boys were good football players. Herb was acknowledged to be the best player in the school and Jack was almost as good. Both boys were criticized for their failure to abide by training rules, for refusing to come to practice as often as they should, and for not playing their best during practice. What they lacked in sportsmanship they made up for in skill, apparently, and played every game no matter how poorly they had performed in practice or how many practice sessions they had missed.

TWO QUESTIONS

Why did the community, the school, and the police react to the Saints as though they were good, upstanding, nondelinquent youths with bright futures but to the Roughnecks as though they were tough, young criminals who were headed for trouble? Why did the Roughnecks and the Saints in fact have quite different careers after high school—careers which, by and large, lived up to the expectations of the community?

The most obvious explanation for the differences in the community's and law enforcement agencies' reactions to the two gangs is that one group of boys was "more delinquent" than the other. Which group *was* more delinquent? The answer to this question will determine in part how we explain the differential responses to these groups by the members of the community and, particularly, by law enforcement and school officials.

In sheer number of illegal acts, the Saints were the more delinquent. They were truant from school for at least part of the day almost every day of the week. In addition, their drinking and vandalism occurred with surprising regularity. The Roughnecks, in contrast, engaged sporadically in delinquent episodes. While these episodes were frequent, they certainly did not occur on a daily or even a weekly basis.

The difference in frequency of offenses was probably caused by the Roughnecks' inability to obtain liquor and to manipulate legitimate excuses from school. Since the Roughnecks had less money than the Saints, and teachers carefully supervised their school activities, the Roughnecks' hearts may have been as black as the Saints', but their misdeeds were not nearly as frequent.

There are really no clear-cut criteria by which to measure qualitative differences in antisocial behavior. The most important dimension of the difference is generally referred to as the "seriousness" of the offenses.

If seriousness encompasses the relative economic costs of delinquent acts, then some assessment can be made. The Roughnecks probably stole an average of about $5.00 worth of goods a week. Some weeks the figure was considerably higher, but these times must be balanced against long periods when almost nothing was stolen.

The Saints were more continuously engaged in delinquency but their acts were not for the most part costly to property. Only their vandalism and occasional theft of gasoline would so qualify. Perhaps once or twice a month they would siphon a tankful of gas. The other costly items were street signs, construction lanterns and the like. All of these acts combined probably did not quite average $5.00 a week, partly because much of the stolen equipment was abandoned and presumably could be recovered. The difference in cost of stolen property between the two groups was trivial, but the Roughnecks probably had a slightly more expensive set of activities than did the Saints.

Another meaning of seriousness is the potential threat of physical harm to members of the community and to the boys themselves. The Roughnecks were more prone to physical violence; they not only welcomed an opportunity to fight, they went seeking it. In addition, they fought among themselves frequently. Although the fighting never included deadly weapons, it was still a menace, however minor, to the physical safety of those involved.

The Saints never fought. They avoided physical conflict both inside and outside the group. At the same time, though, the Saints frequently endangered their own and other people's lives. They did so almost every time they drove a car, especially if they had been drinking. Sober, their driving was risky; under the influence of alcohol it was horrendous. In addition, the Saints endangered the lives of others with their pranks. Street excavations left unmarked were a very serious hazard.

Evaluating the relative seriousness of the two gangs' activities is difficult. The community reacted as though the behavior of the Roughnecks was a problem, and they reacted as though the behavior of the Saints was not. But the members of the community were ignorant of the array of delinquent acts that characterized the Saints' behavior. Although concerned citizens were unaware of much of the Roughnecks' behavior as well, they were much better informed about the Roughnecks' involvement in delinquency than they were about the Saints'.

VISIBILITY

Differential treatment of the two gangs resulted in part because one gang was infinitely more visible than the other. This differential visibility was a direct function of the economic standing of the families. The Saints had access to automobiles and were able to remove themselves from the sight of the community. In as routine a decision as to where to go to have a milkshake after school, the Saints stayed away from the mainstream of community life. Lacking transportation, the Roughnecks could not make it to the edge of town. The center of town was the only practical place for them to meet since their homes were scattered throughout the town and any noncentral meeting place put an undue hardship on some members. Through necessity the Roughnecks congregated in a crowded area where everyone in the community passed frequently, including teachers and law enforcement officers. They could easily see the Roughnecks hanging around the drugstore.

The Roughnecks, of course, made themselves even more visible by making remarks to passersby and by occasionally getting into fights on the corner. Meanwhile, just as regularly, the Saints were either at the cafe on one edge of town or in the pool hall at the other edge of town. Without any particular realization that they were making themselves inconspicuous, the Saints were able to hide their time-wasting. Not only were they removed from the mainstream of traffic, but they were almost always inside a building.

On their escapades the Saints were also relatively invisible, since they left Hanibal and travelled to Big City. Here, too, they were mobile, roaming the city, rarely going to the same area twice.

DEMEANOR

To the notion of visibility must be added the difference in the responses of group members to outside intervention with their activities. If one of the Saints was confronted with an accusing policeman, even if he felt he was truly innocent of a wrongdoing, his demeanor was apologetic and penitent. A Roughneck's attitude was almost the polar opposite. When confronted with a threatening adult authority, even one who tried to be pleasant, the Roughneck's hostility and disdain were clearly observable. Sometimes he might attempt to put up a veneer of respect, but it was thin and was not accepted as sincere by the authority.

School was no different from the community at large. The Saints could manipulate the system by feigning compliance with the school norms. The availability of cars at school meant that once free from the immediate sight of the teacher, the boys could disappear rapidly. And this escape was well enough planned that no administrator or teacher was nearby when the boys left. A Roughneck who wished to escape for a few hours was in a bind. If it were possible to get free from class, downtown was still a mile away, and even if he arrived there, he was still very visible. Truancy for the Roughnecks meant almost certain detection, while the Saints enjoyed almost complete immunity from sanctions.

BIAS

Community members were not aware of the transgressions of the Saints. Even if the Saints had been less discreet, their favorite delinquencies would have been perceived as less serious than those of the Roughnecks.

In the eyes of the police and school officials, a boy who drinks in an alley and stands intoxicated on the street corner is committing a more serious offense than is a boy who drinks to inebriation in a nightclub or a tavern and drives around afterwards in a car. Similarly, a boy who steals a wallet from a store will be viewed as having committed a more serious offense than a boy who steals a lantern from a construction site.

Perceptual bias also operates with respect to the demeanor of the boys in the two groups when they are confronted by adults. It is not simply that adults dislike the posture affected by boys of the Roughneck ilk; more important is the conviction that the posture adopted by the Roughnecks is an indication of their devotion and commitment to deviance as a way of life. The posture becomes a cue, just as the type of the offense is a cue, to the degree to which the known transgressions are indicators of the youths' potential for other problems.

Visibility, demeanor, and bias are surface variables which explain the day-to-day operations of the police. Why do these surface variables operate as they do? Why did the police choose to disregard the Saints' delinquencies while breathing down the backs of the Roughnecks?

The answer lies in the class structure of American society and the control of legal institutions by those at the top of the class structure. Obviously, no representative of the upper-class drew up the operational chart for the police which led them to look in the ghettoes and on streetcorners—which led them to see the demeanor of lower-class youth as troublesome and that of upper-middle-class youth as tolerable. Rather, the procedures simply developed from experience—experience with irate and influential upper-middle-class parents insisting that their son's vandalism was simply a prank and his drunkenness only a momentary "sowing of wild oats"—experience with cooperative or indifferent, powerless, lower-class parents who acquiesced to the laws' definition of their son's behavior.

ADULT CAREERS OF THE SAINTS AND THE ROUGHNECKS

The community's confidence in the potential of the Saints and the Roughnecks apparently was justified. If anything, the community members underestimated the degree to which these youngsters would turn out "good" or "bad."

Seven of the eight members of the Saints went on to college immediately after high school. Five of the boys graduated from college in four years. The sixth one finished college after two years in the army, and the seventh spent four years in the air force before returning to college and receiving a B.A. degree. Of these seven college graduates, three went on for advanced degrees. One finished law school and is now active in state politics, one finished medical school and is practicing near Hanibal, and one boy is now working for a Ph.D. The other four college graduates entered submanagerial, managerial, or executive training positions with larger firms.

The only Saint who did not complete college was Jerry. Jerry had failed to graduate from high school with the other Saints. During his second senior year, after the other Saints had gone on to college, Jerry began to hang around with what several teachers described as a "rough crowd"—the gang that was heir apparent to the Roughnecks. At the end of his second senior year, when he did graduate from high school, Jerry took a job as a used-car salesman, got married, and quickly had a child. Although he made several abortive attempts to go to college by attending night school, when I last saw him (ten years after high school) Jerry was unemployed and had been living on unemployment for almost a year. His wife worked as a waitress.

Some of the Roughnecks have lived up to community expectations. A number of them were headed for trouble. A few were not.

Jack and Herb were the athletes among the Roughnecks and their athletic prowess paid off handsomely. Both boys received unsolicited athletic scholarships to college. After Herb received his scholarship (near the end of his senior year), he apparently did an about-face. His demeanor became very similar to that of the Saints. Although he remained a member in good standing of the Roughnecks, he stopped participating in most activities and did not hang on the corner as often.

Jack did not change. If anything, he became more prone to fighting. He even made excuses for accepting the scholarship. He told the other gang members that the school had guaranteed him a "C" average if he would come to play football—an idea that seems far-fetched, even in this day of highly competitive recruiting.

During the summer after graduation from high school, Jack attempted suicide by jumping from a tall building. The jump would certainly have killed most people trying it, but Jack survived. He entered college in the fall and played four years of football. He and Herb graduated in four years, and both are teaching and coaching in high schools. They are married and have stable families. If anything, Jack appears to have a more prestigious position in the community than does Herb, though both are well respected and secure in their positions.

Two of the boys never finished high school. Tommy left at the end of his junior year and went to another state. That summer he was arrested and placed on probation on a manslaughter charge. Three years later he was arrested for murder; he pleaded guilty to second degree murder and is serving a 30-year sentence in the state penitentiary.

Al, the other boy who did not finish high school, also left the state in his senior year. He is serving a life sentence in a state penitentiary for first degree murder.

Wes is a small-time gambler. He finished high school and "bummed around." After several years he made contact with a bookmaker who employed him as a runner. Later he acquired his own area and has been working it ever since. His position among the bookmakers is almost identical to the position he had in the gang; he is always around but no one is really aware of him. He makes no trouble and he does not get into any. Steady, reliable, capable of keeping his mouth closed, he plays the game by the rules, even though the game is an illegal one.

That leaves only Ron. Some of his former friends reported that they had heard he was "driving a truck up north," but no one could provide any concrete information.

REINFORCEMENT

The community responded to the Roughnecks as boys in trouble, and the boys agreed with that perception. Their pattern of deviancy was reinforced, and breaking away from it became increasingly unlikely. Once the boys acquired an image of themselves as deviants, they selected new friends who affirmed that self-image. As that self-conception became more firmly entrenched, they also became willing to try new and more extreme deviances. With their growing alienation came freer expression of disrespect and hostility for representatives of the legitimate society. This disrespect increased the community's negativism, perpetuating the entire process of commitment to deviance. Lack of a commitment to deviance works the same way. In either case, the process will perpetuate itself unless some event (like a scholarship to college or a sudden failure) external to the established relationship intervenes. For two of the Roughnecks (Herb and Jack), receiving college athletic scholarships created new relations and culminated in a break with the established pattern of deviance. In the case of one of the Saints (Jerry), his parents' divorce and his failing to graduate from high school changed some of his other relations. Being held back in school for a year and losing his place among the Saints had sufficient impact on Jerry to alter his self-image and virtually to assure that he would not go on to college as his peers did. Although the experiments of life can rarely be reversed, it seems likely in view of the behavior of the other boys who did not enjoy this special treatment by the school that Jerry, too, would have "become something" had he graduated as anticipated. For Herb and Jack outside intervention worked to their advantage; for Jerry it was his undoing.

Selective perception and labelling—finding, processing, and punishing some kinds of criminality and not others—means that visible, poor, non-mobile, outspoken, undiplomatic "tough" kids will be noticed, whether their actions are seriously delinquent or not. Other kids, who have established a reputation for being bright (even though underachieving), disciplined and involved in respectable activities, who are mobile and monied, will be invisible when they deviate from sanctioned activities. They'll sow their wild oats—perhaps even wider and thicker than their lower-class cohorts—but they won't be noticed. When it's time to leave adolescence most will follow the expected path, settling into the ways of the middle-class, remembering fondly the delinquent but unnoticed fling of their youth. The Roughnecks and others like them may turn around, too. It is more likely that their notice-able deviance will have been so reinforced by police and community that their lives will be effectively channeled into careers consistent with their adolescent background.

VICTORIA LYNN SWIGERT AND RONALD A. FARRELL

Normal Homicides and the Law

The differential legal treatment of criminal offenders constitutes one of the most controversial areas of study in contemporary criminology. Allegations of racial discrimination or class bias in the judicial system have prompted continued debate and investigation of the issue. Yet the search for patterns of discretionary treatment has generated contradictory findings. Studies of police administration, bail procedures, prosecution and defense, jury selection, and final disposition, while prolific, have failed to surface a definitive statement concerning equality of justice in the United States.[1]

The use of class and race as the primary criteria against which legal treatment has been evaluated may be responsible for the disparity of findings evident in the literature. The criminal justice system is *the* institutional representation of the "American Creed" (Myrdal, 1944) of equality for all. With many stages of the judicial process open to public inspection and legal sanction, violation of this principle through manifest class or racial discrimination would seriously undermine the collective myth.

Given a society characterized by an official commitment to equality before the law, the selective use of discretion in the legal system might better

1. Discussions of the discrepant findings evident in the literature may be found in Hindelang (1969) and Swigert and Farrell (1976:chap. 2).

Source: Swigert, Victoria Lynn, and Farrell, Ronald A. "Normal Homicides and the Law." *American Sociological Review* 42, 1 (1977): 16–32. Permission granted by The American Sociological Association.

be examined along alternative lines. In this regard, it may be noted that law enforcement and adjudication are interpretive processes. At each stage, legal authorities must assess the offender and the offense for evidence that official sanction is warranted. Such evaluation and interpretation may be guided, in part, by popular stereotypes of criminality.

Evidence that stereotypes exist in the general population is abundant. People do, in fact, tend to utilize highly stereotypical characterizations in describing deviants. Furthermore, individual descriptions of specific deviations are remarkably similar in content (Simmons, 1965:226). Thus, "the marihuana smoker stereotype emerges as an insecure escapist, lacking self-control and looking for kicks; the adulterer is immoral, promiscuous, and insecure; the homosexual is perverted and mentally ill; the political radical is ambitious, aggressive, stubborn, and dangerous" (Simmons, 1965:228). Such conceptions are perpetuated in everyday interaction and in the mass media characterizations of comic strips, television, newspapers, books, songs, and advertising. In this manner, even the very young become familiar with stereotypes, images that continue to be reaffirmed throughout adulthood (Cain, 1964: 278-89; Scheff, 1966:64).

Stereotypes not only shape public attitudes and behavior toward deviants, but guide the very choice of individuals who are to be so defined and processed. Persons possessing characteristics associated with the stereotype of a particular deviation are more likely to be identified and reacted to as such (Simmons, 1965:226). Furthermore, since minority groups, lower-class persons, and males more closely approximate stereotypic images, these groups are especially susceptible to their application (Simmons, 1965:226; Hess and Mariner, 1975:255).

Such a pattern also may be observed at the organizational level. Thus, popular beliefs about deviants within social control agencies have been found to influence the application of formal labels regarding criminality. It has been noted, for example, that among legal authorities there is evident a belief that certain groups in the population are inherently criminal. This anticipation of law-violating behavior underlies much of the discretionary treatment accorded the black and the poor. The use of violence against blacks and slum dwellers (Westley, 1953), the cursory disposition of urban vagrants (Foote, 1956), and the differential selection of juveniles for treatment (Goldman, 1963; Piliavin and Briar, 1964) illustrate not so much racism or class discrimination, but a response to a belief that blacks and the poor require rough treatment (Westley, 1953:163), that obvious destitution implies future criminality (Foote, 1956:310), and that black children are more likely to engage in crime than white children (Goldman, 1963:288).

Given the suspicion concerning the behavior of these groups, encounters of legal authorities with black and lower-class individuals are potentially problematic. In such a situation, the decision to invoke legal sanction is a process of determining the extent to which the individuals involved conform to the criminal stereotype. Thus, the arrest and prosecution of juvenile delinquents (Goldman, 1963; Piliavin and Briar, 1964), delinquent bail cases (Skolnik, 1966), shoplifters (Cameron, 1964; Steffensmeier and Terry, 1973), and homosexuals (Farrell and Hardin, 1974) have been shown to be motivated more by the stereotypic appearance of the offender than by evidence of actual criminal behavior; while facial stereotypes of the murderer, robber, and traitor have been found to influence jury evaluations of guilt for each of these criminal categories (Shoemaker, 1973).

Evidence does exist, then, to suggest that stereotypes operate as guiding imageries for action in the treatment of deviance. Applying Goffman's theoretical discussion of the stigma to the adjudication process, it may be observed that the stereotype becomes the "means for categorizing persons and the complement of attributes felt to be ordinary and natural for members of each of these categories," the product of which is to "allow us to deal with anticipated others without special attention or thought" (Goffman, 1963:2). A *legally* problematic situation would seem to be particularly prone to the use of such categorizations. Where constraints of time, personnel, and the sheer number of individuals who must be processed preclude full enforcement or extensive investigation, officials are likely to depend on shorthand methods in administrative decisions. Such methods include inspection of the offender and the offense for conformity to the popular conception of criminality.[2]

That many of the cues perceived by legal authorities are manifestations of class and race cultures has led a number of researchers to conclude that the legal system discriminates against these groups. It is possible to speculate, however, that more than class and race, cultural stereotypes of criminality determine the decisions of legal authorities. While these stereotypes include class- and race-related characteristics, they are not restricted to, nor do they include all members of these groups.

THE DATA

In order to examine this issue, a study of the legal treatment of individuals arrested on general charges of murder was conducted. The records maintained by a diagnostic and evaluation clinic attached to the court in a large urban jurisdiction in the northeastern United States and the indictment files secured from the Office of the Clerk of Courts provided the data used in the research.

2. Quinney (1970) is to be credited with the development of the notion of criminal stereotypes. In his own work, the stereotype is the medium through which powerful segments of society ensure a consistency of definition of criminality. Through the diffusion of the popular conception, individuals become aware of the social characteristics of offenders, the appropriate reaction to crime, and the relevance of crime to the social system.

Established in the mid-1930s, the court clinic has been charged with the diagnosis and evaluation of selected offenders as part of presentence investigation. While most of its long-term efforts have involved the evaluation of sex offenders, in 1955 the clinic established a routine policy of examining cases of criminal homicide. Consequently, all persons arrested for murder in this jurisdiction are seen at the clinic, where an exhaustive study is done of their psychological condition and social background. If the findings indicate that the defendant is insane, the clinic notifies the court and proceedings are initiated for commitment to a mental hospital. Otherwise, the information is summarized and forwarded to the presiding judge for use in sentencing, in the event that the defendant is found or pleads guilty. If the defendant is found not guilty or if the case is dismissed, the sealed envelope is returned to the clinic unopened. In either event, upon its completion, the court notifies the clinic of the specifics regarding the final disposition of the case.

In selecting the cases to be analyzed, an exhaustive list of all persons arrested on general charges of murder in the jurisdiction was compiled from the clinic files. Four hundred and forty-four cases, a 50 percent random sample, covering the period from January 1, 1955, through December 31, 1973, were selected for analysis.

The clinic records provided thorough and systematic data on the social characteristics of the defendant, any prior offense record, the circumstances of the offense, and the results of the psychiatric evaluation. As regards the legal data, however, it was found that the information was not always contained in the clinic reports or that there were certain contradictions in the records concerning award of bail, the identity of the attorney, or the results of postsentence appeals. Because of these lacks, it became necessary to secure the latter data from the indictment records maintained by the Office of the Clerk of Courts. These records supplied information regarding the type of counsel (private, private appointed, or public), bail decisions, the type of trial (jury or nonjury), and the final conviction awarded.[3]

While it is acknowledged that the records maintained by the clinic and court are for other than scientific purposes, it is precisely this information that is used by legal authorities in the determination of the career outcome of the defendant. The data collected for this research, therefore, comprise much of the same information as evaluated by legal representatives in their decision-making processes. The comprehensiveness of the records, the opportunity they present for verification of recorded fact, and their similarity to

3. Since both clinic and indictment records contained a variety of sources of the same information concerning the defendant, victim, and the circumstances of the offense, a multiple check of recorded facts was made possible. Where discrepancies occurred, those sources closest to the legal stage in question were utilized for documentation. Thus, for example, discrepant recordings of final disposition by the clinic and court would result in adoption of the court documents for verification of this fact.

the kinds of information utilized throughout the legal system constitute a data source that may provide a most acceptable basis for the study of adjudication patterns.

THE "NORMAL PRIMITIVE": A CRIMINAL CONCEPTION

Evidence of the role of the criminal stereotype in the legal processing of defendants emerged somewhat serendipitously in the early stages of data collection. In a review of the psychiatric portions of the clinic reports, a diagnostic category surfaced which seemed to reflect an official usage of such a stereotype—the "normal primitive." This category has become part of the standard diagnostic terminology of the staff of the clinic and constitutes a meaningful classification for the court. The characteristics of the "normal primitive" were provided by the clinic and the diagnosis warrants a detailed description here.

> While treated as a diagnostic category, the designation "normal primitive" constitutes a *social* description of a group of people whose behavior, *within their own social setting,* is best described as normal. The "normal primitive" comes largely from the foreign-born and black populations. Their lives are characterized by impoverished economic conditions which, as with their behavior, may be described as "primitive." Occupational achievements center around unskilled, menial labor, and these careers are often sporadic. Educational levels are minimal and testing indicates borderline to low-average intelligence. While the children of the foreign-born do acclimate to a less "primitive" existence, the offspring of the black population seem unaffected by improved educational and social opportunities.
>
> The personality characteristics of the "normal primitive" are childlike or juvenile, the behavior and attitude being similar to that of an eight- to twelve-year-old boy. At the same time, acceptance as a *man* by his group is very important. In this regard, the "normal primitive" is sensitive and takes offense to any question of his masculinity.
>
> Interaction among such individuals often occurs in bars where arguments readily result in aggressive encounters. Compelled to fight any challenger of his masculinity or courage, the "normal primitive" protects himself by carrying a lethal weapon.
>
> While sexual patterns among the foreign-born are relatively stable, promiscuity among the blacks provides additional grounds for aggression. Sexual prowess is a reflection of the masculinity of males, but is denied to females. Thus, when infidelity occurs, "as it inevitably does," the humiliation perceived by the male will result in threats and physical abuse that may produce the death of any one, or all members, of the sex triangle.

In summary:

> The primitive man is comfortable and without mental illness. He has little,
> if any, education and is of dull intelligence. His goals are sensual and
> immediate—satisfying his physical and sexual needs without inhibition,
> postponement, or planning. There is little regard for the future—extending
> hardly beyond the filling of his stomach and the next payday or relief
> check. His loyalties and identifications are with a group that has little
> purpose in life, except surviving with a minimum of sweat and a maximum
> of pleasure. He has the ten-year-old boy's preoccupation with muscular
> prowess and "being a man." Unfortunately, he lacks the boy's external
> restraint and supervision so that he is more or less an intermittent com-
> munity problem and responsibility. (Clinic description.)

The "normal primitive" classification represents a conception of criminality
that combines both class and race characteristics. The imagery suggests a
group of people whose style of life and innate attributes predispose them to
violence. The tendency toward physical aggression over "trivial" issues,
histories of family disorganization, and tenuous marital ties, combined with
a perception by the offender that the violent response is appropriate and
necessary, are manifestations of the volatile life-style in which the "normal
primitive" is said to exist.[4]

The importance of this diagnostic category lies in its expression of a more
general conception of criminality as it operates in the judicial system. In
that the clinic diagnosis is part of the *sealed* information forwarded to the
presiding judge, it is only *following* conviction that it becomes relevant
information in the adjudication process. Evidence that individuals diagnosed
as "normal primitive" receive differential treatment prior to sentencing
would suggest, therefore, a more diffuse operation of the conception. Thus,
an exploration of the effects of such a stereotype on the processing of defendants in the case of homicide becomes the empirical focus of this work.

DESIGN FOR ANALYSIS

Research on the question of differential legal treatment is characterized by
a tradition of limited empirical focus. Concerned almost exclusively with an
examination of specific stages in the legal system, studies have concentrated

---

4. The "normal primitive" criminal conception is remarkably similar to social scientific
depictions of members of the subculture of violence (*see*, e.g., Pittman and Handy, 1964;
Benay, 1966; Wolfgang and Ferracuti, 1967). Elsewhere we have argued that the social
scientific "discovery" of such a subculture may be testimony to the effectiveness with
which the stereotype of violent criminality has been applied (*see* Swigert and Farrell,
1976).

on *either* access to bail (Foote, 1959; Ares et al., 1963), the nature of counsel (Ehrmann, 1962; Sudnow, 1965; Blumberg, 1967; Siegel, 1968), jury selection (Robinson, 1950; Stodtbeck et al., 1957; Erlanger, 1970), *or* final disposition (Johnson, 1941; Garfinkel, 1949; Bensing and Schroeder, 1960; Bullock, 1961; Vines and Jacob, 1963; Wolf, 1964; Forslund, 1969; Farrell, 1971; Chiricos et al., 1972; Burke and Turk, 1975). While intervening relationships involving the status characteristics of the victim (Johnson, 1941; Garfinkel, 1949), the severity of the offense (Bensing and Schroeder, 1960; Wolfgang, 1961; Farrell, 1971; Burke and Turk, 1975), and the extent of prior record (Green, 1961; Farrell, 1971) have been examined, still the empirical treatment of adjudication has been confined to the effects of a limited number of variables on single stages of the legal process.

Such an approach fails to acknowledge the processual nature of adjudication. Differential treatment occurring early in the judicial process may have consequences for final disposition. Thus, the relationships between social characteristics of defendants and disposition may not be direct but, rather, may operate through a number of other variables relevant to the adjudication process. Therefore, it is imperative that the sequence of events leading to the determination of guilt or innocence be incorporated into the study of treatment patterns.

The nature of the data utilized in criminological research has traditionally limited the kinds of investigations conducted. Many of the variables relevant to such studies involve nominal data. Statistical analyses, therefore, have relied upon various cross-tabular schemes. While developments in log-linear techniques (Goodman, 1972; 1973a; 1973b) have introduced the possibility of imposing causal order on nominal data, the usefulness of this method is somewhat restricted. With the addition of each new variable, the possibility of alternative causal interpretations increases exponentially.

It has recently been demonstrated (Knoke, 1975; Goodman, 1976), however, that regression analysis of dichotomous variables produces results comparable to those obtained through log-linear techniques. The argument is that multiple regression may be robust enough to overcome the violation of assumptions produced when a dependent variable is dichotomized. Thus, with the restriction that some degree of variance exists in the dependent variable, the use of regression analysis may be approached with confidence.

The highly structured nature of the judicial system lends itself to a systematic analysis of legal processing. The discrete ordering of events from assignment of counsel, bail decisions, and selection of trial format to final adjudication constitutes a series of stages that allows the researcher to assert the causal sequence of events.

Capitalizing on the nature of the system, then, an effort is made to trace the paths of influence among certain social and legal variables and the final disposition of cases by the court. The path analytic technique is particularly suited for such an exploration. For, having established causal priority among a system of variables, paths of direct as well as indirect influence may be assessed.

The construction of complete recursive path diagrams was executed. Using multiple regression techniques, each stage of the model was fitted to all preceding variables. Paths failing to produce standarized coefficients of at least .100 were deleted and the remaining coefficients were recalculated.[5] The path and correlation coefficients generated by this analysis are presented in Table 1.

HOMICIDE AND THE CRIMINAL CONCEPTION: AN EMPIRICAL MODEL OF LEGAL PROCESSING

Prior Conviction Severity

The first stage of analysis involves the specification of the effects of the social characteristics of homicide defendants on the development of prior conviction records. The importance of a criminal record in the adjudication process has been noted by a number of researchers. The use of this concept, however, has been restricted to an observation of the presence or absence of prior offenses (Farrell, 1971; Burke and Turk, 1975) or, if severity of criminal record is considered, to a simple summation of the number of offenses, felonies, or misdemeanors for which each defendant was found guilty (Bullock, 1961; Green, 1964; Chiricos et al., 1972).

Given the reported significance of the variable, a more sensitive indicant of the seriousness of prior convictions seems required. Toward that end, it was noted that state law establishes the maximum penalty allowable for each degree of felony and misdemeanor. Such penalties would appear to provide an adequate estimate of the seriousness of offenses as officially recognized in a particular jurisdiction. In the present research, therefore, a summation of the prescribed maximum penalties for offenses for

---

5. Coefficients for the abbreviated model were computed using a least-squares estimate (Boudon, 1968:199–235). This procedure utilizes the entire set of antecedent variables in the estimation of path coefficients, rather than deleting the nonsignificant variables from calculations. The adequacy of the abbreviated model was assessed in terms of its ability to reproduce the original correlation matrices. A one-tailed test of the null hypothesis that the original and reconstructed correlations did not differ significantly from zero was utilized. Where these correlations did differ significantly and where the reinstated path produced a coefficient of at least .100, path coefficients were recalculated. This procedure was iterated until all coefficients were adequately reproduced.

Table 1: Standardized Path and Correlation Coefficients for Each Stage of the Analysis

Correlation Coefficients	A Sex	B Race	C Occupational Prestige	D Prior Conviction Severity	E Normal Primitive	F Private Attorney	G Bail	H Jury Trial	I Final Conviction
				Path Coefficients					
Sex (F-M)[a]		—	—	.157	(-.019)	(.038)	(-.061)	(.095)	.159
Race (B-W)[a]	.080		—	(-.051)[b]	-.260	(-.097)	(-.032)	(-.046)	(.048)
Occupational Prestige (L-H)[a]	.057	.352		-.154	-.154	.303	(.072)	(.086)	-.148
Prior Conviction Severity (L-H)[a]	.151	-.081	-.131		(.055)	-.120	-.130	(.001)	.130
Normal Primitive (No-Yes)	-.040	-.311	-.239	.092		(-.096)	-.112	-.171	(.022)
Private Attorney (No-Yes)	.034	.057	.316	.162	-.173		-.199	(-.057)	(-.043)
Bail (No-Yes)	-.065	.042	.153	-.161	.157	.230		(.096)	-.215
Jury Trial (No-Yes)	.093	.034	.104	-.010	-.148	.016	.108		-.123
Final Conviction (L-H)[a]	.167	-.032	-.237	.215	.098	-.165	-.293	-.171	

[a] (F-M) = Female-Male; (B-W) - Black-White; (L-H) = Low to High.
[b] Coefficients before the variable was dropped from the equation are presented in parentheses throughout the table.

383

which the defendant was found guilty constituted a ratio measure of prior conviction severity.[6]

The coefficients calculated for the exploration of this variable are shown in column D of Table 1. The sex and occupational prestige[7] of the defendant do contribute to the development of a prior record. Males and individuals of lower occupational status have more extensive criminal histories, blacks do not.

This latter finding has important implications for earlier explanations concerning the role of race in legal treatment. For, it has been argued that the more severe sentences accorded blacks may be accounted for by the greater extent of prior criminal involvement among black defendants (Green, 1961). Since prior offenses are considered in presentence investigations, the severity of the sentence awarded offenders with extensive records is said to be a reflection of a judicial decision to penalize more severely those whose legal backgrounds indicate a history of recidivism. Thus, if blacks receive longer sentences for their offenses than do whites, it is because of their greater involvement in prior criminal behavior.

The present analysis, however, indicates that race is not directly associated with prior offense record, but operates only through its relationship with occupational prestige ($r = .352$). The usefulness of previous convictions in explanations of racial differences in the adjudication process is therefore not apparent.

The contribution of sex to prior offense severity is presumably in terms of the provision of access to the means for enacting criminal behavior. Social roles and expectations afford males greater exposure to illegal opportunities. The association of this variable with prior offense severity, then, has little theoretical relevance to the exploration of legal treatment. Thus, only the path from occupational prestige to prior offense record is of major concern to this work. In this regard, it may be observed that individuals of lower occupational status accumulate more extensive criminal records.

The Normal Primitive

The "normal primitive" classification, as used by the clinic, designates persons whose violent behavior is said to be normal within their own social setting. Applied largely to minority populations, the label is reflective of a cultural

6. Thus, a defendant with a conviction for robbery (maximum penalty, 20 years) and one for bookmaking (maximum penalty, five years) would receive a prior offense severity score of 25. Penalties ranged from 0 to 20 years, with no prior convictions for first degree murder. Sentences of less than a year were scored in terms of the percentage of the year involved. Persons awarded a 90-day sentence, for example, would receive a severity score of .25.

7. Occupational prestige was measured in terms of Treiman's 1977 classification system. fication system.

stereotype of criminality. Thus, serving as an empirical indicator of a more popular image of individuals who are thought to be prone to the spontaneous expression of violence, the "normal primitive" classification provides the foundations for an analysis of the effects of criminal conceptions on the legal process.

To assess the impact of this conception on legal treatment in the case of murder, defendants were classified according to the absence or presence of the "normal primitive" diagnosis in their clinical evaluations. All prior variables were then examined for their influence in the determination of the diagnosis. Column E of Table 1 shows that the race and occupational prestige of defendants do, in fact, contribute substantially to the designation "normal primitive." Here we note that blacks and individuals of lower occupational prestige are more likely to be designated "primitive" than are whites or higher-status persons.

Such a pattern is not surprising, given the meaning of the concept as formulated by the clinic. For, as noted previously, this conception of crime is based on a number of class- and race-related characteristics. More specifically, the label connotes a predisposition to violence among the black and the poor. An imagery of personal and social disorganization within which these groups are evaluated is said to underlie their tendency toward greater levels of interpersonal aggression.

Access to Legal Resources

The social characteristics of defendants, the severity of their prior conviction records, and the designation "normal primitive" must now be assessed in terms of influence on the availability of private counsel, award of bail, and trial by jury. Differential access to such resources may constitute a crucial link in the determination of adjudication patterns. The nature of the interrelationships at this stage of the analysis, therefore, provides important information for an understanding of legal treatment.

The right to counsel. The system of public defense was developed in order to guarantee the indigent defendant the right to qualified legal representation. Yet the differentials in resources available to private and public counsel (Ehrmann, 1962; Siegel, 1968; Deatherage, 1972), as well as the political milieu within which the latter must operate (Siegel, 1968), have brought into question the quality of defense provided by the public attorney. Of particular concern is the fact that the limitations inherent in appointed counsel seem to affect final disposition patterns in criminal cases (Ehrmann, 1962:21; Chiricos et al., 1972:562-4). Given the apparent centrality of counsel in determining legal outcome, then, it is important to specify the factors that facilitate access to the privately retained defender.

Table 2: Retention of Private Attorney by Normal Primitiveness Controlling for
Occupational Prestige

	Occupational Prestige							
	Low				High			
Access to Private	Normal Primitive				Normal Primitive			
Attorney	No		Yes		No		Yes	
	n	%	n	%	n	%	n	%
No	(80)	57.1	(53)	75.7	(51)	35.7	(5)	19.4
Yes	(60)	42.9	(17)	25.2	(92)	64.3	(12)	70.6
Total			210				160	

$x^2 = 6.203$, df = 3, P $\angle$ .20.

Column F of Table 1 depicts the patterns associated with retention of a private attorney. The best predictor of such retention is the higher occupational prestige of the defendant. Since indigence is the basis for assignment of public defense, this relationship is expected.

In addition to financial ability, the severity of a defendant's prior conviction record has a small but independent effect. That is, individuals with extensive criminal records are more likely to be assigned public counsel. A suggested explanation of this phenomenon involves the decision of private counsel to refuse those cases where successful defense may be problematic. The presence of a criminal history resists the application of an imagery of innocence. When such a presumption cannot be sustained, a defender may be unwilling to risk the courtroom consequences. Protective of his reputation as a successful criminal lawyer and sensitive to his loss of bargaining power with the prosecutor, the private attorney may withhold legal services from those defendants whose prior experiences with the law are seen as predictive of career criminality.

Of special interest is the association between the criminal conception of homicide and retention of a private attorney; the coefficient evident here, although in the right direction, approaches insignificance (P = .096). An explanation of this lack of relationship concerns the number of "normal primitives" who also come from lower occupational positions. Table 2 depicts a cross-tabulation of retention of private counsel and the "normal primitive" designation while controlling for occupational prestige (occupation has been dichotomized according to the mean). The findings indicate that the influence of the popular conception on type of attorney occurs through the financial inability of such persons to retain private counsel, rather than through any direct effect of conformity to the stereotype.

Award of bail. The institution of bail was developed in response to the problem of deterring the accused from fleeing adjudication, while assuring him the right to the presumption of innocence through release from incarceration before trial (Foote, 1959:43). Guided by this principle, bail is to be set in graduated amounts that motivate persons of all income levels to appear in court at the appointed time. Rather than using the financial ability of defendants, however, it has been argued that judges often rely upon the severity of the present offense, as well as the prior conviction record, to determine bail amounts (Foote, 1959). Since these factors are presumed to be associated more often with lower income defendants, bail procedures may be said to have a strong class bias.

Evidence also suggests that the inability to obtain bail has significant effects on final disposition. Studies have shown that defendants jailed before trial were more often convicted than those charged with similar offenses who were able to finance their release (Foote, 1959:47; Louisiana Law Review, 1961:627; Ares et al., 1963:83). Social class, therefore, through the operation of the institution of bail, may have important consequences for adjudication in criminal cases.

An additional word must be said about the nature of the present offense and the decision to set bail. As noted, offense severity is an important consideration in determining the eligibility of a defendant for pretrial release. Indictments often involve an implied statement concerning level of intent and premeditation. Thus, a charge of first degree murder is a more serious offense than a charge of involuntary manslaughter. In the present jurisdiction, however, individuals are arrested and indicted on a general charge of murder. The degree of the offense, along with the guilt or innocence of the defendant, is determined only at the time of the trial. Therefore, offense severity as it is specified in the formal charge is automatically controlled in this study.[8]

The results of an examination of the causal antecedents to award of bail in the case of homicide are shown in column G of Table 1. Occupational prestige was found to have little direct influence. Rather, this relationship occurs through the effects of prior offense record, the nature of counsel, and application of the label "normal primitive."

That a defendant with an extensive prior conviction history is more likely to be detained before trial seems to be a consequence of two related factors. On the one hand, the withholding of bail or establishing its amount

8. Official criteria for determining bail eligibility include an assessment of the "nature of the offense and any mitigating or aggravating factors that may bear upon the likelihood of conviction and possible penalty" (Criminal Code Manual issued by the state in which this study was conducted). It is the determination of the effects of the criminal stereotype on evaluations of mitigating and aggravating factors, when the nature of the charge is held constant, that is the focus of concern in this stage of the analysis.

at excessive levels represents a court decision to detain the repeat offender. On the other hand, there may be operative the belief that individuals who have already been convicted of violating the law are more likely to be guilty of the present offense as well. The question of pretrial release in this case becomes inconsequential.

Another influence in the award of bail is the type of counsel. Privately retained attorneys are more successful in securing bail for their clients than are publicly appointed attorneys. This relationship operates independently from the financial ability of the defendants involved.[9] Thus, access to resources early in the legal process has consequences for the acquisition of additional resources at later stages.

Finally, individuals designated as "normal primitive" are also denied bail. This not only occurs through the nature of the legal services provided them as indigent defendants, but is also a direct effect of their status as "normal primitives." The denial of bail to those whose characteristics conform to a popular conception of the homicidal type suggests that a presumption of guilt is made by the court before official adjudication occurs.

Trial format. The final legal resource variable to be considered is that of trial format. The right to trial by jury is guaranteed all defendants who plead not guilty to the charges against them. Only those who admit their guilt or who waive their right to trial are disposed of by a judge.

An empirical examination of the effects of the several variables discussed thus far on selection of trial format reveals that the only significant path of influence was that generated by the "normal primitive" designation (Table 1, column H).

It is interesting to note that there is no direct path of influence from attorney to trial format. It has been argued that negotiations between prosecutor and attorney will often result in a bargained settlement of the case (Newman, 1956; Alschuler, 1968; Cole, 1970). While all attorneys engage in plea negotiations, such negotiations are most often utilized by appointed counsel (Blumberg, 1967). The absence of a direct relationship between attorney and trial by jury, however, suggests that the origins of the negotiated plea lie outside the initiative of the participating attorneys. Rather, we note that the single most important determinant of type of trial is the "normal primitive" criminal conception.

Once again, we interpret this finding in terms of the impact of the stereotype of criminality on legal outcome. Recalling Sudnow's (1965) discussion of normal crimes, it may be suggested that the characteristics typically associated with homicide have a direct effect on the quality of treatment afforded individuals whose offenses are seen as normal. Thus, the appearance

9. The validity of such a statement, of course, depends upon the adequacy of using occupational prestige as an indicator of financial resources.

of a normal homicide, as one committed by an individual whose culture and characteristics are said to be associated with violent behavior, exerts an influence on trial format which is independent of the nature of counsel.

As with the effects of "normal primitiveness" on the award of bail, the implications of this relationship may be viewed within the context of a presumption of guilt. The denial of bail and the entry of a guilty plea before the court represent a definition of culpability, the criterion for which is conformity to the criminal stereotype. Once that evaluation is made, the legal resources essential for the successful defense of a criminal defendant are, in the eyes of legal representatives, superfluous. Without such advantages, equalitarian legal treatment itself becomes problematic. Public defenders are not able to conduct a pretrial investigation comparable to that initiated by private attorneys; denial of bail not only creates a definition of dangerousness and guilt, but often results in job termination—a factor weighed heavily by the court should probation become a sentencing alternative; and a plea of guilt removes the last vestige of the combative imagery upon which the legal system is founded.

Final Disposition

The last stage in the analysis involves an assessment of defendant characteristics, prior offense record, the "normal primitive" designation, and assess to legal resources as they affect final adjudication. The disposition of a case was measured in terms of the charge for which the defendant was found guilty.[10] Since defendants originally charged with criminal homicide were sometimes convicted of crimes other than the two degrees of murder and two degrees of manslaughter, final conviction was scaled according to felony and misdemeanor levels. Thus, charges included first degree murder, first degree felony (second degree murder), second degree felony (voluntary manslaughter), first degree misdemeanor (involuntary manslaughter), acquittal, and dismissal (including *nolle prosequi* and demurer sustained). Column I of Table 1 displays the coefficients generated in the analysis.

10. Sentencing decisions are dependent upon the conviction awarded defendants. Within each offense category, however, the range of possible sentences is both limited and typically established by formula. Thus, cross-tabular analyses of sentences imposed within each degree of homicide reveal no significant differences. It appears, therefore, that discretionary treatment occurs earlier in the legal processing of criminal defendants. In addition, it is following conviction that the judge has access to the presentence recommendations and diagnoses of the clinic. Since the focus of this research is to ascertain the effects of a shared conceptualization of the violent offender on treatment severity, it is necessary to examine those stages of adjudication that precede official access to diagnostic information.

Figure 1: Final Charge by Legal Resources and Defendant Characteristics

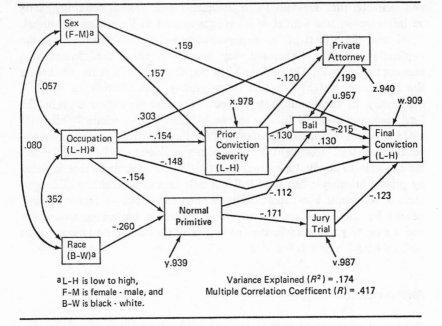

The sex and occupational prestige of defendants are directly related to severity of final disposition. Males and persons of lower occupational status are convicted of the most serious charges.

That women are convicted of lesser offenses than their male counterparts is not surprising. Being female seems to be a mitigating factor in the assessment of criminality in general. It is only in regard to certain moral offenses, especially the sex codes, that women are accorded official recognition as law violators (*see,* for example, Sutherland and Cressey, 1974:126-9). A combination of a social "pedestal effect" as well as the defintion that violent behavior is a male phenomenon contribute, we might speculate, to the less severe treatment accorded women accused of homicide.

Of particular theoretical interest is the direct effect of the defendant's occupational prestige on final adjudication. Individuals of lower status are found guilty of serious crimes more often than those of higher status. Thus, in addition to the advantages that it effects at earlier stages of the legal process, higher occupational prestige also produces a more favorable adjudication before the court.

A defendant's prior conviction record also appears to influence final disposition. Since a decision involving guilt or innocence officially is to be without reference to prior criminal involvement, this relationship is somewhat surprising. It appears, however, that such information enters into the adjudication process through more informal channels. Whether it be the unwillingness of prosecution and defense to consider seriously a reduction of charge for the repeat offender, the judge's awareness of the criminal history of a defendant as he weighs the evidence, or the use of prior record in the attempt to impeach the credibility of one who testifies in his own behalf, the defendant's criminal history becomes an influential factor in the severity of final conviction.

The award of bail and trial by jury are the legal resources which have the most direct effects on the severity of final disposition, while the nature of counsel acts through its influence on bail. The findings, in general, indicate that access to these resources produces the less severe final convictions awarded by the court. Given such a pattern, the antecedents to legal resource acquisition become most relevant. In addition to the operation of social class in the ability to retain private counsel, the two most active determinants of adjudication in the case of homicide are the prior offense record of the defendant and his conformity to an imagery of violent criminality. The completed path diagram generated by this analysis is found in Figure 1.

DISCUSSION

The racial background and social class of criminal defendants traditionally have been the most important factors considered in the study of adjudication. Such attributes, however, have failed to produce conclusive evidence regarding the quality of justice available in the United States. Rather, there appears to be a much more subtle motivation for the discretionary dispensation of justice—the criminal stereotype.

Occupational prestige did emerge as an important factor in the present empirical analysis. It must be noted, however, that the variable most affected by occupational status (that is, attorney) is, in fact, for sale. Little effort is made to disguise the importance of financial status in the ability to retain private counsel. Rather, judicial practices based on economic advantage have become institutionalized to the extent that the inherent inequities are not part of public consciousness. Thus, while the differential ability to purchase defense may elicit concern from those who seek full equality in the legal system, it certainly does not constitute the kind of invidious discrimination charged by the more vocal critics of criminal justice.

As for the relationship between social class and final disposition, we begin to approach the heart of the issue of differential legal treatment. Independent of the financial ability to retain a private attorney, higher social status merits a defendant a more lenient conviction. For an explanation of this pattern, we must look not to an overt attempt by the court to reward the wealthy and penalize the poor, but to the imagery that surrounds the adjudication of defendants. Thus, it may be suggested that the leniency of legal treatment of middle- and upper-class persons is inspired, in part, by the dominant motivations of punishment and deterrence (Farrell, 1971). The offender is to suffer not only in proportion to the severity of his crime, but so that he will weigh the advantages and disadvantages of a repeated offense.

For rich and poor alike, the decision to punish, therefore becomes a calculus of loss and pain. The lower-class defendant, with minimal status in his community, little occupational prestige, and a personal life most frequently described as disorganized, comes to the court with little to lose except freedom from incarceration. The higher status person, on the other hand, simply as a result of arrest is said to have suffered greatly. Suspended professional license, loss of status in the community, personal and familial trauma are seen as being sufficiently punitive and deterrent. Incarceration becomes superfluous when so much is said to have already been lost.

The applicability of this argument is reinforced by observations made within the context of occupational and corporate criminality. For example, while the Incredible Electrical Conspiracy involved losses far exceeding those accrued at the hands of the more conventional criminal, the highest penalty awarded a coconspirator was 30 days (Smith, 1961a; 1961b). Convictions and sentences of the more recently adjudicated Watergate defendants were similarly proportioned. Popular sympathy generated over the loss of job and prestige incurred by those involved in these ventures testifies to the diffusiveness of the ideology of punishment, an ideology shared by laymen and professionals alike.

The distinction between overt discrimination and compliance with an institutionalized imagery is an important one. The credibility of the legal system, as well as that of judicial administrators, would be seriously threatened should evidence of the penalization of persons for reasons of class be substantiated. Legal safeguards of the rights of lower-status persons would make accountable the authorities who flagrantly violate those rights. If, however, the decision to invoke negative sanction occurs within the rationale of a popular ideology of crime and punishment, the legal authority is free to act.

It is already a common practice to take into consideration the presence of a steady job and stable marital ties in the decision to probate or parole the conventional offender. The application of this same notion of "fair play" in the administration of justice to higher status persons is also an acceptable practice and does not generally invoke outrage or allegations of preferential treatment. Rather, in terms of the original logic, justice indeed has been done. The higher status offender, given a middle-class measuring rod, has the most stable ties in the community, is a most productive person socially and, as a result of apprehension, has suffered a threat to that status. "Fair play" mandates that such a person be excused from further degradation.

This approach to an understanding of legal treatment is further substantiated by the effects of race on adjudication. In the present analysis, race did not exercise immediate influence on legal processing. The only theoretically significant effects of race concern its strong associations with social class and the criminal conception, "normal primitiveness."

Here again it may be argued that the exercise of overt discrimination against minority group members is effectively prevented by statutory proscription. When class and race alone are used to determine patterns of legal treatment, therefore, race only appears to operate through its relationship with social class. For reasons cited above, the black defendant is not adjudicated on the basis of skin color; rather, decisions are made in light of his membership in the lower class—a position that earns him the perceived need for a more severe penalty.

Such an explanation of the effects of social status point to the inadequacy of the use of the objective criteria of class and race in the assessment of treatment patterns. The decision to penalize is not likely to be made simply on the basis of skin pigmentation and annual income. The search for such relationships, consequently, may account for the contradictory findings reported in the literature. A more promising effort in this area might lie in an evaluation of the effects of criminal conceptions on legal treatment. It is these conceptions that may be the media through which social and demographic attributes are filtered in judicial decision-making processes.

The evidence generated in the present research would seem to substantiate this assumption. The "normal primitive," as a conceptualization of the typical homicide offender, has emerged as a most important factor influencing final outcome in the court. That certain groups in society are differentially penalized because of the mandates of this conception of criminality becomes valuable information in an analysis of treatment patterns.

Concerning the designation "normal primitive," both race and occupation explained a significant portion of defendants who were found within this category. Blacks and individuals of lower occupational status were more often designated "primitive" than were whites or higher status persons.

The primary effects of such a label appeared in the lack of availability of legal resources. Individuals who were said to conform to this imagery both were denied bail and did not have access to trial by jury. Thus, the presumption of guilt implied by the application of the label became amplified when the court decided that bail should be withheld or when a plea of guilt before the bench was encouraged. In addition, because of the strength of the relationship between occupational prestige and "normal primitiveness," such individuals also lacked the financial ability to retain a private attorney.

These legal resources, in their turn, interacted in such a way as to produce the more severe convictions accorded those with public attorneys, no access to bail, and a nonjury trial format.[11]

The criminal conception of homicide surfaces as a critical variable in the analysis of legal treatment. In addition to the financial inability of certain segments of the population to purchase legal advantages, persons also may be penalized because of their conformity to such an imagery. Those defendants whose personal or social characteristics suggest their participation in a culture where the violent response is said to be appropriate are denied the presumption of innocence constitutionally guaranteed to all. The processing of such persons, consequently, takes on a routine nature. For when guilt is presumed, little justification can be found for providing defendants with the combative tools essential for successful defense of their cases. The lack of legal resources that mediate between initial charge and final outcome is, in turn, instrumental in maintaining an imagery of guilt. Assignment of public counsel identifies the individual with that class of persons, the indigent, out of which the criminal stereotype is formulated; denial of bail defines the defendant as a potential danger to society; and waiver of trial by jury is self-admission of criminal involvement. Those defendants, therefore, whose access to private attorney, bail, or jury trial is blocked, are further confirmed in the stereotype of the crime within which they were originally defined. The sequence of events, from designation as apparently criminal through lack of provision of legal resources for their defense, produces the outcome predicted by legal wisdom—official award of criminal conviction.

11. Such an interpretation involves a departure from the simple evaluation of direct and indirect paths in the determination of causal influence, for both are a function of the original association between independent and dependent variables. The use of this approach, for example, would result in the conclusion that the relationship between race and final charge is a nonsignificant one. Direct and indirect paths of influence, in this case, can only explain a zero-order correlation of -.03.

It is argued here that a far more useful approach to the problem of causality involves a recognition of the importance of variable sequence. Thus, it is possible to envision a series of relationships where the effects of one stage become the causes of another, and where variables which are significant predictors of earlier events appear as nonsignificant causes of later events. (For a discussion of the logic involved in such relationships, *see* Lin, 1976:26–9).

REFERENCES

Alschuler, Albert W. "The prosecutor's role in plea bargaining." *University of Chicago Law Review* 36 (1968): 50–112.
Ares, Charles E.; Rankin, Anne; and Sturz, Herbert. "The Manhattan bail project: an interim report on the use of pre-trial parole." *New York University Law*

Review 38 (1963): 67–95.

Benay, Ralph S. "Study in murder." *Annals of the American Academy of Political and Social Science* 364 (1966): 26–34.

Bensing, Robert C., and Schroeder, Oliver, Jr. *Homicide in an Urban Community*. Springfield, Illinois: Thomas, 1960.

Blumberg, Abraham S. "The practice of law as a confidence game: organizational cooptation of a profession." *Law and Society Review* 1 (1967): 15–39.

Boudon, Raymond. "A new look at correlational analysis." In *Methodology in Social Research*, edited by Herbert Blalock and Ann Blalock, pp. 199–235. New York: McGraw-Hill, 1968.

Bullock, Henry Allen. "Significance of the racial factor in the length of prison sentences." *Journal of Criminal Law, Criminology and Police Science* 52 (1961): 411–17.

Burke, Peter J., and Turk, Austin T. "Factors affecting post-arrest dispositions: a model for analysis." *Social Problems* 22 (1975): 313–32.

Cain, Albert C. "On the meaning of 'playing crazy' in borderline children." *Psychiatry* 27 (1964): 278–89.

Cameron, Mary Owen. *The Booster and the Snitch: Department Store Shoplifting*. New York: Free Press, 1964.

Chiricos, Theodore G.; Jackson, Philip D.; and Waldo, Gordon P. "Inequality in the imposition of a criminal label." *Social Problems* 19 (1972): 553–72.

Cole, George F. "The decision to prosecute." *Law and Society Review* 4 (1970): 331–43.

Deatherage, Bill. "The uncompensated appointed counsel system: a constitutional and social transgression." *Kentucky Law Journal* 60 (1972): 710–26.

Ehrmann, Sara B. "For whom the chair waits." *Federal Probation* 26 (1962): 14–25.

Erlanger, Howard S. "Jury research in America: its past and future." *Law and Society Review* 4 (1970): 345–70.

Farrell, Ronald A. "Class linkages of legal treatment of homosexuals." *Criminology* 9 (1971): 49–68.

Farrell, Ronald A., and Hardin, Clay W. "Legal stigma and homosexual career deviance." In *Crime and Delinquency*, edited by Marc Riedel and Terence P. Thornberry, pp. 128–40. New York: Praeger, 1974.

Foote, Caleb. "Vagrancy-type law and its administration." *University of Pennsylvania Law Review* 104 (1956): 603–50.

———. "The bail system and equal justice." *Federal Probation* 23 (1959): 43–8.

Forslund, Morris A. "Occupation and conviction rates of white and Negro males: a case study." *Rocky Mountain Social Science Journal* 6 (1969): 141–6.

Garfinkel, Harold. "Research note on inter- and intra-racial homicides." *Social Forces* 27 (1949): 370–81.

Goffman, Erving. *Stigma: Notes on the Management of Spoiled Identity*. Englewood Cliffs, New Jersey: Prentice-Hall, 1963.

Goldman, Nathan. *The Differential Selection of Juvenile Offenders for Court Appearance*. New York: National Research and Information Center, National Council on Crime and Delinquency, 1963.

Goodman, Leo A. "A general model for the analysis of surveys." *American Journal of Sociology* 77 (1972): 1035–86.

———. "The analysis of multi-dimensional contingency tables when some variables are posterior to others: a modified path analysis approach." *Biometrika* 60 (1973a): 179–92.

———. "Causal analysis of data from panel studies and other kinds of surveys." *American Journal of Sociology* 78 (1973b): 1135–91.

———. "The relationship between modified and usual multiple-regression approaches to the analysis of dichotomous variables." In *Sociological Methodology*, edited by David R. Heise, pp. 83–110. San Francisco: Jossey-Bass, 1976.

Green, Edward. *Judicial Attitudes in Sentencing.* New York: St. Martin's Press, 1961. "Inter- and intra-racial crime relative to sentencing." *Journal of Criminal Law, Criminology and Police Science* 55 (1964): 348-58.

Hess, Albert G., and Mariner, Dorothy A. "On the sociology of crime cartoons." *International Journal of Criminology and Penology* 3 (1975): 253-65.

Hindelang, Michael. "Equality under the law." *Journal of Criminal Law, Criminology and Police Science* 60 (1969): 306-13.

Johnson, Guy B. "The Negro and crime." *Annals of the American Academy of Political and Social Science* 271 (1941): 93-104.

Knoke, David. "A comparison of log-linear and regression models for systems of dichotomous variables." *Sociological Methods and Research* 3 (1975): 416-34.

Lin, Nan. *Foundations of Social Research.* New York: McGraw-Hill, 1976.

Louisiana Law Review. "The institution of bail as related to indigent defendants." *Louisiana Law Review* 21 (1961): 627.

Myrdal, Gunnar. *An American Dilemma: The Negro Problem and Modern Democracy.* New York: Harper and Brothers, 1944.

Newman, Donald J. "Pleading guilty for considerations: a study of bargain justice." *Journal of Criminal Law, Criminology and Police Science* 46 (1956): 780-90.

Piliavin, Irving, and Briar, Scott. "Police encounters with juveniles." *American Journal of Sociology* 70 (1964): 206-14.

Pittman, David J., and Handy, William. "Patterns in criminal aggravated assault." *Journal of Criminal Law, Criminology and Police Science* 55 (1964): 462-70.

Quinney, Richard. *The Social Reality of Crime.* Boston: Little, Brown, 1970.

Robinson, W. S. "Bias, probability, and trial by jury." *American Sociological Review* 15 (1950): 73-8.

Scheff, Thomas J. *Being Mentally Ill.* Chicago: Aldine, 1966.

Shoemaker, Donald J.; South, Donald R.; and Lowe, Jay. "Facial stereotypes of deviants and judgments of guilt or innocence." *Social Forces* 51 (1973): 427-33.

Siegel, Barry. "Gideon and beyond: achieving an adequate defense for the indigent." *Journal of Criminal Law, Criminology and Police Science* 59 (1968): 73-84.

Simmons, J. L. "Public stereotypes of deviants." *Social Problems* 13 (1965): 223-32.

Skolnick, Jerome H. *Justice without Trial: Law Enforcement in Democratic Society.* New York: Wiley, 1966.

Smith, Richard Austin. "The Incredible Electrical Conspiracy." *Fortune* 63 (4) (1961a): 132-80.

———. "The Incredible Electrical Conspiracy." *Fortune* 63 (5) (1961b): 161-224.

Steffensmeier, Darrell J., and Terry, Robert M. "Deviance and respectability: an observational study of reactions to shoplifting." *Social Forces* 51 (1973): 417-26.

Strodtbeck, Fred L.; James, Rita M.; and Hawkins, Charles. "Social status in jury deliberations." *American Sociological Review* 22 (1957): 713-19.

Sudnow, David. "Normal crimes: sociological features of the penal code in a public defender office." *Social Problems* 12 (1965): 255-76.

Sutherland, Edwin H., and Cressey, Donald. *Criminology.* Philadelphia: Lippincott, 1974.

Swigert, Victoria Lynn, and Farrell, Ronald A. *Murder, Inequality and the Law: Differential Treatment in the Legal Process.* Lexington, Massachusetts: Heath, 1976.

Treiman, Donald. *Occupational Prestige in Comparative Perspective.* New York: Seminar, 1977.

Vines, Kenneth, and Jacob, Herbert. "Studies in judicial politics." In *VIII Tulane Studies in Political Science* (1963): 77-98.

Westley, William A. "Violence and the police." *American Journal of Sociology* 59 (1953): 34–41.

Wolf, Edwin D. Abstract of "Analysis of jury sentencing in capital cases: New Jersey: 1937-1961." *Rutgers Law Review* 19 (1964): 56–64.

Wolfgang, Marvin E. "A sociological analysis of criminal homicide." *Federal Probation* 23 (1961): 48–55.

Wolfgang, Marvin E., and Ferracuti, Franco. *The Subculture of Violence.* London: Methuen, 1967.

ANDREW T. SCULL

Madness and Segregative Control:
The Rise of the Insane Asylum

Three key features distinguish deviance and its control in modern society from the shapes such phenomena assume elsewhere: (1) the substantial involvement of the state, and the emergence of a highly rationalized, centrally administered and directed social control apparatus; (2) the treatment of many types of deviance in institutions providing a large measure of segregation from the surrounding community; and (3) the careful differentiation of different sorts of deviance, and the subsequent consignment of each variety to the ministrations of experts—which last development entails, as an important corollary, the emergence of professional and semiprofessional "helping occupations." Throughout much of Europe, England, and the United States, all these features of the modern social control apparatus are a comparatively recent development.

Prior to the eighteenth century, and in many places as late as the early nineteenth century, the control of deviants of all sorts had been an essentially communal and family affair. The amorphous class of the morally disreputable, the indigent and the powerless—including such elements as vagrants, minor criminals, the insane, and the physically handicapped—was managed in essentially similar ways. Characteristically, little effort was made to segregate such "problem populations" into separate receptacles designed to keep them apart from the rest of society. Instead, they were dealt with in ways which

Source: Scull, Andrew T. "Madness and Segregative Control: The Rise of the Insane Asylum." *Social Problems* 24 (1977): 337-351. Permission granted by The Society for the Study of Social Problems and the author.

left them at large in the community. Most of the time families were held liable to provide for their own, if necessary with the aid of temporary assistance or a more permanent subsidy from the community. Lunatics were generally treated no differently from other deviants: only a few of the most violent or troublesome cases might find themselves confined—in a specially constructed cell or as part of the heterogeneous population of the local jail (Fessler, 1956).

The transformation of traditional arrangements into what we know today as systems of social control is clearly a subject with a profound sociological significance. I shall comment on some aspects of this transition with respect to one major variety of deviance, by examining nineteenth century efforts to "reform" the treatment of the mentally ill. More specifically, I shall try to provide an account of the reasons for the emergence of the asylum as the primary, almost the sole, response to the problems posed by insanity....

Many of the transformations underlying the move toward asylums can be ... tied to the growth of the capitalist market system and to its impact on economic and social relationships. Prior to the emergence of a capitalist system, economic relationships did not manifest themselves as purely market relationships. Economic domination or subordination was overlaid and fused with personal ties between individuals. But the market destroyed the traditional connections between rich and poor, the reciprocal notions of paternalism, deference, and dependence characterizing the old order, producing profound shifts in the relationships between superordinate and subordinate classes, and of upper-class perceptions of responsibilities toward the less fortunate.

Indeed, one of the earliest casualties of the developing capitalist system was the old sense of social obligation toward the poor (Townsend, 1786; Hobsbawm, 1968:88; Hobsbawm and Rudé, 1969:26; Mantoux, 1928:428). At the same time, the increasing "proletarianization" of labor—that is, the loss of alternatives to wage work as a means of providing for subsistence— went together with the tendency of the primitive capitalist economy to oscillate unpredictably between conditions of boom and slump. Obviously, these transformations greatly increased the strains on a family-based system of relief (Polanyi, 1944:92ff.; Hobsbawm, 1968:chap. 3 and 4; Furniss, 1965:211-221). There is, despite its simplification and rhetorical flourish, a profound and bitter truth to Marx's comment that the advent of a full-blown market system:

> has pitilessly torn asunder the motley feudal ties that bound man to his 'natural superiors,' and has left no other nexus between man and man than naked self interest, than callous 'cash payment'.... In one word, for exploitation veiled by religious and political illusions, it has substituted naked, shameless, direct, brutal exploitation (Marx and Engels, 1968: 37-38).

And while the impact of urbanization and industrialization was at this stage geographically limited in scope, by the latter part of the eighteenth century almost all regions of England had been drawn into a single national market economy (Mantoux, 1928:74; Hobsbawm, 1968:27-28). The impact of the universal market of capitalism was felt everywhere, forcing "the transformation of the relations between the rural rich and the rural poor, the farmers and their labor force, into a purely market relationship between employer and proletarian (Hobsbawm and Rudé, 1969:chap. 2).

The changes in structures, perceptions, and outlook marking the transition from the old paternalist order to a capitalist social system triggered a search for an alternative to traditional, noninstitutional methods of managing the indigent. The development of an industrial economy also precipitated a sizable expansion in the number of those receiving temporary or permanent poor relief. This expansion took place at precisely the time when the newly powerful bourgeoisie was least inclined to tolerate it. The industrial capitalists readily convinced themselves that laxly administered systems of household relief promoted poverty rather than relieved it—a position they found well-justified ideologically in the writings of Malthus and others (cf. Malthus, 1798, esp. chap. 5; MacFarlan, 1782:34-36; Temple, 1770:258; Rimlinger, 1966:562-563). Increasingly, therefore, the bourgeoisie were attracted to an institutionally-based response to the indigent. Institutional management would, at least in theory, permit close oversight of who received relief, and, by establishing a regime sufficiently harsh to deter all but the most deserving from applying, would render the whole system efficient and economical (Furniss, 1965:107; Temple, 1770:151-269; Poor Law Report, 1834).

Moreover, just as the vagrancy laws of the sixteenth century had begun to produce the "discipline necessary for the wage labour system" (Marx, 1967 Vol. I:737; also Chambliss, 1964), so too the conditions in the new institutions mimicked the discipline necessary for the factory system. The quasi-military authority structure of the total institution seemed ideally suited to the inculcation of "proper" work habits among those marginal elements of the workforce most resistant to the monotony, routine, and regularity of industrialized labor. As William Temple (1770:266ff.) put it,

> by these means, we hope that the rising generation will be so habituated to constant employment that it would at length prove agreeable and entertaining to them.

Bentham's (1791) Panopticon, which fascinated many of the lunacy reformers (cf. Stark, 1810; Wakefield, 1812), was, in his own words, "a mill to grind rogues honest and idle men industrious . . ." (Bentham to Brissot in Bentham, 1843 Vol. X:226), an engine of reformation which would employ "convicts instead of steam, and thus combine philanthropy with business" (Stephen, 1900 Vol. I:203). And, undoubtedly, one of the attractions of the asylum as a method of dealing with the insane was its promise of instilling the virtues of bourgeois rationality into that segment of the population least amenable to them.

There were, of course, other factors behind the move toward an institutionally focused, centrally regulated system of social control. For the moment, however, I will leave further analysis of these factors to one side and turn to the question of how and why insanity came to be identified and managed as a unique problem requiring specialized treatment in an institution of its own, the asylum. For it should be obvious that before the asylum could emerge as a specialized institution devoted to the problems of insanity, the latter had to be distinguished as a separate variety of deviant behavior not found only among a few upper-class families or confined to cases of furious mania; but existing more pervasively among the lower classes of the community as a distinct species of pathology—a pathology unclassifyable as just one more case of poverty and dependency.[1]

The establishment of a market economy, and, more particularly, the emergence of a market in labor, provided the initial incentive to distinguish far more carefully than heretofore between different categories of deviance. Under these conditions, it was important to distinguish the able-bodied from the non-able-bodied poor. A precondition for the development of a capitalist system, as both Marx (1967 Vol. I:578, 717-733) and Weber (1930:22; 1961:172-173) have emphasized, was the existence of a large mass of wage laborers who were not "free" to dispose of their labor power on the open market, but who were actually forced to do so. But to provide aid to the able-bodied, as frequently occurred under the old relief arrangements, was to undermine the whole notion of a labor market.

Parochial relief for the able-bodied interfered with labor mobility (MacFarlan, 1782:176ff.; Smith, 1776:135-140). In particular, it encouraged the retention of a "vast inert mass of redundant labor," a stagnant pool of under-employed laboring men in rural areas, where the demand for labor was subject to wide seasonal fluctuations (Redford, cited in Polanyi, 1944: 301; cf. also Polanyi, 1944:77-102; Webb and Webb, 1927; passim; Hobsbawm, 1968:99-100). Social protection of those who *could* work distorted the operations of the labor market and, thereby, of all other markets, because of its tendency "to create cost differentials as between the various parts of the country" (Polanyi, 1944:301; MacFarlan, 1782:178; Poor Law Report,

---

1. Of course, I am not suggesting here that prior to this process of differentiation the population at large were naively unaware of any and all differences between the various elements making up the disreputable classes—between, say, the raving madman and the petty criminal, or the blind and the crippled. (Obviously on a very straightforward level such distinctions were apparent and could linguistically be made.) The critical question is rather when and for what reasons such perceived differences became rigid and were seen as *socially significant*—i.e., began to provoke differential responses and to have consequential impact on the lives of the deviant.

1834:43; Mantoux, 1928:450). Finally, by its removal of the threat of individual starvation, such relief had a pernicious effect on labor discipline and productivity (MacFarlan, 1782:169ff.), an outcome accentuated by the fact that the "early laborer . . . abhorred the factory, where he felt degraded and tortured . . ." (Polanyi, 1944:164-165; cf. also Thompson, 1963).

Instead of organizing poor relief in a way which failed to take motivation or compliance into account, it was felt that want ought to be the stimulus to the capable, who must therefore be distinguished from the helpless. Such a distinction is deceptively simple; but in a wider perspective, this development can be seen as a crucial phase in the growing rationalization of the Western social order and the associated transformation of *extensive* structures of domination into the ever more *intensive* forms characteristic of the modern world. In the precapitalist era, domestic populations were generally viewed as an unchangeable given, from which to squeeze as large a surplus as possible. But with the emergence of capitalism and the need for greater exploitation of labor resources, the labor pool came to be viewed as manipulable human material whose yield could be steadily enlarged through careful management and through improvements in use and organization, rationally designed to transform its value as an economic resource. As Moffett (1971:187 et passim) has shown, during this process:

> the domestic population came increasingly to be regarded as an industrial labor force—not simply a tax reservoir as formerly—and state policies came increasingly to be oriented to forcing the entire working population into remunerative employment.

The significance of the distinction between the able-bodied poor thus increases *pari-passu* with the rise of the wage labor system.

The beginnings of such a separation are evident even in the early phases of English capitalism. The great Elizabethan Poor Law (43 Eliz. c.2, 1601), for example, classified the poor into the aged and impotent, children, and the able but unemployed (Marshall, 1926:23); and a number of historians have been tempted to see in this and in the Statute of Artificers (1563) a primitive labor code of the period, dealing respectively with what we would call the unemployed and unemployable, and the employed. But, as Polanyi suggests, in large measure "the neat distinction between the employed, unemployed, and unemployable is, of course, anachronistic, since it implies the existence of a modern wage system which was absent [at that time]" (Polanyi, 1944:86). Until much later, the boundaries between these categories remained more fluid and ill-defined than the modern reader is apt to realize. Moreover, though it is plain that the Tudors and Stuarts did not scruple to invoke harsh legal penalties in an effort to compel the poor to work (cf. Dobb, 1963:233ff.), these measures were undertaken at least as much "for the sake of political security" as for more directly economic motives (Marshall, 1926:17; Mantoux, 1928:443).

Gradually, however, economic considerations became increasingly dominant. As they did, it became evident that "no treatment of this matter was adequate which failed to distinguish between the able-bodied unemployed on the one hand, the aged, infirm, and children on the other" (Polanyi, 1944:94). The former were to be compelled to work, at first through the direct legal compulsion inherited from an earlier period (Marshall, 1926: 37ff.; Furniss, 1965:passim). However, the upper classes came to despair of the notion "that they may be compelled [by statute] to work according to their abilities" (MacFarlan, 1782:105); they became increasingly attracted by an alternative method according to which, in the picturesque language of John Bellers (1696:1), "The Sluggard shall be cloathed in Raggs. He that will not work shall not eat." The superiority of this approach was put most bluntly by Joseph Townsend (1786):

> Hunger will tame the fiercest animals, it will teach decency and civility, obedience and subjection to the most perverse. In general, it is only hunger which can spur and goad [the poor] on to labour; yet our laws have said they shall never hunger. The laws, it must be confessed, have likewise said, they shall be compelled to work. But then legal constraint is attended with much trouble, violence, and noise; creates ill-will, and can never by productive of good and acceptable service: whereas hunger is not only peaceable, silent, unremitting pressure, but, as the most natural motive to industry and labour, it calls forth the most violent exertions.

Or, in the words of his fellow clergyman, T. R. Malthus,

> When nature will govern and punish for us, it is a very miserable ambition to wish to snatch the rod from her hands and draw upon ourselves the odium of the executioner (Malthus, 1826 II:339).

Thus the functional requirements of a market system promoted a relatively simple, if crucial, distinction between two broad classes of the indigent. Workhouses and the like were to be an important *practical* means of making this vital theoretical separation, and thereby of making the whole system efficient and economical. But even though workhouses were initially intended to remove the able-bodied poor from the community in order to teach them the wholesome discipline of labor (Bailey, 1758:1), they swiftly found themselves depositories for the decaying, the decrepit, and the unemployable. And an unintended consequence of this concentration of deviants in an institutional environment was that it exacerbated the problems of managing at least some of them (MacFarlan, 1782:97 ff.). More specificially, it rendered problematic the whole question of what was to be done with those who could not or would not abide by the rules of the house—among the most important of whom were the acutely disturbed and refractory insane.

A single mad or distracted person in the community produced problems of a wholly different sort than those the same person would have produced if placed with other deviants within the walls of an institution. The order and discipline of the whole workhouse was threatened by the presence of a madman who, even by threats and punishment, could neither be persuaded nor induced to conform to the regulations. By its very nature, a workhouse was ill-suited to provide safe-keeping for those who might pose a threat to life or property. In the words of a contemporary appeal for funds to set up a charity asylum:

> The law has made no particular provision for lunaticks and it must be allowed that the common parish workhouse (the inhabitants of which are mostly aged and infirm people) are very unfit places for the Reception of such ungovernable and mischievous persons, who necessarily require separate apartments (St. Luke's Considerations, 1750:1).

The local jail, a common substitute in such cases, proved scarcely more satisfactory; the dislocations produced by the presence of lunatics provoked widespread complaints from prisoners and jailers alike. General hospitals of the period, facing similar problems, began to respond by refusing to accept lunatic inmates "on Account of the safety of other Patients" (St. Luke's Considerations, 1750:2). Clearly, then, the adoption of an institutional response to all sorts of "problem populations" greatly increased the pressures to elaborate the distinctions amongst and between the deviant and dependent.[2]

Initially, with respect to the insane, this situation provided no more than an opportunity for financial speculation and pecuniary profit for those who

2. For primitive mid-eighteenth century examples of this process of differentiation, cf. Marshall, 1926:49ff. On the necessity of such a classification, cf. MacFarlan, 1782: 2-3. The increasing numbers of the poor:

> are thought to arise chiefly from the want of proper general views of the subject, and of a just discrimination of the characters of those who are the objects of punishment or compassion. Thus, while at one time the attention of the public is employed in detecting and punishing vagrants, real objects of charity are exposed to famine, or condemned to suffer a chastisement they have not deserved; at another time, while an ample provision is made for the poor in general, a liberal supply is often granted to the most slothful and profligate. Hence arise two opposite complaints, yet both of them well-grounded. The one of inhumanity and cruelty in our distressed fellow creatures; the other, of a profusion of public charity, and an ill-judged lenity, tending to encourage idleness and vice.

For an elaborate late eighteenth century classification and differentiation of the various elements composing the poor, cf. Bentham, 1797.

established private madhouses and asylums. Such, indeed, was the general character of the eighteenth century "trade in lunacy," a frequently lucrative business dealing with the most acutely disturbed and refractory cases, those who in the general mixed workhouse caused trouble out of all proportion to their numbers. While claims to provide cures as well as care were periodically used as a means of drumming up custom, the fundamental orientation of the system (besides profit) was toward an economical restraint of those posing a direct threat to the social order (cf. Parry-Jones, 1972). In the long run, however, such a differentiation of deviants provided the essential social preconditions for the establishment of a new organized profession, claiming to possess a specific expertise in the management of insanity, and oriented toward a rehabilitative ideal.

On the most general level, the English elite was receptive to the notion that a particular occupational group possessed a scientifically based expertise in dealing with lunacy. This receptivity reflected the growing secular rationalization of Western society at this time; a development which, following Weber, I would argue took place under the dominant, though not the sole, impetus of the development of a capitalist market system. More specifically, it reflected the penetration of this realm of social existence by the values of science, the idea that "there are no mysterious incalculable forces that come into play, but rather that one can, in principle, master all things by calculation" (Weber, 1946:139). Linked to this change in perspective was a fundamental shift in the underlying paradigm of insanity, away from an emphasis on its demonological, nonhuman, animalistic qualities toward a naturalistic position which viewed the madman as exhibiting a defective *human* mechanism, and which therefore saw this condition as at least potentially remediable.

How the "mad-doctors" of the period were able to exploit this favorable cultural environment to secure for themselves the status of a profession is a question dealt with elsewhere.[3] Here I am concerned with one important consequence of the fact that they were able to do so. The growing power and influence of what was to become the psychiatric profession helped to complete and to lend scientific legitimacy to the classification of deviance, transforming the vague cultural view of madness into what now purported

---

3. The negotiation of cognitive exclusiveness on the part of mad-doctors—whereby insanity came to be defined as a disease, and hence as a condition within the sole purview of the medical profession—was necessarily a prolonged and complicated process. As is usual in such cases, "the process determining the outcome was essentially political and social rather than technical in character" (Freidson, 1970:79). Persuasive rhetoric, the symbols (rather than the substance) of expertise, the prestige and ready access to elite circles of the more respectable part of the medical profession—all these resources were employed to secure and maintain a legally enforceable medical monopoly of the treatment of madness. For details, *see* Scull, 1975 and Scull, forthcoming.

to be a formally coherent, scientifically distinguishable entity reflecting and caused by a single underlying pathology.

In a sense, then, one had here a self-reinforcing system. For while the key to the emerging profession's claims to expertise, the new system of moral treatment,[4] did reflect a fundamental transformation in the basic paradigm or perception of insanity, it was not based on a more *scientific understanding* of the subject (cf. Foucault, 1965; Scull, 1974:chap. 5 and 8). Rather, it represented, from one perspective at least, a noval administrative technique, a more efficient means of management. The essence of this innovation lay in its emphasis on order, rationality, and self-control; and much of its appeal, both for the lunacy reformers and their audience, derived from the high value it placed on work as a means to these ends. The new approach could only be fully developed and applied in an institutional setting. So that, just as the separation of the insane into madhouses and asylums helped to create the conditions for the emergence of an occupational group ("mad-doctors") laying claim to expertise in their care and cure, so too the nature and content of the restorative ideal these doctors espoused reinforced the commitment to the institutional approach. Thereafter, the existence of both asylums and psychiatry testified to the "necessity" and "naturalness" of distinguishing the insane from other deviants.

A vital feature of this radically new social control apparatus was how much its operations became subject to central control and direction. As both the Weberian and the Marxist analyses have stressed, precapitalist societies were overwhelmingly localized in their social organization. The mechanisms for coping with deviance in pre-nineteenth century England placed a corresponding reliance on an essentially communal and family-based system of control. The assumption of direct state responsibility for these functions thus marked a sharp departure from these traditional emphases.

4. One cannot readily summarize in a phrase or two what moral treatment consisted of, nor reduce it to a few standard formulae, for it was emphatically not a specific technique. Rather, it was a general, pragmatic approach which aimed at minimizing external, physical coercion; and it has, therefore, usually been interpreted as "kind" and "humane." Instead of merely resting content with controlling those who were no longer quite human, the dominant concern of traditional responses to the mad, moral treatment actively sought a transformed lunatic, remodeled into something approximating the bourgeois ideal of the rational individual. Those advocating moral treatment recognized that external coercion could force outward conformity but never the necessary internalization of moral standards. Instead, lunatics must be induced, by playing on their "desire for esteem," to collaborate in their own recapture by the forces of reason and conformity; and their living environment must be reconstructed so as to encourage them to reassert their own powers of self-control. As moral treatment evolved in the large public asylums, it was increasingly simplified and reduced to a set of internal management devices: the crucial elements here were the development of the ward system, and the creation of an intimate tie between the patients' position in this classificatory system and their behavior—still among the major weapons mental hospitals use to control the uncontrollable.

While administrative rationalization and political centralization are not only or wholly the consequence of economic rationalization, it seems inescapable that the advance of the capitalist economic order and the growth of the central authority of the state are twin processes intimately connected with each other.

On the one hand, were it not for the expansion of commerce and the rise of capitalist agriculture, there would scarcely have been the economic base to finance the expanded bureaucratic state structures. But on the other hand, the state structures were themselves a major economic underpinning of the new capitalist system (not to speak of being its political guarantee) (Wallerstein, 1974:133).

In a very literal sense, institutional control mechanisms were impracticable earlier, because of the absence both of the necessary administrative techniques and also of the surplus required to establish and maintain them.

The creation of more efficient administrative structures, both the precondition and the consequence of the growth of the state and of large-scale capitalist enterprise, possessed a dual importance. On the one hand, it allowed for the first time the development of a tolerably adequate administrative apparatus to mediate between the central and local authorities, and thus to extend central control down to the local level. On the other, it provided the basis for the development of techniques for the efficient management of large numbers of people confined for months or years on end. Without these structures, institutional methods of social control would scarcely have achieved the importance they did. State construction and operation of institutions for the deviant and the dependent was very costly. Hence the importance, as a transitional arrangement, of the state contracting with private entrepreneurs to provide jails, madhouses, and the like. Under this method, the state allows the "deviant farmer" to extort his fees however he can, and turns a blind eye to his methods; in return, the latter relieves the state of the capital expenditure (and often even many of the operating costs) required by a system of segregative control. Movement to a system directly run by the state required the development of large stable tax revenues and/or the state's ability to borrow on a substantial scale. These in turn were intimately tied to the expansion of the monetary sector of the economy and the growth of the sophisticated credit and accounting mechanisms characteristic of capitalist economic organization (Ardant, 1975).

Likewise, the development of national and international markets produced a diminuition, if not a destruction, of the influence traditionally exerted by local groups (especially kinship groups) in the patterning of social life. More directly, the growth of a single national market and the rise of allegiance to the central political authority to a position of over-riding importance undermined the rationale of locally-based responses to deviance, based as they were on the idea of settlement and the exclusion of strangers. As local communities came to be defined and to define themselves as part of a single overarching political and economic system, it made less and less sense for one town to dispose of its problems by passing them on the the the next. There was a need for some substitute mode of exclusion. In combination, these developments contributed to "the monopolization of all 'legitimate' coercive power by one universalist coercive institution . . ." (Weber, 1968 Vol. I:337), and to the development of a state sponsored system of segregative control.

The struggle to legislate and to implement lunacy reform in England involved just such a transfer of the locus of power and responsibility to the central authority and necessarily took place in the face of fierce local resistance (Scull, 1974:chap. 4). This opposition reflected both a parochial defensiveness against the encroachments of the state, and the uneven spread of a new outlook on the insane. Local authorities generally accepted the traditional paradigm of insanity, along with its emphasis on the demonological, almost bestial character of madness. In consequence, they were frequently unable to comprehend why the reformers saw the treatment of lunatics within their jurisdiction as brutal and inhumane; why conditions they saw an unexceptionable produced shock and outrage in others. The reformers had fixed on the fundamentals of a new system for dealing with the insane—asylums constructed at public expense, and regular inspection of these institutions by the central authorities—as early as 1815. But before the plan was given legislative approval in two 1845 Acts of Parliament (8 and 9 Vict. c.100, 126) there were three decades of Parliamentary maneuvering and compromise designed to placate local opposition; a series of official inquiries producing a stream of revelations of the abuses of the old system (1815-1816, 1827, 1839, 1842-1844); and a mass of propaganda in popular periodicals and reviews extolling the merits of their proposed solution.

Most historical writing on lunacy reform perpetuates the illusion that the whole process represented progress toward enlightenment, the triumph of a rational, altruistic, humanitarian response over ancient superstitions, the dawn of a scientific approach to insanity. Yet this is a perspective made possible only by concentrating on the rhetoric of intentions to the neglect of the facts about the establishment and operation of the asylum system. Even a superficial acquaintance with the functioning of nineteenth century mental hospitals reveals how limited was the asylum's concern with the human problems of its inmates.

The consistent structural limitations of the total institution (Goffman, 1961) operated from the asylum's earliest years to reduce its ostensible clients to the level of cogs to be machined and oiled till they contributed to the smooth running of the vast apparatus of which they were each an insignificant part. In such a place, said John Arlidge (1859:102) a patient may be said to lose his individuality and to become a member of a machine so put together as to move with precise regularity and invariable routine; a triumph of skill adapted to show how much unpromising materials as crazy men and women may be drilled to order, but not an apparatus calculated to restore their pristine condition and their independent self-governing existence.

Certainly, the equanimity with which the English upper classes regarded this development cannot have been unrelated to the fact that the inmate population was overwhelmingly drawn from the lower segments of society. Nor can there be much doubt that the influential classes' emphasis on the centrality of efficiency and economy in the daily operations of the asylum (an insistence likewise reflecting the low social status of the bulk of the insane) functioned only to worsen the drab awfulness, the monotonous custodial quality of institutional existence.

Asylums quickly assumed gigantic proportions. Within twenty five years of the establishment of the first state-supported institution of this sort, the larger asylums already contained between five hundred and a thousand inmates. By mid-century, some had facades which stretched for nearly a third of a mile, and contained wards and passages of more than six miles (Quarterly Review, 1857:364). Thereafter, wing was tacked on wing, story upon story, building next to building, as the demand grew to accommodate more and more "lunatics." In the words of one critic, they began to "partake more of the nature of industrial than of medical establishments" (Arlidge, 1859:123), where "all transactions, moral as well as economic, must be done wholesale" (Browne, 1864:18). In such places, the mad-doctors of the period "herd lunatics together in special institutions where they can be more easily visited and accounted for by the authorities" (Bucknill, 1880:122).

In addition to the broader sources of the commitment to the asylum model, the activities of a committed group of lay reformers and of that segment of the medical profession with an interest in the mad business obviously played an important role in legitimizing the institutional approach. In the second quarter of the nineteenth century, such men developed an increasingly elaborate proinstitutional ideology. Moreover, the fact that the asylum was presented as an arena for professional practice had much to do with the stress on rehabilitation and the marked utopian strain so characteristic of its early years. In the process, the defects inherent in the asylum's structure were largely, though not entirely, overlooked (cf., e.g., Browne, 1837).

The drawbacks of choosing an institutional response *were* elaborated, with striking prescience, by a few early critics of the asylum (Hill, 1814; Reid, 1816; Conolly, 1830), and were repeated some years later by a handful of disillusioned reformers (e.g., Bucknill, 1880; Arlidge, 1859). By then, the operations of the system had revealed the basic accuracy of the criticisms; yet the authors of them continued to be ignored. A major source of the resistance to these objections is undoubtedly to be found in the unattractive-ness to the English bourgeoisie of the alternative policies that might have been pursued. In particular, given that many of the conditions which so aroused the lunacy reformers were little or no worse than the conditions large numbers of the *sane* lower classes were forced to endure (cf., e.g., Chadwick, 1842; Engles, 1969), to have attempted to improve the condition of the insane while leaving them in the community would necessarily have entailed questioning the fundamental structure of nineteenth century English society.[5] In view of the social background of the lunacy reformers, and their concern with incremental change, it is scarcely surprising that they failed to do this. But in the absence of a coherent alternative plan, their carpings about the defects of the asylum could be (and were) simply ignored (cf. Scull, 1977:chap. 6 and 7).

Once the asylum was established, the psychiatric profession sought, without success, to secure a clientele not restricted to lower-class marginal elements of the population. The upper classes displayed an understandable reluctance to confine their nearest and dearest in a total institution. With a few exceptions (which in any event bore little resemblance to the con-ventional asylum of the period, save in the number of cures they could claim), the expansion of the English asylum system during the nineteenth century was substantially an expansion of the pauper sector.

Undoubtedly, this circumstance is a major explanation for the low prestige of the psychiatric profession throughout this period. The class focus of institutions at this time had a critical impact on the nature of the asylum itself, reinforcing the pressures to develop low cost custodial warehouses characterized by huge size, routine, and monotony. Under these conditions,

---

5. Thus, improving the conditions of existence for lunatics living in the community would have entailed the provision of relatively generous pension or welfare payments to provide for their support; implying that the living standards of families with an insane member would have been raised above those of the working class generally. Moreover, under this system, the insane alone would have been beneficiaries of something approxi-mating a modern social welfare system, while their sane brethren were subjected to the rigors of a Poor Law based on the principle of less eligibility. Such an approach would clearly have been administratively unworkable, not least because of the labile nature of lunacy itself, and the consequent ever-present possibility that given sufficient incentive (or rather desperation) the poorer classes would resort to feigning insanity. (This possi-bility probably provided an additional incentive for keeping the conditions in the lunatic asylums as unattractive as possible, as "ineligible" as workhouses.) These obstacles presented an absolute barrier to the development of a plausible alternative, community-based response to the problem of insanity—in fact none of the critics of the asylum was ever able to suggest even the basis of such a program: a *sine qua non* if their objections were to receive serious consideration.

moral treatment, never grounded in a well-developed theory of insanity, simply because a system of discipline and a convenient verbal camouflage for the psychiatric profession's questionable expertise.

The formal commitment to rehabilitation remained, but the practical concerns of those running the system were by now far different: the isolation of those marginal elements of the population who could not or would not conform or could not subsist in an industrial, largely laissez faire society. But even as the optimism of the first years evaporated, the usefulness of custody for widely differing segments of society operated to sustain a system that had apparently failed, and helped to prevent the emergence of a constituency objecting to the asylum.

Working-class opposition to the elimination of parish relief and their hatred of the new workhouse "Bastilles" brought only a limited modification of the rigors of the New Poor Law and not its abandonment (Hobsbawm, 1968:229). The poor thus had little alternative but to make use of the asylum as a way of ridding themselves of what, in the circumstances of nineteenth century working-class existence, was undoubtedly an intolerable burden, the caring for their sick, aged, or otherwise incapacitated relatives. From the bourgeoisie's perspective, the existence of asylums to "treat" the mentally ill at public expense could be invoked as a practical demonstration of their own humanitarian concern with the less fortunate. But far from asylums having been "altruistic institutions . . . detached from the social structures that perpetuate poverty," (Gans, 1971) one must realize that they were important elements in sustaining those structures; important because of their symbolic value and as a reminder of the awful consequences of nonconformity.

Ultimately, I contend that we must see the move toward an institutionalized and centralized social control apparatus as primarily the product of closely interrelated *structural* changes, the main driving force behind these changes being the commercialization of social existence and the advent of a full-blown capitalist market economy. What is crucial about the late eighteenth and the first half of the nineteenth centuries is that both the need and the ability to organize the necessary administrative structures and to raise the substantial sums required to establish such a control system were present in this period. . . . [O] ne may view the pervasive anxiety about the stability of the social order . . . as the anxiety of a specific class. It was the way the bourgeois and professional classes made sense of the corrosive effects of capitalism on such traditional precapitalist social restraints as religion and the family. As such, the fears of the professional and entrepreneurial bourgeoisie were mediators through which structural pressures were translated into "reform"; but they cannot plausibly be regarded as the primary or decisive cause of this change.
this change.

REFERENCES

Ardant, G. "Financial policy and economic infrastructure of modern states and nations." In *The Formation of National States in Western Europe,* edited by C. Tilly. pp. 164–242. Princeton: Princeton University Press, 1975.

Arlidge, J. T. *On the State of Lunacy and the Legal Provision for the Insane.* London: Churchill, 1859.

Bailey, W. *A Treatise on the Better Employment and More Comfortable Support of the Poor in Workhouses.* London, 1758.

Bellers, J. *Proposals for Raising a College of Industry of All Useful Trades and Husbandry.* London, 1696.

Bentham, J. *Panopticon; or the Inspection House.* London: Payne, 1791.

_____. *Pauper Management.* London, 1797.

_____. *Works,* edited by J. Bowring. Edinburgh, 1843.

Browne, W. A. F. *What Asylums Were, Are, and Ought to Be.* Edinburgh: Black, 1837.

_____. *The Moral Treatment of the Insane.* London: Adlard, 1864.

Bucknill, J. C. *The Care of the Insane and their Legal Control.* London: Macmillan, 1880.

Chadwick, E. *Report on the Sanitary Conditions of the Labouring Population of Great Britain.* London, 1842.

Chambliss, W. "A sociological analysis of the law of vagrancy." *Social Problems* 12 (1964): 67–77.

Conolly, J. *An Inquiry into the Indications of Insanity.* London: Taylor, 1830.

Dobb, M. *Studies in the Development of Capitalism.* New York: International Publishers, 1963.

Engles, F. *The Condition of the Working Class in England.* London: Panther Books, 1969.

Fessler, A. "The management of lunacy in seventeenth century England." *Proceedings of the Royal Society of Medicine, Historical Section* 49 (1956).

Foucault, M. *Madness and Civilization.* New York: Mentor Books, 1965.

Freidson, E. *Profession of Medicine.* New York: Dodd, Mead, 1970.

Furniss, E. *The Position of the Laborer in a System of Nationalism.* New York: Kelly, 1965.

Gans, H. *Preface to Colin Greer, The Great School Legend.* New York: Basic Books, 1971.

Goffman, E. *Asylums.* Garden City, New York: Doubleday, 1961.

Hill, G. N. *An Essay on the Prevention and Cure of Insanity.* London: Longman, 1814.

Hobsbawm, E. *Industry and Empire.* London: Penguin Edition, 1968.

Hobsbawm, E., and Rudé, G. *Captain Swing.* London: Penguin Edition, 1969.

MacFarlan, J. *Inquiries Concerning the Poor.* Edinburgh: Longmans and Dickson, 1782.

Malthus, T. R. *An Essay on the Principle of Population,* 4th and 6th eds. London: 1798, 1826.

Mantoux, P. *The Industrial Revolution in the Eighteenth Century.* London: Cape, 1928.

Marshall, D. *The English Poor in the Eighteenth Century.* London: Routledge, 1926.

Marx, K. Capital. (3 vols.) New York: International Publishers, 1967.

Marx, K., and Engels, F. "The Communist Manifesto." In *Selected Works.* New York: International Publishers, 1968.

Moffett, J. T. "Bureaucracy and Social Control: A Study of the Progressive Regimentation of the Western Social Order." Unpublished Ph.D. dissertation, Columbia University, 1971.

Parry-Jones, W. Ll. *The Trade in Lunacy.* London: Routledge and Kegan Paul, 1972.

Polanyi, K. *The Great Transformation.* Boston: Beacon Edition, 1944.

Poor Law Report. *Report of the Royal Commission on the Poor Laws.* London, 1834.

Quarterly Review. "Lunatic asylums." 101 (1857): 353-393.

Reid, J. Essays on Insanity. London: Longmans, 1816.

Rimlinger, G. "Welfare policy and economic development: a comparative historical perspective." Journal of Economic History (1966): 556-71.

Scull, A. T. "Museums of Madness: The Social Organization of Insanity in Nineteenth Century England." Unpublished Ph.D. dissertation, Princeton University, 1974.

_____. "From madness to mental illness: medical men as moral entrepreneurs." European Journal of Sociology 16 (1975): 219-61.

_____. Decarceration: Community Treatment and the Deviant—A Radical View. Englewood Cliffs, New Jersey: Prentice-Hall, 1977.

_____. "Mad-doctors and magistrates: English psychiatry's struggle for professional autonomy in the nineteenth century." European Journal of Sociology, in press.

Smith, Adam. The Wealth of Nations. New York: Modern Library Edition, 1776.

St. Luke's Hospital. Considerations upon the Usefulness and Necessity of Establishing a Hospital as a Further Provision for Poor Lunaticks. Manuscript at St. Luke's Hospital, Woodside, London, 1750.

Stark, W. Remarks on the Construction of Public Hospitals for the Cure of Mental Derangement. Glasgow: Hedderwick, 1810.

Stephen, L. The English Utilitarians. (2 vols.) London, 1900.

Temple, W. An Essay on Trade and Commerce. London, 1770.

Thompson, E. P. The Making of the English Working Class. New York: Vintage, 1963.

Townsend, J. A Dissertation on the Poor Laws, by a Well-Wisher of Mankind. London, 1786.

Wakefield, E. "Plan of an asylum for lunatics, etc." The Philanthropist 2 (1812): 226-29.

Wallerstein, I. The Modern World System. New York: Academic Press, 1974.

Webb, S., and Webb, B. English Poor Law History: Part One—The Old Poor Law. London, 1927.

Weber, M. The Protestant Ethic and the Spirit of Capitalism. London: Allen and Unwin, 1930.

_____. From Max Weber: Essays in Sociology, edited by H. Gerth and C. W. Mills. London: Oxford University Press, 1946.

_____. General Economic History. New York: Collier, 1961.

_____. Economy and Society. (3 vols.) Totowa, New Jersey: Bedminster Press, 1968.

RICHARD QUINNEY

The Political Economy of Crime

Social expenditures on criminal justice necessarily increase with the development of advanced capitalism. In the late stages of capitalism the mode of production and the forms of capital accumulation accelerate the growth of the relative surplus population. The state must then provide social expense programs, including criminal justice, both to legitimate advanced capitalism and to control the surplus population. Rather than being capable of absorbing the surplus population into the political economy, advanced capitalism can only supervise and control a population that is now superfluous to the capitalist system. The problem is especially acute when the surplus population threatens to disturb the system, either by overburdening the system or by political action. Criminal justice is the modern means of controlling this surplus population produced by late capitalist development.

The state attempts to offset the social expense of criminal justice by supporting the growth of the criminal justice-industrial complex. The fiscal crisis of the capitalist state is temporarily alleviated by forming an alliance between monopoly capital and state-financed social programs. The social programs of the state are thereby transformed into social capital, providing subsidized investment opportunities for monopoly capital and ameliorating some of the material impoverishment of the surplus population (O'Connor, 1973:221). The new complex thus ties the surplus population to the state

Source: Quinney, Richard. "The Political Economy of Criminal Justice." In *Class, State and Crime*, pp. 131–140. New York: David McKay Company, Inc., 1977. Copyright ©1977 by Longman Inc. Reprinted by permission.

and to the political economy of advanced capitalism. While a growing segment of the population is absorbed into the system as *indirectly productive workers*—the army of government and office workers, paraprofessionals, and those who work in one way or another in the social expense programs—there is also a large surplus population that is controlled by these programs. These unemployed, underemployed, reserve army workers now find themselves dependent on the state. They are linked to the state (and to monopoly capital) for much of their economic welfare, and they are linked in being the object of the social control programs of the state. The criminal justice system is the most explicit of these programs in controlling the surplus population. Criminal justice and the surplus population are thus symbiotically interdependent.

As the surplus population grows with the development of capitalism, the criminal justice system or some equivalent must also grow. An expanding criminal justice system is the only way late capitalism can "integrate" the surplus population into the overall economic and political system. The notion that the social problems generated by capitalism can be solved becomes obsolete. Instead, problems such as crime are dealt with in terms of a *control* model. When the underlying conditions of capitalism cannot be changed—without changing the capitalist system itself—controlling the population oppressed by the existing conditions is the only "solution." Thus as one theorist-strategist of the capitalist state puts it, we must "learn to live with crime"; and the important question then becomes "what constitutes an effective law-enforcement and order-maintenance system?" (Wilson, 1968:199, 204.)

On all levels of the criminal justice system new techniques of control are being developed and instituted. Not only has there been increased implementation of a military-hardware approach to criminal justice, but developing more recently alongside are more subtle approaches. A dual system is developing whereby some actions of the surplus population that are defined as criminal are dealt with harshly by strong-arm techniques and by punitive measures. Other actions by other portions of the surplus population are handled by such software techniques as diversion from the courts and community-based corrections. In general, however, whatever the current techniques, the new model is one of *pacification*. The surplus population is not only to be controlled, but it is to accept this control. As the authors of *The Iron Fist and the Velvet Glove* (Center for Research on Criminal Justice, 1975:54) note, in regard to the law-enforcement aspects of the criminal justice system, the system is developing as follows:

> During the late 1960s, the technical and managerial approach to police work represented by the military-corporate model came under increasing criticism. More sophisticated analyses of crime and urban disorder suggested that massive spending on military hardware, by itself, would not

only fail to stop rising crime rates and urban discontent, but would probably serve to further alienate large sectors of the population. This approach
stressed the need for the police to develop closer ties to the communities
most heavily patrolled by them. The emphasis began to be placed less
on paramilitary efficiency and more on ensuring popular consent and
acquiescence. The idea that police departments should engage in some
sort of "community relations" had, of course, been around for some
time, but community relations programs, in practice, were few, and
those that did exist were generally regarded as ineffective window-dressing.
The new emphasis, on the other hand, represented a serious attempt to
supplement the growing technological prowess of the police with programs
that could make the police role more acceptable to the people most
affected by it.

The capitalist state, in alliance with monopoly capital, must continually
innovate in expanding the criminal justice system.

Whatever the techniques of control, the fact remains that it is the surplus
population that is in need of control, that is being controlled by the criminal
justice system. Control is especially acute in those periods when the economic
crisis is most obvious—during periods of depression and recession. It is during
these times that the surplus population is affected most; and it is during
these times that the surplus population grows through unemployment.

As usual during these periods, the hardest-hit groups are women, blacks,
the young, and unskilled workers. For example, in 1974 the unemployment
rate among nonwhites was twice as high as that of whites; almost half the
unemployed were women, although they occupied only about 40 percent
of the labor force; the unemployment rate of young workers (16-21 years)
was twice the average rate of workers; and the unemployment rate of unskilled workers was several percentage points higher than that for all other
workers (NEPA News, 1976:10–11). Moreover, these figures drastically underestimate the extent of unemployment in the United States. While the official
statistics indicated that 5 million people were unemployed in 1974, this
figure obscures the fact that over 18 million people were out of work at some
time during the year. In 1975 nearly 24 million people were unemployed at
some time during the year, a figure representing one out of every four workers.

Even these figures underestimate the extent of the problem. They systematically exclude the people in the surplus population who have given up
looking for jobs. Unemployment figures likewise do not count people who
are employed part-time but seek full-time jobs. They also exclude the many
people who are "subemployed," those who are not employed in jobs for
which they are qualified. All these situations provide an employment/unem-
ployment picture quite different from that portrayed by the government.

A way of controlling this unemployed surplus population is simply and
directly by confinement in prisons. The rhetoric of criminal justice—and that

Figure 1: Prisons and Unemployment.[a]

Prison Admissions	Unemployment Rate							
16,500	6.0							
16,000	5.5							
15,500	5.0							
15,000	4.5							
14,500	4.0							
14,000	3.5							
13,500	3.0	1960	1962	1964	1966	1968	1970	1972

Source: *NEPA News*, February 1976, p. 16.

[a] This graph shows how prisoner admissions to the federal prison system rise and fall according to how the national unemployment rate rises and falls. The *broken line* shows the unemployment rate, while the *solid line* shows admissions to federal prisons.

of conventional criminology—is that prisons are for incarcerating criminals. In spite of this mystification, the fact is that prisons are used to control that part of the surplus population that is subject to the discretion of criminal law and the criminal justice system. What is not usually presented are the figures and the conclusion that prisons are differentially utilized according to the extent of economic crisis. The finding is clear: the prison population increases as the rate of unemployment increases. As shown in Figure 1, using admissions to federal prisons, the number of prison admissions varies directly with the rate of unemployment. Unemployment simultaneously makes actions of survival and frustration necessary on 'the part of the unemployed surplus population and makes some form of controlling that population necessary by the state. Containment of the unemployed in prison is a certain way of controlling a threatening surplus population. Until other solutions of control are found, the capitalist state will need the certainty of the prison for controlling portions of the surplus population.

From arrest to imprisonment, then, the criminal justice system exists to control the surplus population. During 1975 the police made approximately 9.3 million arrests. This is a rate of 45 arrests for each 1,000 persons in the population. As the FBI notes in its report (1975:37), "arrests are primarily a measure of police activity." An attempt is being made by the police, in other words, to control the population, primarily the surplus population. While the arrest figures "provide a useful index to indicate involvement in criminal acts," they are first a measure of police activity in controlling the population. That the number of arrests has climbed, with the arrests for the major crimes increasing by over 40 percent between 1969 and the mid-1970s, is also an indication of the increasing need to control. As the economic crisis of capitalism grows, the actions generated by this crisis increase. The actions of the surplus population and the actions of the criminal justice agencies are produced by the capitalist system and are increased by the crisis in the system.

Moreover, a large portion of the population is imprisoned, and thereby controlled, at any one time (National Criminal Justice Information and Statistics Service, 1975a:12; 1975b:8; 1975c:1). The total number of prisoners in custody at the end of 1973 was 204,349 held in state and federal prisons, rising to 249,716 as of January 1, 1976. In addition to these figures there are over 45,000 juveniles held in juvenile and correctional institutions. Also there are people confined to local jails, more than half of whom have not been convicted of a crime. In other words, considering only the adult population, about 1 out of every 370 adults is confined at any given time to a penal institution in the United States.

Prisons in this country are used mainly for those who commit a select group of crimes, primarily burglary, robbery, larceny, and assault. Excluded are the criminals of the capitalist class, who cause more of an economic and social loss to the country and the society but who are not often given prison sentences. This means that prisons are institutions of control for the working class, especially the surplus population of the working class.

Another consequence of this use of custody and punishment is that a very large number of prisoners are black. It is estimated that 1 out of every 20 black men between the ages of 25 and 34 is either in jail or prison on any given day, compared to 1 out of every 163 white men in the same age group (Wright, 1973:31-34). About one out of every four black men in their early twenties spends some time in prison, jail, or on probation. Control by the criminal justice system is indeed a reality for a good share of the American people.

The criminal justice system is nevertheless caught in the larger contradiction: late capitalism is producing a rising crime rate and the social expense of criminal justice is more than the state and the capitalist class can afford. Prisons are already dangerously overcrowded, increasing the number of "trouble-makers" within the prison and strengthening the prisoners' movement. From the standpoint of the criminal justice system, either new prisons have to be built to contain the growing number of people controlled by the system, or something has to be done to reduce the size of the prison population at any single time (NEPA News, 1976:3). One direction calls for the construction of roughly 1,000 new prisons, at an estimated cost of $20 billion. The other direction that the capitalist state can move is in the reduction of the prison population by means of sentencing reform.

Sentencing reforms consist mainly of mandatory, fixed, and reduced sentencing schemes. These schemes, of course, apply only to crimes committed by the working class, never the crimes of the government and the corporations. Furthermore, by reducing the length of the prison sentence, and by assuring that a prison sentence will be administered, more people can be imprisoned with certainty. This means that about 50 percent more people could be sent to prison for short terms than can now be sent for long terms.

Viewed this way, sentencing reform is a way for the criminal justice system to have its cake and eat it too. Mandatory or fixed sentences can be introduced, sending larger numbers of people to prison while at the same time the cost of building new prisons can be avoided. Prison officials and legislators can also pose as "good guys" when shortening sentences, while also posing as "tough on crime" because more offenders will be sentenced. (NEPA News, 1976:7.)

Prison reform actually means that control of the surplus population can be increased, for the time being at least, within the social expense limits of the criminal justice system. Future changes in control likewise will be tied to the political economy of criminal justice. Control of the surplus population is a social expense that late capitalism must somehow meet. Built into this, of course, is a dialectic in which control is weakened in the course of class struggle and the economic crisis of the capitalist state. Criminal justice and its transformation are central to socialist revolution.

REFERENCES

Center for Research on Criminal Justice. *The Iron Fist and the Velvet Glove: An Analysis of the U. S. Police.* Berkeley: Center for Research on Criminal Justice, 1975.

Federal Bureau of Investigation. *Uniform Crime Reports, 1975.*

National Criminal Justice Information and Statistics Service. "Prisoners in State and Federal Institutions on December 31, 1971, 1972, and 1973." *National Prisoner Statistics Bulletin.* Washington, D.C.: U.S. Government Printing Office, 1975a.

──. *Children in Custody.* Washington, D.C.: U.S. Government Printing Office, 1975b.

──. *The Nation's Jails.* Washington, D.C.: U.S. Government Printing Office, 1975c.

O'Connor, James. *Fiscal Crisis of the State.* New York: St. Martin's Press, 1973.

"Overcrowding and Sentence Reform." *NEPA News* (February 1976).

Wilson, James Q. "Crime and Law Enforcement." In *Agenda for the Nation,* edited by Kermit Gordon. Washington, D.C.: U.S. Government Printing Office, n.d.

Wright, Erik Ohlin. *The Politics of Punishment: A Critical Analysis of Prisons in America.* New York: Harper & Row, 1973.